# Society and the Internet

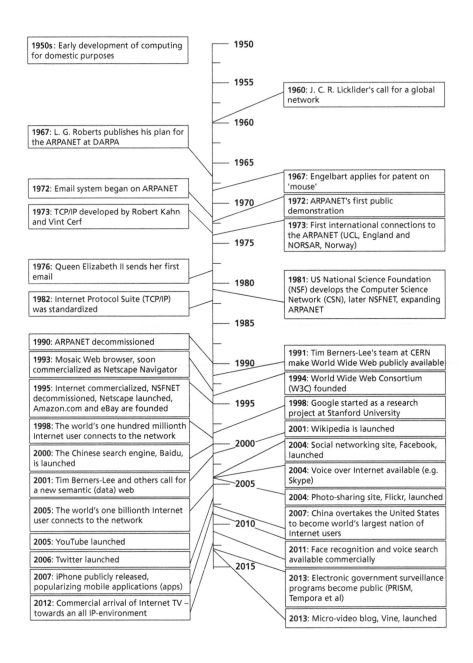

1950

**1950s**: Early development of computing for domestic purposes

1955

**1960**: J. C. R. Licklider's call for a global network

1960

**1967**: L. G. Roberts publishes his plan for the ARPANET at DARPA

1965

**1967**: Engelbart applies for patent on 'mouse'

**1972**: Email system began on ARPANET

1970

**1972**: ARPANET's first public demonstration

**1973**: TCP/IP developed by Robert Kahn and Vint Cerf

**1973**: First international connections to the ARPANET (UCL, England and NORSAR, Norway)

1975

**1976**: Queen Elizabeth II sends her first email

1980

**1981**: US National Science Foundation (NSF) develops the Computer Science Network (CSN), later NSFNET, expanding ARPANET

**1982**: Internet Protocol Suite (TCP/IP) was standardized

1985

**1990**: ARPANET decommissioned

**1993**: Mosaic Web browser, soon commercialized as Netscape Navigator

1990

**1991**: Tim Berners-Lee's team at CERN make World Wide Web publicly available

**1994**: World Wide Web Consortium (W3C) founded

**1995**: Internet commercialized, NSFNET decommissioned, Netscape launched, Amazon.com and eBay are founded

1995

**1998**: Google started as a research project at Stanford University

**1998**: The world's one hundred millionth Internet user connects to the network

**2001**: Wikipedia is launched

2000

**2004**: Social networking site, Facebook, launched

**2000**: The Chinese search engine, Baidu, is launched

**2004**: Voice over Internet available (e.g. Skype)

**2001**: Tim Berners-Lee and others call for a new semantic (data) web

2005

**2004**: Photo-sharing site, Flickr, launched

**2005**: The world's one billionth Internet user connects to the network

**2007**: China overtakes the United States to become world's largest nation of Internet users

2010

**2005**: YouTube launched

**2011**: Face recognition and voice search available commercially

**2006**: Twitter launched

2015

**2007**: iPhone publicly released, popularizing mobile applications (apps)

**2013**: Electronic government surveillance programs become public (PRISM, Tempora et al)

**2012**: Commercial arrival of Internet TV – towards an all IP-environment

**2013**: Micro-video blog, Vine, launched

# Society and the Internet

How Networks of Information and
Communication are Changing
Our Lives

Edited by

Mark Graham and William H. Dutton

with a foreword by Manuel Castells

OXFORD
UNIVERSITY PRESS

# OXFORD

**UNIVERSITY PRESS**

Great Clarendon Street, Oxford, OX2 6DP,
United Kingdom

Oxford University Press is a department of the University of Oxford.
It furthers the University's objective of excellence in research, scholarship,
and education by publishing worldwide. Oxford is a registered trade mark of
Oxford University Press in the UK and in certain other countries

Published in the United States of America by Oxford University Press
198 Madison Avenue, New York, NY 10016, United States of America

British Library Cataloguing in Publication Data

Data available

Library of Congress Control Number: 2014930242

ISBN 978-0-19-966199-2 (hbk.)

ISBN 978-0-19-966200-5 (pbk.)

Printed and bound by
CPI Group (UK) Ltd, Croydon, CR0 4YY

# INTERNET STUDIES: A CRITICAL NEW FIELD IN THE SOCIAL SCIENCES

The Internet weaves the fabric of our lives. It is to the information age what the electrical engine was to the industrial age. We live in, on, and by the Internet, in work, business, education, health, governance, entertainment, culture, politics, social movements, war and peace, and friends and family. It is not really a new technology, as it was first deployed in 1969 as ARPANET, but its widespread diffusion in the planet at large took place in the 1990s after it was privatized and was made user friendly by the World Wide Web created by Tim Berners-Lee in 1990. The explosion of wireless platforms in the last decade has distributed the power of the Internet everywhere. With 2.5 billion Internet users worldwide (over half a billion of them in China), and over 6 billion subscribers of wireless devices, humanity is almost fully connected, albeit with uneven levels of bandwidth, in this network of computer networks that has become the backbone of all activities in all domains. It has made possible the constitution of a new social structure, the network society, that has subsumed the industrial society that characterized the world in the last two centuries. Social networking sites on the Internet, which have spread at an accelerated pace since 2002, have become the social spaces where people meet, socialize, retrieve information, express themselves, work, shop, create, imagine, participate, fight, and shape their experience.

Yet, while everybody acknowledges the tectonic change the Internet represents in communication, the essence of human organization and practice, there is little understanding of the social implications of the Internet in the public mind, and even less so in the mainstream media that specializes in propagating horror stories about the effects of Internet use with little relationship to the actual experience of Internet users. This is a well-known fact in the history of technology: any revolutionary technology is met with fear by the population at large and with rejection by the holders of power and wealth, based on a superseded technological paradigm. The elites that are most opposed to new communication technologies are precisely the intellectuals, the *maîtres à penser*, who are disintermediated by the diffusion of information and the enhanced self-communication capacities of people. They are joined by the guardians of communication, that is the traditional mass media, who fear literally to be put out of business by free communication, and by the governments that have based their power throughout history on the control of information and communication. Thus, the more the Internet, the ultimate technology of freedom, referring to the visionary formulation of Ithiel de Sola Pool, permeates the human experience, the more it is misconstrued in the public perception. Cybersecurity becomes more important for all the powers that be than the creative construction of cyberculture, a new frontier of the human mind.

A veil of ignorance and ideology covers the reality of Internet as a social practice. And yet, social scientists know a great deal about the dynamics, effects, and potential impacts of Internet use. In the last two decades, there has been an extraordinary, cumulative harvest of empirical research and grounded theory on the interaction between social practices and Internet-based communication in every dimension of our experience. Studies have been conducted in multiple cultural contexts, at different points in time, on a wide array of topics, and with diverse methodologies, from formal models of network communication to statistical analysis of surveys on representative samples of the population of many countries, and fine-grain ethnographic and psychological observation. I would go as far as to say that we know more about the Internet as a social phenomenon than about most other communication technologies.

There is a dramatic gap between our scientific knowledge of the Internet and the public's perception of the communication technology that is at the root of their everyday life. The reasons for such a gap are not to be found in the lack of diffusion of the findings of social science. As I argued above, it is in the interest of the elites and of traditional media organizations to accuse the Internet of every possible evil, as if technology could be the cause of our social problems. Because the Internet is embedded in the culture of autonomy, and social autonomy contradicts the disciplinary powers of established institutions, there is a determined effort to undermine the credibility and legitimacy of Internet practices. And so, it is unlikely that producing rigorous knowledge about the Internet could lift the curtain of obscurantism that characterizes the perception of the most revolutionary communication technology in history.

Nonetheless, to conduct research on Internet practices, including the relentless transformation of the technology and its uses, to systematize it and to diffuse it, is a necessary step towards allowing humankind to appropriate the power of the Internet for the projects of individuals and social actors. Thus, the importance of the volume you have in your hands. It represents a methodologically rigorous and intellectually challenging effort to explain the interaction between Internet and society, between the technologies of freedom and the culture of autonomy. The studies contained in this reader, in their plurality, demonstrate the vitality of social sciences when they use the tools of empirical research and innovative theorizing to illuminate the current paths of social transformation.

Manuel Castells

# ▨ PREFACE

How is society being shaped by the diffusion and increasing centrality of the Internet in everyday life? This book addresses this question through a stimulating set of readings grounded in theoretical perspectives and empirical research. It brings together research that examines some of the most significant cultural, economic, political, and other social roles of the Internet in the 21st century.

Together, this research defines some of the basic issues of Internet Studies, a new and thriving field of multi-disciplinary inquiry, which the Oxford Internet Institute (OII) has helped develop since its inception as a department of the University of Oxford in 2001. *Society and the Internet* draws primarily on the work of OII faculty participating in the Institute's evolving series of lectures targeted initially at students of the University of Oxford. The series was expanded, written, and edited for undergraduate and graduate courses.

Contributors and topics were selected to introduce students to some of the most engaging and groundbreaking scholarship in the field. The chapters are rooted in a variety of disciplines, but all directly tackle the powerful ways in which the Internet is linked to transformations in contemporary society. This book will be the starting point for some students, but valuable to anyone with a serious interest in the economic, social, and political factors shaping the Internet and its impact on society.

As this book was nearing completion, we learned of the death of Douglas C. Engelbart (1925–2013), an engineer, and one of the first scholars to envision a future in which computers and telecommunications would be networked worldwide in ways that could augment human intelligence. In 1962, over fifty years ago, he started work on the design of what he called an "oN-Line System" (NLS), which he demonstrated in 1968, one year after his team invented the "mouse"—a device that has since changed the ways in which people interact with computers. He was one of many pioneers who helped shape what we have come to know as the Internet, Web, and related digital technologies, ranging from telecommunication infrastructures to tablets and smart phones. He was inspired by earlier pioneers, such as Vannevar Bush and J. C. R. Licklider, who called for a global system, and in turn inspired others, such as Ted Nelson, who coined the concept of "hypertext" to describe the non-linear pathways that can link text and images in the online world, and which move away from the model of a linear book.

Such early visions of what would become the Internet of the 21st century were formed when nearly all computing was conducted on large mainframe computers so expensive and complex that only governments and the larger organizations possessed such a resource. In the sixties, the very idea that house-holds, much less individuals, would have access to a computer networked with millions of other computers around the world was viewed as folly—completely unrealistic futurology—or what many called "blue-sky" forecasts. Today it is taken for granted.

Of course, many pioneers followed in the steps of Engelbart and other early visionaries to develop the technologies we have access to in the 21st century. They include Vint Cerf and Robert Kahn, inventors of the protocols that define the Internet, and Tim Berners-Lee and his team at CERN, who invented the World Wide Web. Of course there are many more—too many to list, but one of the most unsung pioneers of the Internet is the user—people like yourself who use, view, mediate, edit, and therefore profoundly change the ways that much contemporary knowledge is circulated and re-circulated, and communication is enacted and used. This book provides many examples of how users have shaped the development of the Internet and its application across nearly every sector of society, always coming back to the key issue of what difference the Internet makes to all aspects of our lives.

Pioneers in the design and development of the Internet, such as Doug Engelbart, understood the importance of users. As computing moved from large mainframes to personal computers, to the Internet becoming your computer, it became clear that users were playing a major role in shaping the Internet in ways the designers might not have imagined. Consider the ways in which crowdsourcing—tapping the wisdom of Internet users distributed across the globe—has enabled users to play more important roles in science and society than many anticipated. Wikipedia, for instance, has been so suc-cessful that it has spawned a long-running joke: "The problem with Wikipedia is that it only works in practice. In theory, it's a total disaster." As new uses evolve, there is a need for even greater ingenuity and creativity on the part of developers and users alike to address the problems and risks of the digital age, such as the potential of near-ubiquitous surveillance, and finding ways to authenticate information being created and distributed at Internet speeds.

In the half century since Engelbart envisioned an NLS, the promise of the Internet, Web, and related digital information and communication technolo-gies to truly augment human intelligence has been realized, but so has the centrality of questions concerning the effect of a global Internet on such val-ued outcomes as freedom of expression, privacy, equality, and democratic accountability. In fact, most debates over such central values as freedom of expression in the 21st century are about the Internet.

Well before the 21st century, many people considered the potential societal implications of computing and telecommunications enabled by digital tech-nologies. As early as 1973, computer scientists such as Kelly Gotlieb began to write about some of the key social issues of computing, such as the implica-tions for freedom of expression, privacy, employment, education, and security.

Most of these issues remain critical today in reflecting on the societal role of the Internet. In the early 1970s, Gotlieb and others discussed the idea of an "information utility" and were well aware of J. C. R. Licklider's call for a global network, even though ARPANET—the early incarnation of what would become the Internet—was only at the demonstration stage at the time they wrote, and governments were the primary adopters of computing and electronic data-processing systems. Nevertheless, the issues defined as early as the 1970s remain remarkably key to discussions of the Internet, big data, social media and mobile Internet debates over forty years later.

What is different in the second decade of the 21st century is that the Internet has become an infrastructure of everyday life and work for much of the world. It is no longer simply a vision, but has become increasingly real. The Internet has become so widely diffused and pervasive that we can begin to study seriously the actual societal implications of one of the most significant technologies of our lifetimes.

The central mission of this book is to show you how a multi-disciplinary range of academics seek to understand, both theoretically and empirically, the social roles of the Internet. It is in this spirit that this book brings to bear a variety of methodological approaches to the empirical study of the social shaping of the Internet and its implications for society.

Are those developing and using the Internet creating a system that augments human intelligence, as Engelbart had envisioned, or are we using the Internet in ways that undermine social relationships and the quality and diversity of information resources required for economic, social, and political development? What difference is the Internet making to the quality of our lives, and how can it further enhance our lives in the future? What people, places, groups, and institutions have been able to derive the most benefit from the Internet, and who has been left out? Who gets to control, create, and challenge new flows of information in our networked lives? In the years and decades to come, the answers to these questions will be driven in part by the quality of research on the social shaping of the Internet and its implications for society. We hope this book helps engage you in that enterprise.

# ACKNOWLEDGMENTS

This book is the outcome of collaboration across the Oxford Internet Institute (OII), one of the first multidisciplinary university-based departments of Internet Studies. The founding mission of the OII was to inform and stimulate debate over the societal implications of the Internet in ways that will shape policy and practice.

*Society and the Internet* arose through a lecture series that the editors organized for the department. The series was created initially to reach out to undergraduate students at the University of Oxford, as our teaching programs were aimed at graduate students. We wanted the OII to do more to enable Oxford students to engage with studies of the Internet and its societal implications from whatever field of study they might be pursuing at the University.

The editors took the lead in developing this lecture series over the course of two years. It was launched with a lecture on the cultures of the Internet by Professor Manuel Castells, an OII Distinguished Visiting Professor at that time. We are most grateful for his support and his foreword to this book, as well as to our other professors, fellows, and academic visitors, who contributed to this series.

As this series unfolded, we realized that our actual audience was far broader than the readers we had targeted, since the topics engaged a wide range of students, faculty, and the public. From feedback from those who attended our lecture series or viewed our webcasts, it was apparent that there was serious interest in the societal implications of the Internet. A growing awareness of the value of pulling together the expertise across the OII led to our commitment to reach an even wider audience through this collection.

In addition to the authors contributing to this volume, we are also very grateful to Barbara Ball's brilliant copy-editing, to Steve Russell for his art work for the OII and the cover of this book, Tim Davies for his assistance with our Internet timeline, and to our editors at Oxford University Press, including David Musson, Emma Booth, and their many colleagues, who were professional, skilled, and patient at every stage of the process of producing this book. We could not have asked for better support. Finally, without the enthusiastic and collegial contributions of the OII and all its faculty and staff, this book would not have been possible.

The Editors

*Oxford*
*2014*

# CONTENTS

# ▨ LIST OF FIGURES

# ■ LIST OF TABLES

# ▣ LIST OF ABBREVIATIONS

| | |
|---|---|
| ADR | Alternative dispute resolution |
| AI | Artificial Intelligence |
| APEC | Asia-Pacific Economic Cooperation |
| API | Application Programming Interface |
| ATUS | American Time Use Society |
| COPPA | US Children's Online Privacy Protection Act |
| CPC | Conservative Party of Canada |
| CT | Communications technologies |
| DDoS | Distributed Denial of Service |
| DFID | Department for International Development |
| DUP | Democratic Union Party (Sudan) |
| EEA | European Economic Area |
| FPS | First person shooter game |
| GCIO | Government Chief Information Officer (New Zealand) |
| GOFAI | Good Old-Fashioned Artificial Intelligence |
| GSA | General Services Administration (US Federal Government) |
| GSP | Generalized second price |
| HTML | Hypertext Markup Language |
| IaaS | Infrastructure as a Service |
| ICT | Information and Communication Technology |
| ICT4D | ICT for Development |
| IGF | Internet Governance Forum |
| IM | Instant Messenger |
| IR | Information Retrieval |
| ISP | Internet Service Provider |
| IT | Information technologies |
| ITU | International Telecommunication Union |
| LPC | Liberal Party of Canada |
| MFA | Multi Fibre Arrangement |
| MMORPG | Massively multiplayer online role-playing game |
| NCP | National Congress Party (Sudan) |
| NGU | Next Generation User |
| NIF | National Islamic Front (Sudan) |

| | |
|---|---|
| ODR | Online dispute resolution |
| OECD | The Organization for Economic Co-operation and Development |
| OII | Oxford Internet Institute |
| OLPC | One Laptop per Child |
| OMB | Office of Management and Budget (US Federal Government) |
| OxIS | Oxford Internet Survey |
| PaaS | Platform as a Service |
| PHP | Pre-Hypertext Processing |
| PII | Personally Identifiable Information |
| QA | Question Answering |
| RISJ | Reuters Institute for the Study of Journalism |
| SaaS | Software as a Service |
| SMS | Short message service |
| SNS | Social network site |
| SOPA | Stop Online Piracy Act |
| SW | Semantic (alternatively, Data) Web |
| UGC | User Generated Content |
| UNCTAD | The United Nations Conference on Trade and Development |
| URI | Uniform Resource Indicator |
| URL | Uniform Resource Locator |
| USSD | Unstructured Supplementary Service Data |
| VOD | Video on Demand |
| WIP | World Internet Project |

# ▓ NOTES ON CONTRIBUTORS

**Grant Blank** is the Survey Research Fellow at the Oxford Internet Institute, University of Oxford, where he a co-principal on the Oxford Internet Survey (OxIS).

**Jay G. Blumler** is Emeritus Professor of Public Communication at the University of Leeds and Emeritus Professor of Journalism at the University of Maryland.

**Gillian Bolsover** is an Oxford Internet Institute DPhil student with a Master's degree in Media and Communication from the London School of Economics.

**Manuel Castells** is the Wallis Annenberg Chair in Communication Technology and Society, University of Southern California. Professor Castells was a Distinguished Visiting Professor at the Oxford Internet Institute from 2006 to 2010, and a member of its Advisory Board.

**Stephen Coleman** is a Professor of Political Communication at Leeds University and was the Oxford Internet Institute's Visiting Professor of eDemocracy from 2002 to 2005.

**Laura DeNardis** is an Internet governance scholar and an Associate Professor in the School of Communication at American University in Washington, DC. She is an affiliated fellow of the Information Society Project at Yale Law School.

**Elizabeth Dubois** is a doctoral candidate at the University of Oxford's Internet Institute, where she is a current Clarendon Scholar and member of Balliol College. Previously she studied communications at the University of Ottawa, Canada, and American University, United States, as a Killam Fellow through the Fulbright Foundation (Canada).

**Soumitra Dutta** is the Anne and Elmer Lindseth Dean and Professor of Management in the Samuel Curtis Johnson Graduate School of Management at Cornell University, United States. He most recently served as the Roland Berger Chaired Professor of Business and Technology and was the founder and academic director of INSEAD's eLab, France. He is a co-principal on the OII's Internet Values Project.

**William H. Dutton** is Professor of Internet Studies at the University of Oxford's Internet Institute, where he was founding director, a Professorial Fellow at Balliol College, an Oxford Martin Fellow, and Professor Emeritus at the University of Southern California, United States.

**Sandra González-Bailón** is an Assistant Professor at the Annenberg School for Communication at the University of Pennsylvania and a Research Associate at the OII. She was a Research Fellow at the OII from 2008 to 2013, as well as a Fellow of Nuffield College, University of Oxford.

**Mark Graham** is a geographer and a Senior Research Fellow at the Oxford Internet Institute. He is also a Research Fellow at Green Templeton College, and a Visiting

Research Associate at the University of Oxford's School of Geography and the Environment.

**Scott A. Hale** is an Oxford Internet Institute DPhil student and Research Assistant.

**Bernie Hogan** is a sociologist and Research Fellow at the Oxford Internet Institute.

**Sung Wook Ji** is an Assistant Professor in the Department of Telecommunication, Information Studies and Media at Michigan State University.

**Aleks Krotoski** is an Oxford Internet Institute Research Associate and Visiting Fellow in the Media and Communications Department at the LSE. She holds a PhD in social psychology, and is the author of *Untangling the Web: What the Internet is Doing to You.* She is a broadcaster and journalist for the BBC and *The Guardian* newspaper.

**Ginette Law** is an ICT Researcher and Consultant and associate on the Internet Values Project at the OII, where she obtained her MSc in Social Science of the Internet.

**Miriam Lips** is the first Professor of e-Government at Victoria University of Wellington, in the School of Government. Prior to her position at Wellington, Miriam was a Visiting Fellow, Research Fellow, and then Associate at the Oxford Internet Institute from 2003 to 2010, and on the faculty at Tilburg University.

**Laura Mann** was a postdoctoral researcher at the University of Oxford's Internet Institute from 2011 to 2014. Laura is now a postdoctoral researcher at Leiden University.

**Helen Margetts** is Director of the Oxford Internet Institute, where she is Professor of Society and the Internet, and a Fellow of Mansfield College, University of Oxford.

**Christopher Millard** is Professor of Privacy and Information Law at Queen Mary, University of London, where he leads the Cloud Legal Project. He is also a Research Associate at the Oxford Internet Institute and is Of Counsel to the law firm Bristows, with over thirty years' experience as a technology lawyer.

**Lisa Nakamura** is the Gwendolyn Calvert Baker Collegiate Professor of American Culture and Screen Cultures in the Department of American Culture in Asian/Pacific Islander American Studies, and in the Department of Screen Arts and Cultures at the University of Michigan, Ann Arbor.

**Victoria Nash** is Deputy Director and Policy and Research Fellow at the Oxford Internet Institute. She also serves as a lecturer in Politics at Trinity College, University of Oxford.

**Nic Newman** is a Research Associate at the Reuters Institute for the Study of Journalism at Oxford University and a Senior Research Fellow at City University London. He is a journalist and former BBC senior executive, and was one of the founding members of the BBC News website.

**Eli M. Noam** has been Professor of Economics and Finance at the Columbia Business School since 1976 and its Garrett Professor of Public Policy and Business Responsibility. He has been the Director of the Columbia Institute for Tele-Information, and one of the key advisors to the Oxford Internet Institute, having served on its Advisory Board through the Institute's first decade.

**Ralph Schroeder** is Professor at the Oxford Internet Institute and Director of its Masters degree in Social Science of the Internet.

**Richard Susskind OBE** is an author, speaker, and independent adviser to major professional firms and to national governments. He is President of the Society for Computers and Law, IT Adviser to the Lord Chief Justice of England, and has been Chair of the Advisory Board of the Oxford Internet Institute since 2011.

**Greg Taylor** is a research fellow at the Oxford Internet Institute. He holds a PhD in economics from the University of Southampton.

**David Waterman** is Professor in the Department of Telecommunications, Indiana University, Bloomington, and was a Visiting Fellow at the Oxford Internet Institute in 2011.

**Barry Wellman** is Professor of Sociology and Director of NetLab at the University of Toronto. He is the co-author (with Lee Rainie) of *Networked: The New Social Operating System* (MIT Press, 2012). He has delivered a number of keynote addresses at major Oxford Internet Institute events.

**Yorick Wilks**, a Professor of Artificial Intelligence at the University of Sheffield, is a Senior Research Scientist at the Florida Institute for Human and Machine Cognition, and a Senior Research Associate with the Oxford Internet Institute.

**Taha Yasseri** is the Big Data Research Officer at the Oxford Internet Institute, having completed his PhD at the Institute of Theoretical Physics at the University of Göttingen, where he worked in the Complex Systems Physics research group.

# Introduction

*William H. Dutton and Mark Graham**

As you introduce yourself to this book, you might find it useful to consider many of the significant ways in which (not) having access to the Internet can alter how you interact with the world around you, such as:

- How you create, get, and distribute information: The Internet might enable you to create content and get access to information more easily and quickly, compared to working in the library, but also make a difference to the extent of your knowledge. Internet-mediated access to information, media, and other content might also shape your movement. Being able to access information electronically means that you can get where you want to be, or meet with people with whom it is important to interact face to face.

- How you communicate with people you know, and how you might meet and interact with people you don't yet know in your social and work-life: The Internet, social media, and video communication introduce you to new people, as well as helping you keep in touch with old friends and associates. It will shape whom you know as well as how you communicate.

- How you obtain services, from banking and shopping to entertainment, games, and public services: If you decide to shop on the Internet, for example, you might shop from different companies, or purchase services you might not otherwise have known about.

- What technologies link you to the Internet, from wired and wireless infra-structures to devices you carry with you or wear: This will not only shape what technologies you require, but also what know-how you require to live and work in a world of digital media and Information and Communication Technology (ICTs).

Just as importantly, think of how people use the Internet to get information about you, to communicate with you, to provide you with services, and per-haps even to observe your Internet-mediated behavior. The Internet is shaping access to you, just as you employ the Internet to shape access to the world (Dutton 1999).

* We thank Elizabeth Dubois and Heather Ford for their insightful comments on this introduction.

It is also important to put some of the significant ways that the Internet mediates everyday life into historical perspective. It was only slightly more than two decades ago that the Web was invented; it was impossible to use Google or Wikipedia in order to look up information fifteen years ago; we couldn't use Facebook to connect with friends a decade ago; and even five years ago it was only a small minority of people who had access to the Internet on mobile devices. If the next two decades of Internet time are as transformative as the previous two, it is likely that many of us will be living in a very different technologically, informationally, and algorithmically mediated world. As such, there will be an increased need for sustained inquiry into crucial, critical, and timely questions about the interaction of the Internet and society.

## Reconfiguring Access and the Societal Implications of the Internet

This book seeks to bring to life some of the basic ways in which digital media and technologies reconfigure your access to the world, and the world's access to you. It also examines how these shifting patterns of access translate into significant outcomes in politics, governance, work, and the quality of your life and the lives of people across the globe.

For nearly half a century, academics, pundits, and policy makers have speculated on the future societal implications of the widespread diffusion of computing and telecommunications, which we have come to identify with the Internet and related digital ICTs. Computer and social scientists alike have highlighted social issues arising from computing from the 1960s to the present day (Gotlieb and Borodin 1973; Dutton 1999). Broad theoretical perspectives on the societal implications of the information age were provided by Daniel Bell's (1973) concept of a post-industrial "information society," Fred Williams's (1982) concept of the "communications revolution," and later by Manuel Castells's (1996) trilogy focused on the "network society." These are only three of many scholars—albeit among the most renowned—who have speculated about the social implications of the convergence of computing and telecommunications that has since networked people through the Internet, World Wide Web, and a growing number of devices from smart phones to wearable computing.

However, since the beginning of the 21st century it has become increasingly possible to move beyond speculation and to study the actual implications of the Internet across a wide range of social, economic, and political contexts of use (Howard and Jones 2004; Lievrouw and Livingstone 2006). Instead of anchoring research in early trials of emerging technologies, researchers can study the factors that are presently shaping the development and use of the wide range of technologies that form the Internet; how they are used; and with what effect on everyday life and work, on the creation and consumption of a wide range of cultural products, on politics and government, and on business and industries, as well as on the wider economy (Wellman and Haythornwaite 2002; Hunsinger et al. 2010; Rainie and Wellman 2012). It is also useful to look back at the history of the technologies that define this new infrastructure of society and the policies and regulations that have shaped its development and use (DeNardis 2013).

Business and industry, governments, and academia will continue to speculate on the future of the Internet, since the range of innovations that defines it will continue to fuel discussion of where the technology is headed. Topics such as the Internet of Things (IoT) and big data, for example, are emerging developments that have spawned much speculation about their eventual uses, and implications. Early trials and experiments will remain important. However, increasingly, researchers and students can draw from studies over years of actual use across many social contexts to make more empirically informed judgments about these technologies. The Internet has been shaping societies around a world with 2.5 billion people connected, and will continue to do so with the next 2 billion likely to come online in the near future (Schmidt and Cohen 2013).

In short, the technology and the research communities concerned with the Internet are in a position to assess how information and social networks are changing our lives. This book draws from theoretically informed empirical research to address this issue across many technologies, in many social and cultural contexts, and within major arenas of use and application, from everyday life to policy and regulation.

## Study of the History, Present, and Future: Don't Take the Internet for Granted

If you have studied at a college or university since the turn of the 21st century, then you are likely to take the Internet for granted as a normal part of life. In fact, it may have been difficult to escape using the Internet in a wide variety of areas, particularly in preparing a paper for a course, for example. However, as illustrated by the selected chronological timeline of Internet innovation, the history of this technology has been one of continuing rapid innovation that is likely to extend into the coming decades (see the frontispiece). What you know as 'the Internet' is likely to be transformed in your lifetime.

As we write in 2013, two and a half billion people around the world are using the Internet, leaving four and a half billion people without access. Are those without access disadvantaged? You might at first think that they would, at least, be free from the hassles of responding to messages and updating their profiles, or being overloaded with information. On further reflection, however, you would probably conclude that those without the tools and skills required to access the Internet are truly disadvantaged in a variety of ways—often unable to compete effectively in many arenas of a digitally networked world.

Around the turn of the century, the Internet was emerging from the academic realm to enter the world stage, only to crash after the dotcom bubble burst that followed the flop of the commercial (.com) rush to exploit the Web, which led to many new companies losing huge amounts in a very short time (Smith 2012). This led many commentators and even social scientists to view the Internet as a fad that would soon fade away (Wyatt et al. 2002). Clifford Stoll, an astronomer and author of *Silicon Snake Oil* (1995), is famously quoted in a 1995 interview[1] as saying that the Internet was

not that important. I think it's grossly oversold and within two or three years people will shrug and say, "Uh yep, it was a fad of the early 90's and now, oh yeah, it still exists but hey, I've got a life to lead and work to do. I don't have time to waste online." Or, "I'll collect my email, I'll read it, why should I bother prowling around the World Wide Web or reading the Usenet" simply because there's so little of value there.

In retrospect, it may seem surprising that the Internet was too quickly dismissed by many well-informed people. Of course, there were many who saw it as the future, and not just an interesting innovation that would pass into obscurity.

However, as the Internet permeates many aspects of our lives, can we discern the difference it makes? Will its impact be less evident as the online and offline worlds continue to become more interwoven? Will it be used in ways that enrich our social relationships? Will we have more diverse and high-quality information at our fingertips, or will we use the Internet in ways that might undermine other information resources, such as the quality press? Will the convergence of film, television, and other media around the Internet change the kinds of entertainment we consume? We know that contemporary debates continue to surround the future of the Internet, but can multidisciplinary research that engages the social sciences inform our views of the future of this information and communication infrastructure and its role in societies across the globe?

In the next twenty years, many major issues will arise around the future of the Internet. Will it fade away as some new technologies perform the role

---

[1] Transcript of the interview is available at <http://blogs.mprnews.org/newscut/2012/02/the_internet_futurist_who_thou/> (accessed August 16, 2013).

of the Internet and Web and related ICTs? Alternatively, will the Internet—defined broadly as a network of networks—become even more pervasive and more critical to everyday life and work? There are seven billion people on the planet in 2013, but the designs of digital industries for a network of sensors—an Internet of Things—anticipate networks with over a trillion "things" such as sensors and actuators. With the Internet of people and things generating mountains of data from searches, postings, messages, and just generally moving through life, governments and corporations are hoping to exploit these big data sources to learn more about our behavior, attitudes, and values. Will this be for better or worse?

Questions such as these about the present, past, and future illustrate the importance of understanding the role of the Internet in society, and how society is in turn shaping the Internet and its societal implications. That is why study of the Internet is growing rapidly as a multidisciplinary field, and has become a more central aspect of the curriculum of courses about communication, information, politics, and society (Dutton 2013; Ess and Dutton 2013; Peng 2013).

This reader was written to provide you with insights about the questions raised by the Internet in society, and to show you how social scientists work in collaboration with multiple disciplines to find the answers. You will see how individuals use the Internet in their daily lives and in the workplace, but also how a variety of institutions, such as governments and Internet firms, use the Internet to maintain and enhance their place in society and the economy. You will see that many questions about society and the Internet remain unanswered.

We hope this engages you by informing and stimulating further debate and research on the Internet through the course of your studies and beyond. This is not the time to take the Internet for granted. On the contrary, the choices that people, ranging from users to policy makers and corporate heads, make about the Internet could shape the quality of your life in dramatic ways over the coming years. Everything from the conveniences you find in shopping, the entertainment media you enjoy, the games you play, the news you have access to, to the freedom you experience in expressing your views, will be shaped by the future of the Internet and society.

# Lessons Learned for the Study of the Internet

There are a number of important lessons that have been learned from decades of research on the societal implications of ICTs—increasingly subsumed under broadening conceptions of the Internet. All of the chapters of this book avoid the common faults identified by these issues, but they are valuable to keep in mind as you critically assess the contributions to research in this field.

## MOVING BEYOND CONVENTIONAL PERSPECTIVES ON TECHNOLOGY AND SOCIETY

Journalistic and much public debate about technology in general, and the Internet more specifically, revolves around three almost classic positions that remain true to this day: They are perspectives on technology as an "unalloyed blessing," or an "unmitigated curse," or "not worthy of special notice" (Mesthene 1969). These utopian, dystopian, and dismissive views seldom if ever survive careful empirical scrutiny. Of course they are basic cultural responses to the idea of technology that are very real and infect everyday discussions and public policy, but they do not hold up to careful observation about the actual implications of technologies in real social settings—they are seldom so simple. Therefore, these perspectives are valuable to keep in mind as you consider how technology is shaping your life and work. However, it is necessary to move beyond such extreme generalizations and define exactly what expectations are tied to particular theoretical and critical perspectives on any given technology. This is an example of the role of the social sciences in the study of the Internet—challenging the taken-for-granted.

## CHALLENGING TAKEN-FOR-GRANTED ASSUMPTIONS ABOUT TECHNOLOGY

Discussions of the Internet and related digital technologies, like social media, are filled with taken-for-granted assumptions. Will the Internet lead to social isolation? Will it undermine higher quality information, replacing carefully edited encyclopedias with Wikipedia? Will it democratize nations or be a technology of control and surveillance? These are important questions but conventional wisdom on them should often be challenged rather than taken for granted.

When you hear your friends talking about the impact of digital technologies, or read accounts of the impact of the Internet, you will find it of value to look closely as what these accounts claim and imply. What do they assume about the role of technologies in causing these impacts? What evidence do they provide, or what evidence might illuminate the actual implications of particular technologies in the specific social settings being discussed? Throughout this book you will find excellent examples of how research can challenge assumptions about the role of the Internet in ways that illuminate our understanding of society and the Internet.

## THE FLAWS OF DETERMINISTIC THINKING ABOUT "IMPACTS": SOCIAL-SHAPING PERSPECTIVES

Traditional perspectives on technology—whether utopian or dystopian—and conventional wisdom often embody technologically or socially deterministic logics. Technological determinism—at its most extreme—maintains that a given technology is on a predetermined trajectory towards the one best way of doing something, and that it will have a rationally predictable set of social consequences, such as enhancing productivity or democracy. For example, because the Internet can support more networked systems of communication, rather than only reinforce more traditional hierarchical ones, it has been viewed as a "technology of freedom" (de Sola Pool 1983). However, the very design of the Internet is a matter of national and international debate, such as when governments want intermediaries like service providers to exercise greater control over certain "choke points" to resurrect more hierarchical controls over content. In addition, technologies seldom evolve along a single path, but more often through multiple paths where selections are made on non-technical criteria, driven, for example, by the momentum behind previous choices. Furthermore, how we experience freedom is shaped not only by the technology, but also by such factors as where and how we access that technology, as well as the socio-cultural contexts (Kitchin and Dodge 2011). As such, the impacts are never straightforward. Think of the debate over the role of the Internet in the Arab Spring: Was it a technology of freedom or, as some observers (e.g. Morozov 2011) have argued, a tool for autocracies?

The idea that technologies, and their uses, are on an inevitable path of development and that their impacts are predictable—easily extrapolated from features designed into the technology—has been challenged so often that social scientists rarely use the term "impact" for fear of being branded a technological determinist. At the opposite extreme are the social determinists, who dismiss the technology as not having any impact at all, since people design and respond to technologies in such open and flexible ways. As Judy Wajcman (2014 forthcoming), one of the leading sociologists challenging technological deterministic perspectives, has argued, it is equally flawed to move into a position in which the roles of technology are not considered seriously.

All technologies—the Internet included—are socio-technical systems in that they shape social choices and behavior. As technologies are accepted, for example, they define the best way to do something. Technological change will make some activities more difficult than before, or other activities easier to do.

Think of how the speed bump in a street can regulate the speed of a car (Latour 1999), or of how email can make it easier to communicate with some people and more difficult to communicate with others (for instance, if they have no access to the Internet). Myriad examples of the biases of different ICTs can be called up to illustrate the fact that technologies matter. You will find many examples in this book.

## ANCHORING RESEARCH ON SOCIAL AND INSTITUTIONAL CONTEXTS

In order to move beyond overly simplistic perspectives, and challenge taken-for-granted assumptions from multidisciplinary perspectives, it is critical that research is focused on particular aspects of the Internet in specific social and institutional settings. For example, the role of the Internet in the household is altogether different from that in a government. A household or government department in the US is likely to be significantly different than in China. As the Internet potentially affects everything, enabling so many different activities in so many contexts, the field requires ways to arrive at some cumulative set of overarching themes and conclusions. Some have approached this through meta-theoretical perspectives, such as Manuel Castells's concept of the "network society" that could be extended to many social and institutional contexts. This book does not embrace any single theoretical approach, but brings a set of scholars together who are addressing key questions across a range of disciplines. By focusing on a number of big questions for Internet Studies within and across four very general contexts of use, we seek to convey the excitement and open-ended nature of this emerging field. This work yields many concepts like the "network society" that can be applied to a variety of contexts of research.

## THE VALUE OF MULTIDISCIPLINARY PERSPECTIVES

One lesson that the editors have sought to follow in compiling this volume is that study of the Internet requires a multidisciplinary perspective. Much disciplinary research seeks to develop and refine a particular theoretical perspective. In contrast, most research within Internet Studies is focused on a problem, such as understanding the role of the Internet in a particular social context. The most important issues tied to the Internet cannot be addressed from any single theoretical perspective. Take online voting as one example. Research on Internet voting would need to draw from political science, but would also need to understand the security issues that could undermine its credibility, so computer scientists and security researchers would have a critical input. Problem-driven research is inherently multidisciplinary, and this is the case for most issues regarding the role of the Internet in society.

## The Big Questions Driving Internet Studies

The questions driving study of the societal implications of the Internet are wide ranging, but a few of the big questions can provide a sense of the issues at stake. These questions are important to each of the five separate but overlapping contexts that help organize this collection: (I) *Internet studies of everyday life,* (II) *information and culture on the line,* (III) *networked politics and government,* (IV) *networked businesses, industries, and economies,* and (V) *technological and regulatory histories and futures.* In each case, the central issue concerns whether the design and use of the Internet will be used to reshape access and behavior in ways that have major outcomes for societies along the following dimensions.

### POWER AND INFLUENCE

A core issue of technical change since the advent of computing centers on shifts of power (Castells 2009). Will the Internet empower or dis-empower networked individuals (Benkler 2006)? Whether as consumers or audiences in the household, or readers and producers of news, or as citizens and as activists, a promise surrounding the Internet has been to empower the user to have more choice and influence vis-à-vis intermediaries, news organizations, governments, and business. This issue has local as well as global dimensions, for example whether people can hold local news organizations and politicians more accountable, but also whether the Internet empowers Western sources of news and cultural production—the old information order—or amplifies new sources of content production, such as in low-income countries, that might find a more global audience in a new world information order.

### EQUALITY AND DIVIDES

Will the Internet contribute to an exacerbation or reduction of socioeconomic inequalities (Unwin 2009, Kleine 2013)? The fact that over 2.5 billion people have access to the Internet makes it even more apparent that over 4 billion people do not. How are non-users distributed across countries, cities, class, race, and gender? Are digital divides possible to bridge, or will new technologies continue to exacerbate the inequalities between those who are on and offline (Graham 2011)? We need, ultimately, to understand what a lack of connectivity means for those who aren't connected. Does it mean absence from networks of knowledge, a lack of access to the right nodes in global production chains, an inability to connect with potential employers, and barriers to communication with friends and family? Related to these issues, does the Internet, and the associated technological infrastructures of use, impose particular norms, values, and ideals that are drawn from, and are thus more conducive to, usage in particular socio-economic contexts? And will the Internet actually address any of the core issues about inequality of access, participation, and voice that we are able to observe in almost every place and community on our planet?

## QUALITY AND DIVERSITY

Is the Internet undermining the quality or diversity of information crucial to democratic societies? Prior to advances in searching, for example, the Web was frequently referred to as a giant garbage dump of information. Bloggers have been castigated as rank, unknowledgeable amateurs (Keen 2007), Wikipedia articles and OpenStreetMap edits have been ridiculed for biases and inaccuracies, with untruths and misinformation potentially spreading with astonishing speed and scope through social media. However, others have viewed the Internet as a new source of information that can complement existing sources and help ensure greater accountability. It can do this both by questioning and critically discussing information sources, and by exposing potential untruths and inaccuracies to the gaze of hundreds or thousands of users through what has been dubbed "the wisdom of the crowd" (Surowiecki 2004). As innovations in digital research have become prominent across the sciences and humanities, questions have been raised about its implications for the quality of research (Dutton and Jeffreys 2010). Apart from issues of quality, critics have argued that the Internet and social media will cocoon users in echo chambers and filter bubbles that simply reinforce their beliefs and attitudes (Sunstein 2007; Pariser 2012; Graham et al. 2013), while others see the Internet as a means of enabling people to find new and more diverse sources of information (Rainie and Wellman 2012).

## HIERARCHIES AND NETWORKS

Another theme tied to all social and institutional contexts is the potential for the Internet to undermine hierarchies that are supported by one-to-many networks of communication and information access. The Internet can easily support more diverse one-to-one, many-to-one, and many-to-many networks of communication and information access. This is one idea behind the concept of a network society being ushered in by the digital age (Castells 1996). However, others would counter that digital media are being used to shore up hierarchies and support the continuity of traditional political and economic power structures (van Dijk 2012; Fuchs and Dyer-Witheford 2013). In the production of information and cultural artifacts, for example, the Internet is said to be undermining traditional distinctions between producers and users [former viewers and audiences] (Castells 2009).

Are users being empowered, or are they buttressing the popularity of traditional producers? How key is the role of users in becoming new sources of content, from posting comments to news stories to participating in collaborative citizen science projects? In politics, are networks powerful structures that can move in more agile ways than hierarchies, or are they unable to take decisive actions? Is the Internet advantaging networked groups and political movements, such as in support of collective action? Are businesses and economies able to benefit from the same transformative forces, such as bypassing intermediaries and creating more direct value-chains between producers and consumers, and reconfiguring the workplace to become a more distributed virtual organization (Huws 2003; Susskind 2013)?

## IDENTITY AND COMMUNITY

When you can participate in local and global networks of communication, it is important to ask what exactly an identity is—how do you portray yourself across multiple online and offline contexts (Castells 2010)? Identity construction undoubtedly becomes more important as you codify various facets of yourself and present them in different networks, such as your personal and work life. Here it is important to ask questions, not only about online versus offline identities, but rather about the ways in which identity is variably presented and enacted through a range of digital, networked, and disconnected forms and media. Similarly, it is important to focus ever more inquiry into the digitally augmented nature of our towns and cities (Graham et al. 2013), such as when a village, a monument, a shop, or an event is represented and defined online. As the Internet increasingly evolves from being a digital network that we log into, towards an assemblage of data and infrastructures that permeate all aspects of everyday life, we need to ask what those changes mean for the ways that urban environments and communities are governed, planned, lived in, and challenged (Graham 2004).

## FREEDOM OF EXPRESSION AND CONNECTION

The media have long been subject to concerns over freedom of expression, most often articulated around issues relating to freedom of the press, as enshrined in the First Amendment to the US Constitution but also in many other national, regional, and global documents (Dutton et al. 2011). Increasingly, as more of our everyday life and work is conducted over the Internet, concerns over freedom of expression relate to issues about Internet policy and regulation. Examples include whether nations, Internet Service Providers (ISPs), organizations, or households should filter content on the Internet in order to protect children and various cultural, ethical, or religious sensibilities (Nash 2013), and whether and how this is practiced (Deibert et al. 2010). Should users be disconnected if they violate laws and regulations governing copyright or decency? What penalties are proportionate to the offense? How should we study, critique, and challenge opaque and proprietary filtering and ranking systems that increasingly shape what is visible (and invisible) on the Internet? Will the Internet be a technology that facilitates more freedom of expression, or will it enable governments, corporations, and regulators to block content, and disconnect users, in ways that can have a chilling effect on freedom of expression and connection (Dutton et al. 2011)?

## PRIVACY AND SECURITY

A similar battle rages over privacy and security issues on the Internet (Bennett and Parsons 2013). Most people support efforts that ensure their privacy—their right to be left alone, and for personal information about them not to be disclosed without their permission (Dutta et al. 2011). Yet, people have long been willing to sacrifice their personal privacy for reasons, for example, of public safety, health, or even convenience (Dutton and Meadow 1987). Are people more trusting in providing personal information to companies in the digital age, or is the protection of privacy becoming more complicated and less manageable by individuals? Many worry that big data, social media, and data shadows of everyday practices enable companies and governments to tap into the personal information of Internet users in ways that violate key privacy and data protection principles (O'Hara and Shadbolt 2008). Can privacy be protected in ways that enable Internet service providers to develop sustainable business models, such as through advertising? Must privacy and anonymity be sacrificed to protect people from cyber-bullies, trolls, or fraudsters? How will governments balance concerns over privacy against other key concerns, such as national security or the enforcement of intellectual property rights and other laws and policies?

## THE SOCIAL-SHAPING OF TECHNOLOGY

The "social shaping of technology" has been a broad theoretical approach to science and technology studies since the 1980s (MacKenzie and Wajcman 1985). This perspective takes the details of technology like the Internet as a focus of social inquiry. Technologies do not just spring into being, but are invented, designed, implemented, and used by people in particular social contexts. It is because these technologies matter that it is valuable to understand why technologies emerge and are designed and used in particular ways. Technologies are not on an inevitable path towards a single best design, as time and again less technically optimal designs often win out. Understanding the technical, economic, political, gendered, geographical, and other social factors shaping technologies can help foster better designs, more effective patterns of implementation and use, and more equitable and fair outcomes. While the focus of this volume is on the social implications of the Internet, it is taken as a given throughout this collection that technological innovation is a key focus of inquiry in all of the areas studied. The last section of the book moves this into a more central focus. What factors are shaping the futures of the Internet and its use across multiple contexts?

## INTERNET GOVERNANCE

The development of technologies and their social implications are also dramatically shaped by policy and regulations (DeNardis 2013). The very success of the Internet is in part due to many governments making an effort to encourage technological innovation through investment in computing and telecommunications, but also by not regulating early innovations in these fields. In the first decades of the 21st century, governments around the world are debating whether and how best to govern the Internet in the face of issues around child protection, cybercrime, and national security, in addition to politically charged turf struggles over who governs the Internet. While the outcomes of these debates and policy initiatives around the world are uncertain, it is very clear that policy and governance issues will be increasingly important to the future of the Internet and its societal implications. To put it in the starkest terms, the continued vitality, if not very existence, of a global infrastructure for media, information, and communication services is at stake, making it critical that the Internet be governed in ways that preserve its documented value to global communication while managing to grapple with many issues of safety, security, privacy, and freedom of expression that hang in the balance. Who governs the Internet? Who should govern the Internet?

Changes in policy and governance of the Internet are almost certain to follow from global controversies around who governs the Internet. Therefore, it is important to study empirical relationships and anchor debate in what people actually do through, and on, the Internet, how the Internet and the sites that it contains are themselves designed, governed, and produced, and the social effects of technical designs that pervade our increasingly Internet-mediated world. But it is simultaneously crucial to keep a clear view of future developments in technology and policy that together can reshape the societal implications of the Internet, such as turning a potential technology of freedom into a tool of surveillance, or segmenting a global digital network into a set of national and regionally isolated domains.

## UNCERTAIN FUTURES

The future of each of the issues across all of the contexts discussed above is uncertain in light of the unpredictability of technology, policy, and users in the coming years and decades. The fact that we are in a position to study the actual role of the Internet in multiple contexts does not mean that the Internet and its use and impacts will stand still. Quite the contrary, there are major developments around the Internet, such as big data, cloud computing, the ascendance of new devices like the smartphone, the Internet of Things, the Semantic Web, wearable computing, and more, that could reconfigure many of the ways we get information, communicate with people, navigate through our cities, organize activities, and obtain services in the future (Carr 2008; Zittrain 2008). For these reasons, it is critical that multidisciplinary research should study the social shaping of technologies of the Internet, the factors shaping Internet policy, and the relationships between technical change, patterns of use, and Internet governance.

# Outline of this Book

The book is divided into five parts: (I) *Internet Studies of Everyday Life*, (II) *Information and Culture on the Line*, (III) *Networked Politics and Government*, (IV) *Networked Businesses, Industries, and Economies*, and (V) *Technological and Regulatory Histories and Futures*. Each one of these parts focuses on particular contexts of use and impacts, but also remains closely interrelated to the other parts.

The chapters in Part I center on the important roles played by the Internet in contemporary life. Aleks Krotoski (Chapter 1) kicks off this discussion by introducing many of the social issues raised by the Internet, and how blame is distributed, arguing that the Internet is often a scapegoat that diverts attention from more fundamental reasons why problems, such as bullying online, exist. We then move to a discussion of "next Internet generation users" in which Grant Blank and William Dutton (Chapter 2) describe how people in Britain and other high-income countries use the Internet. They argue that the increased use of mobile smart phones and other portable devices like tablets is complementing rather than substituting for the use of a variety of devices to access the Internet at home, work, and on the move, making the Internet even more central to everyday life and work. This is followed by an analysis of the foundations that drive the popularity of social media, with Bernie Hogan and Barry Wellman (Chapter 3) focusing attention on the centrality of creating a self-portrait through the use of social network sites.

Victoria Nash (Chapter 4) has been involved in ongoing debates over children and the Internet and provides insights concerning the role of children in the politics of Internet policy and practice. In so doing she demonstrates how children have been one of the most politically charged topics of Internet debate, whether they are the focus of online learning initiatives or at risk from bullying or online pornography. In the final chapter in Part I, Lisa Nakamura (Chapter 5) focuses on race and gender online by examining the world of online gaming, where racism and sexism is often dramatically exhibited.

In Part II, the focus turns to the role of the Internet in the creation and accessibility of information that is reshaping global cultural practices, processes, and products. In the first chapter, Mark Graham (Chapter 6) illuminates global geographies of information resources, showing how data on the Internet reflect material places, as well as the digital divisions of labor that produce them. He argues that the geographical distribution of information resources shapes both what we know and the ways that we are able to enact, produce, and reproduce social, economic, and political processes and practices—a central theme of this book. The geography of the Internet is carried forward by Gillian Bolsover, William Dutton, Ginette Law, and Soumitra Dutta (Chapter 7) in describing what they call the "New Internet World," comparing the United States, one of the early leading nations online, and China, the largest emerging nation of the New Internet World. They argue that the center of gravity of the Internet is shifting away from North America and Europe as emerging nations of Asia and other low-income countries come online in far larger numbers.

We then move from chapters focused on the global cultures of the Internet to address some of the major cultural concerns over the Internet: Is the Internet undermining the quality of information and media, such as by destroying the press and mass media? Nic Newman, William Dutton, and Grant Blank (Chapter 8) show that social media have had major implications for the press, but generally are adding to what they call the evolving ecology of news rather than substituting for the press. There is a strong symbiotic relationship between the news and the Internet and social media. Likewise, Sung Wook Ji and David Waterman (Chapter 9) look at the economics of the media industries in a way that challenges conventional wisdom, finding that the film industry is producing more with less, as the Internet and digital technologies seem to be reducing the costs of production, without undermining the number and quality of productions.

Scholarship in the sciences and humanities is another major producer of information where there are also fears that the Internet might be undermining high-quality and grounded research (such as field interviews) in favor of remotely sensed "data shadows". Ralph Schroeder (Chapter 10) highlights how big data and new forms of computational analysis are adding new layers of information to more traditional methods, and therefore augmenting the sciences and humanities in powerful, but potentially problematic, ways.

The next section, Part III, moves to the study of politics and government in a digitally networked world. The idea that the Internet supports more horizontal and interactive networks rather than simply top-down hierarchies within organizations and governments has led to visions of the Internet democratizing government and politics, such as through enhancing the responsiveness of politicians to their constituencies. In governments around the world, major transformational changes have been slow to emerge, if at all, but Miriam Lips (Chapter 11) examines whether moves to provide government services digitally, by default, might well usher in more transformative structures and processes. This chapter provides an excellent overview of the concept of digital government.

This is followed by chapters that focus on the role of citizens in shaping governance and policy in the digital age. Stephen Coleman and Jay Blumler (Chapter 12) critically assess an initiative to use crowd sourcing to inform the UK Government, leading them to question whether governments can orchestrate the crowd from the top down. Their analysis is followed by a synthesis of research on networking and the Internet by Sandra González-Bailón (Chapter 13) that highlights the ways in which the Internet can facilitate networking, but also its limitations. This is followed by an analysis of online petitioning, a particularly promising form of bottom-up politics, by Helen Margetts, Scott Hale, and Taha Yasseri (Chapter 14). They find that the small proportion of successful petitions—those gaining a strong following—are successful almost immediately, underscoring the speed and immediacy of the Internet and the importance of timing in a networked society. Elizabeth Dubois and William Dutton (Chapter 15) move away from collective action to identify the emergence of a new organizational form that they argue to be enabled by the Internet—the Fifth Estate. They argue that the Fifth Estate will be as significant for the digital age as the press was in an earlier era.

In Part IV, the book shifts to the role of the Internet in work, business, and economic development, beginning with a fascinating account of the central role that scarcity of attention plays in the Internet age of millions of Web pages, videos, and blogs. Greg Taylor (Chapter 16) shows how economic theory can

be applied to understanding the scarcity of attention in order to think critically about the business models underlying Internet-mediated information
and services. In the next chapter, Richard Susskind (Chapter 17) draws from
his expertise in applying the Internet within the legal profession to examine
how digital technologies can transform work and learning processes in the
law, where analogies can be drawn with other professions as well.

The last two chapters of Part IV look at the role that the Internet can play
in the contexts of people and places in economic peripheries. Laura Mann
(Chapter 18) focuses on the potential for the Internet to enable job placement
in Africa. Her case study of the Sudanese labor market demonstrates the need
for technical systems to consider the entire process of recruitment and selection, making the design of systems more difficult than many early proponents
anticipated. Finally in this part, Mark Graham (Chapter 19) provides a similarly critical look at the potential of the Internet to empower producers in the
developing world. Instead of disintermediation that might benefit village-level
producers, he finds a new group of intermediaries becoming the primary ben-
eficiaries of Internet-mediated value chains.

Part V concludes the volume by turning to the technologies and regulatory processes that are likely to shape the future of the Internet. Eli Noam
(Chapter 20) looks at the history and future of media consumption and distribution moving toward very fast Internet television via next-generation
networks. Extrapolating trends and technical affordances, Noam speculates
on the content of the future. Another futures perspective is provided by
Christopher Millard (Chapter 21), who looks at the nature and implications of
cloud computing, showing that it opens up a variety of uncertainties over how
to protect and regulate personal data in the clouds. This potential for technical
change to have implications for policy and practice is a central theme for Laura
DeNardis (Chapter 22), who develops the significance of technical designs in
shaping the governance of the Internet. Most people focused on Internet governance are looking at policy processes, but technical decisions, such as in
standard setting, can also have profound implications for such issues as privacy and freedom of expression.

The last chapter by Yorick Wilks (Chapter 23) speculates on the potential
for the next generation of the Web—the so-called Semantic Web—that knows
about its content in ways that will have major implications for who controls
the meaning of terms, and therefore the ability to structure networked knowledge, perhaps one of the most futuristic but significant power shifts that are at
stake in the design of the Internet's future.

This book offers a starting point for those interested in understanding some
of the key interactions of the Internet and society. It provides an overview of
some of the key questions in Internet Studies, and a diversity of data, methods,
and approaches employed to answer them. You will see that much of this work
opens up many new questions while addressing others. The Internet and the

practices that it mediates are constantly evolving, and constantly being reproduced in novel, contingent, and unanticipated ways. As such, Internet research needs to learn from the past, ground itself in a diversity of disciplinary perspectives, and look to the future. In doing so, it can address core questions about equality, voice, knowledge, participation, and power; and it can do so in ways that look to the future, and ask what the ever-changing configurations of technology and society mean for our everyday lives. Armed with such an understanding, it is possible to address the major issues of policy and practice facing societies around the world as we seek to harness the potential of the Internet and avoid the risks that remain very real for our networked society.

## ■ REFERENCES

Bell, D. (1973). *The Coming of Post-Industrial Society: A Venture in Social Forecasting.* New York: Basic Books.

Benkler, Y. (2006). *The Wealth of Networks: How Social Production Transforms Markets and Freedom.* New Haven, CT: Yale University Press.

Bennett, C. J. and Parsons, C. (2013). "Privacy and Surveillance," in W. H. Dutton (ed.), *The Oxford Handbook of Internet Studies.* Oxford: Oxford University Press, 486–508.

Carr, N. (2008). *The Big Switch: Rewiring the World, from Edison to Google.* New York: W. W. Norton & Company.

Castells, M. (1996), *The Rise of the Network Society: The Information Age: Economy, Society and Culture.* Oxford: Blackwell.

Castells, M. (2009). *Communication Power.* Oxford: Oxford University Press.

Castells, M. (2010). *The Power of Identity*, 2nd edn. Oxford: Wiley-Blackwell.

Deibert, R., Palfrey, J., Rohozinski, R., and Zittrain, J. (2010) (eds). *Access Controlled: The Shaping of Power, Rights, and Rule in Cyberspace.* Cambridge, MA: MIT Press.

DeNardis, L. (2013). *The Global War for Internet Governance.* New Haven, CT: Yale University Press.

de Sola Pool, I. (1983). *Technologies of Freedom.* Cambridge, MA: Belknap Press.

Dutta, S., Dutton, W. H., and Law, G. (2011). *The New Internet World: A Global Perspective on Freedom of Expression, Privacy, Trust and Security Online: The Global Information Technology Report 2010–2011.* New York: World Economic Forum, April.

Dutton, W. H. (1999). *Society on the Line: Information Politics in the Digital Age.* Oxford: Oxford University Press.

Dutton, W. H. (2013) (ed.). *The Oxford Handbook of Internet Studies.* Oxford: Oxford University Press.

Dutton, W. H., Dopatka, A., Hills, M., Law, G., and Nash, V. (2011). *Freedom of Connection— Freedom of Expression: The Changing Legal and Regulatory Ecology Shaping the Internet.* Paris: UNESCO, Division for Freedom of Expression, Democracy and Peace.

Dutton, W. H. and Jeffreys, P. W. (2010) (eds). *World Wide Research: Reshaping the Sciences and Humanities.* Cambridge, MA: MIT Press.

Dutton, W. H. and Meadow, R. G. (1987). "A Tolerance for Surveillance: American Public Opinion Concerning Privacy and Civil Liberties," in K. B. Levitan (ed.), *Government Infostructures.* Westport, CT: Greenwood Press, 147–170.

Ess, C. M. and Dutton, W. H. (2013). "Internet Studies: Perspectives on a Rapidly Developing Field," *New Media & Society*, 15(5): 633–643.

Fuchs, C. and Dyer-Witheford, N. (2013). "Karl Marx @ Internet Studies," *New Media & Society*, 15(5): 782–796.

Gotlieb, C. and Borodin, A. (1973). *Social Issues in Computing*. Toronto: Academic Press.

Graham, M. (2011). "Time Machines and Virtual Portals: The Spatialities of the Digital Divide," *Progress in Development Studies*, 11(3): 211–227.

Graham, M. (2013). "Augmented Realities and Uneven Geographies: Exploring the Geolinguistic Contours of the Web," *Environment and Planning A* 45(1): 77–99.

Graham, M., Zook, M., and Boulton, A. (2013). "Augmented Reality in the Urban Environment: Contested Content and the Duplicity of Code," *Transactions of the Institute of British Geographers* 38(3): 464–479.

Graham, S. (2004) (ed.). *The Cybercities Reader*. London, Routledge.

Howard, P. N. and Jones, S. (2004) (eds). *Society Online: The Internet in Context*. London: Sage.

Hunsinger, J., Klastrup, L., and Allen, M. (2010) (eds). *International Handbook of Internet Research*. London: Springer.

Huws, U. (2003). *The Making of a Cybertariat: Virtual Work in a Real World*. London: The Merlin Press.

Keen, A. (2007). *The Cult of the Amateur: How Today's Internet is Killing Our Culture*. Doubleday: New York.

Kitchin, R., and Dodge, M. (2011). *Code/Space: Software and Everyday Life*. Cambridge, MA: MIT Press.

Kleine, D. (2013). *Technologies of Choice? ICTs, Development, and the Capabilities Approach*. Cambridge, MA: MIT Press.

Latour, B. (1999). *Pandora's Hope: Essays on the Reality of Science Studies*. Cambridge, MA: Harvard University Press.

Lievrouw, L. and Livingstone, S. (2006). *Handbook of New Media: Social Shaping and Social Consequences of ICTs*. London: Sage.

MacKenzie, D., and Wajcman, J. (1985) (eds). *The Social Shaping of Technology: How a Refrigerator Got its Hum*. Milton Keynes: Open University Press.

Mesthene, E. G. (1969). "Some General Implications of the Research of the Harvard University Programme on Technology and Society," *Technology and Culture* (Oct.), repr. as "The Role of Technology in Society," in A. H. Teich (1981) (ed.), *Technology and Man's Future*, 3rd edn. New York: St Martin's Press, 91–129.

Morozov, E. (2011). *The Net Delusion*. London: Penguin Books.

Nash, V. (2013). "Analyzing Freedom of Expression Online," in Dutton, W. H. (ed.), *The Oxford Handbook of Internet Studies*. Oxford: Oxford University Press, 441–463.

O'Hara, K. and Shadbolt, N. (2008). *The Spy in the Coffee Machine: The End of Privacy as We Know It*. Oxford: Oneworld.

Pariser, E. (2012). *The Filter Bubble: What the Internet is Hiding from You*. London: Penguin Books.

Peng, T-Q, Zhang, L., Xhong, Z-J, and Zhu, J. J. H. (2013). "Mapping the Landscape of Internet Studies: Text Mining of Social Science Journal Articles 2000-2009," *New Media & Society*, 15(5): 644–664.

Rainie, L. and Wellman, B. (2012). *Networking: The New Social Operating System*. Cambridge, MA: MIT Press.

Schmidt, E. and Cohen, J. (2013), *The New Digital Age: Reshaping the Future of People, Nations and Business*. London: John Murray.

Smith, A. (2012). *Totally Wired: On the Trail of the Great Dotcom Swindle*. London and New York: Simon & Schuster.

Stoll, C. (1995). *Silicon Snake Oil*. New York: Doubleday.

Sunstein, C. R. (2007). *Republic.com 2.0*. Princeton, NJ: Princeton University Press.

Surowiecki, J. (2004). *The Wisdom of Crowds: Why the Many are Smarter than the Few and How Collective Wisdom Shapes Business, Economies, Societies, and Nations*. New York: Doubleday.

Susskind, R. (2013). *Tomorrow's Lawyers*. Oxford: Oxford University Press.

Unwin, T. (2009) (ed.). *ICT4D: Information and Communication Technology for Development*. Cambridge: Cambridge University Press.

Van Dijk, J. (2012). *The Network Society*, 3rd edn. London: Sage.

Wajcman, J. (2014 forthcoming), *Digital Temporalities*. Cambridge, MA: MIT Press.

Wellman, B. and Haythornwaite, C. (2002) (eds). *The Internet in Everyday Life*. Oxford: Blackwell.

Williams, F. (1982). *The Communications Revolution*. London: Sage.

Wyatt, S., Thomas, G., and Terranova, T. (2002). "They Came, They Surfed, They Went Back to the Beach: Conceptualizing Use and Non-Use of the Internet," in S. Woolgar (ed.), *Virtual Society? Technology, Cyberbole, Reality*. Oxford: Oxford University Press, 23–40.

Zittrain, J. (2008). *The Future of the Internet and How to Stop It*. London: Allen Lane.

# PART I

# Internet Studies of Everyday Life

# 1 Inventing the Internet: Scapegoat, Sin Eater, and Trickster

*Aleks Krotoski*

## Introduction

Technology is often greeted with equal degrees of excitement and fear when it's first introduced. In the web wars of the first two decades of the 21st century, the utopians champion the digital world as a panacea, arguing the case for enthusiastic adoption as a widespread social change for good. The web dystopians, on the other hand, warn of the great upset the technology will bring, and in particular how they expect it to undermine the trust bonds that hold family, community, and society together.

The fierce debates that center on arguments at the polar ends of the spectrum are usually divorced from historical experience, focusing only on the now and ignoring concerns that accompanied earlier innovations. In the 1830s, for example, the telegraph, which like the Internet sped up communication between people, countries, and corporations, was at that time expected to "[revolutionize] business practice, [give] rise to new forms of crime, and [inundate] its users with a deluge of information," as Tom Standage wrote in 1998 in his history of the telegraph, *The Victorian Internet*. "Attitudes to everything from newsgathering to diplomacy had to be completely rethought" (Standage 1998: 8). And the popular press at the time of the inventions of the telephone and the electric light was similarly preoccupied with moral panics about how they would transform class, family, and gender relationships (Marvin 1988). Few public conversations consider that very little—or indeed nothing—might happen to individuals or society *because of the innovation*. As Marvin and Standage both argue in their treatments of new technologies, not much change is more often reality.

What these popular social historians also propounded was that the fear surrounding the technology masked the fears surrounding the changes in the interpersonal and societal structures that were already in progress. The technology became the scapegoat, a sin eater, a trickster. The same can be argued for the newest media: the Internet.

A scapegoat is a person, institution, or thing that is singled out and made to bear the blame for others. It is a symbol of the sins of the people and is usually banished. A trickster is a similar psychoanalytic construct, but it is more pro-active: tricksters disrupt the status quo, usually forcing an evolution essential for progress. They are vilified but avoid punishment. This chapter argues that both of these are true in the case of the Web.

The polemic arguments at the ends of the spectrum about the absolute positive or absolute negative impact of the technology on our social and psychological selves obscure the costs and benefits that lie in between. The negotiations about the Web between consumers, developers, corporations, and governments are increasingly responsive to these extreme arguments. The result has been mobilization by special interests groups who put pressure on legislative bodies to take a stand or develop solutions to tackle hot-button issues. Three key areas stand out: debates about the effects of the availability of explicit materials online translate into calls for content regulation; debates about decline in face-to-face communication translate into questions about identity verification and credibility; and debates about radicalization and hate acts translate into negotiations about privacy and surveillance. Rarely is empirical evidence brought to bear in moral panic, despite widespread commentary and assertions about the subject in question (Altheide 2009), and indeed, some claims fly in the face of what empirical evidence there is about the actual social implications of the Internet.

A closer look at the content of these three contentious topics of debate—those hot-button issues of explicit content, community, and radicalization—aims to explore the parameters that are particularly important to the groups and individuals who debate them. It will identify the areas of inevitable change that are encouraged by some and dismissed by others. Although on first sight appearing to be concerned with the technology itself, the arguments are ultimately about the moral and value boundaries at the edges of our social and individual understandings. They provide a lens through which those social and psychological boundaries can be seen more clearly.

## Sex

There is little as socially contentious on the Web as sex. To web dystopians, the technology condones uncontrollable hyperactive pornography production houses that overwhelm the upstanding Internet with dangerous, hardcore, and inappropriate material. Their fear is that the ubiquity of such content threatens to upend the sexual mores of society, and their greatest worry is the perceived effect of children's access to pornography. When they do consider the effects on adults, themes that emerge in their debates center on the "normalization" of kinks and alternative sexual activities, alleged promiscuity amongst women and teenage girls, relationship breakdown, alleged increases in infidelity, and problematic (usually "addictive") use.

Those on the other side focus on the benefits of consumers' access to a wide variety of sexual material. They feel this is shifting sexual mores in a positive way: people with traditionally stigmatized sexual identities can re-assert positive self-esteem by expressing their actualized psychosexual selves in consequence-lite or openly supportive online environments; relationships can be more supportive and fulfilling with open communication between partners and acceptance of each other's interests; women's access to and production of porn is transforming the traditionally heteronormative pornographic industry in general; and their voices are changing offline social norms about gender roles in wider society.

And certainly, the Web's unique technological features fuel both sides of this discussion. As Cooper and his colleagues wrote in 2000 (Cooper 2000: 5), "There are three primary factors which 'turbocharge' online sexuality and make it such an attractive venue for sexual pursuits." He identifies them as access, affordability, and anonymity. This is the Web's "Triple-A Engine," and it affords behaviors for both consumers and producers.

Consumers are able to view, hear, and download sexual content anonymously, and often for free. Imagery, videos, stories, and potential partners that in the past would have required membership of specialist communities or visits to unsavory locations—risking exposure to family, friends, and colleagues—are now easily and cheaply accessible one or two clicks away.

Producers of sexual content are able to distribute homemade or professional materials to a wide audience using recording, editing, and publishing tools that have been built deliberately to deliver the goods at low to no cost. YouTube, iMovie, and the many specialist distribution channels virtually guarantee that anyone can access relevant and interested communities of practice who will consume and feed back.

Access, affordability, and anonymity are the cogs of the machine; web technology lays the foundations for a playground in which social boundaries can be explored. However, the public debate tends to anticipate some kind of transformation through simple exposure. Often, it's framed within a template that views sex as de facto bad or corrupting.

Nowhere is this more apparent than in the issues raised about hypersexualization and children. There is evidence of continuing trends towards earlier sexual activity, promiscuous modes of dress, and more sexually explicit language and interests over the last two decades, yet these trends cannot form the only evidence in the debate about the role of the Internet in evolving social mores. Boynton (2011) argues that children's social milieu are crossed by many influences, including other forms of mass media and interpersonal negotiations; a complex interaction between cultural shifts in the media, the commercialization of sex, and the role of the pharmaceutical industry share responsibility for altering public views on sexuality and sex.

Children's attitudes with regard to sexual content have not changed. Manning (2006) found that sex continues to be compelling, arousing and, frankly, rather confusing for children under the age of sixteen. When they see online porn, they are critical, shocked, disgusted, embarrassed, angry, afraid, and sad. They will tell a friend, then a parent, and then activate the defensive strategies they've learned in school, from parents, and from peers if something upsets them or if something risky is involved (Livingstone et al. 2011). Although the Web has given rise to a different palate of sexually explicit content taste-makers—as Attwood (2010: 72) observes, the new "porn professionals" are "younger, paler, decidedly less straight"—this shift is not based on consumption dynamics, but on the democratization of production for people who previously had no outlet to express their interests (Attwood 2010).

Another social shift levied at the Web is that the language people use to talk about sex has become more explicit. Those critical of the Web use this as an example of its corruptive and dangerous qualities. On the other side of the debate, web proponents reference relationship counsellors who say that the explicit language allows people a much broader lexicon to identify interests and problems (Boynton 2011). The language may be surprising to some, but the underlying issues that pre-teens and teens present to sex counselors and therapists remain the same: boys are concerned with their anatomies; girls are concerned about body image, relationships, and pleasing a partner.

The nature of romantic relationships has also come under scrutiny. Critics fear mobile phones and other portable web-enabled devices that allow for unobserved interactions, dating sites that offer the opportunity for discrete encounters with new partners, and the hidden nooks where strangers can quickly and easily be connected for an intimate moment. They suggest that the bond between romantic partners has weakened because of the access, anonymity, and affordability of a potential affair. Yet relationship counselors maintain that there is an existing problem in a relationship before an individual will begin any kind of affair, online or off (Whitty and Quigley 2008).

What has also remained the same are the expectations of trust between romantic partners. In 2011, the Oxford Internet Institute's *Me, My Spouse and the Internet* report found that looking at online porn or having an online affair—including talking about sex, having cybersex, discussing personal details or a relationship with a person the partner finds attractive—was considered to be an act of infidelity (Hogan, Li, and Dutton 2011). The person conducting the affair may view it as less of a breach (Whitty and Quigley 2008), but the betrayed partner experiences the infidelity in the same way: online or offline, infidelity continues to be viewed as any time and desire taken away from the current partner.

These are only a few areas of concern when it comes to the implications of online sexual content, but they offer evidence that suggests that any recorded effects have not been as dramatic as presented by either side. But the research itself may also be a factor in how the Web is perceived when it comes to the prevalence of uncommon sexual content and practices. The most frequently published studies frame online consumption as problematic by focusing on populations in mental health facilities and hospitals, rather than on the population at large. Their results naturally focus on the correlations between addiction, offenses, and relationships problems, and online sexual content, rather than on the experiences of non-clinical populations.

Jenkins (2007) reminds us that sex and pornography are always central to debates about new, emerging technology, as the public adapts to the larger social shifts that the technology is also part of. New media exposes boundaries between what is public and what is private, and forces new rules about the competing views of sex as liberating or socially destructive. Fear has been heightened in the age of the Internet because explicit materials have become accessible to everyone, particularly audiences who have historically been forbidden them.

# Community

It shouldn't be possible for communities to form online. A conservative working definition of community usually specifies some kind of face-to-face interaction, like clubs that meet in the scout hut, or parents from the local high school who get together to bake cookies for a fundraiser to benefit the football team. Communities are traditionally place-bound, by geography, by neighborhood, by school district, by church.

Town planners responsible for the suburban flight from many post-industrial revolution mega-cities attempted to engineer community by building cul-de-sacs, public parks, and cross streets to encourage accidental encounters. The theory was that they could create flows through the suburbs that would allow people to bump up against one another, to help them develop what environmental psychologists call "place identity" (Proshansky 1978), and what sociologists call "social capital" (Putnam 2000).

Without place identity, no one "owns" or identifies with a place. They won't use it or take care of it. They won't feel comfortable going to the scout hut, or sending their kids there alone. And without social capital, there is no received group wisdom to demarcate the boundaries of the communities, to identify who belongs and who doesn't. It will be irrelevant where someone lies in the pecking order, because no one will have access to anything of interest to anyone else. People will stop speaking a common language, because there will be no symbolic reference points to keep the community together. There will be no pride because no one will feel like they want to belong.

Place identity and social capital are the building blocks of community. They are the ties that bind, and also that gag. They are the adhesive between individuals and their physical and interpersonal environments, a psychological sticky tape that encourages participation and civic-mindedness.

And location-based bias is where the debates about community and the Web arise. If these two features can only be developed and maintained in a physical location, the Web is the antithesis of this, a vacuum of local participation. Those who pose this argument believe the Internet is sucking civic duty away from the neighborhood, school district and church, leaving broken windows and social apathy.

There is some evidence that supports this side of the debate. Using membership rosters of traditional community organizations as a longitudinal metric, Putnam (2000) observed a declining trend in the number of people on the membership rosters of social capital-rich groups, like the Boy Scouts, PTAs, and church congregations in the United States during the 20th century. He suggested that upward trends in crime and antisocial behavior were due to this.

Yet Putnam's work notably focuses on the decline in offline "community" before the Web. He has since considered the potential of new technology for social capital, proposing that the Web can indeed build a version called *bridging* social capital (i.e. it can help connect people who otherwise would not have been connected), but he cautions that it is unable to support another, more long-lasting version, *bonding* social capital (i.e. the type that ties people together). Information exchange is fine; it needs a context, however, to be meaningful.

The web proponents tend to focus on a conceptual community: the feeling of belonging that isn't fabricated from bricks and mortar, grass and mud, or wood and straw, but is the psychological sense that one belongs to part of a whole. This arm of the debate argues that community is, as Goffman wrote in 1959 and Wellman and his colleagues continue to write today, a de-physicalized, conceptual and psychological phenomenon (Wellman and Gulia 1999).

The problem with conceptual communities is that the absence of a tangible thing makes them difficult to measure and therefore to define objectively. They exist in the minds of their members. They are the consensual hallucinations science fiction author William Gibson describes in *Necromancer* (1984). A physical community has clear boundaries, members, and tangible assets; the other is messy: it can't be seen, touched, tasted, or smelled. Yet Goffman argued they serve the same psychological purpose: they give a sense of belonging and offer a safe space for their members to express themselves within the boundaries of the unspoken and spoken rules.

Although Goffman helped to shift the definition of community in the 1960s, the empirical test of conceptual community's value and resilience has been the Internet. Indeed, the anthropologists and sociologists who found themselves in early forums, listservs, and email groups described the emergence of community in this placeless space "as much of a surprise to online participants as...to non-participants" (Haythornthwaite 2007: 125). They also documented how community members described their virtual locations using physical reference points (Correll 1995), and the place identification that emerged in their descriptions of their online assets, like homepages, blogs, and other websites. This identification inspires individuals to volunteer time to "clean up" the virtual asset, whether by documenting group rules, optimizing programming code, or keeping the community's online features generally tidy.

This successful proof of concept for the conceptual community has been an uneasy negotiation for those who believe community demands physical space, and those who do not. In the absence of physical environments that encourage communal experience, argue the web proponents, online groups centered around common practices, beliefs, and concepts fill the gap. And indeed, Whitty and Carr (2005) proposed that an online romantic relationship was considered to be as real as an offline relationship, and work since that time has sought to describe the different ways in which variations in the significance of connections between online-only friends are expressed.

Additionally, there's evidence that individuals can be as influenced by online-only groups and virtual relationships as their offline groups and relationships, particularly in situations in which the group identity of the online group is something the individual identifies with strongly. As in physically based groups, if belonging to a community is important, the individual will step in line with the rules of behavior that group membership dictates (Krotoski 2009).

Wellman's work has also explored the ways online activity can enhance the civic involvement of offline communities, specifically when an offline community uses online tools to extend its practices into the virtual space (Wellman and Gulia 1999).

"Community" has long been under threat; in recent history, the scapegoat was industrialization and urbanization. Later, it became personal technology. In his work on community decline, Putnam argued that the culprit in the decline in social capital is technology—any technology that allows people to function collectively but separately. The car, the telephone, electricity, and the television have all been scapegoated when introduced, as the public negotiates shifts in the nature of connections between members of groups. "Each new disruption in the (imagined) ideals of home and town is met with resistance and fear of the further degradation of our daily experiences," argues Haythornthwaite (2007: 125). We continue to exist in a world away from the computer, and the benefits of online or offline community are apparent if the focus isn't on their differences, but on how people connect and what they get from their communications, whatever the medium.

## Hate

Another area of fierce debate is online behavior, and specifically how anti-social behavior is transforming offline communities by degrading interpersonal interactions. This is an extension of the social capital debate, but it focuses on the ties between individuals rather than those between the individual and the group.

Generally, the accused party in bad behavior online is the anonymity of the medium. Specifically, web critics propose that the ability to hide behind a computer screen removes the social restrictions for pro-social behavior because, in an environment in which an individual can disappear with the flip of a switch, there is no consequence for online action.

Arguing the case for the other side is conceptually difficult: no one can ignore the "flame wars" and other bad behavior that poisons many online comments boards and forums. Bullying behaviors have also naturally found an outlet in social networks. Yet web proponents tend to present two arguments in their favor. First, they look at the research on deindividuation. It initially appears to contradict their view: deindividuation means to be removed from identity, to feel, as Zimbardo (1969) described it, "in a state of organism." Deindividuated people feel a sense of decreased personal responsibility, which in turn inspires impulsivity, irrationality, and disinhibited behavior.

But although deindividuation was considered the root of bad behavior when it was first described in the late 1960s, research since that time suggests that deindividuation need not result in it. Rather, this state can lead to good, caring, and pro-social behavior instead. The key variable isn't the loss of identity, but the social cues in the context in which the deindividuation occurs.

In a classic study, one group of participants was asked to wear a hood and cloak similar to the outfits won by the radical racist organization the Ku Klux Klan (anti-social condition). The other group wore a costume that resembled a nurse's uniform (pro-social condition). Those in the anti-social condition behaved more anti-socially, while those in the pro-social condition behaved more pro-socially. The deindividuation effects of anonymity brought on by the costume was mediated by the social cues woven into the symbolic meaning of the clothing that participants put on (Johnson and Dowling 1979).

Spears and Lea (1992) applied this thinking to the Web. They propose that the online environment has behavioral norms that vary according to online group, sites, and services. It is these social cues that inspire pro or anti-social behaviour, rather than the anonymity of the digital context. According to this theory, sites that have a culture of negativity will engender antagonistic comments, flame wars, and personal attacks, whereas sites that have a culture of positivity will engender supportive comments and positive actions. Online hate, therefore, need not be the result of anonymous web activity: as with offline bullying or in-person hate crimes, the contextual norms are what condone this kind of behaviour.

Web proponents put forward a further argument: they say the online world *isn't* anonymous. Rather, people operate in forums, games, blogs, and social networks under persistent pseudonyms that develop social status and reputations that allow or disallow access to communities, people, and assets. These online selves become as much an identity as a work identity, a school identity, a family identity, a play identity, or any other self an individual adopts that is unique to that context. The pseudonym carries as much social and personal consequence to the individual as their actions at work have to their reputation at work, and so on. If the online identity is a salient part of the individual's life, she or he will work to maintain positive relationships with the other people in the group, which means playing "nice," or according to the status quo. But this can cause problems, particularly if the status quo is antisocial.

A 2012 UK Home Affairs Committee report called *Roots of Violent Radicalisation* argued that the Web is a hate "incubator,"—that it is one of three places in the modern age that encourages and foments unrest and antagonism. Although the report also discussed the role of universities and prisons in recruitment and radicalization, the UK press headlined their coverage with phrases that described the Web as "particularly dangerous" and "one of the few unregulated spaces where radicalisation is able to take place" (Travis 2012).

Such statements naturally fuel the concerns of people worried about the Web's effects on society. The extreme scenario addressed by the Home Affairs Committee report takes the view that vulnerable populations are manipulated by anonymous others who encourage, usually through a campaign of propaganda, radical anonymous activity that can move beyond antagonistic online comments.

Indeed, the previous section of this chapter described how communities can form and influence their members, but the lean computer medium, without the many non-verbal cues apparent in offline interactions, can also lead to misunderstandings. This is where the anonymity of the medium can play a role in changing attitudes and behavior.

Perceptions about what an online group stands for, enhanced by the absence of contrary cues, may lead to a belief that the online group as a whole thinks and behaves in the same way as the individual. In fact, it might not. This phenomenon, known as pluralistic ignorance, can lead to changes in attitudes and behaviors as the individual conforms to those attitudes and behaviors she or he feels are important to belonging to the online group (Wojcieszak 2008).

Web opponents argue that this partial view can be used by people who wish to spread hateful messages and misinformation. The concern is that hate groups will recruit web users, and radicalize them by exclusively showing them content that contains hateful messages. Yet this is rarely the case, according to the Home Affairs Committee report and research from the UK-based counter-radicalization think tank Quilliam (Ali Musawi 2010). Both organizations' results suggest that the Web is not an effective recruitment vehicle: hate sites are generally inward-looking, boundary-defining exercises, in which existing members seek to clarify their messages by excluding others whom they don't trust or who don't represent their beliefs. Such groups are wary of new people, and almost never incorporate them into their group without meeting them face to face.

The implicit suggestion in the critical argument is that humans are naturally badly behaved, and that the Web removes the normative restrictions that keep our instincts in check. It also suggests that we are naturally vulnerable, weak-minded, and potentially threatening. The accusations about the Web and its potential to foment hatred sidestep these attributions, and how they might be addressed offline.

## The Technofundamentalist Trap

In each of these examples, the extreme arguments fall prey to what Siva Vaidhyanathan describes as "technofundamentalism," uncritical and unempirical faith in the machine (Vaidhyanathan 2011). Although their perspectives on the implications of the Web may differ, they share the belief that the technology is, deterministically, doing something *to* them, rather than capable of being shaped by the norms of the system. Certainly, as the Web is increasingly incorporated into daily life at the behest of commercial, government, or social systems, it has become natural to turn to it to solve problems, find information and like-minded others, and express ourselves. It has become an outlet for and a tool with which to achieve our human needs. And web services—from social networks to blogging software, chatrooms, photo and video sharing sites, and other communities—give their users tools that satisfy their needs.

We are in the process of incorporating the Web and other digital technologies into the wider toolbox we use to meet our human needs. These debates, however, stem in fact from innovation-inspired self-reflection about our personal and collective value systems at the beginning of the 21st century. The distress for Web opponents is not their disapproval of technology, but the disapproval of other people.

Technofundamentalism ultimately disempowers the individuals who use the technology. It is a discomfort to the degree to which people feel they have delegated control to the Web that has given rise to the arguments at either end of the debate. The true debate about technology that we should be having is over technofundamentalism, not these parameters.

An important part of recognizing technofundamentalist leanings is accepting that the design decisions of the technologies we use have inbuilt design affordances. Kranzberg's First Law applies here: technology is neither good, nor bad. Nor is it neutral (Kranzberg 1986). Search algorithms, for everything from love to information, include inbuilt assumptions of which results will be relevant or valuable to the person (or computer) that is asking the question. Social networks have inbuilt assumptions about the nature of connections and the value ascribed to them. Technofundamentalism ignores these human paradigms and their natural human failings.

Rather than looking at the nature of our social and personal boundaries, we have chosen to scapegoat a system that appears, at first glance, to be doing something to us.

It is not surprising that a new technology like the Internet has inspired such a response: most people believe they're un-recruitable, un-corruptible, and un-convincible, and that people not like them are vulnerable, weak-minded, and a potential threat. The Internet is a mass medium, and Davidson's "Third-Person Effect" (Davidson 1983) has been used to describe this bias in most other mass media. A psychological motivation towards self-esteem encourages the bias towards positive thoughts of the in-group and negative thoughts of the out-group, and therefore we can imagine others being influenced by sexually explicit content online, while we don't worry how we ourselves might be influenced.

The extreme positions over-simplify the issues, often conflicting with empirical research (as in the case of community). They tend to be fueled by moral panic, and emphasize the need and value of further analyses of the actual role of technological innovations like the Internet.

## ▓ REFERENCES

Ali Musawi, M. (2010). *Cheering for Osama: How Jihadists Use The Internet Forums*. London: Quilliam.

Altheide, D. L. (2009). "Moral panic: From sociological concept to public discourse," *Crime, Media, Culture*, 5(1): 79–99.

Attwood, F. (2010). *Porn.com*. New York: Peter Lang.

Boynton, P. (2011) "Interview: Dr. Petra Boynton, 'The UK's First Evidence-Based Agony Aunt' and researcher at UCL," *The Guardian*, January 31. <http://untanglingtheweb.tumblr.com/post/3030368921/interview-dr-petra-boynton-the-uks-first> (accessed April 25, 2013).

Cooper, A., Delmonico, D. L., and Burg, R. (2000). "Cybersex Users, Abusers, and Compulsives: New Findings and Implications," *Sexual Addiction and Compulsivity*, 7(5): 5–29.

Correll, S. (1995). "The Ethnography of an Electronic Bar: The Lesbian Cafe," *Journal of Contemporary Ethnography*, 24: 270–298.

Davidson, W. J. (1983). "The Third-Person Effect in Communication," *Public Opinion Quarterly*, 47(1): 1–15.

Gibson, W. (1984). *Neuromancer*. New York: Ace Books.

Goffman, E. (1959). *The Presentation of Self in Everyday Life*. Garden City, NY: Doubleday & Company/Anchor Books.

Haythornthwaite, C. (2007). "Social Networks and Online Community," in A. Joinson, K. McKenna, T. Postmes and U. Reips (eds.) (2007). *The Oxford Handbook of Internet Psychology*. Oxford: Oxford University Press, 121–137.

Hogan, B., Li, N., and Dutton, W. H. (2011). *A Global Shift in the Social Relationships of Networked Individuals: Meeting and Dating Online Comes of Age*. University of Oxford: Oxford Internet Institute.

Home Affairs Committee (2012). *Roots of Violent Radicalisation*. London: House of Commons.

Jenkins, H. (2007). "Porn 2.0." <http://henryjenkins.org/2007/10/porn_20.html> (accessed April 25, 2013).

Johnson, R. D. and Dowling, L. H. (1979). "Deindividuation and Valence of Cues: Effects on Prosocial and Antisocial Behavior," *Journal of Personality and Social Psychology*, 37(9): 1532–1538.

Kranzberg, M. (1986). "Technology and History: 'Kranzberg's Laws,'" *Technology and Culture*, 27(3): 544–560.

Krotoski, A. (2009). "Social Influence in Second Life: Social Network and Social Psychological Processes in the Diffusion of Belief and Behaviour on the Web." PhD thesis. Guildford: University of Surrey, Department of Psychology, School of Human Sciences.

Livingstone, S., Haddon, K., Gorzig, A., and Olafsson, K. (2011, September). *EU Kids Online*. London School of Economics.

Manning, J. C. (2006). "The Impact of Internet Pornography on Marriage and the Family: A Review of the Research," *Sexual Addiction & Compulsivity*, 13: 131–165.

Marvin, C. (1988). *When Old Technologies Were New: Thinking about Electric Communication in the Late Nineteenth Century*. New York: Oxford University Press.

Proshansky, H. M (1978). "The City and Self-Identity," *Environment and Behavior*, 10(2): 147–169.

Putnam, R. D. (2000). *Bowling Alone: The Collapse and Revival of American Community*. New York: Simon & Schuster.

Spears, M. and Lea, M. (1992). "Social Influence and the Influence of the 'Social' in Computer-Mediated Communication," in M. Lea (ed.), *Contexts of Computer-Mediated Communication*. Hemel Hempstead: Harvester Wheatsheaf, 30–65.

Standage, T. (1998). *The Victorian Internet*. New York: The Berkeley Publishing Group.

Travis, A. (2012). "Internet Biggest Breeding Ground for Violent Extremism, Ministers Warn," *The Guardian*, February 5. <http://www.guardian.co.uk/uk/2012/feb/06/internet-violent-extremism-breeding-ground> (accessed April 25, 2013).

Vaidhyanathan, S. (2011). *The Googlization of Everything—and Why We Should Worry*. Berkeley. CA: University of California Press.

Wellman, B. and Gulia, M. (1999). "Virtual Communities as Communities: Net Surfers Don't Ride Alone," in P. Kollock and M. Smith (eds.), *Communities in Cyberspace*. New York: Routledge, 167–194.

Whitty, M. T. and Carr, A. N. (2005). "Taking the Good with the Bad: Applying Klein's Work to Further our Understandings of Cyber-Cheating," *Journal of Couple and Relationship Therapy*, 4(2/3): 103–115.

Whitty, M. T. and Quigley, L. (2008). "Emotional and Sexual Infidelity Offline and in Cyberspace," *Journal of Marital and Family Therapy*, 34(4): 461–468.

Wojcieszak, M. (2008). "False Consensus Goes Online," *Public Opinion Quarterly*, 72(4): 781–791.

Zimbardo, P. G. (1969). "The Human Choice: Individuation, Reason, and Order Versus Deindividuation, Impulse and Chaos," in W. T. Arnold and D. Levine (eds.), *Nebraska Symposium on Motivation*. Lincoln, NE: University of Nebraska Press, 17: 237–307.

# 2 Next Generation Internet Users: A New Digital Divide

*Grant Blank and William H. Dutton**

## Introduction: The Post-PC Era?

Many pundits (e.g. King 2012) argue that Internet use has entered a "post-PC" era: mobile devices are becoming the "default gateway" for access to the Web and other services. It is nothing less than a major transformation from the use of desktop PCs and business laptops to small mobile devices, such as smart phones (Perlow 2012). Major computer firms, such as Hewlett-Packard, have responded to this vision with layoffs and new acquisitions that reposition companies for the mobile age in ways similar to the earlier transition from standalone personal computers to the Internet age.

There is no question that the phenomenal growth of smart phones, tablets, and readers has had a major impact on how people access the Internet. However, the argument that we are entering a "post-PC" era is often based on the idea that mobile devices are replacing rather than complementing PCs, often based on the slowing of PC sales figures. This chapter shows that the relationship between PCs and mobile devices is more complex than simple replacement of one device by another.

We will describe this relationship through survey evidence on individuals and households in the UK, but also in the context of comparative surveys in over two dozen other nations that are part of the World Internet Project (WIP). These data enable us to address several key questions: How have devices like smartphones and tablets changed the way people access and use the Internet? Who uses these devices? Are they closing down the Internet, making it less creative, or opening up the Internet to new users and uses? If they are valuable new channels for access, are they more widely accessible, enabling new users, or does access on new devices reinforce existing digital divides?

---

* This chapter is an update and revision of Dutton and Blank (2013).

# Perspectives on Technical Change and its Social Significance

Three alternative theoretical perspectives make contrasting predictions about the social implications of a shift in patterns of access to the Internet. They are all qualitative explanations of relationships, rather than operationally defined models, but these contrasting patterns of relationships capture the major competing perspectives on the role of the Internet in everyday life, which we can compare and contrast with our empirical survey findings.

## TECHNICAL RATIONALITY: DUMBING DOWN THE INTERNET

The technical rationality perspective draws on major features of new technologies to reason about the likely implications of adoption. It characterizes themes of some prominent scholars of the Internet and new technology, such as Lawrence Lessig (1999) and his view that "code is law." The view from this perspective is that the move towards "appliances" such as tablet computers or smart phones is bound up with the adoption of closed applications or "apps" that have a limited set of functions. Jonathan Zittrain (2008) saw this shift as likely to restrict the openness and "generativity" of the Internet, compared to general-purpose personal computers which enable users to program, write code, and not be limited to a secured set of applications and sites. Since those who adopt the new appliance devices, such as tablets, are often satisfied with closed applications, they are likely to be less sophisticated than those who remain anchored to personal computing, and less creative in their use and application of the Internet. Will they move users toward a role as more passive consumers of information and entertainment, with their activity limited to browsing to select content of interest?

## DOMESTICATION: INDIVIDUALS AND HOUSEHOLDS BRING THE TECHNOLOGY TO HEEL

In contrast, a "domestication" perspective on technology argues that the Internet will be shaped by social choices and structures in ways that reconfigure the technology to fit in with the values and needs of the household. The concept of domesticating technology (Silverstone 1996; Haddon 2006) emphasizes the influence of households or workplaces on shaping, taming, or domesticating technologies as users fit them into the values and interests of their particular social context. People adopt and integrate technologies into their everyday routines in ways that follow and reinforce existing practices, which differ across households.

Will mobile devices change the way people incorporate the Internet into their daily routines, or will households domesticate portable technologies to support their patterns of Internet use? Since domestication suggests people shape the Internet to their pre-existing interests and values, we would not expect the adoption of new mobile devices to make much difference in how people use the Internet, nor to have a significant, transformative impact on the social role of the Internet in their lives. Domestication should have a conservative influence on the social uses and impact of the Internet.

## RECONFIGURING ACCESS

A different theoretical perspective focuses on the likelihood of any communication technology "reconfiguring access," but in ways that are not predetermined by the features of the technology (Dutton 2005). From this perspective, it is impossible to determine the implications of technologies in advance, either by rationally extrapolating from the technical features of the innovations or by assessing the interests and values of users. This is distinguished from both a more technologically determinist view of dumbing down the Internet, or a socially determinist position like domestication.

Reconfiguring access takes note of the fact that users often reinvent technologies, employing them in ways not expected by their developers. In addition, the social role of a technology can be influenced by the actions of many actors other than users, and from choices far outside the household, which distinguishes this perspective from the notion of domestication. Control of new technologies, particularly a networked technology such as the Internet, is distributed across a wide array of actors, including users, Internet Service Providers, hardware manufacturers, search engine firms, and social networking companies. Rather than expecting the impacts to be determined by features of the technology, or the values and interests of the household, reconfiguring access places a central emphasis on observing the actual use and impact as it is shaped by a diverse ecology of actors, including users, but not limited to them, to discern emergent patterns of use and impact.

However, like a more technologically determinist model, the concept of reconfiguring access is based on the expectation that technologies do matter—they have social implications—in two major respects. They reconfigure (1) how people do things, as well as (2) the outcome of these activities (Dutton 1999). People adopt and use technologies, such as the Internet, more or less intentionally to reconfigure access in multiple ways, including their access to people, information, services, and technologies, and access to themselves.

From this perspective, the technology does not simply fit into existing practices, but it changes them. If a person enjoys reading the newspaper, they might decide to use the Internet to get access to the news. However, this changes not only how they get the news but what and how much news they can get, as well as how easily they can get it. It reconfigures their access to news, in this case, and therefore influences what they know—a profound social implication.

The Internet can change the outcome of information and communication activities by virtue of changing cost structures, creating or eliminating gatekeepers, redistributing power between senders and receivers, making a task easier or more difficult, changing the circumstances under which a task can be performed, restructuring the architecture of networks (many to one versus one to many), and changing the geography of access (Dutton 1999: 60–69). By changing costs, or eliminating gatekeepers, for example, the Internet can reconfigure access to information, people, services, and technologies, such as by making millions of computers accessible to a user of an inexpensive smart phone in the palm of their hand. The ability of the Internet to reconfigure access can be used to reinforce existing social arrangements, like helping friends stay in touch, or reconfiguring social relations, such as helping a person to meet new people. Technological change can shape these outcomes, as well as social choices.

## Methods and Data

This chapter addresses these issues around new patterns of Internet access by analysing survey data gathered in Britain as part of the Oxford Internet Survey (OxIS). Based on demographic, attitudinal, and Internet use questions it is possible to construct profiles of the survey participants, who include users and non-users of the Internet. These profiles allow us to draw detailed conclusions about who uses the Internet, in what ways, to what extent, and what differences it makes for everyday life and work.

OxIS is a biennial sample survey of adult Internet use in Great Britain, including England, Wales, and Scotland.[1] The first survey was conducted in 2003 and subsequent surveys followed in 2005, 2007, 2009, and 2011. As we write, the 2013 survey is in the field. Each survey has followed an identical sampling methodology. The respondents are selected for face-to-face interviews based on a multi-stage random sample of the population. Professionally trained field-survey staff conduct face-to-face interviews in people's homes. In this chapter, we focus on the 2011 survey, which had a response rate of

---

[1] For a more complete overview of the OxIS methodology, see <http://microsites.oii.ox.ac.uk/oxis/methodology> (accessed April 30, 2013).

51 percent. Our analyses are based either on the full sample of 2,057 completed interviews or on the subset of current Internet users: 1,498 respondents, 72.8 percent of the full sample.[2] Given the design of our probability sample, and high response rates, OxIS allows us to project to the adult (14 and over) population of Britain with a high level of confidence.

## The Emergence of Next Generation Users

In 2011, along with trends in mobile phone use and the diffusion of appliances, such as tablets, we saw two dramatic and interrelated shifts appearing in our survey results. First, the proportion of users using the Internet over mobile devices, such as a smart phone, continued to increase. As late as 2003 this was only a small proportion. At that time, 85 percent of British people had a mobile phone but only 11 percent of mobile phone users said they accessed the Internet over their mobile phone. However, by 2011, 98 percent of British people owned a mobile phone and the proportion accessing the Internet over their phone increased to nearly half (49%) of all users.

Second, by 2011, a larger proportion of Internet users had multiple devices available to access the Internet, such as multiple computers, readers, tablets, laptop computers, and smartphones. Just two years earlier, in 2009, only 19 percent had a tablet. Since then, the development of readers and tablets has boomed, such as with Apple's successful introduction of the iPad. In 2011, almost one-third of Internet users had a reader or a tablet with 6 percent having both devices. Fully 59 percent had access to the Internet via one or more of multiple devices, a trend that has continued since 2011.

Most observers have treated these developments as separate trends. There are even academics who focus only on mobile communication, and others who focus on tablets or the use of smart phones. However, these trends are not just related but are also synergistic. Those who own one device are more likely to own another device, and those who use multiple devices are also more likely to use the Internet on the move and from multiple locations.

Based on this analysis we identified two categories of users. First, we defined the Next Generation User (NGU) as someone who accessed the Internet from multiple locations and devices. Specifically, we operationally defined the Next Generation User as someone who used at least two Internet applications (out of four applications queried)[3] on their mobile and who fit two or more of the

---

[2]  See Dutton and Blank (2011) for a more detailed description of the sample and methodology.

[3]  The four applications are: browsing the Internet, using email, updating a social networking site, or finding directions.

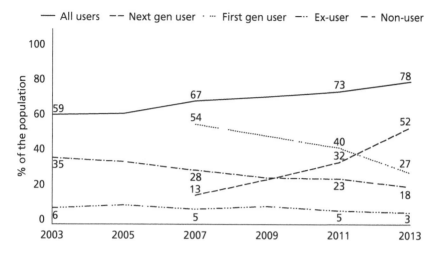

**Figure 2.1** Next Generation Internet Users in Context
OxIS: 2003 N: 2,029; 2005 N: 2,185; 2007 N:2,350; 2009 N: 2,013; 2011 N: 2,057; 2013 N: 2,657

following criteria: they owned a tablet, owned a reader, owned three or more computers. By this definition, in 2011, almost a third of Britons were Next Generation Users (Figure 2.1). Figure 2.1 has been updated with preliminary data from 2013. All other tables and figures, as well as the text, are based only on data through 2011, but you can see these trends have continued into 2013.

Second, from the 2003 OxIS survey of Internet use, access has been primarily via a personal computer in the home. For many, this was complemented by similar access at work or school. While access has moved from using a dial-up modem to using always-on broadband connections to the home, wireless connections have expanded and broadband speeds have continued to increase. Since 2003, most distinctions made among users were between those using a modem with narrow bandwidth and those using faster speed broadband connections who could do more things online. By 2011, almost all users had a broadband connection, so the major difference developed between those whose primary Internet access was from a stationary computer, who we have labeled the "first generation users," and those with multiple devices, some of which are portable, who are the "Next Generation Users."

Figure 2.1 shows the rise of Next Generation Users in the context of overall Internet use. British Internet use grew from just under 60 percent in 2003 to 73 percent in 2011, leaving more than a quarter of the British population without access to the Internet. There has been a steady but slow decline in the proportion of people who have never used the Internet (non-users), and relative stability in the proportion of those who have used the Internet at one time but who no longer do so (ex-users). Despite multiple government and private initiatives aimed at bringing more people online, digital divides remain in access to the Internet, albeit rose to 78 percent in 2013.

This gradual growth in the proportion of British people with access to the Internet contrasts dramatically with the rapid rise of Next Generation Users. They increased from 13 percent in 2007 to 32 percent of the British population by 2011. There is a corresponding decline in First Generation Users from 54 percent to 40 percent of the British population. Clearly, the promotion of new technical devices, such as the tablet, has changed the way households access the Internet. It is hard to see this as simply a process of domestication, rather than a consequence of new product and service offerings.

# What Difference Does a Generation Make?

Access to the Internet shapes the ways in which individuals use the technology, and how people wish to use the Internet shapes the technologies they adopt. This is shown by the contrast between first and next generation use of the Internet in three areas: content production, entertainment and leisure, and information seeking. In each case, a technical rationality might see innovations like mobile phones and tablets reducing the openness and generativity of users, while from a domestication perspective, you would expect to see little change in patterns of use between next and first generation users. We found quite different patterns in our 2011 survey (Dutton and Blank 2011).

## CONTENT PRODUCTION

In contrast to the predictions of technical rationality, with its focus on how the limited openness of new devices restricts users, Next Generation Users were more likely to be producers of content than were first generation users, who concentrated more on consumption rather than production. For many types of content, Next Generation Users were as much as 25 percentage points more likely to be producers. Specifically, Next Generation Users were more likely to update or create a profile on a social networking site (Dutton and Blank 2013). They are also more likely than first generation users to post pictures and videos, post messages on discussion boards or forums, and post stories, poetry, or other creative work. For more demanding types of content, such as maintaining a personal website or writing a blog, Next Generation Users were almost twice as likely to be producers than were first generation users. In such ways, innovations in access have been reconfiguring patterns of use by enabling greater production of content by Next Generation Users, but in a direction opposite to that expected on the basis of the more limited features of appliances.

## ENTERTAINMENT AND LEISURE

Compared with first generation users, the NGU were much more likely to listen to music online, play games, download music, watch videos online, and download, as well as upload, videos or music files (Dutton and Blank 2013). As with content production, these are large differences, often exceeding 20 to 25 percentage points. NGUs were also more likely to bet or gamble online, but this difference is much smaller than with content production. Next Generation Users seem to have integrated the Internet more extensively into their entertainment and leisure activities. In this respect, an association with listening to more music or watching more video productions is in line with the technical rationality of appliances, but is still reconfiguring access in significant respects, which would not be anticipated from the perspective of domestication.

## PORTABILITY AND MOBILITY

Will Next Generation Users access the Internet from more locations? The 2011 survey shows that this was indeed the case. NGUs were no more likely than first generation users to access the Internet from their home, as everyone did, but—importantly—they were no less likely to do so. This underscores the continuing centrality of the household across the generations of users. However, NGUs were far more likely to access the Internet on the move and from all other locations, including another person's home, at work, at school or at university, at a library, or at an Internet café (Dutton and Blank 2013).

This finding might suggest the flaw in a technically rational argument that appliances would undermine the generativity of the Internet (Zittrain 2008). Appliances are generally not substituting for personal computers and other more general-purpose devices, but complementing these technologies, and extending them in time and place. Nearly everyone with a reader or tablet tended to use these technologies to augment rather than replace their other modes for accessing the Internet.

More generally, and in contrast to the technical argument, or the domestication thesis, Next Generation Users appear to have been empowered, relative to the first generation users, in creating content, enjoying entertainment online, and accessing information in ways and at times and locations that fit into their everyday life and work in a more integrated way. Of course, those who want to create content and embed the Internet in more aspects of their everyday life are more likely to adopt mobile technologies, so in that sense, a domestication process could be relevant. Through the social shaping of adoption and the empowerment of users, it is clear that the Next Generation User has a more advantageous relationship with the Internet and the resources it can provide for accessing information, people, services, and other technologies.

This leads to the question, who are the Next Generation Users? Who is empowered by next generation access, and who is not?

## Who are Next Generation Users?

Are Next Generation Users simply the youth of the Internet age—the so-called "born digital"? Not really. Age and life stage were related to next generation use, but primarily in the degree that people who were retired, or of retirement age, were much less likely to be Next Generation Users. Those who were unemployed were also somewhat less likely to be part of the next generation, while students and the employed were equally likely to be Next Generation Users. It is not simply a function of youth or age cohorts. For example, only 52 percent of students were Next Generation Users (Dutton and Blank 2013). In short, domestication is not equal as some are more capable of bending new technologies to serve their needs and interests than are others. In this way, innovations are reconfiguring access by creating a new digital divide across people at different stages of life.

We need to develop a more sophisticated understanding of Next Generation Users that simultaneously considers multiple factors, including non-demographic characteristics of users. This requires two steps. First we will describe variables that influence Next Generation Use beyond demographics. And second, we will summarize the characteristics of Next Generation Users in a more concise fashion, using a multivariate analysis as a means of discerning whether patterns of use have been shaped by being a NGU, independent of one's social and economic background.

Four categories of non-demographic variables relate to Next Generation Users, beginning with experience on the Internet. Dutton and Shepherd (2006) and Blank and Dutton (2012) find that the Internet is an "experience technology," meaning the more people are exposed to the Internet, the more they understand what it can do and the more they use it. People with more experience are more likely to be open to investing in new technologies for accessing the Internet because they are more likely to understand its possibilities and want to explore them in more depth.

OxIS contains several items relating to experience. Two items are number of years on the Internet and self-rated ability, named "technical ability." Experience could also be negative experiences. Bad experiences on the Internet could influence willingness to engage in Next Generation User activities. OxIS asks about six possible bad experiences on the Internet: SPAM, viruses, misrepresented purchases, stolen identity, requests for bank details, and accidentally reaching a porn website. Each variable is a yes-or-no, dichotomous variable. We summed these variables to produce a "bad experiences" index, with values ranging from 0 to 6.

Second, willingness to buy and learn how to use more devices can be influenced by users' broad dispositions toward technology. As general dispositions they represent the default point of view for people who are using the Internet. Their default point of view may be modified by their personal experiences or other factors. Nonetheless, when people are asked about technology these attitudes are the responses that they give "off the top of their heads" (Zaller 1992). As the default perspective it influences the willingness of respondents to learn how to use new technologies and the motivation to overcome problems, such as to become a Next Generation User.

To measure general attitudes toward technology we created an index composed of responses to Likert-scaled items: openness to trying new technology, a view that technology is making things better, plus three reverse-coded items: a belief that it is easier to do things without technology, a lack of trust in technology, and nervousness around technology. The five-item index (called "technology attitudes") has a satisfactory Cronbach's alpha of 0.82, meaning that the items are interrelated and likely to be measuring the same underlying trait.

Confidence in ability to do things on the Internet can also influence willingness to buy new technology. More confident people will be more likely to be willing to invest in new devices because they feel better able to learn how to use the technology. Five OxIS variables ask about confidence: confidence participating in an online discussion, confidence making new friends online, confidence downloading music, confidence uploading photos, and confidence in learning new technology. Cronbach's alpha was 0.90. We summed these items to create a new continuous variable measuring "web confidence."

Finally, much interaction with smartphones and tablets is via apps. Many apps may require revealing personal details about yourself—like your name and email address—that could allow companies to identify you and market products to you. Some users may wish to keep these details private. The extent to which people see this as risky may influence the perceived attraction of mobile devices and, hence, willingness to buy the devices required to become a Next Generation User. Five items ask about comfort revealing personal information: Comfort revealing an email address, a postal address, a phone number, a date of birth, and a name. Cronbach's alpha was 0.88, so we created a measure called "personal data comfort."

# A Multivariate Understanding of Next Generation Users

We can describe the characteristics of Next Generation Users using demographic variables available in the OxIS 2011 dataset. The seven variables include age in years, household income, higher education degree, gender, retired, use of the Internet at work, and married.

In general the demographic results in Table 2.1 show the odds of being a NGU compared to a non-NGU. Thus, the interpretation of age is that every year reduces the odds of being a NGU by 0.96. The strongest variable is retired respondents: retired users are less than half as likely to be NGUs than non-retired respondents (see also Figure 2.2).[4] The next strongest variables are having a higher education degree and using the Internet at work. The Next Generation User activities, like content production and entertainment uses, require particular skills. Content production requires certain abilities, for example, writing a successful blog requires the ability to write interestingly and persuasively. These sorts of persuasive literary skills are most common among people with more schooling, especially a university degree. Using the Internet at work usually indicates a more complex job, possibly managerial or professional, and probably indicates more experience with the Internet (Dutton and Blank 2011). The concept of domestication suggests that some individuals and households would be more disposed to take advantage of technical innovations, and in that way, they are using access to domesticate technologies in ways that can support their needs and interests.

The multivariate analysis indicates that being married reduces the likelihood of being a Next Generation User. This may reflect the fact that many Next Generation User activities are time-consuming activities that often cannot be shared. The coefficient for gender, 0.76, says that women are one-quarter less likely to be Next Generation Users than men. The centrality of the Internet in the household has been associated with a narrowing of the digital divide. It might well be that the diffusion of more mobile devices that can be integrated into everyday life and work are reconstructing gender divides to some degree.

Expanding beyond demographic variables to attitudes and skills, we find that two of three attitude variables are significant: general technology attitudes and web confidence; personal data comfort is not significant. Attitudes and web confidence are both positive, as expected. The lack of significance for personal data comfort is interesting because mobile devices are most useful when

---

[4] Strength is measured by the size of the odds ratio. With an odds ratio of only 0.33, retired respondents are the most important variable in the regression. Similarly, having a higher education degree and using the Internet at work both have odds ratios near 1.50, making them the second most important variables in the regression.

**Table 2.1** Logistic Regression Predicting Next Generation User

| Variable | Demographic variables | Attitudes and skills |
|---|---|---|
|  | Odds ratio | Odds ratio |
| Age | 0.96*** | 0.97*** |
| Income | 1.20*** | 1.20*** |
| Higher education degree | 1.51** | 1.26 |
| Gender | 0.76* | 1.10 |
| Retired | 0.41* | 0.40* |
| Married | 0.71* | 0.80 |
| Use Internet at work | 1.51** | 1.16 |
| Technology attitudes |  | 1.11*** |
| Web confidence |  | 1.05** |
| Personal data comfort |  | 0.98 |
| Bad experiences |  | 1.21** |
| Internet ability |  | 1.23 |
| Years of Internet use |  | 1.03* |
| Constant | 2.31*** | 0.05* |
| N | 1,076 | 1,036 |
| McFadden's R² | 15.3% | 21.6% |
| Correctly classified | 69.8% | 73.5% |

*** p = .001; ** p = .01; * p = .05

used with various subscription services or for buying content, like books or music. One might have expected Next Generation Users to be more sensitive to the dangers of fraud or theft of personal data. The three skills variables also show a mixed effect. The number of bad experiences and years of Internet use are significant, while self-rated Internet ability is not significant. The positive effect of number of bad experiences is particularly interesting. It may reflect the fact that Next Generation Users make more intensive use of the Internet and so are exposed to more bad experiences. The lack of a statistically

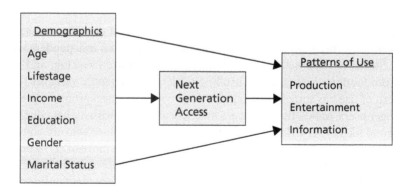

**Figure 2.2** Next Generation Access Shaping Patterns of Use

significant effect for Internet ability may reflect the ease of use of apps and mobile devices in general. Mobile devices may not require the same level of Internet skills as using a personal computer.

Most interesting is that once attitudes and skills are controlled, many of the demographic variables become non-significant. In particular, having a higher education degree, gender, being married, and using the Internet at work are no longer directly significant, but work through their influence on attitudes and skills. Age and income remain highly significant and being retired is also not influenced by the presence of the attitude and skills variables. More specifically, as long as you have certain positive attitudes and certain skills, the education you have, your gender, your marital status, or your use of the Internet at work have no direct effect on whether or not you become a Next Generation User. Their influence is generally through shaping attitudes toward the Internet and associated skills (tables not shown). The mechanism could be that technology attitudes make some people more (or less) receptive to new mobile devices. More receptive people are more likely to buy, learn, and use the devices. A similar mechanism may operate for skills: more (fewer) skills may make people more (less) receptive to new devices. We can summarize these findings by saying that Next Generation Users are shaped by their age, income, and employment status, as well as positive attitudes toward and skills in Internet use.

## The Impact on Patterns of Use

Finally, but most significantly, we need to ask whether the differences in the observed patterns of Internet use between First and Next Generation Users can be explained by these demographic and attitudinal indicators of age, income, employment status, attitudes, and skills. Do they simply reflect the different characteristics of First and Next Generation Users? We test this using the model illustrated in Figure 2.2.

Table 2.2 provides a second multivariate analysis that demonstrates this is not the case. This analysis shows that being a NGU has an independent effect on patterns of use, including entertainment, information seeking, and content production, even when controlling for key demographic variables. Each pattern of use has some direct relationships with these background variables. Younger users, males, those who are married, and users with higher education are more likely to use the Internet for entertainment. Those who are younger, male, employed, and have a higher level of schooling are more likely to pursue information online, such as the news. Finally, younger users, males, and those with higher levels of education are more likely to produce content online. Even when controlling for all of these factors related to being an NGU, there is still

**Table 2.2** OLS Regression Predicting Next Generation User

Logistic Regressions Predicting Patterns of Use

| Dependent variable | Next Generation User | Entertainment | Information seeking | Content production |
|---|---|---|---|---|
| Next Generation User | | 1.433*** | 0.241* | 0.695*** |
| Age | 0.953*** | -0.069*** | -0.020*** | -0.033*** |
| Female | 0.728* | -1.245*** | -0.363*** | -0.315** |
| Income | 1.211*** | -0.063 | 0.018 | -0.014 |
| *Lifestage* | | | | |
| Student | (base) | (base) | (base) | (base) |
| Employed | 1.841* | -0.192 | 0.635** | 0.013 |
| Retired | 0.590 | -0.597 | 0.109 | 0.144 |
| Unemployed | 1.580 | -0.503 | 0.251 | -0.288 |
| *Marital Status* | | | | |
| Single | (base) | (base) | (base) | (base) |
| Married | 0.709 | -0.812** | 0.012 | -0.092 |
| Live with partner | 0.936 | -0.441 | 0.065 | -0.186 |
| Divorced/separated | 0.990 | -0.525 | -0.347 | -0.344 |
| Widow/widower | 2.115 | -0.522 | -0.804* | 0.039 |
| *Education* | | | | |
| No qualifications | (base) | (base) | (base) | (base) |
| Secondary | 1.342 | 0.493 | 0.423* | 0.100 |
| Further education | 1.565 | 0.745* | 0.806*** | 0.199 |
| High Education | 2.268** | 0.640* | 0.983*** | 0.470** |
| Constant | 1.360 | 7.910*** | 4.770*** | 2.776*** |
| N | 1072 | 1072 | 1072 | 1072 |
| $R^2$ | | 0.311 | 0.151 | 0.195 |

*Note:* The regression on Next Generation User is a logistic regression and the coefficients are odds ratios. All the other results are OLS regressions with ordinary regression coefficients.

an independent relationship between being an NGU and patterns of use (as illustrated in the three right-most columns of Figure 2.2). That is, NGUs are more likely to use the Internet more intensively for creating content, entertaining and informing themselves, than are FGUs. The technology does reconfigure access. Use is not simply a function of socio-economic factors as might be expected from a domestication perspective. Also, patterns of use are shaped by Internet use in positive ways, which is the opposite of what one would expect from the technical rationality of a shift to appliances.

# The Future: The Rise of Next Generation Users, or a Transition to Appliances?

The patterns of use and impact uncovered in 2011 tend to contradict the notion of a shift from a PC-based to mobile Internet platform. Instead, we found complementarities across multiple devices. Moreover, the move to Next Generation Access made a difference in patterns of use in ways that undermined the technical rationality and domestication perspectives. The complementary uses of multiple devices, some of which are portable, have tended to help users integrate the Internet more closely into their everyday life and work, and therefore enhance the likelihood of users employing the Internet to create content, find entertainment, and be informed online.

Clearly, more mobile phone users will be accessing the Internet in the coming years, but this forecast misses the broader picture—the twin trends of mobility and the use of multiple devices, and the synergy of these two trends that creates Next Generation Use. As Figure 2.1 suggests, these trends appear to be strong and likely to continue into the foreseeable future. Although our data are based on Internet use in Britain, we expect these findings will apply across Europe and North America. They are less likely to apply in other regions, with emerging economies, where the mobile phone might be the first and primary platform for Internet access. In this case, however, we would also expect a growing diversity of devices to become important.

Perhaps the rise of an NGU is simply a transitional phase, with more users dropping their use of the personal computer in the home or at work. It is clear that some individuals only use a smart phone for Internet access, others only use a tablet. As each of these devices become more powerful and versatile, the centrality of the household personal computer could diminish rapidly. Alternatively, with the rise of what some have called the Internet of Things, where more and more devices will be Internet-enabled, such as via sensors and RFID devices, then every individual is likely to be carrying an increasing number of devices with them as they move through their day. If so, future surveys might discover the Next Generation User employing an even wider array of Internet-enabled devices for a broader range of services.

It is therefore important for research to track such changing patterns of use, and their societal implications. If, as we find, this next generation is truly empowering users in new ways, then it will be equally important to address the new digital divides created between First and Next Generation Users.

This study exposes problems with both technologically and socially deterministic perspectives. Innovations that define the Next Generation User are reconfiguring their access to information, people, and services in ways that are likely to empower them in relation to other users. This is in contradiction to the expectations of a technically dumbed-down Internet, as quite the opposite appears to be emerging. New devices are complementing and building on existing tools. In contradiction to the domestication perspective, some people are better able to domesticate these new technologies than others, and the technologies tend to have systematic implications for their users, such an enabling them to integrate them into their lives in ways that enhance their significance.

One of the most remarkable aspects of the Internet is its dynamic nature. It has never remained the same exact object or ensemble of technologies from year to year; for example, the dramatic rise in the use of social networking sites since 2007 has introduced a whole new way for people to communicate in large numbers. Another example: After more than a decade of languishing as "personal digital assistants" or PDAs, Apple introduced the iPad, and newly renamed "tablets" suddenly became the Next Big Thing. The Internet is a site for multiple ICTs and multiple innovations. A weakness of domestication theory is that it assumes a certain level of stability, specifically that there is an identifiable and stable object that is slowly adapted to fit into the life of the household. But the Internet is not stable, but constantly being reinvented. Each new development has brought with it new challenges for people to incorporate into their routines. Continuing waves of innovation also challenge research. In the midst of continuing change the challenge is to identify patterns of incorporation that have stabilized and will persist for an extended period of time. Next Generation Users are the most recent of these patterns.

## ■ REFERENCES

Blank, G. and Dutton, W. H. (2012). "Age and Trust in the Internet: The Centrality of Experience and Attitudes Toward Technology in Britain," *Social Science Computer Review*: <http://ssc.sagepub.com/content/early/2011/02/21/0894439310396186> (accessed April 30, 2013).

Dutton, W. H. (1999). *Society on the Line: Information Politics in the Digital Age*, Oxford: Oxford University Press.

Dutton, W. H. (2005). "The Internet and Social Transformation: Reconfiguring Access," in W. H. Dutton, B. Kahin, R. O'Callaghan, and A. W. Wyckoff (eds.), *Transforming Enterprise*. Cambridge, MA: MIT Press. 375–397.

Dutton, W. H. and Blank, G. (2011). *Next Generation Users: The Internet in Britain. Oxford Internet Survey 2011*. Oxford Internet Institute: University of Oxford.

Dutton, W. H. and Blank, G. (2013). "The Emergence of Next Generation Internet Users," *International Economics and Economic Policy*, doi: 10.1007/s10368-013-0245-8.

Dutton, W. H. and Shepherd, A. (2006). "Trust in the Internet as an Experience Technology," *Information, Communication and Society*, 9(4): 433–451.

Haddon, L. (2006). "The Contribution of Domestication Research to In-home Computing and Media Consumption," *The Information Society*, 22: 195–205.

King, R. (2012). "Great PC exodus on the Internet," *ZDNet*. Posted 29 October 2012 from <www.zdnet.com/idc-were-in-the-midst-of-the-great-pc-exodus-on-the-internet-7000006532/> (accessed November 23, 2012).

Lessig, L. (1999). *Code and Other Laws of Cyberspace*. New York: Basic Books.

Perlow, J. (2012). "Post-PC means mass extinction for personal computer OEMs," *ZDNet*. Posted 31 May 2012 from <www.zdnet.com/blog/perlow/post-pc-era-means-mass-extinction-for-personal-computer-oems/20514> (accessed November 23, 2012).

Silverstone, R. (1996). "Future Imperfect: Information and Communication Technologies in Everyday Life," in W. H. Dutton (ed.), *Information and Communication Technologies—Visions and Realities*. Oxford: Oxford University Press, 217–231.

Zaller, J. (1992). *The Nature and Origins of Mass Opinion*. Cambridge: Cambridge University Press.

Zittrain, J. (2008). *The Future of the Internet and How to Stop It*. New Haven, CT: Yale University Press.

# 3 The Relational Self-Portrait: Selfies Meet Social Networks

*Bernie Hogan and Barry Wellman*

## Introduction

Social network sites such as Facebook did not emerge by accident. Rather, they evolved from two historical ideas: the idea that a person can be signified by a static object or set of such objects (such as portraits, personals ads, and sculptures), and the idea that one can represent human relationships as discrete person-to-person connections. These ideas may seem obvious at the present moment. Yet, one may just as easily suggest a world in which relationships are defined primarily by one's association with a well-bounded group (such as a clan, tribe, or company), and a culture where static representations of people are seen as vulgar, vain, or even blasphemous, and where any contact other than face-to-face contact is to be regarded with suspicion or painted as inauthentic.

To say that social network sites (SNSs) combine personalizing technologies and person-to-person relations puts them in contrast with a host of earlier media and ways of maintaining relationships. SNSs consist of personalized digital artifacts curated by a third party, such as Facebook, LinkedIn, Twitter, or Weibo (Hogan 2010). Unlike virtual worlds, telephone conversations, or personal interactions, communication is not generally done in *synchronous* (or "real-time") settings. Instead, artifacts are distributed *asynchronously* to specific people in their own time, in their own separate physical settings. While synchronous interaction comes naturally to humans, usually through conversation and body language, asynchronous interaction, whether it is cave paintings, postcards, or tweets, necessarily requires a medium to store this information across time.

Prior to SNSs, there were many ways for individuals to communicate asynchronously, such as via letters, starring in film or television, being on an audio recording, sending email, instant messaging, and chatting on a bulletin board. With these media, we can construct a social network of information flow if we can point to a specific sender and a specific receiver. We can say that Alice emails Bob or that this audience saw Dave in this movie. The difference with

SNSs is that the social network does not merely emerge from the person who is communicating with (or to) whom. Instead the network exists a priori. The network defines who can and does access each other's content.

In this chapter, we follow the trajectory of the two key ideas (static profiles and person-to-person connections) that go into making an SNS. We start by discussing the profile as extension of the self-portrait and then discuss how social networks emerge from person-to-person relations. As these ideas converge on SNSs, we might say these sites exist as sets of relational self-portraits.

This convergence of ideas takes a different shape on different sites. Each site might have a slightly different answer to some fundamental questions: How to label a relationship? Is it necessary to use one's real name? Should friendships be given a numerical value? Should a relationship be directional (where one follows a celebrity on Twitter) or symmetric (where two people are contacts on LinkedIn)? To discuss how the answers to these questions work in concert helps to clarify some of the fundamental qualities of SNSs. After this discussion, we introduce a theoretical lens known as "networked individualism" (Rainie and Wellman 2012) that we hope prompts new research questions about SNSs as they exist today and the practices that will emerge in their wake.

## Profiles: Writing the Self into Being

All SNSs include a profile. A profile is a snapshot of the self: a written "selfie". The profile on an SNS is a shadow of lived experience, selectively looking back at whatever the user (and the user's friends) wishes to attach to it. In Facebook, a profile often includes a person's head-shoulders picture, gender, relationship status, favorite movies, and a self-description. On Twitter, profiles consist of a photo, a location, and terse description. For example, Wellman's profile currently includes an old sepia-toned photo and the following description:

Networked http://amzn.to/zXZg39 = networks+personal internet+mobile availability = networked individualism. RT = inform, ≠ endorse. Favorite ≠ like Block jerks, spam

Wellman's profile also includes nearly forty thousand tweets. Some are his contribution to a larger conversation, while most are links and quotes representing him and his audience.

Profiles offer a strong sense of individualism since the aggregate presentation of so much information linked to a single person helps to define that person. Even if the picture is partial, it is still often very thorough. To note, we do not think that the profile is historically unique, even if it benefits from contemporary technologies. Rather, it is part of a long line of technologies and practices for signifying the self that stretch back millennia. Two antecedents are especially important: the *portrait* and the *personals* ad.

The *portrait*, first sculpted or painted and more recently taken as a photograph, is an early personalizing technology (perhaps second only to grave markers such as tombstones). It was first employed to memorialize the dead (in ancient Egypt and China) and valorize the esteemed and powerful (throughout the world). Recall the crumbling statue in the desert that Percy Bysshe Shelley memorialized in his 1818 poem about a fictional hero:

"My name is Ozymandias, king of kings:
Look on my works, ye Mighty, and despair!"

Shelley's inspired poem simultaneously indicates many notable aspects of portraits (even if, strictly speaking, it is describing a statue). First, portraits persist outside of the self, as this statue purportedly lived on beyond Ozymandias. Second, there is a temptation towards vanity within the portrait. In contemporary language, the portrait is a selective representation of the self, often trying to put forward the best impression. Ozymandias sought this through a proud pose and a hyperbolic warning. And third, although the profile exists outside the self, its permanence is never guaranteed.

A portrait is a means of signifying an individual, and by extension, noting that an individual is worth signifying. Yet, a portrait is also decontextualizing. Unlike epic poems or plays, a portrait lifts an individual out of a specific context aesthetically. The background for a portrait has typically been dark, neutral, or unremarkable in order to draw one's attention to the individual and not the surrounding space. The choices of attire and accoutrements have traditionally been considered as signifiers of individuals, their tastes, and their statuses. In general, these additional features were meant to indicate something about the individual who was the focal point of the portrait. Indeed, people have been listing their "likes" for millennia.

Traditionally, making a portrait has been a laborious task. Painting is a skilled art, and even portrait photography requires scene setting, attention to detail, and often make-up. Particularly prior to the age of technological reproduction (and certainly digital reproduction), the portrait has been a high-fidelity way to signify an individual, but also one that has been resistant to change, expensive to create, and difficult to reproduce.

In the seventeenth century a second significant personalizing technology appeared—*personals* or "lonely hearts" ads. Where a portrait is high fidelity, slow and exclusive, a personals ad is low fidelity, quickly read, and accessible. The ad is meant to be a terse characterization of the self that made a person attractive to others while signifying what the individual is seeking in someone else. Consider this ad, from the earliest known published column:

A Young Man about 25 years of Age, in a very good Trade, and whose Father will make him worth 1000l. Would willingly embrace a suitable Match. He has been brought up a Dissenter, with his Parents, and is a sober Man. (Beauman 2011: 1)

Much like the traditional portrait and the modern profile, there are markers of class (worth the then-notable sum of 1000 English pounds), age (25), values (a "Dissenter" from the established religion), and virtue (sobriety).

Personals have grown in use over the past few centuries, but continue to carry some elements of stigma for several reasons. First, personals may imply some moral failing—that individuals had to resort to a terse characterization of the self rather than meet first in person. Second, personals may be false, or at least misleading. There is much research on how individuals routinely lie on online dating sites, but often in small ways that serve as a form of selective or even aspirational impression management rather than outright deception (Ellison et al. 2012). Third, personals are meant to advertise an individual rather than an individual-plus-social-network. Anonymous ads mean the sender is not subject to the judgments of friends and family, while the reader cannot tell much about the sender's social skills or social connections.

As technology increased, so did the fidelity of the cues available in the personals. For example, the video ads that emerged in the 1980s often operated through an agency that would videotape a client: in short, a personals advertising agency. A matchmaking agency can show the video to appropriate candidates, and it would indicate facial expressions, physical attractiveness, mood, and other subtle paralinguistic cues. Yet, the videos are still decontextualized and individualized. That is, one can infer markers of class, locality, and income from the video, but rarely can a viewer know if this prospective suitor also knows the viewer's friends, family, or any other social connections. The people in these personals are still *strangers* without visible interconnections.

SNSs have overcome the stigmas of the personals by embedding the profile in a large pre-existing social network that includes both the viewer and the viewed. Many sites traditionally expect this social network to reflect existing role relationships. Facebook has especially cemented the notion of the "Real-Name Web" by insisting that people use their own names and identities (Hogan 2012). That said, not every profile photo is necessarily a photo of the real person, nor every name a real name. For example, many Japanese use both pseudonyms and anime cartoons on Facebook and the locally popular Mixi site (Fogg and Iizawa 2008). Under what circumstances individuals decide to use real names versus pseudonyms remains an open question.

Portraits and personals coalesce in the modern SNS profile, as profiles include both photos that signify the individual (often next to messages on the SNS), and selective revelations about the self that a user considers appropriate to that site. By reflecting on portraits of old, we see how photos can valorize the self and drift toward vanity. By reflecting on personals, we see how the modern profile's self-descriptions, taste markers, interests, and past conversations do not simply exist to create a static immortalized self, but a dynamic and selective digital self that can link to and communicate with others.

# From Homepages to Profiles: Simplifying Self-Representation

Prior to the emergence of SNSs, many Internet users were seeking ways to create self-representations online. We argue that this was brought on by the emergence of the World Wide Web in 1991. Prior to the Web, the Internet still functioned as a means for sharing documents (through early systems such as Archie and Gopher) and person-to-person communication (through email, Usenet, and IRC). The Web brought together these technologies in a means for individuals to browse documents that included pictures, text, and a consistent mechanism for linking from one document to another.

Documents on the Web initially began as web "pages" that used Hypertext Markup Language (HTML) to enable people to position images, links, and text together. The technology to do this was a formidable challenge. By the end of 1994 there were approximately 10,000 websites (Gray 1996). In 1995 this number exploded to 100,000 and continued its exponential growth. One of the key contributors to this growth was Geocities—a site that allowed individuals to self-publish a web page as a "homepage."

Homepages function as self-contained sets of documents, often dedicated to a specific theme such as pets, travel, or famous actors. Sites hosting homepages, such as Geocities, Angelfire, and Tripod helped reinforce the Web as a place "out there." People could construct web pages that were singular and self-contained testaments to their interests and technical skills. These sites were reminiscent of a modern portrait: a great deal of effort displaying a specific theme or person, along with signifiers of his or her interests that were difficult to repackage or distribute. Outside of a comments page and a hit counter, homepages consisted almost entirely of content uploaded by the page owner. They often were unsystematic, unwieldy, and borrowed heavily from the copy and paste culture of amateur webpage designers. Such homepages were haphazardly designed bricolage as much as portraiture. They were projections of a *home* in "cyberspace", part of a longstanding (mis)use of spatial metaphors for online data (Star 1996; Graham 2013).

At the turn of the 21st century, the popularity of homepages waned in favor of the profile. Even though Geocities was one of the most visited domains in the world in 1999, by 2009 it was considered defunct and was shut down by its current owner Yahoo! in every market but Japan. The transition away from the homepage was not simply an aesthetic choice for Internet users. It was the culmination of technologies for enabling pages to display on-demand socially relevant information. Some of the key technologies involved include PHP (Pre-Hypertext Processing), MySQL, and JavaScript. Initially these technologies were meant to simplify the process of rendering dynamic content (such as a shopping basket), but in the mid-1990s they blossomed into a dominant framework for interfacing with the masses of data that were being collected and stored in organized databases.

This new potential has been liberating, and a welcome means for meeting the increasing demand to access the burgeoning Web. It has become possible to start searching and finding—a welcome relief in a world that started to become overwhelmed by information overload. But this technology was also constraining. Whereas a homepage is typically a free-for-all of self-representation, databases require rows of well-formed data. On Facebook, for example, the user is expected to fill out a bevy of very specific information requests, such as one's e-mail, age, gender, interests, and location. Providing such well-formed data lowers the barrier to entry for online self-representation, but it also creates more systematic a priori categories for people to use, such as employment, relationship status, or religion.

## Networks and Social Network Analysis

Databases of well-formed data, like date of birth or universities attended make it easy for any user to search for other users. Consequently, a horde of use cases emerged to leverage well-formed data online, such as job listings, auctions, and dating. One need only fill in the keywords and browse the results. But friendship is different. A person's friends are not separate segmented objects plucked from a shelf, but clustered around sites of social cohesion, such as cohorts, churches, voluntary organizations, neighborhoods, and teams (Fischer 1982). Friends are part of a vast interconnected social network.

As a concept, social networks have been around for almost a century in different forms. Their ability to make sense of the world has shed new light on social relationships dating back millennia. Anywhere that a researcher can define specific relationships between two or more people, the relationships can be considered a social network (Wellman 1988).

As a means of representing the world, the study of social networks consolidated in the early sixties out of a confluence of mathematical graph theory, ethnography, and interpersonal "sociometric" psychological studies (Freeman 2004). Since then, the field has emerged as a leading approach to social scientific study and has made rapid inroads in physics, biology, computer science, and other academic and corporate domains.

Networks at their simplest require two sets. The first set is a list of "actors" or people. With that first list of people, one can build a database table with one row for each person and details about the person, such as his or her name and attributes. We can sort this database or filter it down based on keywords. This process of filtering and sorting is precisely what one can do on traditional dating sites or job search sites.

The second set denotes the connections between these people. Where actors represent the dots in a network diagram, connections represent the lines that connect these dots. As users collectively befriend and follow each other, they collectively create a social network rather than merely a very long list of people. Now one can search, for example, for high school friends, fellow co-workers from a particular company, members of the amateur hockey team one is playing next week, and "people who are in a photograph with me." The rationale for these searches is obvious—these relationships come pre-packaged with certain memories, meanings, and sentiments for one user in particular, not all users in general.

Social network analysis has not merely foreshadowed the emergence of technologies for including friendship relations between profiles: it has also presaged the challenge of how to formally encode these relationships. Several approaches exist to encoding, but the most fundamental is whether to consider a relationship as directed or undirected.

A directed relationship suggests a flow. As water and traffic are organized to flow one way through pipes and roads, information can flow from one profile to another. Bob shares a story with Alice, and she then shares this story with Ted. But, information flows may also be reciprocal, where Bob shares a story posted by Alice, and then Alice shares a story posted by Bob.

An undirected relationship suggests a mutual acknowledgment. For example, we could say Alice and Bob know each other, or Bob and Ted were both at the same party. Personal networks have traditionally been measured as undirected networks of acknowledgment. One would ask "Are Bob and Ted close?" referring to their interpersonal closeness. This is simpler than building the network by asking "Is Bob close to Ted?" and "Is Ted close to Bob?" (Wellman 1979).

SNSs embed this fundamental distinction into their products. Arguably, this distinction between directed and undirected is unavoidable, since it is embedded in every relationship on the site. If Twitter moved from being directed "Alice follows Bob," or "Bernie Follows Ted," to an undirected "Bernie and Ted know each other," it would radically change how the site operates. Celebrity Ashton Kutcher has more than 15 million followers but only follows about 700 people (<https://twitter.com/aplusk>). If he had a twitter feed including all 15 million it might become completely unusable. Instead, Kutcher operates as an opinion leader, taking in information from innovators and early adopters and diffusing it to many others (Rogers 1995: 518).

Twitter and Google+ both have directed relations. They are platforms for diffusing information as well as for interpersonal communication. By contrast, Facebook (through "friends") and LinkedIn (through "contacts") have undirected relations. On these latter sites, after a user sends an invitation to be the recipient's friend, the recipient has to agree before the friendship is used to share content. Content sharing can then be linked to personally relevant information one wishes to share with their close friends (such as pictures of weddings, graduations, and newborns). The content is generally meant to be understood in a personally relevant context of other information both on and off the site.

This distinction between directed and undirected relations informs much of the current state of research on Twitter (directed; informational) and Facebook (undirected; identity). Although research on identity exists for Twitter and research on information flows exists for Facebook, these sites tend to have a knack for stimulating certain kinds of discussion that are aligned with these sorts of practices.

Considering Facebook, a large academic discussion concerns the capacity to engage with many audiences and manage competing demands in the same streams of information. Each friend or audience member may be personally relevant, but personally relevant in utterly different ways. Teens, for example, often have competing demands from school friends and authority figures (parents, teachers, etc.) that are in utter conflict (boyd 2007, 2014). Experiencing these multiple audiences at the same time leads to a sense that contexts have collapsed on each other, thereby creating challenges to privacy and impression management.

On the other hand, some information is not person-specific. The "news" is framed as something of collective interest. Twitter's directed links allow individuals to follow hubs of information without having to be followed back. Tracking the flow of information through these links, between news sites, celebrities, everyday Twitter users, and even lurkers, enables questions of a more global scale. This has encouraged studies of large selections of Twitter data analysing collective political action, what happens on the site, and how much influence users have (e.g. Cha et al. 2010).

## Leveraging the Complexity of Networks: Weighting and Clustering

Undirected or directed relationships merely scratch the surface of the complexity of networks. For example, ties in both undirected and directed networks can have a "weighting." That is, Alice may be friends with both Bob and Ted, but she sends five times more messages to Bob than Ted. Relations without values are binary, with a 1 or a 0 marking the presence or absence of a relation: one is either a Twitter follower or not. This is a simplification of a relationship—reducing "best friends," "the popular kids," "casual acquaintances," and so forth to "friends." However, individuals in personal networks may be considered within varying degrees of closeness or personal importance. Some friends are closer than others. But marking this and displaying it publicly (as in MySpace's "Top 8") is not as straightforward as simply knowing whom to call when in need. Social pressures, public face, and interpersonal drama all collude in making the Top 8 a challenging set to manage (boyd 2006).

There have been at least three broad approaches to classifying the relations on an SNS: weighting, tagging, and automating.

*Weighting*: Having individuals weight their impressions of others was one selling point of Orkut, Google's first social network site. A user could rate another user on three presumed dimensions of relevance: trustworthiness (or "trusty"), attractiveness (or "sexy"), and information gain (or "cool"). Users could then see the aggregate scores from all their friends.

*Tagging*: A relationship between two people can have any number of attributes, such as where the two people met, or whether they are family members. Tagging is an approach to labelling these relationships. In an early incarnation, Facebook asked how users knew each other when adding a friend. Google+ currently employs a tagging system referred to as "social circles," that allows individuals to be as identified as members of multiple circles. Perhaps coincidentally, their metaphor of "social circles" dates back to early social network scholar Georg Simmel's notion of partially overlapping sets of acquaintances, or literally, crosscutting social circles [*kreuzung sozialer kreise*] (cf. Simmel 1922).

*Automating:* The third approach to classifying relations is to use an implicit weighting scheme based on user behavior. This is the basis of "EdgeRank," Facebook's black box algorithm for ranking content from a user's friends. It sidesteps the notion of filtering based on social circles, and it minimizes the burden on users. Simply by interacting with one's network, one is training EdgeRank to learn what is important. One notable concern about automated systems is that they may work too well, thereby filtering in only content that someone already considers agreeable. This filtering can theoretically lead to what Eli Pariser calls a "filter bubble" (2011) that passively hides or minimizes dissenting viewpoints.

## Considering SNSs as Networked Individualism

SNSs sit at the intersection of new database technologies for searching and sorting, and the cultural evolution of the profile as a means for representing the self. These technologies are individualizing as profiles tend to be used to represent a single person (even if a single person has multiple profiles). However, these technologies are also networked, since well-formed profiles can be searched, sorted, and linked in creative and efficient ways.

The notion of modern life as "networked individualism" began before the rise of SNSs. It is an attempt to understand how modern media and living conditions are associated with shifts in how people maintain their relationships. It grew out of Wellman's answer to "the community question," the perennial concern about the loss of community. In describing the durable personal networks of support (first in a borough of Toronto, Canada), it became apparent that focusing on networks of relationships rather than bounded local groups (such as community associations) more accurately explained how people get by (Wellman 1979).

The hallmark of networked individualism is that people operate "more as connected individuals and less as embedded group members" (Rainie and Wellman 2012: 12). In short, it is a way of describing the process of initiating and sustaining contact between people based on person-to-person contact, regardless of whether such contact is physical or digital.

Not all ways of sustaining contact are networked individualism, but all of them are a form of networking. The earliest networking was door-to-door. People would physically move from one place to another and often perform some ritual signifying their presence, such as knocking on the front door or clapping at the front of the house. Door-to-door networking is strongly coupled with physical co-presence.

The development of mediating technologies marked a shift from door-to-door towards place-to-place networking. Mediated place-to-place networking can be traced back as far as drum signals, letters, and carrier pigeons. It diffused widely with electricity and internal combustion engines as more places became networked through roads, airline routes, and the telephone grid. In place-to-place networking, contact is oriented around specific places rather than physical co-presence. Mail would be sorted in a mailroom, telephone calls would be received in the kitchen, meetings could be held across town, or, as is the case for many professionals, the world. Nevertheless, to receive a specific communication, someone still had to be at a specific place.

Person-to-person networking involves the direct connection between people regardless of place. While this does not obviate the relevance of space, it does mean that the media used to sustain contact are linked to a person. Most people still communicate with those nearby more than with those far away (Mok et al. 2010), but the communication can be at a grocery store, a pub, or in the middle of a meeting. The technical infrastructure that powers this communication is not hardwired to predetermined places, but to any node connected to the global telecommunication network. Granted, this network is not equally accessible across all places, due to differences in connectivity and censorship. But space has become more of a condition of possibility for access to the network, rather than that which defines how networking takes place.

With the dominance of person-to-person technologies, teenagers may never know the awkwardness of having a friend or potential romantic interest call the house and have to deal with the parent answering the phone rather than the intended recipient. Email, mobile phones, instant messaging, voice, and webcams all directly link people to other people, rather than to people who happen to be at specific spatial coordinates adjacent to a mailbox or landline telephone. Recall that Romeo and Juliet died because they could not find each other to clarify their tragic plans. Now, if Julia had simply texted "fake poison, brb" [be right back], Romeo could have patiently waited out her slumber, and they might have lived happily ever after (Wellman and Rainie 2012).

We consider networked individualism as a practice and praxis rather than a description of a specific set of either technologies or network configurations. It is a practice because individuals who most successfully engage with these social network systems tend to be actively engaged with their profile(s), responsively commanding the interest of both strong and weak ties. As Rainie and Wellman assert (2012), it is a new social operating system for managing the "person-as-portal." But it is more than a set of cultural scripts. It is praxis, in the sense of being an ideologically embedded practice that assumes a strong, if not necessary, bond to the state of technology and media. Facebook (like other SNSs) is not merely a website, but a bundle of specific design decisions about how individuals sustain contact with their friends, family, and (sometimes) fans.

There are both drawbacks and benefits to maintaining contact in a networked individualistic manner. The work of Robert Kraut and colleagues is instructive. In an early, widely cited study (1998), they noted that when the Internet was introduced into homes, feelings of loneliness increased among some people. They dubbed this the "Internet paradox," since loneliness was seemingly induced by a social technology. It is worth remembering that while the Internet is inherently social, this study took place in the late 1990s when people were more likely to come across pseudonyms such as "BeatlesFan82" than to find a long-lost friend from high school or to organize a community barbecue.

A decade later, Burke et al. (2011) found more complex results. While those who passively consumed Facebook still felt disconnected, lonely, and had less interpersonal "social capital," those who actively engaged their friends, communicated, and chatted, felt more connected and reported higher social capital. Their attitude to technology made the difference. The less successful users were acting as passive consumers, while the more successful users of Facebook were being pulled into a virtuous cycle of engagement and connectivity. They were approaching Facebook as networked individuals, with themselves as conduits for information and affect.

# Conclusions

Contemporary SNSs are the confluence of database technologies and cultural logics of how to represent both the self and the connections between selves. By embedding a logic of social networks (and social network analysis) into the very fabric of the site, Twitter, Facebook, and their ilk exhibit a networked individualistic way of organizing relationships based on person-to-person contact. They also prompt us to ponder what comes after person-to-person networking? Based on the preceding discussion we consider several trends for future inquiry.

> *Profile-to-profile networking*: Strictly speaking, profiles are not people but selective representations of people. As Harrison White (2008) has noted, identities are mechanisms for interfacing with networks, not unitary and stable objects. Different profiles for different purposes are already in use, but we may start to see this more explicitly, not unlike Blackberry's recent attempt to create work and personal personae on the same phone.

> *Agent-to-agent networking*: As algorithms get smarter, they may cease to merely curate our content, but manage it on our behalf. Google Now already anticipates searches by, for example, presenting the weather or directions to a hotel when one is in a new city. Will it start to manage invitations on one's calendar? Will we see decentralized systems do this work as well?

> *The rise of graph searching*: The formalization of the profile has led to network-based filtering and content access. Newer graph database technologies are taking this even further by enabling complex queries about friends and friends of friends. One can now ask Wolfram Alpha, "Who is the most popular person in my network?" Using graph searching, people will be able to make complex queries on Facebook (such as "friends-of-friends in London who are single, like Korean food and not friends with my ex-boyfriends"). If networked individualism is in fact a new "social operating system," graph search may be networked individualism's killer app and bring new meaning to the strength of weak ties.

In the end we will be left with many of the same challenges in a new guise: What do these media mean to my sense of self? What do these media mean for my relationships to other people? What do these media mean for the social contexts that help me define myself and learn about the others I consider important? The answer provided by SNSs is very contemporary: systematic profiles, inspired by networks and queried by databases, regulate access to others and their impressions. It is an evolution of cultural ideas and technologies. Yet, cultural evolution is neither deterministic nor necessarily progressive: technologies will surprise.

Like SNSs, newer media will arrive as extensions to existing ideas and constraints (both social and technological). Nevertheless, such media will still have to contend with many of the same practical issues, such as longstanding and stable patterns of human bonds, preferences for spatial locality, a small number of strong, multiplex (multiple context) relationships, and co-presence when practical. Such technologies will also have to contend with inequalities in operating systems, Internet access, and political power. And it is highly probable that, like the SNSs discussed above, they will reconfigure how we maintain access to others and present further challenges for what it means to represent the self.

## ▓ REFERENCES

Beauman, F. (2011). *Shapely Ankle Preferr'd: A History of the Lonely Hearts Ad.* London: Random House.

boyd, d. (2006). "Friends, Friendsters and Top 8: Writing Community into being on Social Network Sites," *First Monday*, 11(12). < http://firstmonday.org/ojs/index.php/fm/article/view/1418/1336 >.

boyd, d. (2007). "Why Youth (Heart) Social Network Sites: The Role of Networked Publics in Teenage Social Life," in D. Buckingham (ed.), *MacArthur Foundation Series on Digital Learning—Youth, Identity, and Digital Media Volume.* Cambridge, MA: MIT Press, 119–142.

boyd, d. (2014). *It's Complicated: The Social Lives of Networked Teens.* New Haven, CT: Yale University Press.

Burke, M., Kraut, R., and Marlow, C. (2011). "Social Capital on Facebook: Differentiating Uses and Users." *Proceedings of the 2011 Annual Conference on Human Factors in Computing Systems.* New York: ACM Press, 571–580.

Cha, M., Haddadi, H., Benevenuto, F., and Gummadi, K. P. (2010). "Measuring User Influence in Twitter: The Million Follower Fallacy." *4th International AAAI Conference on Weblogs and Social Media (ICWSM)*, Washinton, DC: The AAAI Press, 10–17.

Ellison, N., Hancock, J., and Toma, C. (2012). "Profile as Promise: A Framework for Conceptualizing Veracity in Online Dating Self-Presentations." *New Media and Society*, 14(1): 45–62.

Fischer, C. (1982). *To Dwell Among Friends.* Chicago, IL: University of Chicago Press.

Fogg, B. and Iizawa, D. (2008). "Online Persuasion in Facebook and Mixi," *Proceedings of the Third International Conference, Persuasive Technology.* Oulu: Springer, 35–46.

Freeman, L. C. (2004). *The Development of Social Network Analysis.* Vancouver: Empirical Press.

Graham, M. (2013). "Geography/Internet: Ethereal Alternate Dimensions of Cyberspace or Grounded Augmented Realities?" *The Geographical Journal.* 179 (2): 177–182.

Gray, M. (1996). *Web Growth Summary.* Cambridge, MA: MIT Press.

Hogan, B. (2010). "The Presentation of Self in the Age of Social Media: Distinguishing Performances and Exhibitions Online," *Bulletin of Science, Technology & Society* 30(6): 377–386.

Hogan, B. (2012). "Pseudonyms and the Rise of the Real-Name Web," in J. Hartley, J. Burgess, and A. Bruns (eds), *A Companion to New Media Dynamics.* Chichester: Blackwell, 290–308.

Kraut, R., Patterson, M., Lundmark, V., Kiesler, S., Mukopadhyay, T., and Scherlis, W. (1998). "Internet Paradox: A Social Technology that Reduces Social Involvement and Psychological Well-Being?" *American Psychologist* 53(9): 1017–1031.

Mok, D., Wellman, B., and Carrasco, J.-A. (2010). "Does Distance Matter in the Age of the Internet? *Urban Studies*, 47(13): 2747–2783.

Pariser, E. (2011). *The Filter Bubble: What the Internet Is Hiding from You.* New York: Penguin.

Rainie, L. and Wellman, B. (2012). *Networked: The New Social Operating System.* Cambridge, MA: MIT Press.

Rogers, E. M. (1995). *Diffusion of Innovations*, 4th edn. New York: Free Press.

Simmel, G. (1922 [1955]). "The Web of Group Affiliations," in G. Simmel (ed.), *Conflict and the Web of Group Affiliations.* Translated by Kurt Wolff. Glencoe, IL: Free Press.

Star, S. L. (1996). "From Hestia to Home Page: Feminism and the Concept of Home in Cyberspace," in N. Lykke and R. Braidotti (eds), *Between Monsters, Goddesses and Cyborgs: Feminist Confrontations with Science, Medicine and Cyberspace.* London: ZED, 30–46.

Wellman, B. (1979). "The Community Question," *American Journal of Sociology*, 84(5): 1201–1233.

Wellman, B. (1988). "Structural Analysis: From Method and Metaphor to Theory and Substance," in B. Wellman and S. D. Berkowitz (eds), *Social Structures: A Network Approach.* Cambridge: Cambridge University Press, 19–61.

Wellman, B. and Rainie, L. (2012). "If Romeo and Juliet had Mobile Phones," *Mobile Media & Communication.* 1(1): 166–171.

White, H. (2008). *Identity and Control.* Princeton, NJ: Princeton University Press.

# 4 The Politics of Children's Internet Use

*Victoria Nash*

## Understanding Children's Internet Use

### THE DANGEROUS MYTH OF THE DIGITAL NATIVE

From inspection of daily newspaper headlines it could plausibly be assumed that the Internet's main impact on the lives of children has been the deplorable pollution and corruption of impressionable young minds.[1] Clearly this is a very one-sided view. Whilst each headline depicts a legitimate news story in which the well-being of youngsters is at risk, they tell us far more about the media's traditional dependence on bad rather than good news, and, perhaps more interestingly, about public appetite for scare-stories concerning the Internet and its implied risks for children.

One factor which helps to explain some of the moral panic surrounding children's Internet use is the simple point that children are often presumed to be more expert users than either their parents or law-makers. Characterized by Prensky (2001) as the difference between "digital natives" (those who have grown up with the technology) and "digital immigrants" (those who come to it later in life), this makes an assumption that all children born in the digital era are equally adept at using technology, even displaying the capacity to "think and process information fundamentally differently from their predecessors" (p. 1). Unfortunately, this bluntly essentialist dichotomy is damaging on two fronts. First it encourages us to think that it's *impossible* for the older generation to understand or keep pace with children's Internet use, and second, it manages to obscure many policy-relevant variations in Internet use and access between children. In reality, the picture is, of course far more nuanced. Children growing up in Western nations increasingly enjoy near-universal access to the Internet, at least in school, but there remain considerable

---

[1] For the purposes of this chapter, the term "child" will be taken to refer to any person under the age of eighteen, using the same definition as the United Nations for the purposes of the Convention on the Rights of the Child. Where the research described in the text refers only to a particular subset of this age-group, this will be specified.

differences and inequalities in the extent and types of use, whilst some adults share many of the characteristics of supposed "digital natives" in their Internet use (Helsper and Eynon 2010).

The range of influences shaping children's Internet access and use include both internal and external factors. Most obviously, each child brings a different range of skills to their online activities. Necessary skills include basic motor and technical skills, more specific Internet-related abilities such as search techniques, as well as generic skills such as information literacy and emotional intelligence. Unsurprisingly, the wider the child's range of skills, the more variety in their use of their Internet and the more likely they are to benefit from it (Livingstone and Helsper 2010). Self-efficacy, or self-confidence, is also important in explaining differences in children's capacity to take up online opportunities (Eynon and Malmberg 2011).

Amongst the most important external factors that shape children's Internet use are the availability of home access and levels of support. Home (rather than school) access has been shown to affect both the depth and range of online activities undertaken (Facer et al. 2003). Although households with children are much more likely to have Internet access than those without (Eurostat 2010; Dutton and Blank 2011), there are still significant numbers of children who don't enjoy such access, for example the 7 percent of UK twelve- to fifteen-year-olds lacking desktop or laptop use at home (Ofcom 2011). Unsurprisingly, those in the lowest socio-economic groups are most likely to lack home access (Ofcom 2011). In terms of support, it's not just a question of how much, but also from whom and what type. Support from those with positive Internet experience is more valuable in building children's online confidence (Eastin 2005 cited in Davies and Eynon 2012), whilst children whose parents lack confidence about Internet use may come to rely more heavily on peer support, with fewer opportunities for parents to pass on social norms (Palfrey and Gasser 2008) or provide emotional back-up (Ito et al. 2010; Turkle 2011). Building on these findings about the importance of social support we can see that the "digital natives" myth is damaging in a third sense, insofar as its frequent repetition actually risks undermining parents' and educators' confidence in their own ability to provide positive support to the young Internet users in their charge.

Understanding the variability of children's Internet experiences is vital for policy purposes, both because such inequality in access and use may constitute an important injustice, and also because the differences mean that not all children face the same combination of risks and opportunities. In both cases, policy responses that treat all children as equally confident and skilled "digital natives" will be fundamentally inadequate, so policy, parenting, and educational strategies should be adjusted accordingly. The sections below will consider in more detail how this variability plays out in two specific contexts: for educational purposes, and in children's embrace of it in their private lives.

# Hopes and Expectations: Internet Use and Education

Despite the fore-mentioned media focus on the Internet's dark side, technology policy has also been driven by optimistic (and potentially vote-winning) strategies to achieve beneficial social outcomes. Information and Communication Technology have long been seen to offer many valuable opportunities for children, potentially delivering educational benefits such as improved learning outcomes and skills important for workforce participation, and also more personal benefits such as enhanced self-esteem or self-efficacy (Davies and Eynon 2012). These expectations are often visible in the political rhetoric surrounding the launch of new investment programs, albeit frequently colored by a naive technological determinism that drives a fascination with investment in hardware rather than people (Livingstone 2009).

Whatever the rhetoric, governments across most Western nations have invested significant resources in wiring up schools since 2000, and in many cases such programs have played an important role in expanding national broadband infrastructure. Even though this is clearly a positive development, it doesn't mean that all pupils enjoy similar levels of resource, skills, or support. To start with, not all pupils seem to actually use the Internet at school: the EU Kids Online pan-European survey reported that just two-thirds of pupils claim to do so (Livingstone et al. 2011). Even for those children who do go online at school, the quality of experience may vary dramatically, depending on factors such as teachers' proficiency in integrating Internet use into class work or the level of support provided to help children work effectively. The inequity of these conditions is further exacerbated by the fact that schools from richer and poorer areas often face very different educational challenges which technology use in the classroom cannot be expected to overcome (Warschauer et al. 2004).

A further reason to be wary of the grand claims made for the role of the Internet in transforming children's education comes from the constrained nature of its use in schools. Teachers are necessarily limited by pedagogical requirements to cover certain curricula, which in the UK, for example, means that children are more likely to learn word processing than programming (Birmingham and Davies 2005). They are also charged with ensuring safe and appropriate behavior, such that school Internet use is usually filtered and even surveilled (Buckingham 2007). Both constraints mean that youngsters using the Internet at school are likely to face a more limited set of opportunities in terms of what sites or information they can access, albeit also a reduced array of risks. So long as a sizeable number of pupils continue to lack access to the Internet at home—what Buckingham (2007) has called the "digital divide between in-school and out-of-school use"—the restrictions and inequities of Internet use in school will continue to have discriminatory effects.

Unfortunately, expectations of the Internet's improving effect on formal educational outcomes have yet to be fulfilled, with research suggesting neither any obvious positive or negative impact (Livingstone 2009). Nor does it seem to be the case that the Internet's collaborative and creative potential is exploited to the full for academic purposes. As Davies and Eynon note: "the Internet serves most of all as a reassuring quick fix for teenage learners" (Davies and Eynon 2012: 88), providing opportunities to consult, in the preparation of assignments, a variety of information sources whether they be Google, Wikipedia, or friends.

It has been suggested that such a focus on formal educational outcomes is misplaced. An influential study for the MacArthur Foundation argued that teenage Internet users are increasingly engaged in a "participatory culture," namely, " a culture with relatively low barriers to artistic expression and civic engagement, strong support for creating and sharing one's creations and some type of informal mentorship whereby what is known by the most experienced is passed along to novices" (Jenkins et al. 2006: 3). As the next section will make clear, many of the skills required to engage in such a culture may be better learnt through "informal learning" outside schools, meaning (rather ironically) that personal, private Internet use at home which gives rise to so many parenting fears may ultimately be best placed to build the soft skills required in Internet-enabled cultures.

## Personal Internet Use: Risk or Opportunity?

Many aspects of children's personal lives are mediated by the Internet. It offers valued platforms for creating and playing with identities, making and talking to friends, even for living out some of the most mundane aspects of family life. It's not so much that these activities are new in themselves, but rather that children and teenagers "are doing this while the contexts for communication, friendship, play, and self-expression are being reconfigured through their engagement with new media" (Ito et al. 2010: 1). Such reconfiguration is itself helping to re-shape existing *practice*, such as where traditional efforts by teenagers to change their appearance and image give way to the conscious creation and curation of online identities, as well as the revision of existing *norms* (for example, around the use and re-use of third-party created content). As these altered practices and norms play out, the array of risks and opportunities facing children is also transformed, and it's no surprise that many media-driven outpourings of moral panic concern supposed horrors resulting from children's determination to connect with others online. For many parents and policy makers, perhaps the greatest source of anxiety is the extent to which children and teenagers can conduct much of their personal life online, in an environment which is perversely private in the sense that a responsible adult can easily be excluded, but public insofar as the content or communication is effortlessly opened up to unknown others.

According to the EU Kids Online Survey, 60 percent of European nine- to sixteen-year-olds go online almost daily, with an average duration of just under an hour and a half for all nine- to sixteen-year-olds, and more than three hours a day for those aged fifteen to sixteen (Livingstone et al. 2011). Despite the emphasis placed on Internet use in schools, the most common point of access is still home rather than school and increasingly, in the private spaces of the bedroom or using a personal device such as a laptop or a mobile (Livingstone et al. 2011). Apart from schoolwork, the most common uses of the Internet amongst this group are for entertainment and socializing, such as playing online games, watching videos, and using Instant Messenger (IM), email, or social networks to communicate with friends (Livingstone et al. 2011). Although some children are indeed engaged in what Jenkins describes as "participatory cultures" (Jenkins et al. 2006), perhaps blogging or post- ing content for others to share, these activities are undertaken by relatively few, supporting the concept of a "ladder of opportunities" which children may ascend at different rates and to different levels (Livingstone et al. 2011; Livingstone and Helsper 2007). Ito et al. (2010) note that for most teenagers, creativity is mainly expressed in "everyday personal media production" as they document their daily lives through social media, but that for some, this does become a "jumping-off point" for more elaborate forms of creativity (p. 290). And whilst these more creative activities (photography, blogging, music or video production, etc.) may initially be interest-driven, they can develop into intensely social activities, generating their own communities of interest and becoming important forms of self-expression, the latter being a particularly important feature of Internet use for older children and teenagers.

Starting from the premise that identity is not fixed and objective, but fluid and mutable, the Internet enables the "performance" of identity across a range of sites and for different audiences, albeit with imperfectly permeable boundaries (boyd 2007; boyd and Marwick 2011). Although identity perfor- mance takes place across a range of platforms including IM, chat rooms and texting, the rise of social network sites (SNSs), with their central focus on a self-constructed personal profile, has provided a natural home for such activ- ity. While social network sites such as Facebook are currently for use only by those over thirteen, 59 percent of European children between nine and sixteen claim to have a social networking profile, with age-specific practices varying from 26 percent for those aged nine–ten to 82 percent for those at the top of the age range (Livingstone et al. 2011). In the United States, 80 percent of online teenagers between twelve and seventeen use social networks, far more than the 64 percent of online adults using such services (Lenhart et al. 2011). Whilst the use of SNSs for social and expressive purposes is not necessarily problematic, these figures do raise legitimate policy concerns, implying that large numbers of children are using sites not designed for their age group, and potentially without parental consent or knowledge.

Perhaps unsurprisingly in this context, privacy is a concern for both young SNS users and their parents. Although some studies suggest that young SNS users are discriminating in their choice of which personal information to publicize (Patchin and Hinduja 2010), others note that the architecture of such sites can raise particular problems for teens, whose subtle groupings and rankings of offline friends are poorly served by the blunt categorization of "friends" on SNSs, making the practice of privacy in SNSs much harder to negotiate. In one study, teenagers speak of their frustration in trying to signal whom particular content is directed towards, and of how they seek to erect artificial boundaries to separate parts of their networks (boyd and Marwick 2011). Just because material on SNSs is public in the sense that it is accessible to friends (and often friends of friends or the wider world) does not mean that young users want *all* of their network to access it, especially when that network may include parents or relatives.

Whilst children and teenagers may be in thrall to the potential of SNS to help them curate their online identities, they are also reliant on them for communication. This ability to master the affordances of particular platforms or technologies and make them work for a particular end, in this case establishing or maintaining friendships, is a skill which many, particularly older children and teens, manifest. Many studies note how young Internet users seamlessly manage a portfolio of different communication tools to sustain their social and family relationships, such as IM, Facebook, messaging, and texting for quick and intimate conversations, social network status updates to check in with a broader group, or mobile phone calls for private and urgent conversations (Ito et al. 2010; Livingstone 2009; Davies and Eynon 2012). Although some have raised concerns about the burden of managing so many different modes of communication (Turkle 2011), and the strains of managing complex social hierarchies with relatively unsophisticated tools (Ito et al. 2010), the majority of the evidence suggests that Internet technologies play a key role for children and young people in expressing their developing and mutable social selves.

## Internet Regulation: Protecting or Politicizing Children?

In contrast to the panic-laden news headlines that have accompanied children's adoption of the Internet, the more positive aspects of Internet use rarely receive the same media coverage or policy recognition as the risks. This isn't to say that concern for such risks is illegitimate: clearly, states, parents, and educators have a duty to protect. Rather, there are two problems with such a one-sided approach: first, there is a tendency to ignore messy details, such as the fact that some children are more vulnerable than others or that harm is hard to detect, and second, it ignores the possibility that risk and opportunity may go hand in hand.

## RISK AND HARM

Whilst there is a rich and expanding body of literature investigating how children's Internet use shapes their experience of risks and opportunities, there are still some real weaknesses. From a policy perspective, one of the biggest problems is that we know relatively little about the relationship between risk and actual harm, or the way in which different risk factors combine to increase or decrease risks for particular children. Most fundamentally, there are real methodological and ethical challenges involved in measuring harms to children resulting from Internet use; so many studies in this area measure not harm, or even risk, but the "risk of risk" (Livingstone 2010: 4), for example, the likelihood that any one child will access pornography, rather than the likelihood that he/she will be harmed by this experience. This poses a problem for responsible evidence-based policy making, meaning that even with the best of intentions, policies are likely to be constructed on the basis of judgments about the *potential* risk of Internet use.

Despite this limitation, there are many excellent studies investigating the range of risks that children are exposed to online. The risks most frequently encountered by children online are exposure to pornographic content and bullying, although there is a surprising degree of variation in prevalence between studies. For example, in the United States, Wolak, Mitchell, and Finkelhor's representative sample survey (2007) show that 42 percent of American ten- to twelve-year-olds have been exposed to online pornography in the past year—66 percent of which was unwanted exposure, whilst the EU Kids Online Project reports that 14 percent of Europe's nine- to sixteen-year-olds have been exposed to sexual images online. Cyber-bullying has proved particularly hard to measure with prevalence figures for the United States ranging from 9 percent (Ybarra et al. 2006) to an amazing 72 percent (Juvenon and Gross 2008). Although there is no single factor that can explain the huge variation in results, this is likely to result from differences in the studies' operationalization of key concepts such as "cyber-bullying," as well as different survey methods and sampling strategies.

At the other end of the scale one of the most feared online risks—sexual predation by a stranger—appears to be very rare, although the seriousness of this offence means that despite the low number of occurrences it understandably merits extensive policy attention. A lesser variant, online sexual solicitation and receipt of sexual messages (often from acquaintances) is more common, especially for girls, with between 15 and 19 percent reporting such experiences (Baumgartner et al. 2010; Livingstone et al. 2011). Although this figure sounds very alarming, it is worth noting that sexual conversations between *teenagers* are not necessarily a source of concern, indeed, the majority of children do not report being upset or bothered by this, and many take active steps to prevent a recurrence (Livingstone et al. 2011). With the advent of "sexting",[2] however, the potential harms associated with peer-produced content (rather than "stranger-danger") most certainly merit further attention from both researchers and policy makers.

In addition to these long-acknowledged risks, the Internet's capacity to cater for more specialist audiences has seen the rise of online sites and communities exchanging information and advice on issues such as anorexia, bulimia, self-harm, and suicide. Whilst there is little disagreement in the academic literature as to the potential harm of such sites, there is uncertainty about the balance between the dangers of normalizing damaging behavior, and the value for vulnerable youngsters of finding a non-judgmental space to discuss personal problems with similar others. There is also as yet little research which shows that otherwise healthy children or teenagers are at risk from such content; indeed, many studies in this field show that children who are vulnerable offline are more likely to be susceptible to online risks and harms. Acknowledged predictors of exposure to pornography, self-harm material or other online risks include depression, sexual abuse, eating disorders, or risk-seeking behavior offline (Wolak et al. 2007; Mitchell and Ybarra 2007). Such children may be doubly at risk in the sense that they also lack resources or "resilience" to cope with online risks and may also be less likely to seek support from family or other responsible adults. This poses particular challenges for policy, suggesting a need to more effectively target resources at vulnerable groups.

Counter-intuitively though, other studies have revealed that greater opportunities of use also go hand in hand with greater exposure to online risk, meaning that older, more sophisticated users, or those from middle-class households who enjoy better access also encounter more risk (Livingstone 2009). These findings suggest that policy makers seeking to reduce exposure to online risks need to find ways of supporting children who are most vulnerable on other measures, as well as those who are privileged and confident Internet users—potentially two very different groups.

## Policy Responses—Serving our Children Well?

As noted earlier, media and policy pre-occupation with the negative aspects of children's Internet use is problematic if this results in policy outcomes which

---

[2] "Sexting" is the exchange of sexually explicit images or messages via mobile phone.

restrict opportunities at the same time as reducing risks. In the context of communication technologies this is a particular concern, as many available policy tools offer protection only by reducing opportunities for the free exchange of information or speech. The importance of balancing these competing goals is recognized in legal or constitutional protections in many countries and in international instruments such as the United Nations Convention on the Rights of the Child.[3]

Against this backdrop we should question whether policies relating to children's use of the Internet generally do strike the right balance between the protection of well-being and protection of free speech. It is worth noting at the outset that our concern here is online activities which may pose risks for children rather than those which illegally harm children (such as creation or circulation of child-abuse images). It is often argued that in a situation of such uncertainty it's better to employ precautionary principles to minimize the occurrence of possible harms, particularly when seeking to protect potentially vulnerable individuals (Livingstone 2010). It should also be acknowledged that whilst research evidence may be scarce, there are many other factors (moral, cultural, religious, economic, etc.) that can legitimate policy intervention. But it shouldn't be forgotten that there are also some very poor reasons for policy intervention, such as the "symbolism" of being seen to do something even if that "something" fails to ameliorate the original policy problem (Heins 2001; Sandvig 2001).

A standard policy response to many of the risks outlined in this chapter, for example, is that certain sorts of web content deemed potentially harmful to children should be blocked or filtered, a child-protection solution with a long history in other media (Heins 2001).[4] Filtering methods can be applied at different "choke points" across the Internet ranging from state-directed filtering schemes where blocking is carried out at backbone level, to filtering by search engines or Internet Service Providers (ISPs), all the way down to filtering at the level of the household or institution. Although advocates of free speech argue that filtering decisions should be made as close as possible to the individual user, several countries, including Denmark, South Korea, and the United States have introduced legislation requiring publicly funded schools and libraries to install filtering software to protect children using their facilities. Other countries, such as Australia and the UK, have held lengthy public debates concerning whether ISPs should be mandated to block pornographic content by default.

The introduction of such mandatory filters may seem to be a positive step towards reducing access to adult materials by young children but it remains a

---

[3] Available at <http://www2.ohchr.org/english/law/crc.htm> (accessed 20 August 2012).
[4] Discussion of filtering and blocking in this chapter refers only to material deemed *potentially harmful* and not to that which is *illegal*, such as child-abuse images or hate speech.

controversial policy, both because it restricts access to otherwise legal content, often for adults as well as children, but also because no filter is ever 100 percent effective, either over-blocking legitimate content or under-blocking undesirable content. Over-blocking is particularly problematic if the material has educational or informational value, such as that pertaining to relationships, sexual health, or even art. There is also a danger that when filtering mechanisms are in place, parents or educators may be lulled into a false sense of security, believing that no further risks exist. Unfortunately, calls for mandatory filtering are politically attractive as they articulate a decisive policy response, and are more clearly understood by both the media and the public than subtle calls for improved digital literacy training or more effective parental interventions. A more moderate approach is the introduction of "active choice" policies such as those being introduced in the UK, whereby households signing up to new broadband contracts are asked whether they wish to have filters installed at the household level. This is a positive step insofar as it places the decision with parents, but even so it remains a rather blunt tool that cannot distinguish between the differing degrees of protection needed for various members of the household.

If we are to question whether filtering policies effectively protect children from significant risk or harm without undue damage to their rights to freedom of expression and information, we must also ask whether access policies do enough to support *equal* rights. Although sections of this chapter noted the near-universal efforts in Western developed countries to get schools online, there are still significant inequalities of provision, and children lacking home access remain at a disadvantage. To this extent, policies such as the UK's now-defunct Home Access Programme, which sought to provide laptops for low-income families, could make a great contribution to equalizing opportunities, but are as yet all too rare. In the absence of wide-scale investment in home access, it is vital that better support is provided for school implementation of Internet-supported learning, including teacher training and curriculum development; just as importantly though, it would be highly beneficial if after-school and holiday provision could find ways of making Internet access available in ways that better mimic home use.

To a large degree, policy debates around children's Internet use have long been dominated by concerns about harmful content and access, but other newer policy issues are emerging rapidly, and to do justice to the next generation of Internet users these must be given more consideration. With the current array of tools for creation, use, re-use, and sharing of content, concerns about children's respect for intellectual property and copyright laws have gained new importance. As noted above, the most sophisticated forms of content creation are only engaged in by a minority of children, but large numbers are enjoying simpler uses, such as portraying their everyday lives and relationships through the crafting of SNS profiles or photo-sharing. However, many of the most exciting new opportunities for digital creativity leave children "at risk for ongoing copyright liability" (Palfrey and Gasser 2008: 117). Given that there have already been several high-profile cases of under-18s being pursued by property-owners for abuse of copyright, this risk is all too real. Although it's clearly unrealistic to expect intellectual property regimes to change overnight, there is a bifurcated danger, either that the creative potential of today's most digitally literate children will be stifled, or that their online norms and practices will simply further depart from the current state of the law. Both would seem undesirable.

Children's online practices are similarly ill served by privacy laws (Matwyshyn 2012). At risk both of personal damage that can result from context collapse, as when parents or future employers obtain information from public SNS pages, and also corporate misuse of their data, this is another area where current norms and practice by under-18s do not fit neatly within existing frameworks of legal protection. Whilst there have been efforts to introduce legislation to address the specific needs of those too young to contract on their own behalf, such as the US Children's Online Privacy Protection Act 1998 (COPPA) or the EU's proposed revisions to the Data Protection Directive, in practice this has just meant that popular services such as Facebook apply a minimum age limit of thirteen, but lack effective means of policing this, leaving young users with little protection. Although the proposed EU "right to forget" reinforces privacy policy in ways that might help those who post vigorously in their youth but seek more anonymity later on, it is hard to imagine a straightforward solution (Millard, chapter 21 this volume).

## Conclusion

For many, there could be no better illustration of the "dark side of the Internet" than the media's hysterical portrayal of children's daily exposure to paedophiles, pornography, and gambling. Yet, although such risks undoubtedly do exist and merit serious-minded attention from policy makers, the moral panic surrounding their prevalence serves to obscure another dark corner in this debate, namely the misrepresentation of children in Internet policy and regulation, and the tendency to favor policy measures that restrict, rather than expand, access to information and speech. This chapter has sought to clarify how purported concern for the well-being of our children and teenagers is shaping the future of the Internet. Although there's certainly nobility in such concern, it's unfortunately not obvious that children's interests are necessarily well served by the dominant trends in Internet policy which seem to promote protection but not empowerment (Lunt and Livingstone 2012).

First, too much emphasis is placed on reducing some of the most feared (but not necessarily most harmful) risks by introducing technical fixes such as filtering, rather than engaging with the messy realities of parenting, education, and child development. Second, there is little acceptance of children's rights to freedom of expression and information, too often regarded as less important than their rights to protection from harm, even when that harm is uncertain or unlikely. Such an imbalance may be partly understood as a result of a general failure to accept that childhood is itself a socially defined construct, and that media portrayal of children as helpless, vulnerable victims of online harms is outdated at a juncture where youngsters are capable of both perpetrating online abuse and helping to protect themselves against it. Third, more effort must be made to support positive use or help those who are most vulnerable rather than the easy-to-reach middle-class children with anxious parents. Finally, and perhaps more importantly, there needs to be a wider recognition that no one is well served if genuine concerns for child protection are manipulated and misused in the pursuit of other less noble political goals, such as the quiet pursuit of moral conservatism and social control. Many of those who oppose heavy-handed content filtering might be more easily appeased if significant policy resources were also devoted to promoting access and positive Internet use, underscoring a genuine political commitment to supporting children's well-being. The Internet, quite simply, poses both risks and opportunities for young users, and a serious-minded policy approach should embrace the resulting trade-offs and complexities.

## ▓ REFERENCES

Baumgartner, S., Valkenburg, P., and Peter, J. (2010). "Unwanted Online Sexual Solicitation and Risky Sexual Online Behavior Across the Lifespan," *Journal of Applied Developmental Psychology*, 31(6): 439–447.

Birmingham, P. and Davies, C. (2005). "Implementing Broadband Internet in the Classroom: Key Issues for Research and Practice." Oxford Internet Institute Research Report No. 6, University of Oxford. <http://www.oii.ox.ac.uk/resources/publications/RR6.pdf> (accessed January 22, 2012).

boyd, d. (2007). "Why Youth (Heart) Social Network Sites: The Role of Networked Publics in Teenage Social Life," in D. Buckingham (ed.), *Youth Identity and Digital Media*. Cambridge, MA: MIT Press, 119–142.

boyd, d. and Marwick, A. (2011). "Social Privacy in Networked Publics: Teens' Attitudes, Practices and Strategies" (paper presented at the Oxford Internet Institute conference "A Decade in Internet Time," September 22, 2001). <http://papers.ssrn.com/sol3/papers.cfm?abstract_id=1925128> (accessed August 15, 2012).

Buckingham, D. (2007). *The Impact of the Media on Children and Young People with a Particular Focus on Computer Games and the Internet* (Annex G of the Byron Review). <www.lloydminster.info/libdocs/byronreview/annex_g.pdf> (accessed August 28, 2012).

Davies, C. and Eynon, R. (2012). *Teenagers and Technology*. New York: Routledge.

Dutton, W. H. D. and Blank, G. (2011). *Next Generation Users: The Internet in Britain 2011*. Oxford: Oxford Internet Institute, University of Oxford. <http://www.oii.ox.ac.uk/publications/oxis2011_report.pdf> (accessed 14 January 2013.

Eastin, M. (2005). "Teen Internet Use: Relating Social Perceptions and Cognitive Models to Behavior," *Cyberpsychology and Behavior*, 8(1): 62–75.

Eurostat (2010). "Internet Access and Use in 2010," *Eurostat News Release*. <http://epp.eurostat.ec.europa.eu/cache/ITY_PUBLIC/4-14122010-BP/EN/4-14122010-BP-EN.PDF> (accessed August 6, 2012).

Eynon, R. and Malmberg L. (2011). "Understanding the Online Information Seeking Behaviours of Young People: The Role of Networks of Support," *Journal of Computer Assisted Learning*, 28(6): 514–529.

Facer, K., Furlong, J., Furlong, R., and Sutherland, R. (2003). *Screenplay: Children and Computing in the Home*. London: Routledge Falmer.

Helsper, E. J. and Eynon, R. (2010). "Digital Natives: Where is the Evidence?" *British Educational Research Journal*, 36(3): 503–520.

Heins, M. (2001). *Not in Front of the Children*. New York: Hill and Wang.

Ito, M., Baumer, S., Bittanti, M., boyd, d., Cody, R., Herr-Stephenson, B., Horst, H., Lange, P. G., Mahendran, D., Martinez, K., Pascoe, C. J., Perkel, D., Robinson, L., Sims, C., and Tripp, L. (2010). *Hanging Out, Messing Around, and Geeking Out*. Cambridge, MA: MIT Press.

Jenkins, H., Clinton, K., Purushotma, R., Robison A. J., and Weigel, M. (2006). *Confronting the Challenges of Participatory Culture: Media Education for the 21st Century*. The MacArthur Foundation. Cambridge, MA: MIT Press.

Lenhart, A., Madden, M., Smith, A., Purcell, K., Zickuhr, K., and Rainie, L. (2011). "Teens, Kindness and Cruelty on Social Network Sites," Pew Internet and American Life Project. Online. <http://pewinternet.org/~/media//Files/Reports/2011/PIP_Teens_Kindness_Cruelty_SNS_Report_Nov_2011_FINAL_110711.pdf> (accessed August 15, 2012).

Livingstone, S. (2009). *Children and the Internet*. Cambridge: Polity Press.

Livingstone, S. (2010). "e-Youth: (Future) Policy Implications: Reflections on Online Risk, Harm and Vulnerability" (paper presented at e-Youth: Balancing Between Opportunities and Risks, 27–28 May 2010, UCSIA and MIOS University of Antwerp, Antwerp, Belgium). <http://eprints.lse.ac.uk/27849/> (accessed August 28, 2012).

Livingstone, S., Haddon, L., Görzig, A., and Ólafsson, K. (2011). *Risks and Safety on the Internet: The Perspective of European Children. Full Findings*. London: EU Kids Online, LSE.

Livingstone, S. and Helsper, E. J. (2007). "Gradations in Digital Inclusion: Children, Young People and the Digital Divide," *New Media and Society*, 9(4): 671–696.

Livingstone, S. and Helsper, E.J. (2010) "Balancing Opportunities and Risks in Teenagers' Use of the Internet: The Role of Online Skills and Internet Self-Efficacy," *New Media & Society*, 12 (2): 309–329.

Lunt, P. and Livingstone, S. (2012). "Media Literacy." Chapter 6 in *Media Regulation: Governance and the Interests of Citizens and Consumers*. London: Sage.

Matwyshyn, A. (2012). "Generation C: Childhood, Code and Creativity," *Notre Dame Law Review* 87 (5): 1979–2030.

Mitchell, K. and Ybarra, M. (2007). "Online Behavior of Youth who Engage in Self-Harm Provides Clues for Preventive Intervention," *Preventive Medicine*, 45(5): 392–396.

Ofcom (2011). *UK Children's Media Literacy Report*. London: Ofcom. <http://stakeholders.ofcom.org.uk/binaries/research/media-literacy/media-lit11/childrens.pdf> (accessed August 28, 2012).

Palfrey, J. and Gasser, U. (2008). *Born Digital*. New York: Basic Books.

Patchin, J.W. and Hinduja, S. (2010). "Changes in Adolescent Social Networking Behaviours from 2006 to 2009," *Computers in Human Behaviour*, 26(6): 1818–1821.

Prensky, M. (2001). "Digital Natives, Digital Immigrants: Part 1," *On the Horizon*, 9(5): 1–6.

Sandvig, C. (2001). "Unexpected Outcomes in Digital Divide Policy: What Children Really Do in the Public Library," in B. M. Compaine and S. Greenstein (eds), *Communications Policy in Transition: The Internet and Beyond*. Cambridge, MA: MIT Press, 265–293.

Turkle, S. (2011). *Alone Together*. New York: Basic Books.

Warschauer, M., Knobel, M., and Stone, L. (2004). "Technology and Equity in Schooling: Deconstructing the Digital Divide," *Educational Policy*, 18(4): 562–588.

Wolak, J., Mitchell, K., and Finkelhor, D. (2007). "Unwanted and Wanted Exposure to Online Pornography in a National Sample of Youth Internet Users," *Pediatrics*, 119(2): 247–257.

Ybarra, M., Mitchell, K., Wolak, J., and Finkelhor, D. (2006). "Examining Characteristics and Associated Distress Related to Internet Harassment: Findings from the Second Youth Internet Safety Survey," *Pediatrics*, 118(4): e1169–e1177.

# 5 Gender and Race Online

*Lisa Nakamura*

Videogames are one of the world's most popular and profitable forms of media. Though sales of hardware, software, and accessories in US retail stores "fell in 2013 to $810 million from $1.09 billion the same time a year prior," according to a report issued by NPD Group, largely due to declining hardware sales, *global* sales of video games were projected to grow "from $67 billion in 2012 to $82 billion in 2017" (Gaudiosi 2012). Much of this growth is due to mobile and "casual" games like *Angry Birds* and the like, a trend that is likely to continue, but for the time being blockbuster First Person Shooter (FPS) games like *Modern Warfare: Call of Duty Black Ops 2*, a 2012 release that earned $1 billion in fifteen days, continue to set records and to define the industry (Sliwinski 2012).

The gamer culture that characterizes console games such as *COD: Modern Warfare* is, in Mia Consalvo's words, often extremely "toxic" to women and minorities. How has this come to pass? What can be done about it? This chapter will evaluate the racial and gender climate in the world of console gaming, identify some causes for the pervasive sexism and racism to be found there, and assess the potential for change.

Race is a famously contentious topic, particularly in the United States. Because overt acts of racism have become less common in recent years, there is always a troubling tendency to view racism as disappearing, if not in fact completely eradicated. This view of racism as an unfortunate artifact of the past, always as something that is dying out, characterizes the "post-racial ideology." Subscribers to this ideology believe that racism manifests itself most commonly as isolated incidents of hateful speech directed from one person to another, that racism is the result of "ignorance" rather than harmful intent, and that it is ultimately personal rather than culturally systemic.

However, those who doubt that racism (and its frequent companion, sexism) is still a serious problem or who believe that it is "personal" rather than pervasive throughout societal institutions need only look to the Internet for proof that this is *not* so. This chapter will discuss how racism and sexism have continued to flourish on the Internet, and indeed to some extent have even come to *define* it, despite our supposedly "post-racial" historical moment. The title of Saul Levmore and Martha Nussbaum's book *The Offensive Internet: Speech, Privacy, and Reputation* (2010) attests to the often outrageous amounts of outright misogyny, racism, and other discriminatory types of communication to be found in the digitally mediated world: one chapter on Google and Free Speech is entitled "Cleaning Cyber-Cesspools." This book is written from the perspective of legal scholarship and philosophy and is a welcome corrective to earlier work that glosses over the unpleasant realities of unbridled digital communication and its victims, who are predominantly women and minorities.

The Internet is undoubtedly a powerful tool in the quest for democracy and fairness, as other chapters in this volume eloquently attest; how did it simultaneously become a media platform practically defined by its egregious sexism and racism? Online gaming offers a unique opportunity to study this phenomenon, for as Mia Consalvo, a leading scholar in the field of gender and video games, writes in her essay "Confronting Toxic Gamer Culture: A Challenge for Feminist Game Studies Scholars,": "Of course harassment of female players has been occurring for quite some time—perhaps the entire history of gaming—but it seems to have become more virulent and concentrated in the past couple of years" (Consalvo 2012). Consalvo discovered that gaming culture was far less toxic, paradoxically, when there were *fewer* women playing:

Slowly but surely and building upon one another in frequency and intensity, all of these events have been responding to the growing presence of women and girls in gaming, not as a novelty but as a regular and increasingly important demographic. ... The "encroachment" of women and girls into what was previously a male-gendered space has not happened without incident, and will probably only become worse before it (hopefully) improves.

While the rest of the Internet became more gender-balanced years ago (Wakeford 2000), the world of video games self-identifies and is seen by many of its players of both genders as fundamentally masculine despite evidence to the contrary. Despite the immense popularity of games such as *The Sims* among female players (Gee and Hayes 2010: 207), as Adrienne Shaw's 2011 ethnographic study shows, "there is a definite correlation between gender and gamer identity. Male interviewees were much more likely to identify as gamers than female, transgender, or genderqueer interviewees were" (Shaw 2011: 34). As Shaw notes, her findings are far from unusual: many other game scholars have "found that women tend to underestimate the amount of time they play and do not generally identify as gamers" (p. 34).

Conversely, men who do not play as often as women may identify with gaming and as gamers in order to solidify claims to masculinity. The identification between gaming and masculinity has become so strong that a new type of male identity, that of "geek masculinity," has acquired popular currency. John Scalzi's essay on white privilege, "Straight White Male: the Lowest Difficulty Setting" attests to the ways that the vocabulary of gaming addresses men, particularly white men, in ways that other discourses cannot (Scalzi 2012). As Scalzi writes, "men think in the language of gaming...or at least wish to *appear* to do so in front of other men and women."

Feminist game scholar Nina Huntemann employs a media industries studies' approach to this problem: her work documents how the practice of requiring workers to perform compulsory unpaid overtime at game studios, or "crunch time," produces female- and family-unfriendly workplaces. These institutional environments ensure that game production culture remains male, and this plays a role in perpetuating racist and sexist game content (Huntemann 2010). However, while women are far less likely to claim membership or standing within gamer culture or claim the identity of "gamer," this is not true for non-white players (Shaw 2011).

Dmitri Williams (Williams et al. 2009) and Craig Watkins (2009: 272) have gathered data that showed that Latino, African American, and Asian and Asian American males are better-represented in the gaming world than white males, and Rideout, Lauricella, and Wartella's study of media use among youth in the United States found that non-white youth spend significantly more time playing video games at home (Rideout et al. 2011). However, as Anna Everett and Craig Watkins have found in a qualitative study of video games, games continue to represent black and brown bodies predominantly as criminals, gangsters, and athletes (Everett and Watkins 2008).

Representations of black people as evil zombies, drug dealers, and criminals perpetuate some of the worst images found in other media, while the exclusion of images of blackness and black avatar characters from fantasy games such as *World of Warcraft* creates an artificially "blackless fantasy," as Higgin (2009) puts it. Racist representation within games can be found in every genre: simulation games like the immensely popular *Civilization* series depict non-Western culture as shot through with superstition, cruelty, and irrationality (Galloway 2006). *World of Warcraft's* Tauren, Troll, and Blood and Night Elf player classes reprise classic racist imagery of Native Americans, Caribbeans, and Orientals from previous media (Corneliussen and Rettberg 2008). It is probably not surprising that so-called casual video games, (defined by Jesper Juul as games which are "easy to learn, hard to excel at") generally lack this type of racial and gender stereotyping. The runaway success of games like the 2009 Game of the Year *Plants Versus Zombies, The Sims*, the classic *Tetris, Angry Birds, Bejeweled*, the sidescroller *Braid*, and the beautiful *Passage* may appeal to women partly for this reason.

## Video Games as "Racial Discourse"

Sociologist Ashley Doane defines "racial discourse" as the "collective text and talk of society with respect to issues of race" (Doane 2006: 256). Video games are both textual objects and channels for real-time networked communication that platform racial discourse. As such, they are prime examples of racial ideology. Doane defines "racial ideologies" as "generalized belief systems that explain social relationships and social practices in racialized language" (Doane 2006: 256). Video games, particularly networked games, create social practices and belief systems that license and permit uses of racialized and racist speech that are not believed to apply to or carry over into the "real world," but instead stay within the "magic circle" of the game.

Many gamers are resistant to critiquing racism, sexism, and homophobia within their favorite games, displaying a range of responses "from blatant racism to racial tolerance or inclusion," as Everett found in her analysis of online player discussions about race and racism in *Grand Theft Auto*. Black and brown bodies are represented and treated as expendable targets and violent stereotypes within the "urban/street" games that Everett and Watkins studied in their essay "The Power of Play: the Portrayal and Performance of Race in Video Games." They argue that these games produce "racialized pedagogical zones" that teach young players the proper place for raced and criminalized bodies (Everett and Watkins 2008).

As the Rideout, Lauricella, and Wartella study shows, youth of color spend more time playing games than white youth do, thus they are more vulnerable to the racial discourses within games and game-enabled communications. Doane identifies two dominant ways of understanding and talking about race in the United States. The first defines racism as the product of individual attitudes or behaviors motivated by personal hatred, stereotyping, and prejudice against people of color. The second defines racism as a set of *systemic* and institutional practices such as de facto segregation and persistent inequality and unequal access to resources such as education and safe housing (p. 267). Doane claims that the first definition is by far the most common. Individual examples of person-to-person prejudice and harassment are ubiquitous within networked video games, but it must also be remembered that systemic practices such as the exclusion of non-stereotyped characters of color and women from the game texts and storylines themselves are part of a harmful racial discourse as well.

Games scholars have spent less time or energy studying telepresent and copresent racial and sex harassment occurring in game culture, focusing instead on racist and sexist messages within the games themselves. While demographic work such as Williams et al. analyzes game content in order to trace the ways that video games as a whole exclude the experiences of people of color and women, most studies of racism in video games have focused on racial content and themes within selected game texts (Williams et al. 2009). Anna Everett (2009), David Leonard (2006), Jessica Langer (2008), Tanner Higgin (2009), David Golumbia (2009), and Alexander Galloway (2006) have written excellent essays on racism in video game imagery, narratives, and game mechanics.

In their 2009 study of profanity in video games Ivory, Williams, Martin, and Consalvo cautioned that networked play added a new and as yet understudied dimension to the study of profanity and merited additional studies. The study analyzed several popular video games representing a variety of age ratings and found that one out of five games contained one of the "seven dirty words" which are regulated in network television, as well as "words that evoke strong emotion and offense (e.g. bitch)." No mention is made of racist language, but the study cautioned that player-produced profanity may be a greater cause for concern in the age of networked gaming than pre-scripted profanity programmed into games: "The increasing popularity of multiplayer games and optional multiplayer game modes featuring voice interaction between players suggests that future studies should also examine the prevalence of profanity in online voice chat sessions" (Ivory et al. 2009).

While users have been playing with strangers on networked computers since the early days of the Internet, console gamers are newer to the world of online gaming and have been exposed to a different style of socialization. Despite this, there is plenty of remarkably racist, sexist, and even nationalist behavior to be found in Massively Multiplayer Online Role-Playing Games (MMORPGs), many of which have been in operation well before consoles became popular, some of which has been documented by Douglas Thomas and Constance Steinkuhler. Thomas and Steinkuehler's groundbreaking essays on anti-Korean and anti-Chinese racism in MMORPGs such as *Diablo 2* and *Lineage 2* demonstrate the remarkable prevalence of discriminatory behavior in process-based video games, and the insights and methods employed in their work would enrich studies of television-based console gamers (Steinkuehler 2006; Thomas 2008).

The networking of the Microsoft Xbox, the Sony PlayStation, and the Wii saw the first really large group of users playing with networked strangers, a state of affairs that has become commonplace for gamers, and one that bears close watching by media scholars, sociologists, psychologists, and critical race and gender scholars. In-game communications are very challenging to study. However, it is crucial that scholars produce research on online interaction in console gaming, for since 2009 the most popular games for platforms like the Xbox 360 and the PS3 have been networked military FPS games, with *Call of Duty: Modern Warfare* and its expansions leading the way.

These games not only represent race and gender in one-dimensional ways, usually within a "negative fiction," they are also seedbeds for abusive racial discourse. Player–to-player voice communications via networked FPS games like the *Halo* series, the Microsoft Xbox's original tentpole AAA game title, are known for their profane and often abusive quality and are often described as "trash talk" by players and the industry alike. However, gamers themselves make a distinction between "trash talk" and discourse that crosses the line, such as use of the word "nigger."

A professional black female gamer known as "BurnYourBra," a nationally ranked *Mortal Kombat* player, explained in an interview on a gaming website that "At tournaments players talk [crap] to each other. That's just the way tournaments are. People get hyped. Players get salty when they lose, which is fine. But there is a difference between trash talking and calling other players disrespectful names. For me, I've been called a dyke, a butch, a slut, a bitch...I was even called a black bitch to my face along with being called a lesbian, a gorilla, and a monkey."[1]

BurnYourBra's interview produced a lengthy comment stream on the Eventhubs.com website; many of the contributors debated where the "line" between trash talking and racism lay. Some agreed that "trash talk" was inevitable, indeed an intrinsic part of the competitive culture of video game tournaments, but that it was "not the same" as racism. Others maintained that racism is best ignored and is of little consequence in a "post-racial" world, leaving it to the receiver to "shake it off." A key paradox of race, gender, and game studies rose to the top: while profanity and abuse are "trash talk," a form of discursive waste, lacking meaningful content that contributes to the game, many defended it as a distinctive and inevitable aspect of video game multiplayer culture. If it is indeed trash, the consensus opinion among gamers on this discussion board is that it is the responsibility of the receiver to "take it out."

Trash-talking is common in shared-world games in non-US contexts as well. As Holin Lin has shown in her 2011 study of Asian *World of Warcraft* players, clashes between Taiwanese and Chinese players sharing Taiwanese servers have often resulted in "open nationalist confrontations," with "indigenous" Taiwanese players dubbing Chinese "immigrants" to the gamespace "locusts" (Lin and Sun 2011).

As digital media theorists Galloway and Thacker (2007) write, "trash, in the most general sense, implies remnants of something used but later discarded...trash is the set of all things that has been cast out of previous sets." Once trash talk has been used to intimidate or bully another player, it is supposed to disappear, absolving its user of responsibility or even memory of the event.

If "trash" doesn't deserve notice or interpretation, as some players maintain, it is because it lacks meaning. Yet like the omnipresent trash icon on the computer desktop, a fixture of personal computer use, trash talk is part of the media ecology of digital culture. Just like videogame cheating, in-game economies, and online gender identities, all of which have been the subject of important book-length monographs in game studies (Castronova 2005; Consalvo 2007; Nardi 2010), the discursive environment of sexism, racism, and homophobia deserves critical attention because it is central to game culture.

---

[1] <http://www.eventhubs.com/news/2011/apr/15/dmgburnyourbra-discusses-difficulties-being-female-gamer/>, April 15, 2011 (accessed April 21, 2013).

BurnYourBra is not a particularly famous figure in video game culture, nor would she most likely define herself as a video game activist or a feminist. However, by sharing her experience of racism and sexism within the culture of gaming she is contributing towards a small but growing media campaign against video game racism and sexism, a form of speech that is often defended as just "trash talking." Likewise, user-generated blogs that are devoted to the task of confronting racism, sexism, and homophobia work to prevent us from forgetting or ignoring online "trash talk" by preserving and archiving it, using old and new media.

## "Fat, Ugly, or Slutty?" Crowdsourced Campaigns Against Racism and Sexism in Gaming

As Dyer-Witheford and DePeuter (2009) write, "Games not only cultivate the imagination of alternative social possibilities; they also present practical tools that may be useful for its actualization." Gamers who love the culture but hate its racism and sexism create websites that aim to expose some of its worst excesses. Sites like *Fat, Ugly or Slutty Racialicious, The Border House: Breaking Down Borders in Gaming, Not in the Kitchen Anymore*, and *The Hathor Legacy* dedicate themselves to critiquing and publicizing game culture's problems with race, gender, and sexuality while asserting the pleasure, aesthetic value, and social importance of games. These media often flag themselves as "safe spaces" where these often-unpopular minority critiques can be expressed.

For example, *The Border House: Breaking Down Borders in Gaming* describes itself as "a blog for gamers. It's a blog for those who are feminist, queer, disabled, people of color, transgender, poor, gay, lesbian, and others who belong to marginalized groups, as well as allies." In its policies about posting, it asks users to include "trigger warnings" about content that "involves sexual assault or violence towards women and other marginalized groups, which may distress or cause readers to be triggered."

Though anti-sexist and anti-racist gaming blogs often encourage users to report abuse to game moderators before posting, the sites work to address what the game industry can't or won't by publicizing sexist interactions on popular game platforms and exposing abusive gamers to public ridicule. Most screenshots of abusive discourse in-game include the gamer-tag or in-game identity of the abuser, thus linking the behavior to a semi- (but not fully) anonymous individual. In this, their strategy resembles *Hollaback!*, a "movement dedicated to ending street harassment using mobile technology." *Hollaback!*

encourages women to take pictures of sexual harassers and catcallers on the street or in public places with their cellphones and to share them on their website, thus creating an archive for other users to access, as well as a form of accountability: "By collecting women and LGBTQ folks' stories and pictures in a safe and share-able way with our very own mobile phone applications, *Hollaback!* is creating a crowd-sourced initiative to end street harassment."

*Hollaback!* breaks the silence that has perpetuated sexual violence internationally, asserts that "any and all gender-based violence is unacceptable, and creates a world where we have an option—and, more importantly—a response." Similarly, the "Fatuglyorslutty site" relies exclusively on crowdsourcing to produce a rich sampling of sexist and racist "trash talk" sent from one gamer to another in the course of gameplay on game consoles, mobile devices, within PC games like *World of Warcraft,* and on every imaginable gaming device that permits strangers to contact other strangers.

The site's successful use of humor has helped it to garner positive attention in the gaming community, quite a feat given how unpopular and divisive the topic of sexism has been in recent years. *Kotaku,* a popular and widely read gaming blog owned by Gawker Media, wrote the following in 2011: "The casual racism, snarling sexism and random belligerence one encounters in online play, particularly in a first-person shooter over Xbox Live, is not at all a new phenomenon. It's sadly accepted as par for the course, in fact. But the three curators of *Fat, Ugly or Slutty,* have chosen to archive it, not so much for a high-minded ideal, but to hold a mirror up to idiots worthy of ridicule."

Indeed, *Fat, Ugly or Slutty* embodies Henry Jenkins's "critically optimistic" theories about the power of participatory media to increase tolerance and respect for diversity (Jenkins 2006).

As the *Kotaku* post above noted, racism, sexism, and homophobia are commonplace in networked console video gameplay. Though the Xbox 360, PS2/3, and Wii all require users to sign off on Terms of Service agreements regarding the use of profanity and hate speech in live gameplay, these regulations are enforced through a system of victim-reported "tickets" that are acted upon well after the fact, if at all.[2] Users who engage in hate speech can be banned from the service, but are able to log back on after the ban period has passed. The ineffectiveness of industry regulation of hate speech has created a need for victims of gamer abuse to create their own participatory outlets to engage a wider public and increase awareness of this serious issue.

The front page of *Fat, Ugly or Slutty* features a banner headline decorated with an image of a white woman wearing a dress, pearls, a conservative hairstyle, and a wink (see Figure 5.1). The header reads "So you play video games?

---

[2] Computer-based online games have come up with some novel solutions to the problem of moderation. For example, *League of Legends,* a popular PC-based real-time strategy game, has a system that invites users to act as moderators of player disputes around inappropriate speech and behavior.

**Figure 5.1** "Fat, Ugly or Slutty" front page

Are you...Fat, Ugly, or Slutty?" There are radio buttons that invite users to submit their own material, read archives, learn about the site's staff, and read "press" or media coverage that further explains the site's mission to expose in-game harassment. The side bar on the right categorizes posts under labels that express the most common expletives that users have reported hearing or seeing, including of course the old standbys, "Fat," "Ugly," or "Slutty," as well as additional ones such as "Crudely Creative," "Lewd Proposals," "Unprovoked Rage," "Sandwich Making 101," and "Pen15 club." Perhaps the most disturbing category, "Death Threats," is well-populated by posts threatening female players with specific forms of violence.

Though online gamers almost never use their real names when creating avatars or identities for themselves, many of them have invested significant amounts of time, energy, and real capital in these gaming identities. "Fat, Ugly, or Slutty" publishes gamers' online identities along with the racist and sexist messages that they have sent to its readers, thereby helping these readers to avoid grouping or playing with these abusive players while simultaneously exposing them to semi-public ridicule and shame. For example, "xXSTONERXx1690," the author of a message posted to the site that reads "u will always b a spastic cunt cause ur black ya dirty slave" is unlikely to find that readers of *Fat, Ugly or Slutty* will accept his requests to play with him, and he or she may suffer other repercussions. *Fat, Ugly or Slutty*'s front page offers features radio buttons that allow readers to re-post its content to

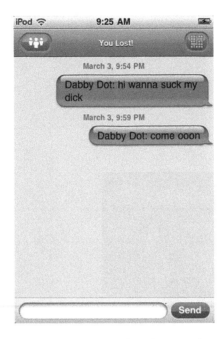

**Figure 5.2** Sexism in casual games: user-contributed capture from FatUglyorSlutty documenting harassment in *Words With Friends*

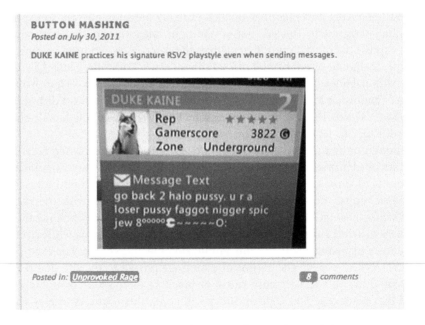

**Figure 5.3** "Go back 2 halo pussy, u r a loser pussy faggot nigger spic jew"

Facebook and Twitter, and an RSS link for those who wish to add it to their newsfeeds.

The naked racism and sexist aggression displayed by xXSTONERXx1690 is far from rare on the site or in gaming culture, but neither is it the norm. While it has been argued elsewhere that fighting games like *Mortal Kombat* and *Street Fighter* and FPS games like the immensely popular *Modern Warfare: Call of Duty* and *Halo* series promote violent and abusive behavior or even real-world violence (Nielsen et al. 2008), the range of game platforms that *Fat, Ugly or Slutty* displays shows the reader that racism and sexism are global behaviors that can be found on *all* platforms within *all* genres of networked play. For example, after winning a game of *Words With Friends* on the iphone app, "Dabby Dot" sent a *Fat,Ugly or Slutty* contributor a message that reads "hi wanna suck my dick?" followed four minutes later by another reading "come ooon" (see Figure 5.2). *Words With Friends* is a casual game based on Scrabble with no gamic texts, images, or negative fictions that might refer to gender, race, or violence in any way.

Another post, filed under "Unprovoked Rage," simply lists a spate of racist and sexist words, demanding that the reader "go back 2 halo" (see Figure 5.3). Similarly, other posted messages threaten to rape, kill, or otherwise violate or harm their recipients. A particularly disturbing example sent by "MrWinnipeg" to another player in *Draw Something*, a very popular casual game based on *Pictionary*, depicts a female figure labeled "slut" performing fellatio on a smiling male figure labeled "me."

## "Shall We Play a Game?" How Calling Someone a Racist Is Like Starting a Thermonuclear War

There is no doubt that the word "nigger" is "a racial insult with a special status and unique strength". In Randall Kennedy's definitive book on this topic, entitled *Nigger: The Strange Career of a Troublesome Word*, he asserts that "it has long been the most socially consequential racial insult" (Kennedy 2002: 25). He cites writer Farai Chideya who concurs, calling it "the All-American trump card, the nuclear bomb of racial epithets" (p. 22). This word is frequently found in *Fat, Ugly or Slutty*, and though the site collects samples of abuse that users found noteworthy enough to send in and is thus not a representative sample of what users commonly hear while playing, its casual use is cause for concern. For this word *cannot* be used casually, for it defines racism itself.

What can be worse than sending someone an in-game message calling them a "nigger bitch" or calling someone a "nigger" over a voice-enabled headset? Calling someone a racist has almost an equivalent charge. (Sadly, calling someone a sexist lacks this ability to shock or anger.) Doane writes that "Today, charges of "racism"—or the use of the label "racist" –carry an extremely negative connotation and serve as perhaps the ultimate rhetorical weapon in public discourse on racial issues." The discursive act of calling someone a racist is viewed as almost equally transgressive as actually using racist language: it is deemed so devastating that presumably no thing or body can survive it.

Doane also writes that there is "significant disagreement about what racism is." This is no less true within the gaming community. Gamers greatly resent charges of racism despite its prevalence within the community. Many gamers often define racism and sexism very differently than non-gamers do, distinguishing between "trash talk" and "real racism." Many gamers who use sexist or racist language do not see themselves or their peers as racist. *Fat, Ugly or Slutty*'s goal is to collect overwhelming evidence that this speech is pervasive, harmful, and indeed both sexist and racist.

On 28 February 2012, *Kotaku* reported that a "firestorm of drama" had been set off in the already drama-laden world of video game reality television. Another popular gaming blog, *Penny Arcade*, followed suit, reporting in a story entitled "Sexual Harrassment as ethical imperative: how Capcom's Fighting Game reality show turned ugly" (PennyArcade.com, 28 February 2012) that during a recent Capcom sponsored event "contestants took part in sexual harassment and in fact argued that sexual harassment is an important part of the fighting game community that needs to continue." In a video podcast entitled Capcom's *Cross Assault*, aired on Twitch.tv, professional Tekken player Aris Bakhtanians repeatedly asked female player Miranda Pakodzi about her bra size, talked about her breasts, and otherwise made inappropriate and abusive remarks while watching her play. When she protested that he was making her uncomfortable and acting "creepy," he responded that she needed to "toughen up." Pakodzi withdrew from the tournament, Bakhtanians apologized on Twitter, but the story continued to draw attention.

This incident went viral, and Baktanians was later interviewed about it by Twitch.tv community manager, Jared Rae. When Rae asked him, "Can I get my *Street Fighter* without sexual harassment?" Bakhtanians replied bluntly, "You can't. You can't because they're one and the same thing. This is a community that's, you know, 15 or 20 years old, and the sexual harassment is part of a culture, and if you remove that from the fighting game community, it's not the fighting game community."

In this interview Baktanians retreats from his earlier position that women need to "toughen up," thus minimizing the effects of sexism, a common post-feminist claim that represents the orthodox opinion on harassment in the gaming world. Rather, this time, Bakhtanians took an entirely different tack, asserting that video game sexism may be harmful, but that it is an intrinsic part of a long-standing culture and needs to be preserved and protected as such. His argument is that the "fighting game community" has the right to engage in sexual harassment because it is "part of the culture," regardless of the harm suffered by women. There are some obvious weaknesses in this argument—and in the wake of the controversy hundreds of gamers stepped forward to disavow their membership in this "culture," or claimed that Bakhtanians was misrepresenting it. However, few challenged the notion that gaming constitutes its own sphere of convention and condoned behaviors: that it was, in short, a "culture" with different norms, forms of speech, and customs than culture at large.

## Conclusion

There is no intrinsic reason that the culture of gaming must retain its customary sexist and racist discourse, no matter how "traditional" it may be. Traditions change. Gaming culture has tremendous potential for acts of creativity, kindness, collaboration, and as Jane McGonigal (2011) writes in *Reality is Broken*, an eloquent explanation of the productive value of play in an overworked world, the "gamification" of social life can result in novel solutions to social and scientific problems. In short, she asserts that games are fundamentally *good* for us.

Indeed, digital networked games are where both the worst *and* the best behavior on the Internet are to be found. How can we honor players' legitimate claims to belonging to a distinctive and fascinating "gamer" culture while working to address its toxicity to women and minorities? There is much scholarly research on the challenges of honoring and preserving indigenous cultural traditions with fairness to marginalized populations. This work often weighs the value of "cultural authenticity" against basic human rights (McPherson 2000).

As gamer culture continues to struggle with racial and sexual difference, those of us who love to play but who do not fit the traditional gamer identity envision an expanded community based on skill, pleasure, engagement, and collaboration.

## ▨ REFERENCES

Castronova, Edward (2005). *Synthetic Worlds: The Business and Culture of Online Games.* Chicago, IL: University of Chicago Press.

Catalyst (2011). *BurnYourBra Discusses the the Difficulties of being a Female Gamer.* <www. Eventhubs.Com> (accessed April 21, 2013).

Consalvo, Mia (2007). *Cheating: Gaining Advantage in Videogames.* Cambridge, MA: MIT Press.

Consalvo, Mia (2012). "Confronting Toxic Gamer Culture: A Challenge for Feminist Game Studies Scholars," *Ada: Journal of Gender, New Media, and Technology,* 1(1). doi:10.7264/N33X84KH.

Corneliussen, Hilde and Walker Rettberg, Jill (2008). *Digital Culture, Play, and Identity: A World of Warcraft Reader*. Cambridge, MA: MIT Press.

Doane, Ashley (2006). "What is Racism? Racial Discourse and Racial Politics," *Critical Sociology*, 32(2–3): 255–274.

Dyer-Witheford, Nick and de Peuter, Greig (2009). *Games of Empire: Global Capitalism and Video Games*. Electronic Mediations. Minneapolis, MN: University of Minnesota Press.

Everett, Anna and Watkins, Craig (2008). "The Power of Play: The Portrayal and Performance of Race in Video Games," in Katie Salen (ed.), *The Ecology of Games: Connecting Youth, Games, and Learning*. Cambridge, MA: MIT Press, 141–166.

Everett, Anna (2009). *Digital Diaspora: A Race for Cyberspace*. Albany, NY: State University of New York Press.

Galloway, Alexander R. (2006). *Gaming: Essays on Algorithmic Culture*. Minneapolis, MN: University of Minnesota Press.

Galloway, Alexander R. and Thacker, Eugene (2007). *The Exploit: A Theory of Networks*. Electronic Mediations. Minneapolis, MN: University of Minnesota Press.

Gaudiosi, John (2012). "New Reports Forecast Global Video Game Industry Will Reach $82 Billion by 2017," *Forbes*, 18 July. < http://www.forbes.com/sites/johngaudiosi/2012/07/18/new-reports-forecasts-global-video-game-industry-will-reach-82-billion-by-2017/> (accessed December 3, 2013).

Gee, James Paul and Hayes, Elisabeth (2010). *Women and Gaming: The Sims and 21st Century Learning*. New York: Palgrave Macmillan.

Golumbia, David (2009). *The Cultural Logic of Computation*. Cambridge, MA: Harvard University Press.

Higgin, Tanner (2009). "Blackless Fantasy: The Disappearance of Race in Massively Multiplayer Online Role Playing Games," *Games and Culture* 4(1): 3–26.

Huntemann, Nina (2010). "Irreconcilable Differences: Gender and Labor in the Video Game Workplace," 22 January. FLOW TV. <http://flowtv.org/2010/01/irreconcilable-differences-gender-and-labor-in-the-video-game-workplace-nina-b-huntemann-suffolk-university> (accessed June 19, 2013).

Ivory, James, Williams, Dmitri, Martins, Nicole, and Consalvo, Mia (2009). "Good Clean Fun? <A Content Analysis of Profanity in Videobr />Games and its Prevalence Across Game Systems and Ratings," *CyberPsychology & Behavior* 12(4): 457–460.

Jenkins, Henry (2006). *Convergence Culture: Where Old and New Media Collide*. New York: New York University Press.

Kennedy, Randall (2002). *Nigger: The Strange Career of a Troublesome Word*. 1st edn. New York: Pantheon Books.

Langer, Jessica (2008). "The Familiar and the Foreign: Playing (Post) Colonialism in World of Warcraft," in Hilde B. Corneliussen, Hilde and Jill Walker Rettberg, Jill Walker (eds.), *Digital Culture, Play, and Identity : A World of Warcraft Reader*. New York: Routledge, 87–108.

Leonard, David J. (2006). "Not A Hater, just Keepin' it Real: The Importance of Race- and Gender-Based Game Studies," *Games and Culture* 1(1): 83.

Levmore, Saul X. and Nussbaum, Martha Craven (2010). *The Offensive Internet: Speech, Privacy, and Reputation*. Cambridge, MA: Harvard University Press.

Lin, Holin and Sun, Chuen-Tsai (2011). "A Chinese Cyber Diaspora: Contact and Identity Negotiation on Taiwanese WoW Servers," *Proceedings of DiGRA 2011 Conference: Think Design Play.*

McGonigal, Jane (2011). *Reality is Broken: Why Games Make Us Better and How They Can Change the World.* New York: Penguin Press HC.

McPherson, Tara (2000). "I'll Take My Stand in Dixie-Net," in Beth Kolko, Lisa Nakamura, and Gil Rodman (eds), *Race in Cyberspace.* New York: Routledge, 117–131.

Nakamura, Lisa (2002). *Cybertypes: Race, Identity, and Ethnicity on the Internet.* New York: Routledge.

Nakamura, Lisa (2013). "Queer Female of Color: The Highest Difficulty Setting there is? Gaming Rhetoric as Gender Capital," *Ada: Journal of Gender, New Media, and Technology* 1(1). doi:10.7264/N37P8W9V.

Nardi, Bonnie A. (2010). *My Life as a Night Elf Priest: An Anthropological Account of World of Warcraft.* Technologies of the Imagination. Ann Arbor, MI: University of Michigan Press.

Nielsen, Simon Egenfeldt, Heide Smith, Jonas, and Pajares Tosca, Susana (2008). *Understanding Video Games: The Essential Introduction.* New York: Routledge.

Rideout, Vicky, Lauricella, Alexis, Wartella, Ellen (2011). *Children, Media, and Race: Media Use among White, Black, Hispanic, and Asian American Children.* Northwestern University: Center on Media and Human Development.

Scalzi, John (2012). "Straight White Male: The Lowest Difficulty Setting There Is?" *Whatever Blog.*<http://whatever.scalzi.com/2012/05/15/straight-white-male-the-lowest-difficulty-setting-there-is/> (accessed December 3, 2013).

Shaw, Adrienne (2011)."Do you Identify as a Gamer? Gender, Race, Sexuality, and Gamer Identity," *New Media and Society,* 14(1): 28–44.

Sliwinski, Alexander (2012). *Call of Duty: Black Ops 2 Sales Reach $1 Billion in 15 Days. Kotaku* (5 December). <http://www.joystiq.com/2012/12/05/call-of-duty-black-ops-2-1-billion/> (accessed April 16, 2013).

Steinkuehler, Constance (2006). "The Mangle of Play," *Games and Culture,* 1(3): 199–213.

Thomas, Douglas (2008). "KPK, Inc.: Race, Nation, and Emergent Culture in Online Games," in Anna Everett (ed.) *Learning, Race and Ethnicity: Youth and Digital Media.* Cambridge, MA: MIT Press, 155–173.

Wakeford, Nina (2000). "Networking Women and Girls with Information/Communication Technology," in David Bell and Barbara Kennedy (eds.) *The Cybercultures Reader.* London: Routledge, 350–359.

Watkins, S. Craig (2009). *The Young and the Digital: What the Migration to Social Network Sites, Games, and Anytime, Anywhere Media Means for our Future.* Boston, MA: Beacon Press.

Williams, Dmitri, Martins, Nicole, Consalvo, Mia, and Ivory, James (2009). "The Virtual Census: Representations of Gender, Race and Age in Video Games," *New Media and Society,* 11: 815–834.

# Part II
# Information and Culture on the Line

# 6 Internet Geographies: Data Shadows and Digital Divisions of Labor

*Mark Graham*

All my characters were white and blue-eyed, they played in the snow, they ate apples, and they talked a lot about the weather, how lovely it was that the sun had come out. Now, this despite the fact that I lived in Nigeria. I had never been outside Nigeria. We didn't have snow, we ate mangoes, and we never talked about the weather, because there was no need to. My characters also drank a lot of ginger beer because the characters in the British books I read drank ginger beer.

Adichie, 2009

## Introduction

The Internet is not an amorphous, spaceless, and placeless cloud. It is characterized by distinct geographies. Internet users, servers, websites, scripts, and even bits of information all exist somewhere. This chapter focuses on those geographies. It begins by discussing why Internet and information geographies matter and how they influence our everyday lives. It focuses on two important facets of Internet geographies, which might be called:

- *Data shadows*: the layers of digital information about places (see Graham 2010).
- *Digital divisions of labor*: the distinct and uneven geographies of the production of digital information (see Graham 2014).

The data shadows of our material cities, towns, and villages, and the digital divisions of labor that produce them shape more than just the content of a few popular websites. These geographies of information shape both what we know and the ways that we are able to enact, produce, and reproduce social, economic, and political processes and practices.

The chapter then moves to a discussion of some of the most significant geographies of connectivity and how they are changing in the twenty-first century. By 2013 the Internet was used by over 2.5 billion people around the world. The fact that so few parts of the world are disconnected and over a third of the world's population are Internet users means that there is both a figurative and literal space for more locally relevant information to be produced about much of the world.

Finally, the chapter explores some of the mappable data shadows and digital divisions of labor that we can observe across much of our planet, asking what people and places are left out of the digital and material augmentations that we produce and reproduce. Even in an age of almost ubiquitous potential connectivity, online voice, representation, and participation remain highly uneven. The chapter then ends by asking why in an age of almost ubiquitous potential connectivity, so many people are still left out of global networks, debates, and conversations. It is ultimately important to understand that the linguistic, cultural, political, and economic processes and barriers that shape many contemporary data shadows and digital divisions of labor cannot simply be transcended by the Internet alone.

## Augmented Realities

We shape our tools, and thereafter our tools shape us.

McLuhan, 2001: xi

The authorial and geographic biases in information shape not just what we know and do, but also what we are able to know and do. We see this with representations of markets (MacKenzie 2009), economic flows (Ouma, Boeckler, and Lindner 2012), tourism, and many other facets of life. In short, geographic information is implicated in how we produce space (Graham et al. 2013; Pierce et al. 2010). It is therefore important to begin to understand both the geographies of information (or *data shadows*) and the geographies of the production of that information (or *digital divisions of labor*). However, before discussing contemporary information geographies, it is instructive to explore older patterns and their geographic inequalities.

First, on the topic of information geographies, it is useful to begin with a look at historical maps because they illustrate some of the geographic limitations to knowledge transmission. Traditionally, information and knowledge about the world have been highly geographically constrained. The transmission of information required either the movement of people or media capable of communicating that knowledge. We see this if we look at the world's oldest surviving navigational chart: a map from the thirteenth century called the *Carta Pisana* (you can see a detailed reproduction of the map at <http://en.wikipedia.org/wiki/Carta_Pisana>). The *Carta Pisana* was produced somewhere on the Italian peninsula, depicts relatively accurate information about the Mediterranean, less accurate information about the fringes of Europe, and no information about any other parts of the world that are farther afield.

This example starkly illustrates some of the constraints placed on knowledge by distance. Thirteenth-century transportation and communication technologies (in other words, ships and books) allowed some of the constraints of distance to be overcome by the map's Italian cartographers. But in the 13th century those technologies were not effective enough to allow detailed knowledge about the Americas, East Asia, and much of the world to be represented on the map.

Second, on the topic of information production, it is important to note that not only have some parts of the world traditionally been left off the map, but some parts of the world produce far more codified and transmittable knowledge than others, bringing into being and reproducing powerful forms of "knowledge dependence" (Ya'u 2005 in Carmody 2013). If we look at present-day patterns of the geographies of information and knowledge, we see some very uneven patterns. For instance, if you examine the geographies of academic publishing in the cartogram in Figure 6.1 you can see that outside of North America and Western Europe, most of the rest of the world scarcely shows up in these rankings. One of the starkest contrasts is that there are more than three times as many journals published in Switzerland than in the entire continent of Africa. We therefore see a stark form of knowledge dependence.

The problem is that these two types of information inequality (information production and information geographies) can potentially start to reinforce each other as information and physical places become increasing intertwined. This is because the networked, iterative, and relational ways that we experience everyday life and enact places is increasingly experienced in conjunction with, produced by, and mediated by digital and coded information (Pierce et al. 2010). These intersections between the material and the digital are often so intertwined and so co-dependent that they are rendered invisible.

Following Wright's (1947) presidential address to the Association of American Geographers on "Terrae Incognitae" and the potentially uneven geographies of knowledge, it is important to examine the ways in which virtual representations of place are implicated in the ways that we produce and experience places as augmented realities. The term *augmented reality* here is used to describe "the indeterminate, unstable, context dependent and multiple realities brought into being through the subjective coming-togethers in time

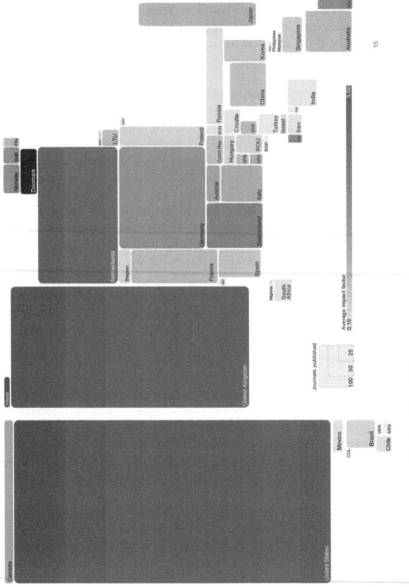

**Figure 6.1** The location of academic knowledge

and space of material and virtual experience" (Graham et al. 2013; Graham and Zook 2013).[1]

When talking about the coming-togethers of information and place, it is important to point out that geographical knowledge—whether by design or by the unintended consequences—has always been associated with power (Driver 1992). Representations of space entail power-laden stabilizations of understanding (Pickles 2004), and absences and silences in representations of place "are more than simply 'blank spaces' on maps, but are integral and deliberate parts of map construction" (Brunn and Wilson 2013). In other words, representations of place are never neutral or objective and are always created in order to serve particular purposes (Harley 1988; Crampton 2001). Representations (and augmentations) of places therefore have, and can exert, power. As Harley argues: "Once embedded in the published text the lines on the map acquire an authority that may be hard to dislodge. Maps are authoritarian images. Without our being aware of it maps can reinforce and legitimate the status quo" (1989: 14).

It is also important to realize that while places can always be characterized by relatively fixed and sedimented social relations and structures, augmented places remain bundles of space–time trajectories that have no homogeneous identity or ontological security (i.e. objective fixity and stability) (Massey 1994; Pierce et al. 2010; Kitchin and Dodge 2007). In other words, augmented realities are not immutable mobiles: they are always "of-the-moment, brought into being through practices (embodied, social, technical), *always* remade every time they are engaged with" (Kitchin and Dodge 2007: 335). So, geospatial content enacted in augmented realities is necessarily spatially, temporally, and personally context-dependent.

Ultimately, the uneven geographies of information that we've seen can all shape what is known and what can be known, which in turn influences the myriad ways in which knowledge is produced, reproduced, enacted, and re-enacted. It is not just Italian navigational maps from the Middle Ages that display such uneven patterns. Almost all mediums of information (e.g. book publishing, newspaper publications, and patents) in the early twenty-first century are still characterized by huge geographic inequalities: with the Global North producing, consuming, and controlling much of the world's codified knowledge, and the Global South largely left out of these processes. This is a fact that only increases the importance of information created in the world's cores, and reinforces what Manuel Castells (1998) refers to as the black holes of informational capitalism that make it difficult for the South to be competitive in the markets for any advanced services.

But, as we increasingly engage with practices of technology and information usage that I've just described, in which we're augmenting our material

---

[1] This is in contrast to Castells' (1989) assertion that information technologies are causing many places to become increasingly meaningless.

worlds with digital content, there is undoubtedly a literal and metaphorical space for more locally relevant information about all of the rest of the world. The remainder of this chapter, therefore, turns to a closer examination, both of where augmented digital content is produced,and who is producing it. It does this with a particular focus on how ICTs might enable new geographies of knowledge in and about some of the world's most disadvantaged places.

## Internet Geographies

Before talking about the geographies of online information, it is useful to first review some of the patterns of Internet use and Internet infrastructure. As recently as 2002, there were only 6 million Internet users in all of Sub-Saharan Africa, and only 16 million in India (compared to 130 million in 2012). A lot of this dramatic unevenness in Internet use came about because of the actual geographies of Internet infrastructure. Some parts of the world simply lacked the physical connections necessary to be well connected to the global grid. In 2009, for instance, not only were some parts of the world much better connected than others, but some parts simply weren't connected at all (East Africa, for instance, was one of the last parts of the world to have any fibre-optic cables connecting it to the wider world). This lack of fibre-optic connectivity meant that Internet access was significantly slower and much more expensive than access in much of the rest of the world.

However, only a few years later, many of these infrastructural constraints have been addressed, and there are only a few parts of the planet remaining absent from the global grid of connectivity. We have thus seen concomitant changes in the geographies of Internet use over time. Internet penetration and mobile growth rates in poor countries are impressive. For the first time in history, we are approaching a state in which a majority of humanity have an ability to communicate or access information non-proximately. At the end of 2011, there were six billion mobile connections globally (<http://data.worldbank.org> (accessed January 9, 2013)), meaning that about 85 percent of humanity is connected in some way.[2] There are now also over two and a half billion people who are Internet users (this is shown in more detail in Figure 6.2). While the geographies of Internet access are still very uneven, we still see that a majority of Internet users live in poor countries. China, for instance, despite its relatively low penetration rate, has the world's largest population of Internet users.

---

[2] The actual figure is likely somewhat lower due to the fact that a significant number of people have more than one connection. However, there are also many cases of multiple people sharing the same connection.

# Internet Population and Penetration

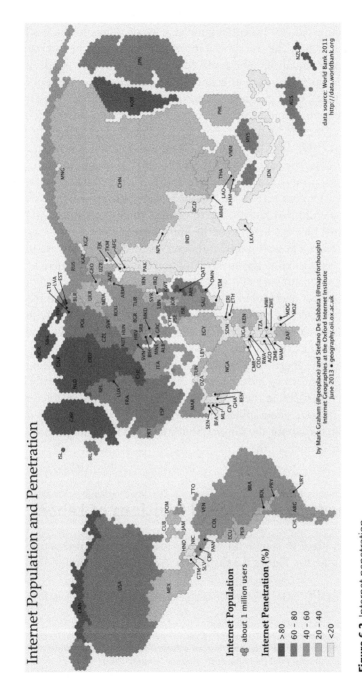

data source: World Bank 2011
http://data.worldbank.org

by Mark Graham (@geoplace) and Stefano De Sabbata (@mapsforthought)
Internet Geographies at the Oxford Internet Institute
June 2013 • geography.oii.ox.ac.uk

**Internet Population**
🔴 about 1 million users

**Internet Penetration (%)**
>80
60 – 80
40 – 60
20 – 40
<20

**Figure 6.2** Internet penetration

In 2012, Sub-Saharan Africa had 120 million users (which is more Internet users than the online populations of the UK and France combined).

Being connected can potentially mean a lot of things to the world's poor (Marker et al. 2002). The free flow of information through the Internet is often seen as a "great equalizer" (Best and Maier 2007). In other words, by allowing people to take advantage of economic, political, and social opportunities, improved connectivity can help empower these capabilities (Sen 1999). The planet's changing connectivity is also seen as central to providing what the World Bank deems to be the missing link (i.e. knowledge) to the Global South (World Bank 1999 in Kleine 2013). These sentiments were more recently echoed in a 2012 speech given by the Secretary-General of the International Telecommunication Union, Hamadoun Touré.[3] He noted that once the world's disconnected are connected then "all the world's citizens will have the potential to access unlimited knowledge, to express themselves freely, and to contribute to and enjoy the benefits of the knowledge society."

Touré 's idea is a powerful one, and deserves further scrutiny. An important question to ask is whether the now 200 million users in Latin America, 100 million in Africa, and almost a billion Internet users in Asia means that people are using this new connectivity to address many of the informational inequalities that have characterized modern media.[4] Are all of these relatively new users represented by relevant information? Are they able to access the information they need? Are they contributing to global discussions that are taking place?

Because of the increasing amount of Internet access we're seeing around the world, with over two billion people online now, and theoretically low barriers to entry, we need to then ask whether the Internet has enabled new, and maybe less uneven, geographies of knowledge. Has it given space for information produced about the Global South and for information produced by people in the Global South?

## Data Shadows and Digital Divisions of Labor

The obvious place to start is to begin by looking at where these new layers of information[5] are. Figure 6.3 displays a measure of the online content that

---

[3] Dr. Hamadoun I. Touré, Secretary-General of the International Telecommunication Union, November 2012.

[4] Because the geographies of traditional media have traditionally been characterized by such stark core-periphery patterns (Norris 2001), the spread of new telecommunications technologies and ICT-mediated practices have thus far only increased inequalities by disproportionately benefiting the already privileged and powerful (Forestier et al., 2002 in Carmody 2013).

[5] *Information* is generally used to refer to codified descriptions that can answer questions such as 'who,' 'what,' 'where,' and 'why.' *Knowledge*, in contrast, usually refers to the structuring, process, organizing, or internalization of information (e.g. see Habermas 1978).

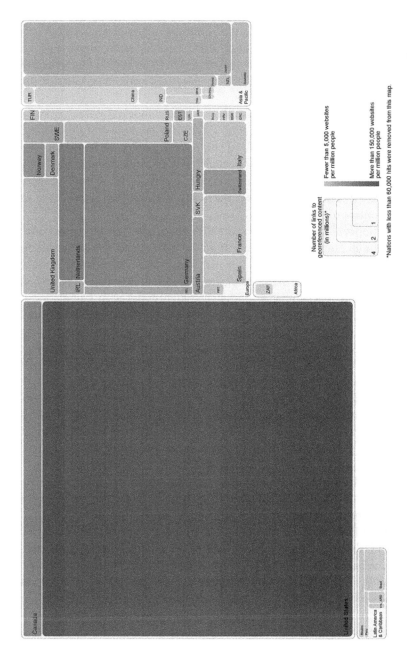

**Figure 6.3** Content indexed in Google Maps

27

people are creating about anywhere on Earth and gets indexed by Google Maps. In other words, it is a measure of what Google knows about the world (and, in turn, what we are able to know about the world by using Google as an intermediary) (for more information about the methods employed to collected these data, see Graham and Zook 2011). Looking at the map, we get an indication of the massive amount of unevenness in these layers of information that surround us. Dense clouds of information exist over some parts of the world and very little over other places.

Norway has the most content per person, with 434 indexed places per every 1,000 people in the country. The rest of Scandinavia and most of Europe and North America also have high levels of content per person. If we move to the bottom of the list we see Afghanistan, which has only 1 indexed place for every 33,000 people in the country. Maybe even more surprising is the fact that there is more indexed content layered over the Tokyo metropolitan region than in the entire content of Africa.[6]

It is also important to note that Figure 6.3 only displays an aggregate count of content in all languages. In order to get a better sense of who is able to read and make use of this content, we can also explore the relative amount of content produced about the same places in different languages. Figure 6.4, for instance, compares Flemish and French content indexed by Google Maps about Belgium (a full description of methods can be found in Graham and Zook 2013).

A dark dot on the map indicates that there is more French content than Flemish content about that particular place, while a lighter dot indicates that there is more Flemish content than French content. What we see is that the map very closely reflects "offline" geolinguistic practices. Interestingly, this pattern almost perfectly mirrors the divisions between Flemish-speaking Flanders and French-speaking Wallonia. We can see similar patterns in much of the rest of the world (e.g. in Eastern Canada there is generally more French-language content about Quebec and more English-language content about Ontario.)

However, this geolinguistic mirroring that we see breaks down when we look at parts of the world in which there are more unbalanced power-dynamics between different linguistic groups. If we perform a similar analysis of Israel and the Palestinian territories (see Figure 6.5), then we see that while Arabic and Hebrew content tends to annotate the same physical places, there is a much denser cloud of Hebrew content over almost all of those places. These have shown us that not only is there a paucity of online information about many of the world's economic peripheries, but of the information that exists, much of it remains inaccessible to many people. This matters

---

[6] This is a fact reminiscent of statistics from the 1990s demonstrating that there were more landline telephones in Tokyo than in all of Sub-Saharan Africa combined (e.g. see Carmody 2013).

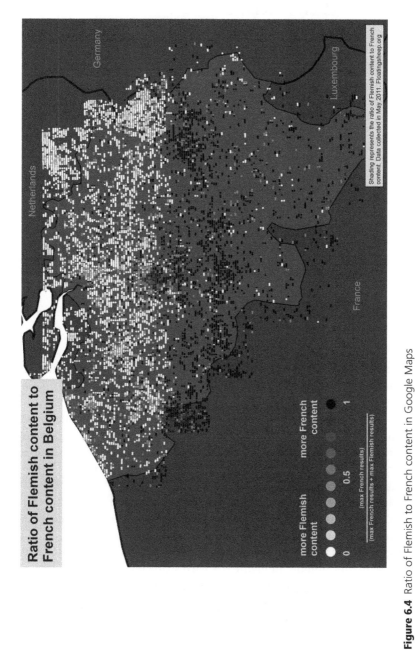

**Figure 6.4** Ratio of Flemish to French content in Google Maps

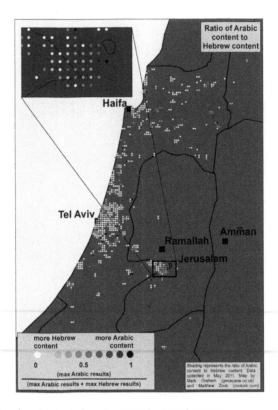

**Figure 6.5** Ratio of Arabic to Hebrew content in Google Maps

because these digital representations can start to define and become part of the augmentations of place.

However, we haven't yet looked at the geographies of explicitly user-generated content on the Internet. Doing so can give us a better sense of what a broader segment of Internet users want to create content about (in contrast to what a large company creates content about). Arguably, the largest, most used, and most influential single web platform on which people are creating layers of information about our planet is Wikipedia.

Wikipedia is by far the world's biggest and most used English encyclopedia, and 1,600 times larger than Encyclopaedia Britannica. On any given day, 15 percent of all Internet users access it. It exists in 282 languages; 40 of those language versions have over 100,000 articles, and the English one alone contains close to four million. In Figure 6.6, each shape represents a country, and the size of the shapes indicates the total number of Wikipedia articles written about each country (i.e. articles about cities, battles, parks, festivals, monuments, buildings, etc.).

We can see that representations within the platform are also highly uneven. Some parts of the world are characterized by highly dense virtual

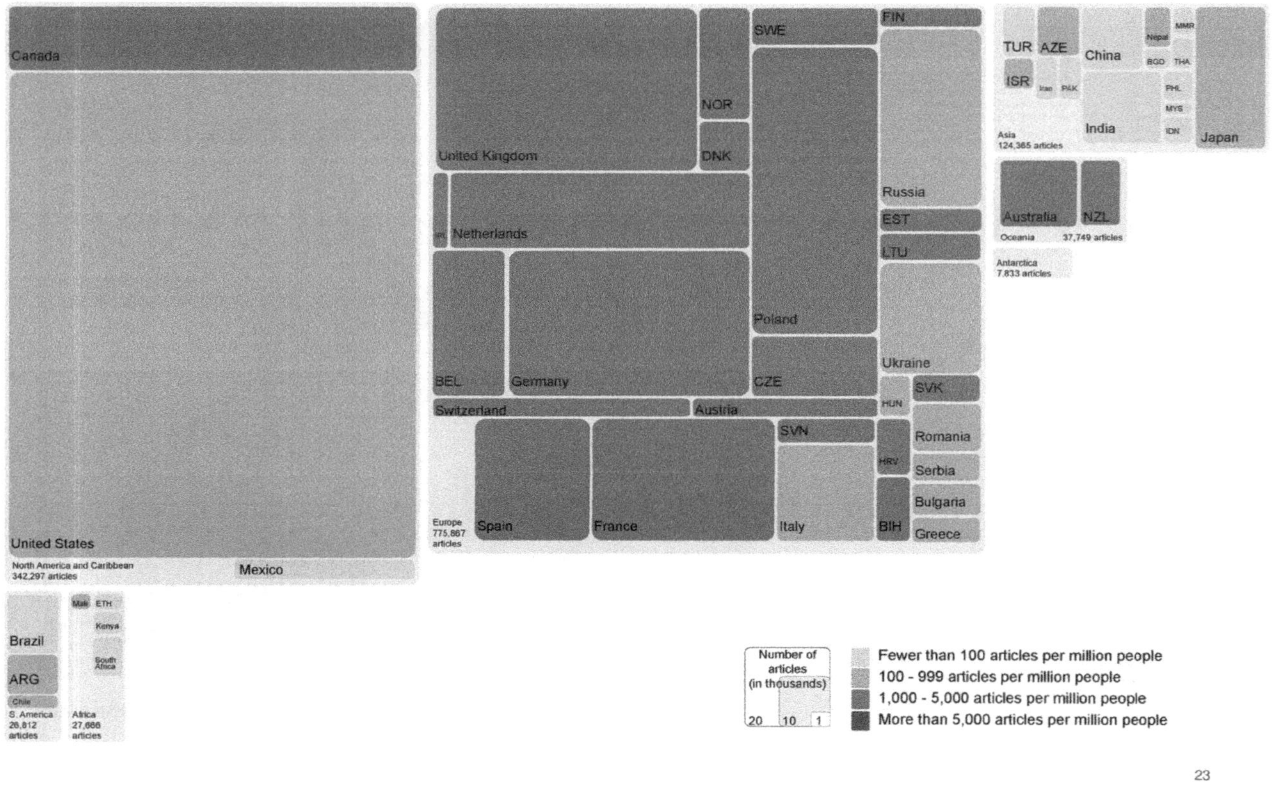

Canada
United States
North America and Caribbean
342,297 articles
Mexico
United Kingdom
NOR
DNK
SWE
FIN
Russia
EST
LTU
Netherlands
Poland
Ukraine
BEL
Germany
CZE
SVK
HUN
Switzerland
Austria
SVN
Romania
HRV
Serbia
Bulgaria
Europe
775,867
articles
Spain
France
Italy
BIH
Greece
TUR
AZE
China
Nepal
MMR
BGD
THA
ISR
Iran
PAK
PHL
MYS
India
IDN
Japan
Asia
124,365 articles
Australia
NZL
Oceania
37,749 articles
Antarctica
7,833 articles
Brazil
ARG
Chile
S. America
26,812
articles
Mali
ETH
Kenya
South Africa
Africa
27,666
articles
Number of articles (in thousands)
20
10
1
Fewer than 100 articles per million people
100 - 999 articles per million people
1,000 - 5,000 articles per million people
More than 5,000 articles per million people
23


**Figure 6.6** The World According to Wikipedia

**average number of edits to Wikipedia**

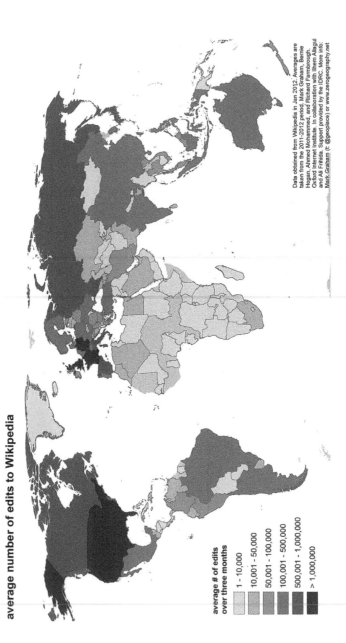

average # of edits
over three months

1 - 10,000
10,001 - 50,000
50,001 - 100,000
100,001 - 500,000
500,001 - 1,000,000
> 1,000,000

Data obtained from Wikipedia in Jan 2012. Averages are
taken from the 2011-2012 period. Mark Graham, Bernie
Hogan, Ahmed Mohammed, and Richard Farmbrough.
Oxford Internet Institute. In collaboration with Ilhem Allagui
and Ali Frihida. Support provided by the IDRC. More info:
Mark Graham (t @geoplace) or www.zerogeography.net

**Figure 6.7** Average Number of Edits to Wikipedia

representations, while others are barely represented at all. The relative absence of Africa is again quite notable here. There are more articles on the Netherlands or Poland or the Ukraine than the entire continent of Africa. Maybe even more shocking is the fact that there are more articles written about Antarctica than most countries in Africa, and many in Latin America and Asia.

The map also displays the number of articles per person in each country (with dark shades representing more articles per person and lighter shades indicating fewer per person). We see that Europe, in particular, has a lot written about it on a per-capita basis. Most of Africa, Asia, and South America, in contrast, is characterized by only a small number of articles per person. Although one of Wikipedia's aims is "to contain the sum of human knowledge," we see that we are far from that important goal. Uneven data shadows of places exist, not just in Wikipedia and Google, but also in all other important Internet platforms of information (e.g. OpenStreetMap, Twitter, Flickr, etc.).

Importantly, we are able to see clearly that not only are there uneven data shadows over much of the world, but that these data shadows are produced in uneven ways. Figure 6.7, for instance, displays the number of Wikipedia edits originating from each country over the 2011–12 period. We see distinct digital divisions of labor. Africa, for instance, produces only a small amount of the content in Wikipedia (the entire continent combined has slightly fewer edits than Hong Kong, and only 4 percent of the edits that originating in the US). Unbalanced digital divisions of labor exist in other parts of the world as well. Israel, for instance, contributes more to Wikipedia than the rest of the Middle East and North Africa put together. Again, the focus here is on Wikipedia, but similar inequalities in online voice and participation can be seen in almost all other platforms.

## Conclusions

In sum, we see that the production and subjects of knowledge have very distinct and uneven geographies. There remain significant silences and uneven geographies of knowledge at a range of scales stretching from the local to the national levels. We also see that Internet penetration rates or numbers of connected persons in each country (Figure 6.2) only explain some of the unevenness that we see. The fact that over a third of the world's population now uses the Internet does not yet seem to have lessened the centrality of the world's informational cores. It is, therefore, a social risk to imagine that we are even getting close to having platforms that contain the sum of human knowledge. Rather, we need to keep a focus on some of the significant biases embedded in this knowledge that plays a key role in shaping our understandings of the world.

These uneven data shadows and digital divisions of labor matter because they shape more than just the contours of websites. They influence what we know and what we can know about the world. They shape how we augment and bring our everyday lives into being. While these broad, national-scale information geographies may seem unimportant to, say, a bus driver in Birmingham or a postman in Pittsburgh, they are but one scale at which informational imbalances and inequalities exist. Even at the most local level, the voice and representation of some people and places will be more visible and more dominant.

More broadly, what do the maps presented in this chapter tell us? Not only is there not a lot of content created from the Global South, but there also isn't a lot of content created *about* the South. A lot of people and places are both literally and figuratively left off the map. The work presented in this chapter inevitably only provides a limited, partial, and selective snapshot of geographies of knowledge. However, the incomplete nature of this inquiry does not lessen the need for deeper research into issues of power, representation, and voice. For instance, the near absence of Arabic, Swahili, Hindi, Bengali, and many other large African and Asian languages on Wikipedia means that we need sustained new inquiry into old questions about power and representation.

So the question then is why? Why when the world is getting wired, and when Internet penetration rates are rising rapidly, are there still these massive absences? The Internet undoubtedly reconfigures processes of creativity and generativity, and, for many, does indeed democratize both the production and consumption of knowledge. But this does not mean that a necessarily causal or determinist relationship exists in which the Internet will "do" any of those things.

Connecting the previously disconnected in order to solve these digital divides is undoubtedly only part of the solution. Equally important[7] are interrelated issues of literacy and education, digital architecture, physical infrastructure, governance of online communities and platforms, cultural, religious, gendered, and other socially constructed barriers, politics and political interference, and language. The demands of persistent poverty are also likely reflected in the geographies of information discussed in this chapter.[8] The role of these social barriers is nothing new, and previous rounds of ICT innovation and upgrading, such as the invention of the printing press or the telegraph, equally failed to democratize voice and power/knowledge.[9] It is, therefore, important to realize that digital media and technological solutions alone can never erase the sorts of spatial patterns highlighted in this chapter.

---

[7] These factors emerged from a two-day workshop that I hosted (with my colleagues Heather Ford, Bernie Hogan, Ahmed Medhat, and Ilhem Allagui) in Cairo in late 2012. The workshop provided a forum for Wikipedians who write articles about the Middle East and North Africa to voice their concerns about barriers to participation and representation for local actors. See also Lessig (2006) for a similar discussion of the complex constraints on Internet-mediated behaviors.

[8] Such demands have been highlighted by Wyche et al. (2013) in their study of social media use in rural Kenya.

[9] Gurumurthy (2004: 7), for instance, notes "the fact that centuries after ICTs such as cheap printing appeared, a vast section of humanity lacks literacy, testifies to our failure to prioritize the social role of technology."

In other words, there is no simple and singular answer to the very uneven geographies of information and voice that we see. Improved Internet connections alone are unable to democratize participation and knowledge, and it can be easy to forget about a lot of underlying structural and social barriers in the context of the expectations, buzz, and hype surrounding the changing connectivities in the Global South. A lot of these unrealistic expectations see the arrival of the Internet and broadband Internet as panaceas for participation and knowledge sharing.

It is also important to remember that despite changing and deepening connectivities for much of the world, most people on our planet are still entirely disconnected. Even amongst the two and a half billion people who are Internet users, a significant number are still left out of global networks, debates, and conversations. While the Internet enables selective connections between people and information, it remains characterized by highly uneven geographies, and in many ways has simply reinforced older global patterns of visibility, representation, and voice.

## ■ REFERENCES

Adichie, C. (2009). "The Danger of a Single Story." *Ted Global*. <http://www.ted.com/talks/chimamanda_adichie_the_danger_of_a_single_story.html> (accessed January 9, 2012).

Best, M. L. and Maier, S. G. (2007). "Gender, Culture, and ICT Use in Rural South India," *Gender, Technology, and Development*, 11(2): 137–155.

Brunn S. D. and Wilson, M. W. (2013). "Cape Town's Million Plus Black Township of Khayelitsha: Terrae Incognitae and the Geographies and Cartographies of Silence," *Habitat International*, 39: 284–294.

Carmody, P. (2013). "A Knowledge Economy or an Information Society in Africa? Thintegration and the Mobile Phone Revolution," *Information Technology for Development*, 19(1): 24–39. doi :10.1080/02681102.2012.719859.

Castells, M. (1989). "The Informational City: A New Framework for Social Change." Research Paper 184 in *The City in the 1990s Series*, Centre for Urban and Community Studies, University of Toronto. <http://www.citiescentre.utoronto.ca/Assets/Cities%2BCentre%2BDigital%2BAssets/pdfs/publications/Research%2BPapers/184%2BCastells.pdf.>

Castells, M. (1998). *The Information Age: Economy, Society and Culture, Volume 3: End of Millennium*. Malden, MA: Blackwell.

Crampton, J. (2001). "Maps as Social Constructions: Power, Communications and Visualization," *Progress in Human Geography*, 25: 235–252.

Driver, F. (1992) "Geography's Empire: Histories of Geographical Knowledge," *Environment and Planning D: Society and Space*, 10(1): 23–40.

Forestier, E., Grace, J., and Kenny, C. (2002). "Can Information and Communication Technologies be Pro-Poor?," *Telecommunications Policy*, 26: 623–646.

Graham, M. (2010). "Neogeography and the Palimpsests of Place: Web 2.0 and the Construction of a Virtual Earth," *Tijdschrift voor economische en sociale geografie* 101(4): 422–436.

Graham, M. (2014). "The Knowledge Based Economy and Digital Divisions of Labour," in V. Desai, and R. Potter (eds.), *Companion to Development Studies*, 3rd edn. London: Hodder, 189–195.

Graham, M. and Zook, M. (2011). "Visualizing Global Cyberscapes: Mapping User Generated Placemarks," *Journal of Urban Technology*, 18(1): 115–132.

Graham, M. and Zook, M. (2013). "Augmented Realities and Uneven Geographies: Exploring the Geo-linguistic Contours of the Web," *Environment and Planning A* 45(1): 77–99.

Graham, M, Zook, M., and Boulton, A. (2013). "Augmented Reality in the Urban Environment: Contested Content and the Duplicity of Code," *Transactions of the Institute of British Geographers* 38(3): 464–479. doi: 10.1111/j.1475-5661.2012.00539.x.

Gurumurthy, A. (2004). "Gender and ICTs: BRIDGE Overview Report," Institute of Development Studies, September: 1–52.

Habermas, J. (1978). *Knowledge and Human Interests*. London: Shapiro.

Harley, J. B. (1988). "Silences and Secrecy: The Hidden Agenda of Cartography in Early Modern Europe," *Imago Mundi*, 40: 57–76.

Harley, J. B. (1989). "Deconstructing the Map," *Cartographica*, 26: 1–20.

Kitchin, R. and Dodge, M. (2007). "Rethinking Maps," *Progress in Human Geography*, 31(3): 331–344.

Kleine, D. (2013). "Development 2.0 or imposition n.0—Geographers engaging critically with ICT4D rhetoric and practice." Unpublished Manuscript.

Lessig, L. (2006). *Code 2.0*. New York: Basic Books.

MacKenzie, D. (2009). "The Credit Crisis as a Problem in the Sociology of Knowledge," *American Journal of Sociology*, 116(6): 1778–1841.

McLuhan, M. (2001). *Understanding Media: The Extension of Man* (2nd edn). Cambridge, MA: MIT Press.

Marker, P., McNamara, K., and Wallace, L. (2002). *The Significance of Information and Communication Technologies for Reducing Poverty*. London: Department for International Development. <http://www.dfid.gov.uk/documents/publications/ictpoverty.pdf> (accessed January 9, 2012).

Massey, D. (1994). "A Global Sense of Place," *Marxism Today*, June: 315–323.

Norris, P. (2001). *Digital Divide: Civic Engagement, Information Poverty, and the Internet Worldwide*. Cambridge: Cambridge University Press.

Ouma, S., Boeckler, M., and Lindner, P. "Extending the Margins of Marketization: Frontier Regions and the Making of Agro-Export Markets in Northern Ghana," *Geoforum*, 48: 225–235.

Pickles, J. (2004). *A History of Spaces*. London: Routledge.

Pierce, J., Martin, D. G., and Murphy, J. T. (2010). "Relational Place-Making: The Networked Politics of Place," *Transactions of the Institute of British Geographers*, 36: 54–70.

Sen, A. (1999). *Development as Freedom*. New York: Alfred A. Knopf.

Wright, J. K. (1947). "Terrae Incognitae: The Place of the Imagination in Geography," *Annals of the Association of American Geographers*, 37: 1–15.

World Bank (1999). *World Development Report: Knowledge for Development*, Washington, DC.

Wyche, S. P., Schoenebeck, S. Y., and Forte, A. (2012). "Facebook is a Luxury: An Exploratory Study of Social Media Use in Rural Kenya." ACM Conference on Computer Supported Cooperative Work and Social Computing (CSCW 2013), San Antonio, US.

Ya'u, Y. (2005). "Globalisation, ICTs and the New Imperialism: Perspectives on Africa in the Global Electronic Village," *Africa Development*, 30 (1–2): 98–124.

# 7 China and the US in the New Internet World: A Comparative Perspective*

*Gillian Bolsover, William H. Dutton, Ginette Law, and Soumitra Dutta*

## The Internet's Shifting Center of Gravity

The Internet was an American invention and it was in the Western context that the technology was built and matured, but US users no longer drive online developments. China's online population surpassed that of the United States in 2008, and today there are more Chinese Internet users than there are Americans on the planet. With more than half the Chinese population still offline, this shift in the Internet's centre of gravity is likely to continue to accelerate over the next decade.

While China, with its massive population, accounts for much of the Internet's shift away from the West, the trend is not limited to the Asian giant alone. As the percentage of worldwide Internet users located in North America and Europe has halved over the past decade, from 66 percent in 2002 to 33 percent in 2012, the percentage located in Asia has grown from only 5 percent in 2002 to 45 percent in 2012. Other regions in the Global South have also seen their influence grow dramatically. The percentage of worldwide Internet users located in Latin America and the Caribbean has risen from less than 1 percent in 2002 to 10 percent in 2012, and users in the Middle East and Africa, who collectively accounted for approximately 2 percent of the world's Internet population in 2002, made up more than 10 percent of the total by 2012.

* An earlier version of this paper was presented at China and the New Internet World, an International Communication Association (ICA) Preconference, Oxford Internet Institute, University of Oxford, June 14, 2013.

These changes are set to accelerate rather than abate. The extension of Internet connectivity to five billion new users over the next decade, the vast majority of whom will be located in non-Western countries (Schmidt and Cohen 2013), will likely prove as, or more, revolutionary than the changes seen in the developed, Western countries that first adopted this technology. However, despite the scale and importance of these changes, the bulk of academic scholarship in Internet Studies has yet to account for, or fully understand, the significance of this changing population.

One concept that foregrounds this shift and invites a reconsideration of established theories in light of these changes, is our conception of the New Internet World (Dutta et al. 2011). The theory proposes that the Old Internet World, dominated by the English-speaking West and developed East Asian countries, has become less prominent as we are moving into a New Internet World that is increasingly shaped by the users, companies, and conditions in rapidly developing areas such as China and the Global South.

A key, but as yet unanswered question, is how this influx of new users might change the way that we understand the Internet and its effects. Reflecting the conditions of its development, key American values of privacy and freedom of expression were built into the code and structure of the technology (Norris 2001: 232). The Internet was seen as a technology that would spread American values of freedom of expression across the globe, embodied by Bill Clinton's famous comment, in reference to China, that trying to control the Internet was like trying to nail jello to the wall. However, this optimism has proven premature. While the Internet has undermined government control of the flow of information and increased official responsiveness to local grievances, China has largely succeeded in constructing an Internet with Chinese characteristics behind the so-called Great Firewall.

Using data from an online survey of Internet users in more than sixty countries, this chapter will provide empirical evidence to support the concept of the New Internet World and describe the nature of this new world.

The first section of this chapter will illustrate the concepts of the Old and New Internet worlds by asking what similarities and differences exist between users in nations that were prominent in the Old Internet World and those that are driving its transition into the New.

The second section of this chapter will turn its focus to the two countries that were most influential in shaping the Old and New Internet Worlds, the United States and China. It will ask whether, given their distinctive Internet sphere, Chinese users differ from other users, both in established and emerging Internet nations, in terms of their Internet uses and values. Will the influx of users in China, operating in what might be an increasingly different Internet sphere to Western users, result in a fundamental shift in net global understandings of the Internet as a place for free organization, information sharing, and discussion?

# Methods

Two world-leading online research companies, Toluna and comScore, fielded our survey online between July and September 2012. The 209-question survey was offered in nine languages (Arabic; English; French; German; Italian; Japanese; Korean; Spanish, both traditional and Latin American; and Simplified Chinese) and garnered 11,225 respondents in sixty-three countries (Table 7.1).

Online surveys are not without limitations; however, given that our research sought to study the opinions and practices of Internet users, this methodology was deemed the most appropriate. Surveys also often suffer from self-selection and non-response bias, however by utilizing two major commercial survey companies, each with a user base of more than five million, and by employing mandatory answers, we sought to mitigate these limitations.

Despite our efforts at global reach, few panelists could be found in many small countries and countries with low Internet penetrations, limiting our coverage to certain parts of the global Internet population. This made it difficult

**Table 7.1** Countries represented in dataset

| | |
|---|---|
| North America | Key Countries: Canada (n = 512) and the United States (n = 800) |
| Europe | Key Countries: Germany (n = 328), United Kingdom (n = 307), France (n = 303), Italy (n = 301), and Spain (n = 303)<br>Supplementary Countries: Denmark, Finland, Ireland, the Netherlands, Norway, Poland, and Portugal |
| Oceania | Key Countries: Australia (n = 327)<br>Supplementary Countries: New Zealand |
| Asia | Key Countries: China (n = 527), India (n = 507), Japan (n = 319), and Korea (n = 301)<br>Supplementary Countries: Bangladesh, Hong Kong,[1] Malaysia, Pakistan, Singapore, Sri Lanka, Taiwan,[2] and Thailand |
| Latin America | Key Countries: Argentina (n = 301), Brazil (n = 305), Colombia (n = 306), Mexico (n = 305) and Peru (n = 307)<br>Supplementary Countries: Belize, Bolivia, Chile, Costa Rica, Guatemala, Nicaragua, Panama, Paraguay, Uruguay and Venezuela |
| Middle East | Key Countries: Jordan (n = 243), Saudi Arabia (n = 511) and the United Arab Emirates (n = 245)<br>Supplementary Countries: Afghanistan, Bahrain, Israel, Iran, Iraq, Kuwait, Oman, Qatar and Yemen |
| Africa | Key Countries: Algeria (n = 229), Egypt (n = 529), Morocco (n = 270) and South Africa (n = 332)<br>Supplementary Countries: Ghana, Kenya, Nigeria and Tunisia |

[1] Hong Kong and Taiwan are examined as independent units for the purposes of this paper due to their substantially different Internet development histories compared to Mainland China.

[2] See footnote 1.

to collect samples that were large enough for a country-level analysis in some countries. Within our dataset we restricted country-level analysis to nations with more than 200 survey respondents, giving us the ability to compare users in twenty-four individual nations (Table 7.1).

Notwithstanding these limitations, this survey is one of the most comprehensive studies of cross-national Internet uses and attitudes conducted and, thus, provides unique and valuable insights into the Internet's changing geographic and demographic characteristics.

## A Schema for Categorizing Countries According to Internet Development

In order to address our first research question of whether there is a significant difference between Internet users in countries that were prominent in the Old Internet World and those that only joined in the New, it was necessary to divide counties in our dataset based on their historical Internet development. Five distinct patterns of development stood out, when the sixty-three countries in our dataset were compared (Figure 7.1).

The group that we have called Early Leaders represents the most prominent nations of the Old Internet World, Western, and developed East Asian countries that played a major role in shaping the Internet's development (Table 7.2). These nations have had more than half their population online for the past decade and currently have at least three-quarters of their population online.

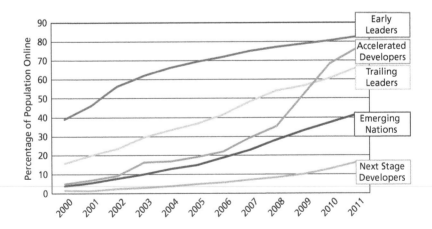

**Figure 7.1** Average Internet penetration rates by developmental group
*Source:* ITU

**Table 7.2** Breakdown of Internet development groups for surveyed countries

| | |
|---|---|
| Early Leaders | Europe: Germany, Norway, Finland, Denmark, The Netherlands, UK<br>East Asia: Japan, Hong Kong, Taiwan, South Korea, Singapore<br>North America and Oceania: Canada, US, Australia, New Zealand |
| Trailing Leaders | Europe: Poland, Ireland, Italy, France, Portugal, Spain<br>Middle East: Israel, Bahrain, United Arab Emirates<br>South America: Chile<br>Asia: Malaysia |
| Accelerated Developers | Middle East: Kuwait, Oman, Qatar |
| Emerging Nations | South and Central America: Argentina, Brazil, Colombia, Costa Rica, Mexico, Panama, Peru, Uruguay, Venezuela<br>Middle East and North Africa: Egypt, Jordan, Tunisia, Morocco, Saudi Arabia<br>Asia: China |
| Next Stage Developers | Africa: Kenya, Nigeria, Ghana, South Africa, Yemen, Algeria<br>South and South East Asia: Iran, India, Afghanistan, Pakistan, Bangladesh, Iraq, Thailand, Sri Lanka<br>South and Central America: Bolivia, Paraguay, Belize, Guatemala, Nicaragua |

Complementing the Early Leaders were Trailing Leaders, countries that were online in the Old Internet World, but due to their more modest Internet populations, did not play a major role in shaping it. This includes countries in Southern and Western Europe as well as early non-Western adopters such as Israel, Chile, and Malaysia.

Accelerated Developers were a small group of nations in the Middle East whose Internet penetration has risen from approximately 5 percent in 2000 to 76 percent in 2011, primarily in the last five years. They became connected only in the New Internet World period, but the Internet is likely to be more integral to everyday life in these countries compared to other newly connected countries with lower penetration rates.

The Emerging Nations are those whose populations are driving the transition of the Old Internet World to the New, rapidly developing countries such as Brazil, Mexico, Egypt, and China, with relatively new but rapidly expanding Internet populations. The countries in this category are particularly relevant to understanding the potential effects of the Internet's changing demographics on global Internet users and values.

The final group within our dataset were the Next Stage Developers. This group, which includes most of Sub-Saharan Africa, much of South and South East Asia, and later developing countries in Central and South America, are likely to play an increasingly influential role in the future Internet, but their current influence is outweighed by the earlier developers and the Emerging Nations group.

Examining the development of the global Internet across these five developmental categories raises many interesting questions. For example, how did Kuwait, Oman, and Qatar achieve such accelerated Internet development, and what are the effects of this unusual path? Also what changes might we expect in the future as a larger percentage of users in Next Stage Developing countries moves online? However, this chapter will focus on the two most influential of these developmental groups, Early Leaders and Emerging Nations and, within these groups, the influential nations of the US and China, asking whether a significant difference exists between users in these two categories, why this might be the case, and what this might mean for the future of Internet policy and practice.

## Emerging Nation Users: More Sociable, Produce More Content

Previous research conducted in 2010 by our team found that users in Emerging Nations produced more online content, and were more willing to explore and meet new people online rather than using the Internet only to support and solidify their offline connections (Dutton et al. 2011). However, this research was limited to fourteen countries and was conducted only in English, so we sought to further investigate these initial findings using a larger sample and more robust methodology.

In order to investigate sociability and online openness, we asked respondents to indicate their willingness to be friends or make connections with someone they did not know offline, whether they would meet someone online that they had not met in person, and whether they would meet someone offline that they had first met online. For each of these three measurements, Internet users in Emerging Nations were significantly more sociable online ($p < 0.00$) than their counterparts in Early Leading countries.

A similar result was found regarding content production: users in Emerging Nations were significantly more active in producing online content. Survey respondents were asked how frequently they contributed eleven different types of content online (Figure 7.2). In each of these areas, users in Emerging Nations produced significantly more content ($p < 0.00$) than those in Early Leading countries. On average, users in Emerging Nations contributed about three times as much content than users in Early Leading Nations.

While some argue that differences between users in emerging and established Internet countries could be due to early adopter effects, or demographic and structural differences in online populations, we found that these differences remained when controlling for age, gender, education, income, time using the Internet, and reported interest in the Internet. Furthermore, we found that while in Early Leading Nations, like the United States, content production falls dramatically for users who have been using the Internet for longer, this is not the case for users in Emerging Nations, where content production remains both high, and stable regardless of how long a person has been using the Internet (Figure 7.3).

These findings lend more support to the conclusion that differences between these two groups are not simply a matter of yet-to-be-domesticated technologies

**Figure 7.2** Percentage of respondents who perform selected content production activities at least monthly

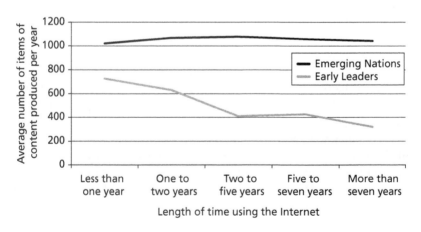

**Figure 7.3** Average number of items of content produced per year

and early adopter effects, and may instead be related to the cultural, social, economic, and political conditions of typical countries in these groups.

Given these findings, it is even more important to understand how users in particularly influential nations, such as China, differ from their counterparts in the Old Internet World, offering explanations for why this might be the case and predictions for how these differences are likely to affect the future of the global Internet.

## Chinese Users Lead The World in Online Entertainment and Shopping

Our survey asked users about the frequency of a wide variety of Internet activities as well as their opinions on these activities. Within our dataset, we were able to compare users in twenty-four nations, representing a diversity of geographic locations and developmental histories.[3] Compared to users in other nations, Chinese users clearly stood out for their high levels of Internet use for entertainment, leisure, and commerce.

Chinese respondents were the most frequent online shoppers of any country surveyed, with 60 percent reporting making online purchases at least weekly, twice the worldwide average (Table 7.3). They also engaged in many types of online entertainment and leisure activities significantly more frequently than non-Chinese, reporting, for instance, more frequently getting music online (gamma = 0.47), and more frequently watching videos online (gamma = 0.31). In contrast, American respondents used the Internet much more infrequently for entertainment and leisure activities, with 23 percent reporting making an online purchase, 19 percent getting music and 39 percent watching videos online weekly.

While many of the most frequent online shoppers were located in the economic powerhouses of the Emerging Nations, there was little difference overall between the frequency of online shopping for users in the Early Leading and Emerging Nation groups, with online shopping in frequent in Mexico, Algeria, and Jordan, and very frequent in Brazil, India, and China. Levels of online shopping were also very high in South Korea, an Early Leading nation with 54 percent of respondents reporting making a purchase at least weekly, second only to China. One possible explanation for this is the economic and cultural closeness of China and South Korea, which could have created a similar and potentially shared online marketplace.

---

[3] Countries were analyzed individually if there were at least 200 valid survey respondents in that country. These countries were Algeria, Argentina, Australia, Brazil, Canada, Colombia, China, Egypt, France, Germany, India, Italy, Japan, Jordan, Korea, Mexico, Morocco, Peru, Saudi Arabia, South Africa, Spain, the United Arab Emirates, the United Kingdom, and the United States.

**Table 7.3** Leisure, entertainment, and shopping in Early Leading countries, Emerging Nations, China, and the United States

|  | Early Leaders | United States | Emerging Nations | China |
|---|---|---|---|---|
| Percentage of respondents reporting making an online purchase at least weekly | 27% | 23% | 30% | 60% |
| Percentage of respondents reporting using the Internet to get music at least weekly | 30% | 19% | 69% | 80% |
| Percentage of respondents reporting using the Internet to watch videos at least weekly | 46% | 39% | 83% | 85% |
| Number of respondents | 3567 | 800 | 3857 | 527 |

Chinese respondents were also more likely than respondents in many other nations to report using the Internet to download music. However, unlike shopping, which was not associated with the Early Leading and Emerging Nations categories, the frequency of downloading music was significantly higher among users in Emerging Nations compared to those in Early Leading countries (gamma = 0.60).

A similar result was found for the frequency of watching videos online. Chinese respondents had the third highest percentage of respondents who reported watching online videos at least weekly (85 percent), after Saudi Arabia (87 percent), and Egypt (86 percent). Watching videos online was a much more frequent activity among respondents in Emerging Nations compared to respondents in Early Leading countries (gamma = 0.63).

Differences in the enforcement of copyright could potentially explain these differences. In many Emerging Nations, and China in particular, copyright is enforced much less strictly than in Western countries, meaning more content is available for consumption and download online, leading to more frequent use. This interpretation is supported by the fact that respondents in Emerging Nations were significantly more likely to report using the Internet to download content than their counterparts in Early Leading countries (gamma = 0.65).

However, another potential explanation is that in Early Leading countries, the use of online resources is more likely to be complementary to an existing pattern of consumption that includes television and portable music devices, reducing the reliance on the Internet for entertainment and leisure activities, whereas in Emerging Nations devices are likely to offer a greater range of programming and choice than that which is otherwise available to the user.

While further research is necessary to investigate the reasons for the more frequent use of the Internet for entertainment, leisure, and commerce in Emerging Nations, one thing is certain. China's rapidly developing consumer culture, supported by online shopping and entertainment activities, will shape the economic and environmental fortunes of the early 21st century (Garth 2011), possibly to a greater extent than any other nation in the world.

On November 11, 2012 (Singles' Day or Chinese Valentine's Day), Chinese online shoppers broke records, spending nineteen billion yuan, approximately three billion US dollars, in twenty-four hours (CCTV 2012). This is three times more than the amount spent online by US consumers during Black Friday on November 25, 2012 (Rao 2012). Although Chinese consumer culture is often said to be attempting to mirror that of the United States, Chinese Internet users far outstrip Americans as well as other nations in their online commercial activities.

The Internet was introduced in China as a means to facilitate economic development and trade, and our survey results confirm that this technology has become an integral part, not just of the nation's economy, but of the everyday lives of the majority of Chinese Internet users in a way that surpasses that of any of the other nations that we surveyed.

## Driving the Transition to a Mobile Internet

At the same time as the Internet's shift from the Old to New Internet Worlds another shift has occurred from fixed machines towards more mobile, multi-platform usage patterns. Across Emerging Nations, Internet users engage in more activities on their mobile phones than their counterparts in Early Leading nations such as the United States (Table 7.4).

Chinese users were the most likely of those in all the twenty-four countries examined to own a smart phone, with 86 percent reporting owning a device, compared to only 35 percent of users in the United States. Again, South Korean respondents displayed remarkable similarities to those in China with 85 percent reporting owning a smartphone. This widespread adoption is not limited to young people; while in the West and Japan, smartphone ownership drops dramatically among those older than 34, smart phone ownership in China and South Korea remained high among older users.

Compared to smartphone users in other countries Chinese (and South Korean) respondents also used their phones more frequently for entertainment

**Table 7.4** Mobile Internet in Early Leading countries, Emerging Nations, China, and the United States

|  | Early Leaders | United States | Emerging Nations | China |
|---|---|---|---|---|
| Percentage of respondents who own a smartphone | 51% | 35% | 59% | 86% |
| Percentage of respondents reporting playing games on their phones | 50% | 34% | 76% | 88% |
| Percentage of respondents reporting listening to music on their phones | 47% | 30% | 83% | 92% |
| Percentage of respondents reporting using their phones to browse the Internet | 57% | 40% | 79% | 91% |
| Number of respondents | 3567 | 800 | 3857 | 527 |

and leisure activities, with 90 percent reporting that they used their phones to listen to music, compared to 30 percent in the United States. Clearly, Internet users in the Emerging Nations, led by the Chinese, use ICTs more frequently for entertainment and leisure activities compared both to countries that were earlier adopters of the technology and to the worldwide average.

While the percentage of respondents reporting using their phones for playing games and listening to music declines with age, it declines much faster among users in Early Leading nations. While in the 18–24 age group 82 percent of users in Emerging Nations reported playing games on their cell phones compared to 77 percent in Early Leading nations (a difference of five percent), in the 45–54 age group the difference rises to 19 percent (61 percent in Emerging Nations and 42 percent in Early Leading countries). This is further evidence that ITCs play different social roles in established and emerging Internet nations, and that the variables that affect ICT uses have different effects in these two populations.

It could be argued that those who use their mobile phones heavily for entertainment and leisure activities in Emerging Nations might do so because they do not have access to other technologies that perform this function; however, individuals who play games on their phones are also likely to report owning a personal gaming system, and those who listen to music on their phones are likely to report owning a portable MP3 player, supporting the conclusion that mobile phones generally do not offer new functionalities to users but rather enable them to do more of the things that they already do using other devices (Blank and Dutton, chapter 2 this volume).

These results suggest that Internet users in Emerging Nations, led by China, are driving the Internet's transition towards a more mobile pattern of Internet use. This is particularly significant in China, where more than half the country's population remains offline, particularly in rural areas. These individuals are expected to be connected over the next decade and will likely rely more on mobile devices, than on fixed machines, to access the Internet. In catering for these populations, China will likely lead the way in shaping the new, more mobile Internet. Already mobile Internet innovations developed in China, such as the text and voice messaging service WeChat, are diffusing worldwide, in line with this thesis.

## A Global Internet Culture

In contrast to the previous sections that focused on Internet uses, finding that users in China and other Emerging Nations were more sociable, innovative, and mobile, this section shifts its focus to consider the attitudes and values of these Internet users towards issues such as privacy, government control, and freedom of expression.

The Internet has been hailed as a technology of free expression, but the Chinese government, among others worldwide, actively seeks to control online speech, employing many censors and rapidly responding to sensitive posts (Zhu et al. 2013). Both the press and academics have produced varied assessments of Chinese Internet policy. Some have argued that policy is becoming more conservative (Qiu 2013), while others have argued that the Internet is having a liberalizing effect (Yang 2009). Few of these studies, however, address the attitudes of ordinary Internet users, particularly in comparison to users worldwide.

We found that a majority of Chinese respondents (70 percent) believed the Internet was free. However, this is lower than average for users in Emerging Nations and the lowest of all the twenty-four countries examined except South Korea (62 percent). Additionally, more than half of Internet users in China agreed that the government should monitor content online, although this is not significantly different from users in other countries (Table 7.5).

Despite operating within an Internet that is significantly more controlled than the majority of survey respondents, Chinese users tended to mirror the values and concerns of others in both Early Leading and Emerging Internet Nations. We found little difference between Chinese and non-Chinese

**Table 7.5** Attitudes toward key Internet values in Early Leading countries, Emerging Nations, China, and the United States

|  | Early Leaders | United States | Emerging Nations | China |
|---|---|---|---|---|
| Percentage of respondents who say they think the Internet is free | 89% | 92% | 80% | 70% |
| Percentage of respondents who agree that the government should monitor content posted on the Internet | 47% | 43% | 46% | 52% |
| Percentage of respondents who agree that the government should not censor political content online | 56% | 65% | 42% | 50% |
| Percentage of respondents who say they are concerned about their online communication being monitored | 68% | 68% | 59% | 64% |
| Number of respondents | 3567 | 800 | 3857 | 527 |

respondents on the subject of Internet control and censorship, and no major difference between respondents in Emerging and Early Leading Nations on these issues (except on the issue of the censorship of racist or discriminatory content where respondents in Emerging Nations exhibited slightly greater levels of agreement).

The remarkable similarity across surveyed nations suggests that there is a distinctive set of global Internet values, supporting privacy and freedom of expression that cuts across geographical, economic and social boundaries. These values are rooted in the Internet's development in the United States and are intertwined with its rhetoric as it spreads worldwide, demonstrating that despite distinct policy priorities of national governments, Internet users largely adhere to the principles the technology has come to embody.

However, some differences exist between Chinese and non-Chinese users on the question of the censorship of political information. When asked whether they agreed or disagreed with government, authorities, or regulators tracking their online activity, censoring political content, or knowing whom they communicate with offline, Chinese respondents were, on average, more likely to express a neutral view, and were also less likely to respond that they strongly agreed or strongly disagreed when compared to non-Chinese respondents, or with respondents from other Emerging Nations or Early Leading countries.

This result could be indicative of a pragmatic view towards government control and censorship on the part of Chinese respondents. Living in a society where they must consider the arguments both for and against Internet censorship, they might see both its pros and cons more strongly than those for whom government control is less expansive and overt, and political-administrative traditions oppose censorship. However, another possible explanation is that of acceptance of the status quo: knowing that they cannot change the state of government regulation within China they choose a neutral view, unlike respondents in more democratic societies who take a more polarized view because they feel that their opinions can shape policy and practice with respect to freedom of expression, and also feel freer to be critical of government policy.

Consistent with attitudes toward censorship of the Internet, Chinese respondents did not stand out in their concern over the monitoring of online activity. Instead it was users in liberal democratic countries in both Early Leading and Emerging Nations, such as Brazil, France, India, the UK, and the United States, with the exception of users in Germany, who showed the highest levels of concern about their online behaviors being monitored. In Japan, Korea, China, and Germany, most respondents expressed moderate, but not high, levels of concern about their online activity being monitored. A third pattern, evidenced in the Middle Eastern and North African countries of Algeria, Egypt, Jordan, Morocco, and Saudi Arabia, showed the greatest number (between 30 and 40 percent of respondents) expressing no concern for their online activity being recorded (Figure 7.4).

Countries fell into four categories based on the distribution of concern over online monitoring (Figure 7.4). Those skewed towards "high concern" included Australia, Brazil, Canada, France, India, South Africa, Spain, the United Kingdom, and the United States. A more "moderate concern" level was expressed in China, Germany, Japan, and Korea. A more distributed range or "divided concern," almost bimodal-skew towards high and low concern, was found in Argentina, Columbia, Italy, Mexico, Peru, and the United Arab Emirates. Relatively "low concern" was expressed in Algeria, Egypt, Jordan, Morocco, and Saudi Arabia.

Figure 7.4 suggests that respondents' concern about their online activities being recorded may have a cultural basis that is separate from whether they live in early or later adopting countries, and separate from opinions about the desirability of monitoring. There was no correlation between whether respondents, either in China or elsewhere, agreed that governments, regulators, and authorities should know with whom they communicate online, and concern about whom they email or about a message online being recorded.

Respondents in China had very similar views to their neighbours in South Korea and Japan, despite a greater realistic chance that their online activities might be monitored. Chinese respondents who reported posting about politics online and those with more education were no more likely to be concerned

Concern About What You Read or Download Online Being Recorded

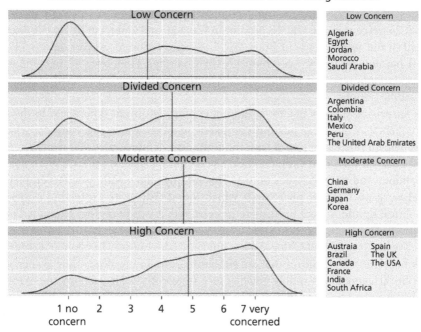

**Figure 7.4** Concern about online monitoring cuts across developmental groups

about online monitoring than others. However, younger Chinese respondents, particularly those in the 25–34 age group, were more likely to express concern about online monitoring.

Concern about one's personal activity being monitored had no correlation with support for the monitoring of the same activity, and countries in which the Internet is generally seen to be free exhibited statistically significant, higher levels of concern about monitoring than countries where more monitoring takes place. Although concern had little correlation with actual reality, it will likely have a strong influence over individual behaviors.

## Political Expression Online

Another important aspect of online civil society is the ability for the Internet to facilitate information sharing, information seeking, and discussion on political and social issues. Studies in the West have consistently shown low levels of participation in online politics (Hindman 2009), reflecting low levels offline.

In contrast to the staggeringly low numbers of users in Early Leading countries who reported expressing a political opinion online (25 percent in the US, 26 percent in the UK, 15 percent in Canada, and 7 percent in Japan), over half of the respondents in Emerging Countries reported expressing a political opinion online at least monthly. In Emerging Countries 40 percent of respondents reported posting weekly, compared to only 15 percent in Early Leading nations.

Surprisingly, users in China, did not exhibit significant differences in their frequency of political posting compared to other Emerging Nations, with 48 percent posting online at least monthly. This demonstrates that restrictions on political speech in China do not have a chilling effect on the ability to post opinions and discuss issues online. This finding aligns with previous empirical work on Chinese microblogs which found that posts expressing critical political opinions were unlikely to be censored; it was posts that attempted to mobilize participants offline that were censored (King et al. 2013).

We have found that Chinese users hold attitudes towards freedom of expression, privacy, and control that are similar to users in the West. They also post political expressions online much more frequently than users in the West. Thus we can conclude that there is a strong social foundation in China that supports freedom of expression online.

We also found that the Internet has become integral to the Chinese economy. Chinese companies and Chinese Internet users are as much, if not more, reliant on the Internet as users in the West. China also exhibits a particularly well-developed mobile culture and Chinese netizens use the Internet frequently for entertainment, shopping, and leisure.

Taken together, these findings provide a basis for greater optimism about the future freedom of the Chinese Internet than is evidenced on the basis of policy rhetoric, given that the infrastructure that exists to support entertainment and commerce in China can also potentially support the free expression and information-seeking activities that a majority of Chinese users support.

## Conclusion: Innovative Users, Persistent Values

Internet users in Emerging Nations, such as China, are significantly different from those in Early Leading Nations, such as the United States. They are more likely to produce new online content and more likely to establish new social connections online. While a smaller proportion of the population in Emerging Nations are currently online, these new Internet users are using this technology in more innovative and varied ways than the users in early adopting nations. These differences remain when controlling for demographic and structural factors known to affect Internet uses and values in the Old Internet World, including age, gender, education, income, time using the Internet, and reported interest in the Internet. This suggests that these differences are likely to persist as the Internet population in these nations grows. In short, the centre of gravity of the Internet is shifting, not only in numbers but also in patterns of use, with Emerging Nations, such as China, moving in directions that could make them central to future innovation in the production and use of online technologies.

While Internet users in China are among the world's leaders in Internet use for entertainment, leisure, and commercial purposes, they align with other nations in their levels of political discussion, and views on government censorship and online monitoring. Based on these patterns of public attitudes, values, and uses, China's policy makers are likely to value the unusually strong commercial and economic significance of the Internet. In combination with the support of users for the traditional values and attitudes underpinning the Internet, there may be more reason to be optimistic about the future of an open Internet in China and across the New Internet World than might be expected on the basis of the rhetoric surrounding national policy.

However, while the values and attitudes of Internet users are important, they are only one element shaping the future of the Internet and its societal implications cross-nationally. These opinions need to be tracked over time and examined in the context of other factors shaping the use of the Internet, including Internet policy and governance cross-nationally and globally, in order to fully evaluate how the Internet's changing demographics will shape its future.

## ■ REFERENCES

CCTV. (2012, November 11). *China's e-Shoppers Break Record on Singles' Day*. http://english.cntv.cn/program/newsupdate/20121112/103465.shtml (accessed March 28, 2013).

Dutta, S., Dutton, W. H., and Law, G. (2011). *The New Internet World: A Global Perspective on Freedom of Expression, Privacy, Trust and Security Online: The Gobal Information Technology Report 2010–2011*. New York: World Economic Forum, April. <http://papers.ssrn.com/sol3/papers.cfm?abstract_id=1810005> (accessed July 22, 2013).

Dutton, W., Dutta, S., and Law, G. (2011, September 18). *Emerging Contours of a New Internet World: Shifting Patterns of Adoption, Attitudes and Behaviour*. iCS-OII Symposium on "A Decade in Internet Time," an OII-iCS Symposium on the Dynamics of the Internet and Society, University of Oxford, September 21–24, 2011. <http://ssrn.com/abstract=1929791> (accessed July 17, 2013).

Garth, K. (2011). *As China Goes, So Goes The World: How Chinese Consumers Are Transforming Everything*. London: Hill and Wang.

Hindman, M. (2009). *The Myth of Digital Democracy*. Princeton, NJ: Princeton University Press.

King, G., Pan, J., and Roberts, M. (2013). "How Censorship in China Allows Government Criticism but Silences Collective Expression," *American Political Science Review*, May 2013: 326–343.

Norris, P. (2001). *Digital Divide: Civic Engagement, Information Poverty and the Internet Worldwide*. Cambridge: Cambridge University Press.

Qui, J. L. (2013). "China's Network Society: A Three-Phase Trajectory—Asteroids, Bees, Coliseums." Talk given at the Centre for Study of Global Media and Democracy, Goldsmiths, University of London, May 29.

Rao, L. (2012, November 25). "E-Commerce Spending On Black Friday Tops $1B For The First Time; Amazon Is The Most Visited Retailer." <http://techcrunch.com/2012/11/25/e-commerce-spending-on-black-friday-tops-1b-for-the-first-time-amazon-is-the-most-visited-retailer> (accessed July 22, 2013).

Schmidt, E. and Cohen, J. (2013). *The New Digital Age*. London: Random House.

Yang, G. (2009). *The Power of the Internet in China*. New York: Colombia.

Zhu, T., Phipps, D., Pridgen, A., Crandall, J., and Wallach, D. (2013). *The Velocity of Censorship: High-Fidelity Detection of Microblog Post Deletions*. <http://arxiv.org/abs/1303.0597> (accessed June 19, 2013).

# 8 Social Media and the News: Implications for the Press and Society

*Nic Newman, William H. Dutton, and Grant Blank*

## Introduction

The Internet's increasing centrality to everyday life and work has raised many questions over its implications for the production and consumption of news (Mitchelstein and Boczkowski 2013). Much focus has been directed at whether online news will complement or substitute for, and displace, print newspapers. Concern over displacement is often tied to the loss of the business models, often built on advertising, that support high-quality journalism. The fear is that weakness in the economic basis of journalism could lead to a decline in the quality and diversity of news coverage (Chyi and Lasorsa 2002).

These concerns are added to by the potential for the Internet to open up new ways for individuals and groups to participate in the news. Fuelled by the growth of powerful social networks like Facebook, Twitter, and YouTube, individuals are increasingly able to create, collaborate, and share their own media—often to the bemusement of governments and traditional news organizations. Big Media has lost its monopoly on the news, and events such as the Arab Spring have demonstrated that in many cases the quickest and most compelling reports can come from ordinary people closest to the action (Rane and Salem 2012).

Citizen journalism and social media haven't replaced professional journalism, but the line has become increasingly blurred amid an overwhelming tide of interlinked sources and outputs. Beyond breaking news, there has been an explosion of comments, blogs, votes, and petitions that add vibrant new voices and perspectives to what has traditionally been the preserve of a small number of news professionals (Shirky 2008). This in turn has led to concerns about both the quality and reliability of the information available in social networks like Twitter, and the dumbing down of the news agenda by amateurs (Keen 2007).

The dramatic rise in the use of social media, such as Facebook, compounds these issues by raising questions about whether, and how, social media might reinforce or transform developing patterns of substitution and exposure. This led Sunstein (2001) to raise the possibility of a virtual "echo chamber" where audiences seek out only information that supports their viewpoints and filter out contervailing information in ways that reinforce their existing prejudices (Zillman and Bryant 1985; Tewksbury and Rittenberg 2009).

Debate over whether the Internet might undermine the print newspaper has been a dominant issue around the social implications of the new media. But the main issue is not whether the news is on paper or electronic, but whether the rise of the Internet and related information and communication technologies, such as social media, will undermine the ability of news organizations to produce quality journalism on a range of important issues and hold the rich and powerful to account. Journalism has been seen as a key underpinning of liberal democratic societies ever since the 18th century, when Edmund Burke observed that the role of the press in holding governmental institutions to account through their watchdog function was that of a "Fourth Estate" (Carlyle 1905; Sunstein 2001).

These considerations of economics, participation, quality, and governance combine to touch directly on the role of information, the media, and the news in contemporary society. For example, social media might reinforce online news, and further displace traditional media such as printed newspapers. Alternatively, time spent using social media could substitute for more traditional uses of the Internet, including searching for online news, exacerbating problems with print and online news provision and the business models supporting them (Donsbach et al. 2011). Such an effect could create additional risks for high-quality journalistic coverage and worsen the decline of traditional news organizations. Alternatively, the use of social media could lead users to find new and more diverse sources of information about the topics that interest them in ways that support quality journalism in local and global arenas.

These questions led us to examine empirically the role of the Internet and social media in changing patterns of the production and consumption of news, and their significance for the institutionalized media. We have drawn on data including the Oxford Internet Surveys (OxIS), conducted biennially since 2003, which enable us to develop overtime indicators of trends in online news consumption, and the use of social media. Outside the UK, we have used survey evidence primarily from the Pew Research Center and from the Reuters Institute for the Study of Journalism (RISJ 2012), which has looked at the role of social media as part of a wider multiple-country study of the use of digital and traditional news sources. We have combined this with interviews and references to leading practitioners and commentators.

# Consumption Trends around Online News and Social Media

Over the past decade the Internet has become an increasingly important source of news and information—beginning to rival television in some countries. For example, in the United States, which has often been first to show new patterns of digital behavior, the growth of digital and social media has been accompanied by falling circulation for traditional print media such as newspapers.[1] These trends appear to be accelerating, in part driven by the increasing ubiquity of smartphones and tablets since 2007. By 2008, for example, a larger percentage of US respondents (40%) cited the Internet as a main source of national and international news than cited the newspaper (35%), and the proportion of those relying on a newspaper continues to erode over time, dropping to 31 percent in 2011, compared to 43 percent relying on the Internet. That said, in the United States, television remained well ahead when consumers were asked about their main source of news: 66 percent of respondents in 2011 said they relied on television news (Pew Research Center 2012).

This data is supported by research data from other countries with commercial or public service media. A study of the plurality of media sources found that that 41 percent of UK adults used the Internet regularly for news—although young people in particular have embraced digital media (Ofcom 2012). Reading the news online is more prevalent among men than women and among students and employed than retired people or the unemployed (reflecting general patterns in levels of Internet use and media consumption (Dutton and Blank 2011).

In the United States, where newspapers rely heavily on advertising, rather than direct sales, many newspapers have closed and journalists have been thrown out of work. In other parts of the world, such as Europe, which rely more on the sale of papers rather than advertising, the impact has not been as severe. A multi-country survey of online news users by the Reuters Institute for the Study of Journalism showed that some European countries like Germany are showing a strong allegiance to traditional media, with 68 percent of Germans accessing a newspaper every day and more than 90 percent watching TV compared with only 61 percent accessing online news. Moreover, it also shows that in all countries the majority of Internet news consumption is still tied to traditional news brands—via the websites of newspapers and broadcasters.

There have been shifts in usage, particularly around reading print newspapers, but the Internet has primarily provided more ways for audiences to access news (Pew Research Center 2012; RISJ 2012). For example, in the UK, most

---

[1] Pew Research Center, *State of the News Media 2012*, <http://stateofthemedia.org/2012/overview-4/> (accessed January 18, 2013).

individuals who read the news online also read newspapers offline (Dutton and Blank 2011). Likewise, 83 percent of tablet users in the UK also watch TV news every month, 65 percent also listen to radio news, and 60 percent also read a printed newspaper (RISJ 2012). This reinforces the thesis that online news more often complements rather than substitutes for offline news sources (Vayas et al. 2007). People who like news tend to look for it on multiple media.

## The Role of Social Media

There has been a dramatic increase in the use of social media in the UK and worldwide. OxIS has tracked the rise of message boards and blogging in the early 2000s—and more recently the growth of social networks like Facebook and Twitter. Between 2007 and 2011 the number of people regularly maintaining profiles on social network sites rose from 17 percent to 60 percent—as they connected with friends, posted comments, and shared photographs—although the most substantial rise in the adoption of social media occurred between 2007 and 2009. That said, more time has shifted to social media, with UK Internet users averaging around thirty minutes each day on Facebook, mirroring worldwide trends (Nielsenwire 2010).

One of the biggest impacts of social media has been in the area of breaking news, where an amateur with a camera is routinely closer to the story than a professional journalist. One early example was a picture of a plane crash in the River Hudson, taken by a tourist from a ferryboat and posted to Twitpic—scooping mainstream journalists like the *New York Times* by several hours. Since then, networks like Twitter, Facebook, and YouTube have routinely been at the center of stories from the Iranian election protests (2009) to the Japanese earthquake (2011), the death of Osama Bin Laden (2011), and the uprisings in Tunisia, Libya, Egypt, and Syria (2011 and 2012), providing a stream of eye-witness material in the form of comments, pictures, and videos.

In many cases, such as Syria and Iran, social networks like Twitter and YouTube have exposed news stories that otherwise might have stayed hidden, but detractors question the way rumor as well as truth can be spread in seconds around the world. A case in point was pictures of the dead body of Osama Bin Laden that were relayed by social and digital networks and picked up by newspapers and television networks—before they were later found to be fakes.[2] At the same time, social media like Twitter enable users to correct

---

[2] See <http://www.guardian.co.uk/world/2011/may/02/osama-bin-laden-photo-fake> (accessed January 18, 2013).

misinformation and rumors very rapidly, as documented in research on Tweets during the England riots of 2011 (Procter et al. 2013).

Social media has contributed to a speed-up of the news cycle, and this has increased pressure on traditional media organizations engaged in breaking news (Newman 2009). One critic has argued that the "Cult of the Amateur" (Keen 2007) is undermining the quality of information and threatening traditional journalism. Keen suggests that professional news organizations have traditionally acted as gatekeepers, analyzing and regulating information before it reaches the masses. He views this expert-based filtering process as beneficial, improving the quality of popular discourse.

But evidence suggests that social media is complementing rather than replacing traditional gatekeepers. Although many Americans found out about Bin Laden's death via social networks, 56 million people still watched President Obama's address on nine different US TV networks.[3] Rather than replace core news outlets, social media acted like a cheerleader, getting the ball rolling and stimulating interest in the main event—which was still delivered in a fairly traditional way. Also, genuine scoops in social networks like Twitter tend to be the exception rather that the rule—with the majority of news emanating from the breaking news feeds of a relatively small number of traditional news organizations such as the CNN, the *New York Times* and the BBC (Bernardo et al. 2011). Survey data shows that while consumers do look to social media as a source of news, traditional media still dominates actual consumption (RISJ 2012).

A second key way in which social media is affecting news relates to its role in distribution and discovery, where it is beginning to rival search in terms of importance to news organizations. About one in five online news users in the UK (20%) come across a news story through a social network like Facebook and Twitter, but almost half (43%) of young people are much more likely to access news this way (RISJ 2012). Overall, search engines are still more important than social media, but the fact that young people are almost twice as likely to discover a news story through social media rather than search marks a significant generational change. And across all age ranges, 57 percent say they are more likely to click on a news link that comes from someone they know—compared with a link from elsewhere (RISJ 2012).

These developments have also been fuelled by a greater focus on news by Twitter and Facebook in particular, with the development of trending algorithms, social plugins for websites, and the launch of social news reading applications. Market research company Experian Hitwise tracked the data for visits to news stories in the UK between 2008 and 2011, a period that coincided with the fastest growth of social networks like Facebook and Twitter. During that

---

[3] "Obama Drew TV Crowd," *Wall Street Journal Online*, May 4, 2011 (<http://online.wsj.com/article/SB10001424052748703834804576301821550865988.html>, accessed January 18, 2013).

time, the share of visits to traditional news sites increased slightly, whilst visits to social media sites grew by 58 percent. Far from cannibalizing news and media traffic, social media appears to have helped drive traffic to news sites.[4]

More widely, we've seen a rapid growth in the number of people multi-tasking, using social media at the *same time* as another form of media such as television. UK media regulator Ofcom (2010) reports that 20 percent of time spent with media each day is now spent using two or more forms of media simultaneously. OxIS finds multitasking to be increasingly prominent among younger Internet users, with more than 90 percent of students saying they multitask (Dutton et al. 2009: 37). These trends are reinforced by spikes of social media activity during live events such as the 2012 London Olympics,[5] with similar peaks being seen around key moments during the UK elections in 2010 and the US presidential elections in 2012.

Multi-tasking is one pattern behind claims that the Internet is encouraging media snacking rather than deeper understanding: what Nicholas Carr (2010) has labeled the "shallows"—but it is interesting to note that data from news organizations suggests time spent with news and media websites has increased slightly over the period. Overall, it appears that—for at least some people interested in the news—snippets of information in social networks are stimulating further interest in news events and encouraging further exploration of key stories.

## The Impact of Social Media on the Traditional News Media

The growth of social networks and the emergence of personal media—such as that provided by YouTube, Flickr, Facebook and Twitter—might be rebalancing the traditional relationship between news producers and consumers. Paul Saffo (2005) has reflected on this change:

The Mass Media revolution 50 years ago delivered the world to our TVs, but it was a one-way trip—all we could do was press our nose against the glass and watch. In contrast, Personal Media is a two-way trip and we not only can, but also expect to be able to answer back.

Some of the early manifestations of this two-way relationship were the commenting and message boards around news websites, but in the early days there was very little connection or integration into wider mainstream coverage. In

---

[4] Data and conversations with Hitwise UK market analysts.
[5] <http://blog.twitter.com/2012/08/olympic-and-twitter-records.html> (accessed January 18, 2013).

the UK, this changed during the Asian tsunami of December 2004 and the London bombings of July 2005, with footage shot on digital cameras and mobile phones incorporated into prime time television coverage for the first time. Within hours of the explosions on the London underground and bus network on July 7, 2005, the BBC had received more than 1,000 photographs, 20 pieces of amateur video, 4,000 text messages, and 20,000 emails. According to the BBC's Head of News at the time, Richard Sambrook (2005), this led to a rethink of how news organizations connect to audiences:

When major events occur, the public can offer us as much new information as we are able to broadcast to them. From now on news coverage is a partnership.

One result of this partnership was the formation of production teams within news organizations such as the BBC to manage and filter this new wave of User Generated Content (UGC) and to distribute the best material to output teams. By 2012, the BBC's user-generated hub was a team of around twenty people monitoring, verifying, and filtering UGC. CNN took a slightly different approach, launching an independent website iReport for user contributions and encouraging a community of global contributions.

## BLOGGING JOURNALISTS

However, these initial developments went only so far. They did not change the way most journalists worked or got involved in social interactions with audiences. The real change happened with the adoption of blogs and later Twitter by mainstream journalists (Thurman and Walters 2013).

Early blogs were seen as brash and outspoken—incompatible with the more measured and balanced tone in many broadsheet newspapers and broadcasters. The informal style and conversational nature of a blog did not always sit comfortably with some journalists, whilst the frequent updates made it hard to apply the normal second level checks around publication of updates. Gradually, however, senior journalists began to see the merits of these tools.

The BBC Business Editor, Robert Peston, began his blog as a tool for communicating to the wider BBC business team, but it soon became required reading for a broader public during the unfolding banking crisis of 2008 and economic turmoil that followed (Newman 2009). Speaking at the Edinburgh TV festival, Robert Peston explained his motivations:

For me, the blog is at the core of everything I do…The discipline of doing it shapes my thoughts. It disseminates to a wider world the stories and themes that I think matter…and connects me to the audience in a very important way.

(Peston speech to Edinburgh TV Festival 2009)

Underlying these trends was a deeper concern, that in an era where anybody could publish an opinion or become a "citizen journalist," the value of sifting and checking facts was being diminished. However, citizen journalism complements mainstream news, and the notion of "five- or twenty-minute activism" enabled online captures the potential of small contributions by networked individuals, adding up to a collective impact (Earl and Kimport 2011).

One specific example of this approach followed the UK parliamentary expenses scandal in 2009 when *The Guardian* newspaper launched an online tool that allowed citizens to examine the full records of their member of Parliament. Using the tool, individuals could flag up issues of concern which were them investigated by professional journalists at *The Guardian*. Another example of mutualized journalism in action has been the emergence of a new form of live blogging, where major news organizations host a live conversation incorporating breaking news and verified facts, with eyewitness material and audience opinion from social media channels like Twitter and Facebook.

Live blogs are just one example of how both the content and format of social media has infiltrated and changed the practice of mainstream journalism on a daily basis. Another example comes from the Telegraph Media Group, where during the 2010 UK election, journalists were encouraged to use Twitter rather than their own production tools to send rapid updates from the campaign trail, which were then incorporated back on the newspaper website. In this way, Twitter helped correspondents to file copy more regularly throughout the day (Newman 2010).

But not all news organizations are able to fully realize the benefits of social media. Newspapers that have chosen to place at least some of their content behind a "paywall" in search of a more sustainable business model limit their potential to build credibility through these networks and make it harder for correspondents to be part of the global conversation.

Overall, in the UK and many other nations, newspapers and broadcasters have normalized their use of social media as source material, filtering the best for a mass audience. News organizations have gradually worked through the dilemmas associated with social media, and have published guidelines and undertaken training programs on how to embrace these new formats whilst protecting their principles and brands. Many news companies have turned their community editors into social media editors and have developed strategies for distributing content in social networks and for using social data to drive more readers to their own websites. In the process, both the practice of journalism and the resulting output has become more open and more iterative—with many more opportunities for dialogue with audiences.

# New Models for News, Community Building, and Accountability

Mainstream media may still be powerful, but they no longer have a monopoly of the means of production or distribution. The ease of creating and publishing information via digital media has enabled individuals, voluntary groups, and others to enhance their "communicative power"—using digital technologies strategically to form their own online networks. Individuals can now source their own information with less dependence on any particular news outlet—and network with each other across the globe using social networking sites, email, instant message, and other avenues.

Similar connections are also made within and across organizational and institutional boundaries in ways that create opportunities for individuals and groups to provide content of value to the mass media, and further enhance their communicative power. The UK election in 2010 offered a number of examples of how these new trends might be affecting accountability in politics—through the activities of Mumsnet, the Straight Choice, and Vote Match.

Mumsnet is a discussion and information site for parents founded in 2000 by sports journalist Justine Roberts and TV producer Carrie Longton. It has over 1.25 million unique users every month and users post around 20,000 contributions every day, sharing information and experience on parenting issues (Henderson 2011). At first glance the site does not seem political, but it has created an infrastructure that can be turned to political purposes. For example, it gained influence by organizing national campaigns on parenting issues, by syndicating the best of its discussion forums to national newspapers, and by inviting politicians to interact with its community. During the 2010 UK election, all three major party political leaders took part in webchats with members, and these encounters were widely reported in the mainstream media. After the 2010 election, Mumsnet was instrumental in focusing the attention of the government on the issue of "phone hacking," after members of the tabloid press tried to access phone messages of a young woman who had disappeared and was later found to have been murdered. A collaborative network organized to support professional women became a source of political empowerment.

Also during the 2010 UK election, there were several successful independent initiatives, not orchestrated by news organizations, to try to use digital and social media to increase transparency and democracy. The Straight Choice was an initiative to digitize local election leaflets—so the statements within them could be more visible and permanently accessible. Over 4,000 leaflets were uploaded by volunteers around the country co-ordinated by software engineer and democracy campaigner Julian Todd, who said that the value of this activity would grow over time: "These spent shells of the campaign were never meant to be seen online. We've left our cameras running, and (now) we can show the newsreel of the ground war" (Todd 2010).

The Internet is enhancing the information available to citizens in other ways as well. Vote Match was an online blind test survey of the policies of all the political parties—part of an initiative by voluntary group Unlock Democracy to raise turnout and political awareness. The initiative was supported by academic institutions and used statements submitted by the political parties themselves. Overall, more than a million people completed the Vote Match survey, with a quarter taking part in the final two days of the campaign.[6] The application was focused on eighteen- to thirty-five year olds, and included a strong tie-in with Facebook, which integrated it into their Democracy UK portal. Additional interest was driven through a partnership with the Daily Telegraph newspaper and its website.

In these examples we see varying forms of involvement in politics by networked individuals. Sites like Mumsnet are so large that their audiences alone attract the attention of vote-seeking politicians. Focussed on a single topic, they have an interest in political issues related to that topic. Straight Choice shows how a single website can create a historical record and make it available. Vote Match illustrates the way an independent website can become involved in non-partisan political issues like voter registration, a straw poll, and links to traditional media, thereby raising awareness and enthusiasm.

The diversity of these sites indicates some of the complexity of the three-way relationship between politics, traditional journalism, and social media. It could be very difficult to generalize about "typical" social media influence on traditional journalism or politics, but in all of these cases, networked individuals were able to use social media to enhance the significance of their messages with the traditional media and the networked public.

## LOCAL AND NICHE COVERAGE

Away from straight politics, there are other examples where digital and social media are helping to widen the amount and range of news available: hyper-local websites and niche websites. These sites are often staffed by volunteers using cheap or free blogging technology. A local site in East London, as one example, offers a regular mix of news, aggregated live transport and weather information, reviews of shops and restaurants, stories about local history, and pictures of nearby beauty spots. Twitter is used to aggregate comments and source stories, while Facebook and email have become the main forms of distribution

---

[6]  1,014,028 completed surveys between March 31 and polling day, May 6, 2010 (Matthew Oliver interview with Nic Newman).

and marketing.[7] Another local example is a site based in the city of Lincoln run by three students who struggled to find work after leaving university. Less than a year after launching in May 2010, the *lincolnite.co.uk* gained a readership of 15,000 and launched an iPhone application.[8] With a focus on immediacy and user-generated content, these hyper-local sites are often providing a complementary service to local newspapers—which necessarily need to take a wider view and focus their limited resources on the biggest news stories in their patch.

Elsewhere, networked organizations such as Avaaz and 38 Degrees are using social media to engage millions of people in petitions and campaigns on subjects as diverse as gay rights in Uganda, climate change, and press freedom. Following allegations of phone hacking in the UK, a loose coalition of academics, celebrities, and others set up a campaigning organization, Hacked Off, to campaign for a public inquiry and a new system of press regulation. Their use of social and digital media—in combination with interviews on mainstream media—helped keep the pressure on Rupert Murdoch's News International and led to the appointment of Lord Leveson to investigate the activities of the press. In such ways the current use of the Internet and other digital ICTs is establishing the potential for another independent source of accountability—something that been called the "Fifth Estate" (see Dubois and Dutton, chapter 15 this volume).

The quality and reliability of information and the numbers viewing these sites and channels often remain relatively small—but as these examples demonstrate, the influence can be significant and complementary, rather than an alternative, especially where the stories or comments are picked up and amplified by the mainstream media, and vice versa. And as described here, there are many instances in which the Fifth Estate has filled niches not being served by the traditional news media, such as in hyper-local news, or has held the traditional press to account for their practices.

## Conclusions

The emergence of digital and social media needs to move beyond simple models of substitutions versus complementarities, as they have created a much more complex ecosystem for the creation and distribution of news (Newman et al. 2012). Similarly, any simple view of competition versus substitution of

---

[7] See <http://www.wansteadium.com/> (accessed January 18, 2013). Wansteadium website is one of thousands of sites listed on the Openly Local directory which lists some of the best <http://openlylocal.com/hyperlocal_sites> (accessed January 18, 2013).

[8] <http://thelincolnite.co.uk> (accessed January 18, 2013).

the Fourth and Fifth Estates needs to be refined to encompass this more inter-related ecology. Both draw from, and contribute to, the strength of the other, while holding each more accountable, such as when Hacked Off and Mumsnet questioned the nature of phone hacking by the tabloid press. Increasingly, pro-fessional journalists rub shoulders with bloggers, citizen journalists, academ-ics, pressure groups, part-time and semi-professional writers, and personal media—and vice versa—in an increasingly transparent and connected world. This is the new ecology of news production and consumption.

But the relationship with mainstream media is complex. In some cases these voices have been brought into the mainstream institutions with developments such as live blogging and the commissioning of external bloggers to write for sites like the *Huffington Post* and *The Guardian*'s "Comment is Free." In other cases, blogs and Twitter accounts by networked individuals are used by the mainstream media as a source of stories or opinions to be checked, validated, and then brought to the attention of a mass audience. But the overall story of social media does not indicate that these new sources are replacing traditional sources, rather they live side by side as an additional layer of information and comment, and in some cases, possibly displacing search as a portal to the news, particularly with young people.

None of this detracts from the economic difficulties affecting many tra-ditional publishers. Without innovations in the business models supporting traditional newspapers, for example, there remains a possibility that financial issues will at some point diminish the ability of the press to employ sufficient journalists to hold the rich and powerful to account. But at this stage there is little evidence that this is happening to a significant extent (also see Ji and Waterman, chapter 9 this volume). The press are experimenting with new business models, such as online advertising, and consolidating their opera-tions in ways that could maintain quality and diversity. Moreover, this chapter points to ways in which digital media are forcing a new transparency in a way that combines the continued professionalism of traditional media with the networked power of individuals and groups.

Given the limitations of our study, with a focus on the UK and United States, there is a need for more systematic research on the actual practices of journalists, networked news organizations, and networked individuals over time and across an extended range of countries. Nevertheless, our study high-lights the degree to which online news and social media are being reflected in the practices of mainstream news organizations of the Fourth Estate, as well as the practices of networked individuals of the Fifth Estate. Both are using the Internet to enhance their communicative power in an increasingly complex ecology of news production and consumption. The interaction and possible synergies among these actors is possibly the most engaging aspect of these developments. These observations led us to suggest the need to move beyond the dominant questions about the uptake of online news and the displacement of traditional media, to look more closely at the rapidly evolving ecology of news production and consumption in the online world. From this perspective, the new news ecology should be supportive of greater democratic accountability, if reinforced and protected by media and Internet regulation and public policy.

## ■ REFERENCES

Bernardo A., Huberman, B. A., Szabo, G., and Wang, C. (2011). "Trends in Social Media: Persistence and Decay." Unpublished manuscript, Social Computing Lab, HP Labs, and Department of Applied Physics, Stanford University. <http://www.scribd.com/doc/48665388/Trends-in-Social-Media-Persistence-and-Decay> (accessed January 8, 2013).

Carlyle, T. (1905). *On Heroes: Hero Worship and the Heroic in History*. London: H. R. Allenson.

Carr, N. (2010). *The Shallows: What the Internet is Doing to Our Brains*. New York: W. W. Norton and Company.

Chyi, H. I. and Lasorsa, D. L. (2002). "An Explorative Study on the Market Relation between Online and Print Newspapers," *Journal of Media Economics*, 15(2): 91–106.

Donsbach, W., Rentsch, M., and Walter, C. (2011). "Social Media as News Sources—Empirical Evidence from Four Countries." Paper presented to the 61st Annual Conference of the International Communication Association, Boston, MA, May 26–30.

Dutton, W. H. and Blank, G. (2011). *Next Generation Users: The Internet in Britain 2011, Oxford Internet Survey Report*. Oxford: Oxford Internet Institute, University of Oxford.

Dutton, W. H., Helsper, E. J., and Gerber, M. M. (2009). *The Internet in Britain 2009*. Oxford: Oxford Internet Institute, University of Oxford.

Earl, J. and Kimport, K. (2011). *Digitally Enabled Social Change: Activism in the Internet Age*. Cambridge, MA: MIT Press.

Henderson, N. (2011, January 20). *When Mumsnet Speaks, Politicians Listen*. BBC News. http://www.bbc.co.uk/news/uk-12238447 (accessed May 5, 2011).

Keen, A. (2007). *The Cult of the Amateur: How Today's Internet is Killing Our Culture*. New York: Doubleday.

Mitchelstein, E. and Boczkowski, P. J. (2013). "Tradition and Transformation in Online News Production and Consumption," in Dutton, W. H. (ed.). *The Oxford Handbook of Internet Studies*. Oxford: Oxford University Press, 378–400.

Newman, N. (2009). "The Rise of Social Media and its Impact on Mainstream Media." Working Paper. Reuters Institute for the Study of Journalism. <http://reutersinstitute.politics.ox.ac.uk/fileadmin/documents/Publications/The_rise_of_social_media_and_its_impact_on_mainstream_journalism.pdf> (accessed July 9, 2013).

Newman, N. (2010). "*#UKelection2010, Mainstream Media and the Role of the Internet: How Social and Digital Media Affected the Business of Politics and Journalism*." Reuters Institute for the Study of Journalism, Oxford University (July). <http://reutersinstitute.politics.ox.ac.uk/fileadmin/documents/Publications/Working_Papers/Social_Media_and_the_Election.pdf> (accessed January 18, 2013).

Newman, N., Dutton, W. H., and Blank, G. (2012). "Social Media in the Changing Ecology of News: The Fourth and Fifth Estates in Britain," *International Journal of Internet Science*, 7(1): 6–22.

Nielsenwire (2010). "Led by Facebook, Twitter, Global Time Spent on Social Media Sites up 82% Year over Year" (January 22). Message posted to <http://blog.nielsen.com/nielsenwire/global/led-by-facebook-twitter-global-time-spent-on-social-media-sites-up-82-year-over-year/> (accessed January 18, 2013).

Ofcom (2010). "Halt in Decline of Flagship TV News Programmes" (June 30). Message posted on <http://media.ofcom.org.uk/2010/06/30/halt-in-decline-of-flagship-tv-news-programmes/> (accessed January 18, 2013).

Ofcom (2012), Office of Communications, "Measuring Media Plurality: Ofcom's Advice to the Secretary of State for Culture, Media and Sport" (June 19). London: Ofcom.

Pew Research Center (2012). "State of the News Media 2012," Pew Research Center, March 19. <http://www.pewresearch.org/2012/03/19/state-of-the-news-media-2012/> (accessed January 15, 2013).

Procter, R., Vis, F., and Voss, A. (2013). "Reading the Riots on Twitter: Methodological Innovation for the Analysis of Big Data," *International Journal of Social Research Methodology*, 16(3) (Special Issue: Computational Social Science: Research Strategies, Design and Methods): 197–214.

Rane, H. and Salem, S. (2012). "Social Media, Social Movements and the Diffusion of Ideas in the Arab Uprisings," *Journal of International Communication* 18(1): 97–111.

RISJ (2012), Reuters Institute for the Study of Journalism, "Digital News Report." Oxford: University of Oxford. July 2012: <http://reutersinstitute.politics.ox.ac.uk/publications/risj-digital-report.html/> (accessed January 18, 2013).

Saffo, P. (2005, December). "Farewell Information, it's a Media Age." Message posted to <http://saffo.com/wp-content/uploads/2012/01/essay_farewellinfo.pdf.> (accessed January 18. 2013).

Sambrook, R. (2005). "Citizen Journalism and the BBC," *Niemen Reports*, Niemen Foundation for Journalism at Harvard University. http://www.nieman.harvard.edu/reportsitem.aspx?id=100542 (accessed May 10, 2011).

Shirky, C. (2008), *Here Comes Everybody*. New York: Allen Lane.

Sunstein, C. (2001). *Republic.com*. Princeton, NJ: Princeton University Press.

Tewksbury, D., and Rittenberg, J. (2009). "Online News Creation and Consumption: Implications for Modern Democracies," in A. Chadwick (ed.), *The Handbook of Internet Politics*. New York: Routledge, 186–200.

Thurman, N., and Walters, A. (2013). "Live Blogging—Digital Journalism's Pivotal Platform?" *Digital Journalism*, 1(1): 82–101.

Todd, J. (2010). "How Dirty was the Election Ground War?" (April 30).Message posted to http://blog.thestraightchoice.org/author/goatchurch.

Vayas, R. S., Singh, N. P., and Bhabhra, S. (2007). "Media Displacement Effect: Investigating the Impact of Internet on Newspaper Reading Habits of Consumers," *Vision: The Journal of Business Perspective*, 11(2): 29–40.

Zillmann, D. and Bryant, J. (1985). "Selective-Exposure Phenomena," in D. Zillmann and J. Bryant (eds.), *Selective Exposure to Communication*. Hillsdale, NJ: Lawrence Erlbaum, 1–10.

# 9 The Impact of the Internet on Media Industries: An Economic Perspective*

*Sung Wook Ji and David Waterman*

## Introduction

Robust media industries are critical to ensuring availability of the high quality and variety of media products that are essential to a vibrant democracy and modern society. It is thus imperative to understand the economic effects of new technologies on the media industries that produce and distribute these products. Much of the commentary about the Internet's impact on the media has focused on its destructive effects on established industries, such as news and music. Thus, the Internet has raised major concerns about the quality and diversity of news and entertainment productions. Is the Internet undermining the quality of media content? If so, this would be a major societal concern, since the media are the key source of information, educational content, and entertainment the world over.

In this chapter, we address this general concern with a study of the economic effects of the Internet on the US media industries. To varying degrees since the mid-1990s, audiences and revenues are migrating from established "offline" media to Internet-distributed online media. On the premise that the economic effects of this transition are best understood in context, we observe a broad group of media industries together over a long period to time. We analyze economic trends in ten major US media categories (books, newspapers, magazines, recorded music, movie theaters, radio, television broadcasting, multichannel television delivery systems, home video, and video games)

---

* This chapter is adapted from Waterman, D. and Ji, S. W. (2012). "Online Versus Offline in the United States: Are the Media Shrinking?" *The Information Society*, 28(5): 285–303. More complete methodological details and citations to previous research appear in that article.

over six decades, from 1950 to 2009 or 2010 (the latest data available at the time of our study).

The first of the main research questions we pose is: how have online media affected media industry revenues overall? We also ask how the balance of advertiser vs direct payment support of media (e.g. consumer purchases of songs, video-on-demand (VOD), or monthly subscriptions to news and entertainment) may be shifting as Internet media grow. The viability of advertising and direct-payment business models, especially on the Internet itself, is important to understanding the industry trends. The balance of advertising vs direct-payment support also affects the pricing and thus consumer access to media. Of most interest, however, is a third question: how is the Internet affecting the overall quality and variety of media products themselves? That is, are offline plus online media a negative or a positive sum game with respect to content production? At this stage we can offer only speculative answers to this last question but it motivates our research.

Our main focus in this chapter is on professionally produced commercial media products. User-generated blogs, video-sharing websites such as YouTube, and Facebook along with other social networks have an important economic role, however, and we include these media in some of our measures. This study is in the tradition of Machlup (1962), Rubin et al. (1986), OECD (1981; 1986), and Jussawalla and Lamberton (1988); previous research that has sought to measure the size of the larger "information economy."

The next section begins with our main statistical investigation of economic trends. The following section considers reasons for the observed trends, followed by a summary and conclusions.

# Economic Effects of the Internet in Historical Context

## A. AN OVERALL DECLINE IN MEDIA INDUSTRY REVENUES SINCE THE ADVENT OF BROADBAND PENETRATION

The broad historical picture is set out in Figure 9.1. This graph shows trends in total US revenues (or turnover) of ten major professionally produced consumer media, from advertising and direct payment support combined, as a percentage of GDP, from 1950 to 2009.[1] Following the methodology of the

---

[1] Only software revenues are included. Hardware sales, such as computers, televisions, and game equipment obviously facilitate consumer use, but are excluded since they do not directly contribute to the resources for media production.

**Figure 9.1** Total US Media Revenue as a Percentage of GDP, 1950–2009

* "lower bound" estimate: includes newspaper websites; digital music/movies; television station/network websites; Internet radio; e-books

*Sources:* US Census; trade associations; industry analysts; 10-K reports; author estimates.

previous studies cited above, the GDP metric is used to give comparative meaning to the size of the media industries as a proportion of overall economic activity. The various media are generally ordered from bottom to top in terms of the dates of their commercial development: "old" media on the bottom, and "new" on top. Note that as presented in Figure 9.1, the stacked graphs for the ten media do not include their Internet revenue components; these are combined in the top bars labeled "Internet" as the sum of all the Internet-distributed media for which we could obtain data.

Selection of these ten media is necessarily limited by available data, but they represent the economically most significant and distinct forms of consumer entertainment and information media in the United States. The data are compiled from a variety of sources: primarily continuous series published by the US government, industry associations, reports of industry analysts, press reports, or in a few cases, the authors' estimates. The data remain incomplete. In particular, we do not have data for recorded music before 1973, or videogames before 1998, and as discussed below, revenue data for some Internet media were not available. The data nevertheless provide an overall picture of broad trends.

Several observations about the broad historical trends can be made from Figure 9.1. First, in spite of missing early data for recorded music, it is apparent that from the 1950s to the mid-1970s, total media revenue as a percent of GDP fell moderately, or remained relatively flat, as ad-supported television displaced movie theaters, and to a lesser extent, radio, magazines, and newspapers. The pronounced rise from the mid-1970s to about 1990 can be attributed to rapid growth of multi-channel cable TV and home video movies, both of which are primarily supported by direct payment, and had remarkably mild negative economic effects on theaters, broadcast TV, or other media. The revenue peak was reached in 1999, after which media revenues as a percent of GDP fell from 2.68 percent to 2.12 percent of GDP in 2009—a relative decline of 21.0 percent. In US dollar terms, the ten media industries earned total revenue of $301.9 billion in 2009, a 20.5 percent increase from $250.6 billion in 1999 for the same industries, but that contrasted with a 52.4 percent increase in GDP.

The 1999 peak of media revenues as a percent of GDP corresponds approximately to the advent of consumer Internet broadband adoption, which reached 3 percent in 2000 (the first year it was reported), then 66 percent in 2010 (Pew Research Center 2010). We use the 1999 year as a benchmark for discussion and that year is labeled on all historical figures.

The combined Internet revenue estimates used in Figure 9.1 significantly understate total Internet media revenues because they omit data for non-newspaper-operated news sites, magazine websites, and online video games, for which information was unavailable. We therefore defined an alternative "upper bound" Internet revenue total which includes *all* Internet advertising, except search and email, in addition to the direct payment revenues included in the Figure 9.1 estimate. This measure includes all Internet

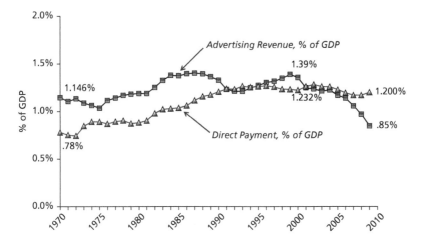

**Figure 9.2** Total US Media Revenue as a Percentage of GDP (Internet upper bound\*), 1950–2009
\* Internet lower bound, not including video game software

advertising that directly supports professionally produced commercial media products distributed over the Internet, plus the great majority of revenues accruing to user-generated media such as YouTube and other video-sharing sites, Facebook and other social-networking sites, and news blogs. Search and email, which accounted for 48 percent of all Internet advertising in 2009, are excluded because these categories do not appear to support consumer media content directly. The "upper bound" measure does, however, include all non-search and email advertising on e-commerce sites, etc., which are unrelated to media, so that measure is likely to substantially overstate Internet media revenues, whether or not user-generated and social-networking media are included.[2]

Using the Internet "upper bound" measure results in significantly higher Internet revenues in all years than the lower bound measure (e.g. $19.4 billion compared to $10.7 billion in 2009). Our main result, however, is little changed: a decline from 1999 to 2009 in total media revenues as a percent of GDP from 2.73 percent to 2.27 percent—or a relative decline of 20.5 percent (see Figure 9.2).

---

[2] It is unlikely that including direct-sales revenue from online videogames could outweigh the overestimate of Internet media advertising by the "upper bound" estimate. One report indicates total spending by Facebook subscribers on online virtual goods (the only significant component of direct consumer spending on games) to be $800 million in 2010 (Takahasi 2011). Facebook apparently accounts for the overwhelming majority of this spending. Revenue for 2009 was unavailable, but presumably lower. Data for mobile media, and sales to consumers of news were also not available, but were probably very minor for 2009 or earlier years.

In conclusion, the role of the Internet in reducing the economic size of the commercial media in the United States, at least in terms of their revenues, seems evident.

## B. A SHARP FALL IN ADVERTISER SUPPORT OF MEDIA SINCE 1999

Figure 9.2 shows trends in advertiser vs direct-payment support of the nine media for which we have continuous data, plus Internet media, since 1973. While there has been relative parity throughout most of this thirty-six year period between advertiser and direct-payment support, there was a precipitous fall in advertiser support of media from its local peak in 1999 of 1.39 percent of GDP to 0.85 percent in 2009—or a relative fall of 38.9 percent, reaching by far the lowest level since 1973. Meanwhile, direct-payment media remained relatively steady over this same period (1.23% to 1.20%).

Based on the Internet upper bound definition, the decline from 1999 to 2009 in total media advertising as a proportion of GDP was about the same amount, from 1.44 percent to 0.90 percent of GDP, or a relative decline of 37.5 percent.

A further analysis also reveals that Internet media by themselves have increasingly relied on direct-payment support: from virtually zero in 1999 to a 44.78 percent share in 2009. (The Internet upper bound estimate shows a smaller change, from nearly zero in 1999 to 23.7 percent in 2009.)

## C. CONSISTENT TRENDS FOR MOST INDIVIDUAL MEDIA

Inspection of Figure 9.1 indicates declines in "offline" revenues from the benchmark year of 1999 to 2009 for eight of the ten media—books, magazines, movie theaters, radio, broadcast television, and home video—but especially newspapers and recorded music. Bucking the downward trend were multi-channel television, by far the largest segment in 2009, and video games, the smallest segment, for which revenues remained approximately constant.

Trend data we were able to compile for the offline + online revenue components of separate media or media groups also confirmed that digital media revenues fell short of compensating for the 1999–2009 declines in the offline media components. Combined revenues as a percent of GDP for five media/media groups—books, newspapers, recorded music, radio, and motion pictures (theaters and home video + digital movie sales and rentals)—all declined. Combined revenues for all television (broadcast and multichannel + digital television sales, rentals, subscriptions, and advertising) increased over the period, but the digital components remained relatively small in size (0.9% of total television revenue in 2009).

Regarding sources of support, motion picture theaters and home videos, recorded music and books have always relied almost entirely on direct payment. Over the 1999–2009 period, revenues for television, newspapers, and radio also shifted toward direct payment. In television, the main factor was a continuing conversion from advertiser-supported broadcasting to multichannel subscriptions. The shift in radio, formerly an almost exclusively ad-supported service, was caused by development of satellite radio in the early 2000s, a subscription service which accounted for 18.4 percent of industry revenues by 2009. Also notable is the shift in newspaper revenues. Partly due to steep declines in advertising revenues, especially from classified ads, the proportion of total newspaper revenues accounted for by subscription and single copy sales increased from 18.4 percent in 1999 to 28.9 percent in 2009. Newspapers also, however, raised subscription (or newsstand) prices over this period, as indicated by an increase in total revenues per subscriber of 19.8 percent.

# Reasons for the Recent Economic Trends

In this section, we discuss four explanations that might account for the post-1999 decline in total media revenues.

## 1) SHIFTS IN CONSUMER USE AWAY FROM PROFESSIONALLY PRODUCED MEDIA

Survey research makes clear that individuals, especially youth, are turning away from offline media to pursue other forms of entertainment or news consumption (Pew Research Center 2008; 2011). While it is obvious from traffic counts alone that Internet media are attracting increasing usage, the available evidence is that the Internet's overall impact on the consumption of professionally produced commercial media has been relatively minor to date.

Table 9.1 reports the earliest and latest available years, plus the year 2000, from a long-running recreation time use study by CBS/Wilkofsky Gruen Associates (Vogel 1994; 2004; 2011). The data are annually assembled from a variety of sources. "Internet" use is defined to include all non-work related activity, including Internet media (e.g. online television watching), while "television" includes only standard delivery TV. Note also that estimated hours for each category listed include both primary and secondary activity; that is, vin

**Table 9.1** Leisure Time Use in the US, hours per person per week, major media 1970–2009

|  | 1970 | 2000 | 2009 |
|---|---|---|---|
| TV | 23.5 | 30.7 | 34.0 |
| Radio | 16.7 | 20.4 | 19.9 |
| Print media* | 8.7 | 6.2 | 5.1 |
| Recorded music** | 1.3 | 6.1 | 2.9 |
| Theater/home video | 0.2 | 1.3 | 1.1 |
| Video games | -- | 1.5 | 2.9 |
| Cultural/sports events | 0.1 | 0.4 | 0.5 |
| **Total except Internet** | **50.5** | **66.7** | **66.4** |
| Internet*** | -- | 1.0 | 14.5 |
| **Total per week** | **50.5** | **67.6** | **80.8** |

\* newspapers, magazines, leisure books
\*\* including digital in 2009; includes only legitimate transactions
\*\*\* includes all Internet use except work-related
*Source:* Vogel (1994, 2004, 2011)

Table 9.1, therefore, add to more than the average individual's total amount of leisure time.

The long-term growth in leisure time use from 1970 to 2000 can be largely attributed to an expansion of available hours for leisure and to higher per capita income for leisure spending (Vogel 2011). The shorter-term growth from 2000 to 2009 suggests that while estimated time use has shifted among media, total media use, excluding the Internet, was stable between 2000 and 2009. The rise in total time use including the Internet also suggests a substantial increase in multi-tasking.

Other time use studies corroborate relatively minor effects of the Internet on television and other media use. Using the longitudinal American Time Use Survey (ATUS), Wallsten (2011) found that an average hour of online leisure displaced only about .27 hours of other leisure activities, and suggested multi-tasking to be a factor. Other studies showing limited displacement of media or other leisure time use included Robinson (2011) and Robinson and Martin (2009).

Internet media and consumer habits are rapidly developing, but it appears that overall, time displacement accounts for relatively little of the revenue displacement of US media that we have reported.

The next two possible explanations—weakened intellectual property protection, and shortcomings of the Internet advertising business model—fall under the economic rubric of "appropriability" problems. Basically, appropriability means the ability of copyright owners to appropriate, or extract, the full value of an information product from consumers. Fundamentally, information products are subject to appropriability problems because it can be hard to exclude those who do not pay for information from consuming it. The Internet may worsen these problems, and thus reduce media industry revenues, either due to piracy or otherwise weakened copyright enforcement, or because advertising or direct-payment revenue systems don't work as well as they do on older, offline media. We consider these in turn.

## 2) WEAKENED INTELLECTUAL PROPERTY PROTECTION

Illegal file-sharing has been widely blamed for the dramatic decline in music sales since 1999, the year that the notorious P2P file-sharing site, *napster.com* was launched. Most of several empirical studies have found negative effects of file-sharing on legitimate music sales (e.g. Peitz and Waelbroeck 2004; Zentner 2006; Rob and Waldfogel 2006; Liebowitz 2008).[3] Recent evidence of declining rates of P2P piracy suggests, however, that file-sharing could not account for the continuing decline in legitimate music sales. An NPD survey reported, for example, a decline in the number of Internet users who use P2P networks to pirate music from 16 percent in 2007 to 9 percent in 2010 (Indvik, 2011). One reason may be that, as Lessig (2002) predicted, legitimate channels for Internet music distribution have become more prevalent and easy to use, as well as low-cost.

The Motion Picture Association, the Hollywood studios' trade association, has blamed a sharp decline in digital video disc (DVD) sales since about 2005 on piracy, but only a few independent empirical studies have informed the issue. Rob and Waldfogel (2007) found a negative effect of file-sharing on legitimate sales in an experimental context. Smith and Telang (2010) found that broadband access actually had a net positive effect on legitimate DVD sales, but the time period of their study was mostly prior to the 2003 introduction of BitTorrent technology, which made movie file-sharing far easier. While there seems little doubt that illegal movie file-sharing has reduced studio revenues at least to some extent, there is little evidence to date of a measurable net effect.

Another industry with apparently serious information appropriability problems in the Internet age is news. As one prominent example, Google's news aggregation service posts headlines and the first few sentences of news articles from a variety of news sources, such as major newspapers, with links to the full story at the news source website. Only a fraction of Google news readers, however (44% according to one report (Wauters 2010)), click through to the full story, stimulating a series of complaints and legal actions by newspapers

---

[3] One academic study, Oberholzer-Gee and Strumpf (2007), using German data, found no relationship between file-sharing and album sales.

and other news producers against Google, claiming violation of their copy-right. More broadly, the Internet lowers the cost of copying news facts and the ideas embodied within news analysis, neither of which can be copyrighted. In sum, the ability of news creators to appropriate the value of their product is reduced,[4] thus threatening incentives to invest in news creation. The effec-tive crumbling of copyright protection for news has undoubtedly contributed to the newspaper industry's myriad economic difficulties (see Newman et al., chapter 8 this volume). Among other major US media, television has probably escaped major damage. IP protection has been relatively strong for online TV, and since many of the most popular shows are free (with advertising), the incentive to pirate them is limited.

## 3) SHORTCOMINGS OF THE INTERNET ADVERTISING BUSINESS MODEL

As we have seen, the overall decline of media industry revenues since 1999 can mostly be attributed to a sharp decline of media advertising. Much of that decline has involved the disintegration of some established media adver-tising models, especially for newspapers, as well as a continuing ascent of direct-payment technologies in some other established industries, especially multi-channel television. As the parallel shift toward direct-payment support of online-distributed media in the past decade that we discussed earlier sug-gests, however, the advertising business model has also performed less well on the Internet itself.

On one hand, Internet technology offers potentially important improve-ments in the advertising business model; based on their past browsing or pur-chase behavior, individuals can be more efficiently targeted, reducing waste circulation, and enabling fast click-through retail purchases. However, adver-tising will not in the end generate more revenues if consumers can easily evade the ad, if they don't notice it, or if it otherwise does not have an impact.

One interpretation of the shortfall in Internet media advertising revenues is that the targeting prowess of Internet advertising has mostly been siphoned off by search engines, leaving relatively ineffectual banners, display, or other models to directly support online media. Again, Internet news sites, which have mostly relied on banner and display-type advertising, offer a prominent example. It remains uncertain how well in-program advertising will fare in Internet television distribution. At least, the model directly transfers from standard television to the Internet.

---

[4] Boczkowski (2010) relates vivid narratives and analysis of news imitation by two Argentinian newspapers.

Turning to the other side of the coin, increasingly, direct payment can be handled very efficiently by Internet content suppliers—from the posting of large arrays of single and bundled product prices that can be instantly changed, to relatively secure electronic collection via credit cards or payment services like PayPal. These technologies have undoubtedly advantaged growing à la carte or monthly subscription sales of digital music, movies, TV programs, books and other Internet-distributed media. News publishers have long asserted that direct-payment models, or "pay walls" as they are often known, do not work well for them either. Those shortcomings, however, can reasonably be attributed to excessive competition among news providers, who face no geographic barriers and extremely low costs of online distribution, a subject we now turn to.

## 4) LOWER COST/MORE EFFICIENT DISTRIBUTION SYSTEMS

It may be that even though media industry revenues are declining, distribution costs are also falling—perhaps faster than revenues. This possibility is important to consider, because our most basic interest is in the resources available to invest in media production, and thus ultimately the variety and quality of media products themselves.

A number of established media, notably cable television and DBS, require large capital infrastructure investments to distribute their products. Similarly, newspapers typically have capital investments in printing presses and they maintain geographic networks for physical distribution of papers. In other cases, such as recorded CDs and DVDs, the process of physical production of copies, then distribution and retailing, are a substantial proportion of total costs.

It is difficult to compare costs of Internet media product distribution with established media systems because costs depend on economies of scale, quality differences, and other factors. Some examples make it evident, however, that Internet media distribution can be far cheaper than distribution of the same basic information via established channels.

As Table 9.2 illustrates, editorial content creation costs made up only about one-sixth of total expenses in 1994 for a typical 33,000 circulation newspaper (approximately the average size of a newspaper in the US), while 40 percent were accounted for by the physical production and distribution of printed papers. Although classified advertising is not itself a consumer media product, the dramatically more efficient distribution of online news information via the Internet is suggested by recent trends in classified advertising. From its historical peak in 2000 to the year 2009, print newspaper classified ad revenues fell by $13.4 billion; by 2009, however, all classified advertisement spending on the Internet was reported by the Internet Advertising Bureau

**Table 9.2** Distribution of Printed Newspaper Costs (an average 33,000 circulation paper, 1994)

| | |
|---|---|
| News-editorial | 16% |
| Advertising | 11% |
| Production/printing | 29% |
| Circulation | 11% |
| Building/depreciation | 32% |
| **Total** | 99% |

*Source:* Inland Press Association

to account for only $2.3 billion in total revenues (PriceWaterhouseCoopers 2011). There seems no doubt that far more classified ads are now available on the Internet than newspapers have ever offered. Often zero costs for posting ads on the Internet reflect that difference. Internet news distribution surely realizes similarly lower costs in comparison to print or standard television alternatives.

A second example, falling costs of à la carte movie rentals vs Internet downloads, is shown in Table 9.3. Only a third of the average DVD rental price in 2002 (when brick and mortar stores like Blockbuster were the norm) was collected by the movie studios at the wholesale level, reflecting the high costs of video shipping, plus retail inventory and transactions at rental stories. Studios also incurred a $1 to $2 per unit cost of DVD (or VHS) manufacturing, making the studios' effective share of retail revenues even less. In 2010, the average price of an Internet video on demand (VOD) offering was $4.41, but the studio share reportedly averaged over two thirds, with no (DVD) manufacturing costs involved.

Neither case necessarily means lower total distribution costs for copyright owners due to the transitional or perhaps permanent need to maintain both established and IP distribution operations, for example. It is evident, however,

**Table 9.3** A La Carte Movie Distribution Cost Comparisons

| | Rental price | Studio % share* |
|---|---|---|
| 2002 (Video stores) | $3.25 | 33 |
| 2010 (online) | $4.41 | 70 |

* Before duplications/distribution cost.
*Sources:* Author calculations based on Adams Media Research and SNL Kagan Research data for 2002 and 2010 respectively.

that distribution and exhibition costs of most established media can be greatly streamlined by Internet technology. The relatively low revenue streams coming from IP distribution that were reported for most media above are thus likely to involve substantially lower unit costs of distribution/exhibition. Low Internet news, music, and other media revenues, that is, need to be balanced against lower costs to distribute that information—thus suggesting high economic promise for the industries as the transition to Internet media continues.

To the extent that media distribution costs are falling due to the Internet, greater economic resources should be available for production of media products, suggesting higher quality and variety of professionally produced media products.

## Summary and Conclusion

Measured as a proportion of overall economic activity (GDP), the media industries in the US have been shrinking in size fairly steadily since about 1999, at least through 2009, the end date on our study. Trends of revenue decline in individual media sectors are generally consistent, with the exception of multi-channel television and video games, which have continued to expand slightly or at least keep pace with US GDP. We also observed a strong shift over the past decade in the means of support for media in the US from advertising to direct payment—including for Internet media themselves.

We have discussed four possible explanations for the recent decline in US media revenues: shifts in consumer usage, weaker IP protection, the decline of media advertising, and lower costs due to the greater efficiency of Internet distribution, although these factors have apparently affected the individual media quite differently.

Our study has evident limitations. It is based mostly on descriptive historical data from a variety of different sources, and our explanations for the trends are generally speculative. Also, we have not attempted to provide detailed or complete explanations for trends in particular media. Our main purpose has been to paint a broad picture in order to bring attention to sweeping economic changes in the US media industries, and to provide a framework for thinking about the future of the media and consumer access to them.[5]

---

[5] It would also be useful to construct similar data for other countries. The European Commission has recently produced a valuable series of reports about economic effects of the Internet on the content and media transition in the member countries of the European Union (European Commission, various). Although long-term historical data of the kind we gathered for the United States is generally lacking for European countries, these studies point to a number of parallel trends for recent years.

Two of the explanations we advance for the trends of the last decade—reduced IP protection and the decline of media advertising—suggest reduced incentives for commercial media production investment, and thus a fall in the quality and variety of professionally produced media products available to American consumers. In addition, the shift of professionally produced media support from reliance on advertising to direct payment models suggests a reduced accessibility of media products to society. But the last, and admittedly most speculative of the reasons we identified in this paper for the decline of media industry revenues—greater efficiency due to lower costs of Internet distribution—promises the opposite effects of stimulating media production and reducing media prices, both to consumers and advertisers. If the interpretation of greater efficiency is correct, then much of the conventional wisdom that the Internet is undermining the quality and diversity of media content needs to be reconsidered. That is, due to lower costs, the Internet may in the longer term be leading to greater quality as well as diversity of media productions. Our society and our democratic institutions thus stand to benefit from the economic impact of the Internet.

## ■ REFERENCES

Boczkowski, P. J. (2010). *News at Work: Imitation in an Age of Information Abundance*. Chicago, IL: University of Chicago Press.

European Union (various). <http://ec.europa.eu/index_en.htm> (accessed January 13, 2013).

Indvik, L. (2011). "U.S. Internet Piracy is on the Decline," *Mashable*, March 25, 2011. <http://mashable.com/2011/03/25/internet-music-piracy-study/ > (accessed November 14, 2011).

Jussawalla, M. and Lamberton, D. M. L. (1988). *The Cost of Thinking: Information Economies of Ten Pacific countries*: Norwood, NJ: Ablex.

Lessig, L. (2002). *The Future of Ideas: The Fate of the Commons in a Connected World*. New York: Vintage.

Liebowitz, S. J. (2008). "Research Note: Testing File-Sharing's Impact on Music Album Sales in Cities," *Management Science*, 54(4): 852–859.

Machlup, F. (1962). *The Production and Distribution of Knowledge in the United States*. Princeton, NJ: Princeton University Press.

Oberholzer-Gee, F. and Strumpf, K. (2007). "The Effect of File Sharing on Record Sales: An Empirical Analysis," *Journal of Political Economy*, 115: 1–42.

OECD (1981). *Information Activities, Electronics and Telecommunications Technologies: Impact on Employment, Growth and Trade*, volumes I and II. Paris: OECD.

OECD (1986). *Trends in the Information Economy*. Paris: OECD.

Peitz, M. and Waelbroeck, P. (2004). "The Effect of Internet Piracy on Music Sales: Cross-Section Evidence," *Review of Economic Research on Copyright Issues*, 1(2): 71–79.

Pew Research Center (2008). "Key News Audiences Now Blend Online and Traditional Sources," *Pew Research Center Biennial News Consumption Survey*. <http://www.people-press.org/files/legacy-pdf/444.pdf> (accessed April 17, 2012).

Pew Research Center (2010). "Broadband and Dial-up Adoption, 2000-2011," *Pew Internet and American Life Project* [online site] <http://www.pewinternet.org/Trend-Data/Home-Broadband-Adoption.aspx> (accessed November 3, 2011).

PricewaterhouseCoopers (2011). *IAB Internet Advertising Revenue Report*. PricewaterhouseCoopers, April, 2011. <http://www.iab.net/media/file/IAB_Full_year_2010_0413_Final.pdf> (accessed August 11, 2011).

Rob, R. and Waldfogel, J. (2006). "Piracy on the High C's: Music Downloading, Sales Displacement, and Social Welfare in a Sample of College Students," *Journal of Law and Economics*, 49: 29–62.

Rob, R. and Waldfogel, J. (2007). "Piracy on the Silver Screen," *Journal of Industrial Economics*, 55(3): 379–395.

Robinson, J. P. (2011). "IT, TV and Time Displacement: What Alexander Szalai Anticipated but Couldn't Know," *Social Indicators Research*, 101(2): 193–206.

Robinson, J. P. and Martin, S. (2009). "Of Time and Television," *ANNALS of the American Academy of Political and Social Science*, 625(1): 74.

Rubin, M. R., Huber, M. T., and Taylor, E. L. (1986). *The Knowledge Industry in the United States: 1960–1980*. Princeton, NJ: Princeton University Press.

Smith, M. D. and Telang, R. (2010). "Piracy or Promotion? The Impact of Broadband Internet Penetration on DVD sales," *Information Economics and Policy* 22(4): 289–298.

Takahasi, D. (2011). "U.S. Virtual Goods Revenue on Facebook to Grow 32 Percent to $1.65B in 2012," *GamesBeat*, September 20, 2011. <http://venturebeat.com/2011/09/20/u-s-virtual-goods-revenue-on-facebook-to-grow-30-percent-to-1-65b-in-2012/> (accessed October 20, 2011).

Vogel, H. L. (1994). *Entertainment Industry Economics: A Guide for Financial Analysis*, 3rd edn. New York: Cambridge University Press.

Vogel, H. L. (2004). *Entertainment Industry Economics: A Guide for Financial Analysis*, 7th edn. New York: Cambridge University Press.

Vogel, H. L. (2011). *Entertainment Industry Economics: A Guide for Financial Analysis*, 8th edn. New York: Cambridge University Press.

Wallsten, S. (2011). "What are We Not Doing When We're Online?" <http://ssrn.com/abstract=1966654>, <http://dx.doi.org/10.2139/ssrn.1966654>.

Waterman, D. and Ji, S. W. (2012). "Online Versus Offline in the United States: Are the Media Shrinking?" *The Information Society*, 28(5): 285–303.

Wauters, R. (2011). "Report: 44% Of Google News Visitors Scan Headlines, Don't Click Through," *Techcrunch*, January. <http://techcrunch.com/2010/01/19/outsell-google-news/>, (accessed May 3, 2011).

Zentner, A. (2006). "Measuring the Effect of Music Downloads on Music Purchases," *Journal of Law and Economics* 49(1): 63–90.

# 10 Big Data: Towards a More Scientific Social Science and Humanities?

*Ralph Schroeder*

Researchers' uses of the Internet have transformed knowledge. This transformation has taken various forms, including how scholars communicate, how they access information, and how they perform their analyses (Borgman 2007; Dutton and Jeffreys 2010; Meyer and Schroeder 2013). Here I will focus only on the last of these: how the Internet and computing are changing the production of knowledge. This area has come to be known under a variety of labels, including e-Science, cyberscience, e-Infrastructures, computational science, and digital research. It has also moved through a number of phases, including Grids, web services, and cloud computing. The latest incarnation of this movement is "big data," which entails computational approaches to the sciences and humanities. Big data has generated considerable excitement, not just in academia, but also for applications in the public and private sector (Manyika et al. 2011). In the sciences, big data is regarded as potentially transformative, with data streams from sensor networks, telescopes, and health, to name only a few. Here, I will focus on big data in areas that are less well documented and more relevant for Internet researchers: the social sciences and humanities.

For each of the labels and phases mentioned, a recurring question has been: what is novel about big data research? Isn't the Internet just making research easier and faster, while it is not fundamentally changing the nature of research questions that are being asked? This chapter examines three cases where computational approaches to big data have driven new research agendas: search engine behavior, the large-scale analysis of text, and micro-blogging. These areas illustrate quite different aspects of the opportunities and challenges of big data. In the case of the analysis of search engine behavior, this allows social scientists to examine what people are searching for. Second, computational approaches to the large-scale analysis of text have been used in the humanities and social sciences, for example, to detect patterns of cultural, literary, or historical change. Finally, analysis of micro-blogging services such as Twitter—which has become a most popular object of study—has raised new questions about how information is transmitted in different media. All three examples involve the analysis of large corpora of key words or text—produced by information seekers in one case, authors in the second, and microbloggers in the third. Yet, as we shall see, they raise important questions about computational approaches to research.

One criticism that has been leveled in these areas has been to ask whether the availability of "big" data and computational methods is being put ahead of asking the right questions. In short: is the tail (of readily available data) wagging the dog (of good questions—which some say should come *before* considering what kinds of data are available)? This question can be seen as part of a broader concern about big data in the social sciences and humanities (as indicated in the title of this chapter), namely whether big data can be regarded as a trend, seen as positive by some and negative by others, to shift social science and humanities in the direction of more quantitative and computational, and thus in a specific sense (to be discussed in the conclusion), scientific approaches? In what follows I will argue that, while there are legitimate worries about whether big data is hijacking or being hijacked by the wrong questions, there are more useful questions to be asked about how it is transforming what we know, and about the social implications of the resulting advances.

The chapter will briefly describe the three cases, going through some of the major advantages/innovations and the disadvantages/limitations of each of these three types of computational approaches to big data research. The aim is simply to assess the contributions of these studies to the advance of knowledge, to raise problematic issues around these approaches, and thereby to gauge the role of big data in setting current and future research agendas. Once these three examples have been discussed, the chapter will then turn to more general themes and issues raised by computational approaches to big data.

Big data can be defined as research that is made possible by means of the capture, aggregation, and manipulation of data about a given phenomenon on an unprecedented scale and scope. Note that unlike other conceptualizations of big data, which typically focus on computer processing and storage power (for example, "terabyte" size), this definition centres on the relation between the object being investigated and the digital tools and materials that are available for the analysis of this object or phenomenon. In short, the definition is not just about the technology or the data, but about the object of study. I will come back to this point. In any event, it is worth noting that there is little by way of a social science understanding of the role of data in society (the main exceptions relating to digital data will be discussed below), though there has been some discussion about the implications of big data research (Savage and Burrows 2007; boyd and Crawford 2012). I shall argue in the conclusion that the key to these implications lies in understanding how research technologies drive knowledge advance. Hence the question: do research technologies and big data enable research to take new directions, or do they complement and extend existing research directions? This larger question will be addressed in the conclusion; but first, let us take each of the three cases in turn.

## Search Engine Behavior

The analysis of search engine behavior has become a major area of research. Here it will be useful to single out just one example that crystallizes both the opportunities and the limitations of big data. Vivienne Waller (2011) had access to "transaction logs to provide an analysis of the type and topic of search queries entered into the search engine Google (Australia) in April 2009," where it can be added that Google has an almost 90 percent market share in Australia (2011: 761). She also had data from the marketing company Hitwise Experian about which of eleven lifestyle groups—broadly comparable to socio-economic stratification groups—searched for which search terms. She analyzed almost 1 percent of all search terms entered for that month, extracting a sample of 60,000 different search terms which accounted for 28.7 percent of all search queries (a query typically consists of two or three terms. She thus captured "every search term that appeared more than once in April, as well as what amounted to a random selection of those that appeared only once;" 2011: 764). She then used seventy-eight codes and amalgamated these into fifteen broad subject groupings, such as "high culture" and "popular culture," "Ecommerce," "weather/time/public transport," and several others.

Her findings include the fact that "queries about popular culture and Ecommerce account for almost half of all search engine queries" and "somewhat surprisingly, the distribution of topics of search query did not vary significantly across different Lifestyle groups for the broad subjects of popular culture, Ecommerce, cultural practice and adult" (2011: 767). This is quite surprising since it might be expected that different lifestyle groups, or demographics, or expert versus skilled Internet users, would search for different things (see Tancer 2009 and Dutton and Blank 2011 for examples). Yet it seems that, in Australia at least, users from different socio-economic groups have similar queries. Waller has other interesting findings, which include the fact that people looking for information "on particular contemporary issues accounted for less than 1% of all search queries. Queries about government, including programs, and policies, accounted for less than 2% of all Web search queries" (2011: 769; Hindman 2010 has similar findings). Overall, she argues that search engines are mainly a technology for leisure or consumption, and less one for seeking knowledge and information.

What new insights do big data provide here? In the case of search, there are data about a whole month's worth of all searches for a population which, because of Google's near monopoly share, can be seen as an unequalled and powerful dataset and analysis even if the sample is just 1 percent. Note the fit with the definition given earlier: it is not the size of the data, but the fact that the data provide fairly comprehensive evidence about a particular phenomenon (what Australians search for). If big data is defined as advancing knowledge with a dataset of a size and scope of a magnitude larger than any previously available for a given domain, then these data count as big data. Tancer (2009), who is head of research at Hitwise Experian, has much bigger samples, including about 10 million Americans for many years' worth of searches, though his analysis is published in a non-academic book, whereas Waller's (2011) paper is published in the top peer-reviewed journal in information science. It could, of course, be possible to obtain a representative sample for Australian search queries by other means, such as surveying users (asking them to record their search queries), or by asking a large sample of users to log their search queries on their computers over the course of a month or more. But it is interesting to imagine the resources required to gather data on this scale (as opposed to using ready-made data, which is often what big data refers to), which are likely to be prohibitive for academic social scientists. It is also interesting to reflect on the research ethics constraints involved in this research (how would researchers get access? Or ethics approval to pry into people's searches?). Instead, Waller's paper is a case of data that was not intended for social science research and which has nevertheless been used to advance social scientific knowledge about what particular groups of search engine users search for. It has provided an analysis of data on an unprecedented scale, both in the domain of search engine behavior and as regards which social group is searching for what (it is "unprecedented" relative to what was known before about people's search for information—although there are datasets with an even greater scale and scope, such as in the research that Tancer reports).

For search engine behavior, there are applied or pragmatic reasons for this research: figuring out how to enhance the user experience, where people's attention is directed to target advertising at them, and ultimately predicting what they are interested in buying. But there are also powerful social science insights that Waller derives from these data which include, as mentioned, that most searches are for leisure and that search engine behavior is generally similar across lifestyle groups. One problem highlighted by Waller's study (and those that use similar methods) is that it is based on proprietary data. This means that, even if these data were made accessible to other researchers, we do not know precisely how search engines work (this, after all, is Google's "secret"), and thus how the data are arrived at. Second, the classification of groups of information seekers is based on marketing company categories ("lifestyle groups"): these are similar to, but not the standard categories used by, social scientists.

Commercial data also raises the question: which part of the population does not use Google, and does this give rise to the issue of representativeness? Put differently, who is being left out when the Australian population is being analyzed as Google users? In short, the research, though it provides new and very powerful insights, is not replicable and cannot be built upon with standard classifications. It could be built upon only inasmuch as others, inspired by Waller's striking findings, could see if they obtain similar results. As we shall see, these and similar studies raise the concern recently articulated by Savage and Burrows (2007) about whether private companies with this type of data are able to do more powerful research than academic social scientists. Finally, the new insights provided by Waller's study, regarding what Australians search for or what information they are interested in, and also Tancer's research, raise the prospect that companies and governments can use this knowledge to target and tailor services for consumers or citizens, perhaps even changing what people are interested in in the first place.

## Large-Scale Textual Analysis

The analysis of cultural patterns using digital data have grown and received a lot of attention recently. Here we can focus on the analysis of text from collections of books, which has made incursions, among others, into history and literary studies. This will allow us to ask (unlike with Twitter, discussed below, which is arguably a new domain) whether these studies contribute novel questions in well-established domains or disciplines. The example that can be used here is a study of more than 5 million digitized books (~4% of all books ever printed) that have become available through the Google Books project (Michelet et al. 2010). The study used a corpus of more than 500 billion words in several languages (though the website for the project, <http://www.culturomics.org/home>, notes that the quality is highest for the English language and for last 200 years) and so easily fits the definition of big data used here (data of a magnitude larger than any previous research in the domain, simply by virtue of covering a larger corpus of printed material than any available before).

In this case, again, there are novel insights: for example, charting the English word "feminism" and the French equivalent "feminisme" over the course of the 20th century, which can provide clues about the changing cultural significance of this phenomenon: for example, does the rise and fall of the term's popularity give an indication about how strong of a movement "feminism" has been? Do the French and English terms move in lockstep in this regard, or according to different rhythms? This is just one of several examples in the paper. More generally, the paper claims that this is a "new science"—hence they call it "culturomics"—and they claim that "culturomic results are a new type of evidence in the humanities." The Michelet et al. study encountered criticisms (see below) but since it was not undertaken by humanities scholars, we can add another example of "quantitative methods" (Heuser and Le-Khac 2011) from within literary studies: the Litlab at Stanford University analyzed word frequencies in 2,779 nineteenth-century British novels (from a commercial database of digitized books) and found over the course of the century a decline in "abstract values words" and a rise in "concrete, physical, specific, and non-evaluative" words, which the authors, Heuser and Le-Khac, call the "hard seed" (2011: 83). This study, again, claimed new findings since the authors hypothesized that these shifts in words could be linked to social change, and particularly rapid urbanization, in British society (2011: 85).

Whereas "culturomics" promotes a scientific approach to the humanities, the quantitative methods of the Litlab have championed a new approach within literary studies: "distant reading" (Moretti 2000) in contrast with the "close reading" of highly interpretive approaches to literature. The "distant reading" and "culturomics" studies do not have the replicability problem of Waller's study of search behavior; in fact, one of the promising aspects of this research is that others will add to and extend these studies: comparing these with other bodies of texts, comparing the results for other key words, and so on. Indeed, unlike the Litlab study which requires access to a commercial database of literary texts, the n-gram viewer of Google Books (<http://books. google.com/ngrams>) allows anyone to search this corpus for word frequencies. Thus, whatever one may think of these two studies, they hold the promise of a rigorous, quantitative, hypothesis-driven and -generating, and systematic approach to the study of culture and literature using patterns of words on a large scale; in short, a computational and scientific (again, in a sense to be specified) approach.

Yet these studies have also drawn criticisms: for example, one criticism is that the link that Heuser and Le-Khac's make between word frequencies in novels and British culture is too large a leap for which more evidence and interpretation would be needed (Stauffer 2011: 65). Questions have also been raised about the quality of the data in Google Books (Duguid 2007; Nunberg 2009). Perhaps the main concern here, however, has been the challenge of scientificity to cultural and literary interpretation, which can be seen as a question of defending disciplinary turf. This is why "distant reading" has provoked more reaction than "culturomics": since the challenge from the Heuser and Le-Khac study has come from within the study of literature and published in humanities journals, it has ruffled feathers among literary scholars (e.g. Fish 2012), whereas the "culturomics" team published in the journal *Science* and therefore the study perhaps seems less threatening. It can also be noted, however, that criticism in this case can be seen as a variant on the fears about how analyzing search behavior is a scientific window into people's minds: in the case of the analysis of literature, there is a defensiveness against this type of scientific reductionism (Wellmon 2012), though of course what can be seen as defensiveness from one perspective can be seen as legitimate concern from another.


## Analyzing Twitter

A third case that can be examined here are the social science uses of Twitter, which have also exploded in recent years. Here it is obvious that one of the reasons for using this type of data is that it is easily available. Anecdotally, there are two typical reactions in discussions of Twitter research—both from academics and from a wider public: excitement and scepticism. The excitement comes from the possibilities of using Twitter as a research tool, which is also reflected in the news coverage of Twitter research (for example, Giles 2012). The basis for this excitement is partly the idea of having real-time (or near real-time) data about how information spreads among users, which can be uniquely tracked in this medium since the data are publicly available, although with limits, as discussed below. Email can be studied in a similar way (though the content is not normally available in the same public way), but it consists of interpersonal communication. With Twitter, in contrast, it is possible to measure public information-sharing. As we have seen, search engine behavior gives an indication of individual information needs, but again, in the case of Twitter, we can, instead, see the spread of news or information exchange about newsworthy events and so on—though, as we shall also see, the question whether Twitter is a news or an interpersonal medium is still open.

The second reaction to Twitter research is scepticism along the lines of: "the Twitterverse is rather insular and so studying it for convenience's sake misses that Twitter is unrepresentative and mostly consists of pointless celebrity gossip" (see, for example, the responses to a blogpost on the website of the *New York Review of Books* about the research uses of Twitter, by James Gleick <http://www.nybooks.com/blogs/nyrblog/2013/jan/16/librarians-twitterverse/>). This response also has some basis: celebrities do attract a lion's share of followers—though arguably, this is itself a phenomenon worthy of research. But this viewpoint is also misleading insofar as there are some data available for who uses Twitter (although many studies do not address this question). For example, according to the Pew Internet and American Life project (<http://pewinternet.org/Reports/2012/Twitter-Use-2012.aspx>), in the United States, "as of February 2012, some 15% of online adults use Twitter, and 8% do so on a typical day." Add to this the fact that Twitter is often used by media professionals and opinion leaders, and it is clear that this medium is not a marginal or trivial pursuit.

However, Twitter also needs to be contextualized in a larger media ecology: for example, does it lead, or merely follow mainstream media? And what type of medium is it—again, "news," or information exchange within small networks? So, for example, if we restrict our consideration of Twitter to political communication, inasmuch as this medium is one among many, how does Twitter fit into the context of the whole media ecology of political communication (see Newman et al., chapter 8 this volume)? Further, one could ask, how do media shape politics generally, not just in terms of Twitter, but in terms of the limited attention given to political news as a whole?

When we move from analyzing a particular topic or aspect of political communication on Twitter to the most comprehensive macro level, even if all tweets and retweets relevant to politics are captured and analyzed, the totality of these data is still a drop in the ocean. And these data are limited in their own terms: What are the constraints and possibilities of disseminating 140 text characters, or sending links and their contents? (and what proportion of tweets are links to longer texts, or video?) Who tweets and who follows these tweets? What is different when, instead of using 140 characters, items are "retweeted" or passed on to other users—are these different forms of media use? Nevertheless, as with the other two examples, Twitter in a sense offers a more powerful tool or domain of research for political communication because the results can be built upon: they provide a way of focusing attention on analysing data from a medium in a way that can be improved upon, and so provide the means to advance political communication as a field.

Against this background, we can take a concrete example: Kwak et al. (2010) produced the "first quantitative study on the entire Twittersphere and information diffusion on it." They have "crawled 41.7 million user profiles, 1.47 billion social relations, 4262 trending topics, and 106 million tweets" (2010). Again, these are not necessarily "big data" in technical terms, but they are big data in terms of capturing and being able to analyze "social relations." But what are these "social relations?" Social relations in this case are "1.47 billion directed relations of following and being followed" (2010). This prompts a further question about the nature of these directed relations: Indeed, the authors pose this question in the title of their paper: "What is Twitter, a Social Network or a News Media?" However, this is a question that the authors of the study can only answer in a narrow way: they provide figures, for example, for how many users have how many followers (a power law distribution is found, whereby a very few users have very many followers), how many relations are reciprocal or one way (among other findings, Twitter is less reciprocal than Flickr), and what proportion of users (approximately two-thirds) are not followed by any of those who they follow, making Twitter more a "source of information rather than a social networking site." They can also rank the users by followings, and establish that celebrities (Britney Spears, Oprah), politicians (Barack Obama), and news (CNN, *New York Times*) are among the top twenty by number of followers. They can also compare the top "trending topics" on Twitter with topics on CNN Headline News, finding, among other things, that "more than half the time, CNN was ahead in reporting. However, some news broke out on Twitter before CNN" (2010). In other words, in answer to the question posed earlier, whether Twitter merely follows other news media (here, television news) or also breaks news earlier than other media, the answer is mixed.

It will be readily apparent that, while these are powerful findings which can be built upon and refined, they need to be contextualized, as argued earlier, within a larger ecology of media: we need to know what these relationships signify or what kind of medium Twitter is. If we consider political communication again, Twitter is not a broadcast technology like traditional ones since there are no gatekeepers (apart from signing up to the service). But even if Twitter "breaks news," the news-making function needs to be put in the context of what can be disseminated within the constraints and possibilities of this medium. As ever, new technologies tend to add to and complement, rather than displace and supersede, existing ones like print and broadcasting (Schroeder 2007). And here, as elsewhere, it is difficult to gauge the social impact of new technologies early on, and it is important to conceptualize these impacts by identifying where and how the extension of existing media is taking place within an overall media ecology. The same goes, incidentally, for Twitter as a social medium (as opposed to a news or political medium): the Kwak et al. (2010) study can tell us about the number of followers, but while Twitter allows large audiences for some users (in this sense, broadcasting-like), we need to know how many users are using Twitter more in the manner of a social-networking site or blog for conveying "status updates" to a group of friends or members of offline networks.

Again, Twitter provides a more comprehensive and larger dataset than those that were previously available in terms of how information is shared in a population (for interpersonal communication, a similar dataset are emails, or Facebook). But to understand the value of these data, the context is essential. A further challenge is that while Kwak et al. were able to analyze the whole of the Twittersphere, as Bruns and Liang (2012) document, this kind of access to the whole of the Twittersphere is no longer allowed by Twitter. Instead, the company allows restricted access and otherwise provides the data for a fee. Further, there are many problems with both the freely available and the commercially available data, and Bruns and Liang provide a discussion of how researchers can cope with these problems—within limits. Thus, as with the data from Google Books and search behavior, in the case of Twitter it is not clear how the analyses can be replicated and validated, especially as the quality of the data are not transparent. Finally, using Twitter as a window into people's thoughts and their relationships raises unsettling prospects of how this service can be used in a manipulative way, namely, the scandals about "buying" followers on Twitter (see, e.g. Furnas and Gaffney 2012).

## Conclusions

The studies described here have one feature in common: they are all lenses into people's minds and behavior with powerful new tools. Such studies are not unprecedented in the social sciences: there is a long tradition of quantitative analysis in various social science disciplines (Porter 2008), in marketing, and in polling, surveys and censuses—though in literary studies, quantitative approaches are quite recent. The key point here is that quantification and scientificity have often been seen as going hand in hand. At this stage, therefore, it is important to specify what is meant by "scientific." A widespread view is that science relates to epistemological questions. A more sociological view is that research technologies (Schroeder 2007; 2008), mathematization (Collins 1998: 523–569), and the use of a common symbolic language, have been critical to driving the advance of modern science and cumulative knowledge. They do this partly because they focus communities of researchers on a research front which consists of certain tools and data and objects, and which can be extended because of the use of a common symbolic language.

Social science has not had many such research technologies in the past (Collins 1994)—we can think here of recording devices such as tape recorders for interviewing—but computing tools have clearly changed this. Furthermore, as we have seen, in the realm of big data, a number of platforms (search engines, Google Books, and Twitter) provide large datasets, unprecedented in scale and scope (recalling the definition of big data provided at the outset) for specific phenomena, that are readily available for mathematical—or here, statistical—analysis, by means of digital tools (or research technologies). In short, the idea that quantification and scientificity go hand in hand is warranted in this case, and big data provide a good illustration of how research technologies advance scientific knowledge.

In both the social sciences and in cultural studies, the main theoretical approach in recent decades has been interpretivist "social constructivism," which argues (among other things) that data and knowledge are never simply "out there," and that science can never achieve objectivity—indeed, perhaps it should not strive to do so: put differently, that "truths" are socially constructed. Thus a scientific and highly quantitative approach can be regarded as a challenge to this dominant paradigm. Yet the trend towards big data can also be seen as part one of the periodic swings from a more qualitative and interpretive to a more quantitative and scientific approach in the social sciences, enabled by new techniques (big data could of, course, also be used for quali-tative analysis, but this is typically not the point for studies using large data-sets). These swings take place because of the low task certainty and low mutual dependence (Whitley 2000) in social science, which allows new directions to move into a vacuum. Literary studies and history also have low task certainty and low mutual dependence (Fuchs 1992), but since quantitative approaches are novel, at least for literary studies, there is also more defensiveness towards new approaches. This defensiveness is understandable but also unwar-ranted: it can be foreseen that distance reading or quantitative approaches will only ever be a specialty within—and complement—close reading and other non-computational approaches to culture and history. In the social sciences, similarly, both quantitative and qualitative approaches will continue to be used, sometimes in combination, and big data will merely be one input that shifts social science in a more quantitative and scientific direction.

Novel big data methods have opened up new lines of enquiry: as we have seen, there is not just a quantitative leap but also a leap in kind in the scale, scope, and sources of data and in computational methods; or a break in terms of the questions that can be asked relative to what could be asked before in relation to particular phenomena. The implications are not what they are nor-mally thought to be, which is that some see this number-crunching or scienti-ficity as an impoverishment of research. New data (which as we have seen here is also big data), and technologies and techniques for analyzing these data also lead to new questions, and these must be evaluated in relation to the existing research front and whether they contribute—or not—to our ability to grasp phenomena that extend and advance this research front (hence, again, basing the novelty of big data not just on tools and data, but on the object of study).

The prospect for big data is therefore not so much that the tail of data is wagging the dog of questions, but rather that the advance of knowledge, as ever, brings new directions, with benefits as well as new limitations. In all three cases, it is not the "wrong" question that is the problem with big data approaches. Rather, these data raise specific issues, including about their sci-entificity: replicability is another feature of science, which is problematic here due to the commercial nature of the platforms studied (Google, Twitter). Or again, we have seen issues with data quality that cannot be checked (in the case of Google Books), or categories that do not fit with existing research categories (classifications used in marketing, as opposed to those used in research, in Waller's study), or restricted access to commercial data (Google search behav-ior, Twitter).

There are many other implications of big data that could have been dis-cussed here, including privacy and anonymity (see Rule 2007), but, for rea-sons of space, this has not been done. Here I have focused on a single issue, posed in the question in the title of this chapter, to which the answer is: yes, big data contributes in a specific sense to a more scientific social science and humanities. But it behoves us to consider the implications of this scientificity, instead of mainly challenging big data on epistemological grounds (boyd and Crawford 2012), or foreseeing the relative decline of academic social science in view of the fact that commercial companies have more access to digital data than do academic social scientists (Savage and Burrows 2007). Rather, it is crucial to assess the advances and challenges of this renewed effort at a scientific approach to the study of society, and where these new directions complement and extend existing research fronts. The implication of this scientificity for academic research is limited, and can be pinpointed by examining which new phenomena are uncovered at the research front. These implications may be "small" rather than "big;" but they contribute to cumulative advances of knowledge, with all its gains and challenges.

## ■ REFERENCES

Borgman, C. (2007). *Scholarship in the Digital Age: Information, Infrastructure, and the Internet.* Cambridge MA: MIT Press.

boyd, D. and Crawford, K. (2012). "Critical Questions for Big Data: Provocations for a Cultural, Technological and Scholarly Phenomenon," *Information, Communication and Society,* 15(5): 662–679.

Bruns, A. and Liang, Y. E. (2012). "Tools and Methods for Capturing Twitter Data During Natural Disasters," *First Monday,* 17(4). <http://firstmonday.org/htbin/cgiwrap/bin/ojs/index.php/fm/article/viewArticle/3937/3193> (accessed February 3, 2013).

Collins, R. (1994). "Why the Social Sciences Won't Become High-Consensus, Rapid-Discovery Science," *Sociological Forum,* 9(2): 155–177.

Collins, R. (1998). *The Sociology of Philosophies: A Global Theory of Intellectual Change.* Cambridge MA: Harvard University Press.

Duguid, P. (2007). "Inheritance and Loss? A Brief Survey of Google Books," *First Monday* 12(8). <http://firstmonday.org/htbin/cgiwrap/bin/ojs/index.php/fm/article/view/1972/1847> (accessed February 3, 2013).

Dutton, W. H. and Blank, G. (2011). *Next Generation Users: The Internet in Britain. Oxford Internet Survey 2011.* Oxford Internet Institute, University of Oxford. <http://www.oii.ox.ac.uk/events/?id=453> (accessed April 16, 2012).

Dutton, W.H. and Jeffreys, P.W. (2010). *World Wide Research.* Cambridge, MA: MIT Press.

Fish, S. (2012). "Mind Your P's and B's: The Digital Humanities and Interpretation," *The New York Times Opinionator* [Online Commentary]. January 23. <http://opinionator.blogs.nytimes.com/2012/01/23/mind-your-ps-and-bs-the-digital-humanities-and-interpretation/?hp> (accessed February 3, 2013).

Fuchs, S. 1992. *The Professional Quest for Truth: A Social Theory of Science and Knowledge.* Albany, NY: State University of New York Press.

Furnas, A. and Gaffney, D. (2012). "Statistical Probability That Mitt Romney's New Twitter Followers Are Just Normal Users: 0%," *The Atlantic,* July 31. <http://www.theatlantic.com/technology/archive/2012/07/statistical-probability-that-mitt-romneys-new-twitter-followers-are-just-normal-users-0/260539/> (accessed August 31, 2012).

Giles, J. (2012). "Making the Links: From E-mails to Social Networks, the Digital Traces Left by Life in the Modern World are Transforming Social Science," *Nature*, 488: 448–450.

Heuser, R. and Le-Khac, L. (2011). "Learning to Read Data: Bringing out the Humanistic in the Digital Humanities," *Victorian Studies* 54(1): 79–86.

Hindman, M. (2010). *The Myth of Digital Democracy*. Princeton, NJ: Princeton University Press.

Kwak, H. et al. (2010). "What is Twitter, a Social Network or a News Media?" *Proceedings of the 19th International World Wide Web (WWW) Conference*, April 26–30, 2010, Raleigh, NC.

Manyika, J., Chui, M., Brown, B., Bughin, J., Dobbs, R., Roxburgh, C., and Hung Byers, A. (2011). "Big Data: The Next Frontier for Innovation, Competition and Productivity," *McKinsey Global Institute*. Available at <http://www.mckinsey.com/insights/mgi/research/technology_and_innovation/big_data_the_next_frontier_for_innovation> (accessed August 29, 2012).

Meyer, E. T. and Schroeder, R. (2013). "Digital Transformations of Scholarship and Knowledge," in W. Dutton (ed.), *The Oxford Handbook of Internet Studies*. Oxford: Oxford University Press, 307–327.

Michelet, J. et al. (2010). "Quantitative Analysis of Culture Using Millions of Digitized Books," *Science*, 331(6014): 176–182.

Moretti, F. (2000). "Conjectures on World Literature," *New Left Review*, 1: 54–68.

Nunberg, G. (2009). "Google's Book Search: A Disaster for Scholars," *The Chronicle Review*, August 31, <http://chronicle.com/article/Googles-Book-Search-A/48245/> (accessed February 3, 2013).

Porter, T. (2008). "Statistics and Statistical Methods," in T. Porter and D. Ross (eds.), *The Modern Social Sciences*. Cambridge: Cambridge University Press, 238–250.

Rule, J. (2007). *Privacy in Peril: How We are Sacrificing a Fundamental Right in Exchange for Security and Convenience*. New York: Oxford University Press.

Savage, M. and Burrows, R. (2007). "The Coming Crisis of Empirical Sociology," *Sociology*, 41(5): 885–899.

Schroeder, R. (2007). *Rethinking Science, Technology and Social Change*. Stanford, CA: Stanford University Press.

Schroeder, R. (2008). "e-Sciences as Research Technologies: Reconfiguring Disciplines, Globalizing Knowledge," *Social Science Information*, 47(2), 131–157.

Stauffer, A. (2011). "Introduction: Searching Engines, Reading Machines," *Victorian Studies* 54(1): 63–68.

Tancer, B. (2009). *Click: What Millions of People are Doing Online and Why It Matters*. New York: HarperCollins.

Waller, V. (2011). "Not Just Information: Who Searches for What on the Search Engine Google?" *Journal of the American Society for Information Science and Technology*, 62(4): 761–775.

Wellmon, C. (2012). "Why Google Isn't Making Us Stupid…or Smart," *The Hedgehog Review*, 14(1): 66–80.

Whitley, R. (2000). *The Intellectual and Social Organization of the Sciences*, 2nd edn. Oxford: Oxford University Press.

# Part III

# Networked Politics and Governments

# 11 Transforming Government—by Default?

*Miriam Lips*

## Introduction

With the widespread diffusion of the Internet, scholars and practitioners have become convinced that Information and Communication Technology (ICTs) will play an increasingly important role in government (e.g. Dunleavy et al. 2006; OECD 2009; Lips 2011; Weerakkody and Reddick 2012; European Commission 2013). Visions, theories, and strategies have been championed on how government would be re-engineered and transformed in the digital age, but with limited success thus far (Lips and Schuppan 2009). Since 2011, governments around the world have pronounced that they will become "digital by default." In general, this means that they will be using digital channels and platforms as the standard way, or as their "default setting" if you wish, for providing information and services to citizens, businesses, and other stakeholders of government.

Not unlike other ICT-enabled public-sector reform waves in the past, general expectations are that this digital by default modernization effort will lead to a re-engineered government that finally will achieve the cost savings promised by ICTs. However, many of the earlier ICT-enabled modernization programs did not meet the expectations placed on them for a variety of reasons. For example, expected savings or efficiency gains were not achieved, new innovative services were provided in the mistaken belief that uptake would follow, digital solutions were not user-friendly, the uptake of digital channels turned out to be limited, or much higher costs were involved than originally expected (Kraemer et al. 1981; Heeks 2006; Institute for Government 2010).

Since 2011, however, the context has changed in ways that could make a difference in the outcome of digital government initiatives. Specifically, this time, the impact of the global financial crisis may have put more pressure on financially belt-tightening governments to not only explore, but also deliver on innovative cost-effective solutions.

The question, therefore, has become, not only whether these digital by default reform programs will end up any differently compared with their predecessors, but also what the outcomes of these programs might be. By 2013, many Anglo-Saxon and Scandinavian countries, including the UK, United States, Norway, Denmark, New Zealand, and Australia, had started to implement strategies to achieve digital by default. Interestingly, the UK had also signed a Memorandum of Understanding with Estonia, one of the world's leading countries in digital government, which will see the two countries collaborate on developing digital services. At the same time, countries in other parts of the world are also rapidly developing digital government. For instance, countries like India, Indonesia, Thailand, and Vietnam have started to replace traditional human-based public service channels with standardized digital channels in order to move away from corruption and achieve good governance.

In this chapter, before empirically exploring digital by default reform programs in several Anglo-Saxon and Scandinavian countries, the concept of digital government is introduced, and different perspectives on the role of ICTs in administrative reform are explained. Looking at various digital transformation strategies, six basic reasons are provided for why governments want to become digital by default, and variations between strategies are further explored. Subsequently, issues emerging from these digital transformation programs are discussed. And finally, the chapter addresses the role of digital technology in administrative reform.

## What is "Digital Government"?

Digital government can be broadly defined as "the introduction, management and use of ICTs in the public sector and its external relationships with citizens, businesses, NGOs, and other organizations." Acknowledging the expanding use of ICTs in government and its external relationships, digital government to date includes, and touches upon, the many and varied roles, functions, and activities government undertakes in its unique relationship with society.

However, the arrival of new technologies has always captured the lively imagination of reformists. So when the public Internet was introduced in the early 1990s, there were clear expectations that it would re-engineer government (Fountain 2010). That is, governments would change the ways they did things in order to take full advantage of the Internet and electronic service delivery. Although Information Technologies (IT) and communication technologies (CT) had been used separately in government since the 1960s (Kraemer et al. 1981), the converging, digitized, decentralized, networked, and ubiquitous nature of the Internet led people to believe that a new era had arrived where ICTs would shape and deliver the government of the future (Castells 1996).

Initially, the dominant expectation was that the new technology would drive the transformation of government and democratic governance, leading to revolutionary utopian visions of a "virtual government" that would be 24/7 accessible to citizens from anywhere in the world (Fountain 2010), or a direct democracy where citizens would be connected with one another and their political representatives, leading to enhanced practices of political participation and engagement (Chadwick 2006; Coleman and Blumler 2001). At the same time, dystopian revolutionary visions about the future state of government emerged, pointing at government becoming a "Big Brother" or a "surveillance state" by using the "panoptic" capabilities of the ubiquitous Internet (Lyon 1994).

Since the emergence of these revolutionary visions, and on the basis of empirical evidence, scholars have argued for evolutionary perspectives on changes related to the introduction of ICTs in government (Lips and Schuppan 2009; Fountain 2010). Moreover, governments started to acknowledge digital technology as a useful instrument or *enabler*, rather than a *driver*, of transformation (Lips 2011) (see Table 11.1). As an example, especially in the 1990s, many governments saw an opportunity to use ICTs in line with New Public Management reform ideas, such as establishing modernized, efficient, and customer-focused government services. Other examples are administrative reform initiatives focused at establishing "Citizen-Centric Government" by using ICTs to meet the unique service demands and needs of an individual citizen in a more holistic way (OECD 2009) and, more recently, "Open Government" by using ICTs to open up existing government data sets to the general public and, with that, create opportunities for improved transparency, public participation, collaboration, and innovation (Linders et al. 2012).

In considering these administrative reform perspectives, an important question is what the actual outcomes of the use of ICTs have been. For instance, from a comparative point of view, the nature and extent of ICT-enabled transformational change in government can be quite different, even if we consider similar-type reform projects. O'Neill (2009) makes a useful distinction between

**Table 11.1** ICTs and Administrative Reform

| *Revolutionary Visions:* Technology as *driver* of transformational change | *Evolutionary Visions:* Technology as *enabler* of transformational change |
| --- | --- |
| • Virtual government | • Customer-focused public service provision |
| • Direct democracy | • Citizen-centric government |
| • Surveillance state | • Open government |

*instrumental* transformation, or "doing things differently," and *systemic* transformation, or "doing different things." Whereas instrumental transformation means a radical change in the existing administration, information management, and service delivery practices of government organizations, systemic transformation means a radical change in existing governance arrangements in the public sector, including constitutional responsibilities and accountabilities, fiscal management, regulation, and decision-making rights over public resources (O'Neill 2009: 71).

Another interesting possibility is that ICTs have not been used as instruments for administrative reform, but have been used to reinforce existing power distributions in government organizations. This so-called "reinforcement thesis" was confirmed by research findings from the United States, which showed that ICTs were used to maintain and enhance the interests of the political and administrative leaders in government (Kraemer and King 2006).

Whether such outcomes present themselves in the end depends on the *actual use*, in a particular institutional and social context, of the digital technologies and the information they generate or facilitate (Lips 2011: 254). Technology does not *determine* the outcome of administrative reform: the technological capabilities shape, but are equally shaped by, the social environment in which they are used. Consequently, the outcome of technology-enabled administrative reform is in fact determined by an ecology of games, that is, the interplay of the technological application, policy choices and regulation, management strategies, available resources and implementation, organizational and cultural responses, and social use and non-use of an ecology of actors (Dutton 1999).

## What is Different about Government Becoming "Digital by Default"?

Around the world, governments have recognized the potential offered by digital transformation and many have decided to become "digital by default." Generally, this means that not only will digitized service provision become the norm or the standard way for government in interacting with its multiple relationships, and replace paper-based or face-to-face interactions, but digital services will also be provided in a customer-centric way. For example, the UK Cabinet Office defines "digital by default" as "digital services that are so straightforward and convenient that all those who can use them will choose to do so whilst those who can't are not excluded" (Cabinet Office 2012a: 5). Several governments have presented their digital by default reform ambitions in digital strategies, which reveal many commonalities but also some notable

**Table 11.2** Six Main Reasons for Governments to Adopt Digital by Default

1. To follow fundamental changes in society and seize the digital opportunity to transform itself
2. To promote substantial efficiency and cost savings
3. To become customer-centric and provide better quality services
4. To improve the availability and accessibility of public data
5. To move away from siloed approaches and duplications across the public sector by introducing common technology platforms
6. To promote the adoption of digital services through enhanced security and privacy protection

differences. Looking at these reform strategies, there are six basic reasons (Table 11. 2) why governments want to become digital by default:

1) Governments acknowledge the fact that society has fundamentally changed as a result of the uptake of digital technologies, and that, consequently, government should seize this digital opportunity to transform itself. For example, the Norwegian Government's Digitizing Public Sector Services Strategy makes the following observation: "People born in 1993 and later have never experienced a world without the Internet. This generation of Norwegians was born not only fitted with skis on their feet, but also holding a web tablet in their hands. Mobile telephones are just as natural for them as electricity. Digital solutions have become a natural part of everyday life for adults as well" (Norwegian Ministries 2012: 3). Another example of the digital transformation of society is provided in the US Federal Government's Digital Government Strategy, which also particularly emphasizes the rapidly changing mobile landscape (The White House 2012).

   Examples of how government might be able to seize this digital opportunity can be found in Norway and Denmark, where all paper-based communication between government and businesses is replaced by digital service provision. For citizens in Denmark, it will be mandatory to use a personal digital mail box for all correspondence with government by 2015. Moreover, once printed forms and letters have been phased out, all Danish citizens will have to use online self-service (Danish Agency for Digitization 2011).

2) Governments see the opportunity of making substantial efficiency savings by becoming digital by default. Several digital strategy documents provide insights into the enormous cost savings that are potentially to be gained from using digital channels, compared to traditional public service channels. For example, the UK Cabinet Office estimates that digital government transactions will be about twenty times cheaper than by phone, and fifty times cheaper than face to face (Cabinet Office 2012a). However, these savings assessments do not include the costs involved in creating digital services, or costs related to the transition from traditional to digital channels (National Audit Office 2013).

Based on these calculations, the UK Central Government aims to save GBP £1.2 billion by 2015. In addition, they expect a further GBP £1.7 billion in annual savings from 2015 onwards by redesigning the UK Central Government's seven biggest websites which, together, account for more than 90 percent of all UK Central Government transactions, by digitizing services which cope with more than 100,000 transactions annually, and by further improving other government websites used for interaction with the general public.

3) Governments want to be customer-centric and provide better quality, more convenient, easy-to-use, and less time-consuming services to citizens and businesses. Moreover, they want customers to be shielded from the internal complexities of government. As an example of providing better quality, customer-centric services, under the Australian Digital First initiative, the aim is for government agencies to provide their customers with user-friendly online access to priority services, allowing end-to-end processing for those services through a choice of a single authentication method that enables access to a range of services without needing multiple passwords or multiple tests of credentials (Department of Broadband, Communications and the Digital Economy 2013: xi). Another example is from the UK, where the UK Cabinet Office's Government Digital Service team recently introduced a Digital by Default service standard to ensure that customers receive a consistently high-quality digital experience across government.

In several countries, the aim to be customer-centric is supported by delivering more integrated services via unified online transaction and information hubs to citizens and businesses. This development often goes together with a consolidation of non-digital channels and the removal of duplicating or "redundant" websites. For example, in New Zealand, non-digital channels, such as call centers and face-to-face government counters, will become "operator assisted" interfaces into the self-service digital channel, and will be rationalized as transaction volumes reduce over time (Department of Internal Affairs 2013: 13). In 2011, the UK Central Government closed down seventy-four "redundant" government sites in order to further slimline its web presence and focus on its remodelled, unified GOV.UK portal, which replaced the central hubs Directgov and Business Link as a single domain for government on the Internet.

4) Governments want to improve the availability and accessibility of public-sector data. Usually, government's aim of making public data accessible and more broadly available is to facilitate reuse in new ways for social, economic, and democratic benefit. Some governments, including the New Zealand Central Government, view public information, that is, non-personal and unrestricted data, as a national asset that must be open by default.

Similarly, the US Federal Government wants to better leverage the wealth of public data for new innovative applications and services by ensuring that data is open and machine-readable by default (The White House 2012: 2).

5) Governments are introducing common technology platforms to underpin and support digital services. In most countries, moving away from siloed approaches and duplications across the public sector and accelerating the adoption of new technologies, these common technology platforms are shared across government organizations. In New Zealand, besides common technology platforms, also other common capabilities, such as a digital identity verification service and a shared service for digital engagement with the general public, must be shared by default across the New Zealand Central Government. The Norwegian and Danish Governments also use common public registers and other authoritative core data sets across government to support digital services.

6) Governments recognize the need to ensure security and privacy protection in the development and delivery of digital services. Their expectations are that enhanced security and privacy protection will promote the adoption of technology-enabled services and increase trust in digital government by default. The New Zealand Central Government even goes one step further with its ambition to build security- and privacy-by-design into the provision of new digital services.

In order to further facilitate the use of digital services, governments are removing legislative barriers which prevent the development of digital by default services, such as existing laws made before the digital age. For example, existing legislation in the UK required the provision of tax coding notifications on paper rather than via digital channels (Cabinet Office 2012a: 35).

# Variations in Digital Government by Default

There are also some important differences to observe in the digital by default strategies from the various countries.

## SERVICE- VERSUS INFORMATION-CENTRIC APPROACHES

Some countries, such as the UK, use a *service-centric* approach in advancing their digital by default strategy, for instance converting paper-based transaction services into web-based equivalents, whereas other countries, such as the United States, use a more radical *information-centric* approach. For example, rather than primarily considering the management of documents and, with that, the final presentation of digital information, the US Federal Government decouples information from its presentation by focusing on managing discrete pieces of open data and content, which can be tagged, shared, secured, mashed up, and presented in the way that is most useful for the consumer of that information (The White House 2012: 3). By using open standards and web Application Programming Interfaces (APIs), the US Federal Government is able to make data assets freely available for use by various internal and external stakeholders, and in a program- and device-agnostic way. Consequently, the same web APIs can be used, and reused, to present information to customers through multiple channels (e.g. websites, mobile applications), and to release the information to external developers who then can use it to create new information products, services, or applications.

As an example of this information-centric approach, the City of San Francisco releases its raw public transportation data on train routes, schedules, and location updates directly to the general public through web services. This has enabled citizen developers to write over ten different mobile applications to help individuals navigate San Francisco's public transit systems and, with that, to provide more information services than the City of San Francisco could have provided (The White House 2012: 5–6).

## IMPLEMENTATION STRATEGIES

Countries demonstrate substantial differences in their implementation focus on establishing digital by default. Some countries, such as the UK and Australia, focus on developing digital by default services at the level of individual government organizations, in particular those organizations providing the bulk of transactional services in the public sector. Other countries, such as the United States and Denmark, focus on developing government-wide digital by default solutions (e.g. open datasets, public registers), which can be used in government-agnostic, program-agnostic, and device-agnostic ways. New Zealand is an example of a country where an implementation focus at both administrative levels can be observed: with the New Zealand Government Chief Information Officer (GCIO) as the functional leader for government ICT, the New Zealand digital by default strategy is led by the GCIO and delivered in collaboration with government agencies.

## ACCESS STRATEGIES

To ensure fair access to public services for all individuals entitled to them, countries like the UK, Norway, and Denmark recognize the importance of

actively supporting people who are not online or are less capable of accessing digital services. For example, acknowledging that the majority of the UK
population is online (82%) but only 27 percent use online government services
(Cabinet Office 2012b), the UK Central Government introduced an "assisted
digital" program as part of their digital by default strategy. Assisted digital
aims to develop and apply customer insights about those who use digital services, and those who can't, and identify the support requirements needed for
people who are not online, and to provide assistance to those who need it.
Moreover, both by improving the quality of services offered through digital
channels and making people aware of available services, those who are online
will be persuaded to use digital services. Or, in UK Cabinet Office Minister
Francis Maude's own words: "We are developing digital services that are so
good people will prefer to use them, while ensuring that those who are not able
to go online are given the support they need to do so" (Price 2013).

Assistance for those who are not online or those less capable of accessing digital services could involve providing help to use the digital channel,
and offering services in non-digital ways, such as face-to-face, by phone, and
through intermediaries. Departments are responsible for determining how
they will provide assistance at the same time as they are digitally transforming their services (Cabinet Office 2012a: 16). Furthermore, in order to ensure
that those who need assistance receive a consistent service across the multiple
services they use, the UK Cabinet Office collaborates with government departments to develop a cross-government approach.

## Issues Emerging from Digital by Default Strategies

Governments seem to take this administrative reform opportunity of establishing digital by default very seriously, as illustrated for example by the following opening statement by President Obama on the US Federal Government's
Digital Government Strategy: "I want us to ask ourselves every day, how are
we using technology to make a real difference in people's lives" (The White
House 2012: 1). In order to jump-start the transition process towards digital
by default, US Federal Government agencies needed to identify at least two
major customer-facing systems containing high-value data and content, with
the highest priority given to those systems that contain the most valuable
information from a customer's perspective; expose this information through
web APIs to appropriate audiences; apply metadata tags in compliance with
US Federal Guidelines; and publish a plan to transition additional systems
as practical. This transition process is closely monitored by the US Federal

Government's Office of Management and Budget (OMB). Also, the US Federal Government's General Services Administration (GSA) is helping government agencies to develop web APIs through its Digital Services Innovation Center where digital solutions can be developed and shared with other government agencies in accordance with the principle of "build once, use many times" (The White House 2012: 7). Similarly, in the UK, the high priority of the digital by default reform strategy is reflected by both the monitoring and actively supporting role of the UK Cabinet Office as well as the requirement for UK government organizations to appoint a digital leader to their executive team, who will lead on the development and delivery of the organization's digital strategy.

As earlier attempts of ICT-enabled administrative reform have demonstrated, digital transformation will not happen overnight and, if it happens, it often does so with quite different and unexpected outcomes (Foley and Alfonso 2009; Lips and Schuppan 2009). It therefore remains the question at this stage if, and if so, how and to what extent, countries will be able to achieve their digital by default strategies. Taking into account lessons learnt from ICT-enabled reform initiatives in the past, the following issues around the implementation of digital by default can be observed.

Many studies of ICT-enabled administrative reform initiatives point at the importance of leadership to achieve transformation (Fountain 2010; Institute for Government 2010). Although this critical condition for success has been recognized by governments like the US Federal Government and the UK Central Government in their digital by default strategies, there are several reasons why the right leadership for successful digital government transformation may not be attained. An important reason is the fact that, in many countries, senior government leaders, with the exception perhaps of the Chief Technology Officer and Chief Information Officer, demonstrate a lack of understanding of the public management implications of digital transformation. One explanation is the current generation of senior leaders in government: besides the fact that they usually were born a long time before the introduction of digital technologies, including the Internet, into society and are not "digital natives" therefore (Palfrey and Gasser 2008), they also often do not actively use these technologies (Dutton and Blank 2011: 15). A further explanation is that they usually see digital transformation as a technology issue which does not belong to their own managerial portfolio, and therefore do not recognize and understand the public management aspects of ICT-enabled reform initiatives (Lips 2011). Similar observations can be made for the current generation of political leaders in many countries, with an additional issue that political leaders usually like to see "quick wins" in terms of efficiency gains, preferably during the time that they are in office. Usually, they do not understand the (longer-term) investments needed to achieve digital transformation, including the costs involved with managing and implementing the transformational change process. Also, political leaders commonly want to stay away from risky government IT initiatives which might attract negative media attention (Heeks 2006).

Another reason is that, as a result of a lack of capability and skills in government in the area of channel shift and digital transformation, leadership is often brought in from the private sector. However, the unique characteristics of government compared to private-sector organizations, such as the political dimension, the multiple and varying interests that need to be met, and strong media attention, usually lead to additional complexities and requirements, which private-sector leaders are not always aware of, or have experience with. Ian Watmore, a top UK public servant with extensive experience in the private sector, was once quoted as saying: "IT in government is as difficult as it gets" (Institute for Government 2010: 9). This statement also applies to the complexity of public services compared to commercial services, for instance. As public services are often intangible, led by rules and regulations aimed at achieving fairness, and required to meet the varying needs and demands of all those citizens entitled to them, the standardization and simplification processes needed for digitization are difficult to achieve. This, then, may lead to substantial additional cost investments in order to realize digital transformation.

In general, an important issue for the achievement of digital by default is the transition process from traditional public service provision to digital services. Varying fundamental changes will need to be managed during this process, including digitizing tasks and work processes; redesigning and coordinating common capabilities across government; changing job requirements for frontline public servants; managing cultural change within government organizations; managing the shift from existing IT systems, also called "legacy systems," to new digital systems that are suitable for digital transformation; consolidating digital channels; introducing common technology platforms; creating open data sets; establishing interoperability so that end-to-end digital solutions can be provided; realizing a user-friendly digital service design; establishing partnerships with commercial and voluntary-sector organizations; regulatory changes needed to achieve digital transformation; changing privacy and security requirements as a result of introducing new digital solutions; and assistance for targeted customer groups.

Managing these complex changes in order to achieve digital by default can be compared to managing ICT-enabled public-sector innovation. This raises the problem for many governments of not having the right levels of digital capability and specialist skills in-house. Moreover, a favorable culture and supporting conditions for innovation are often missing in public-sector organizations, especially when invested innovation efforts fail to achieve clear outcomes in the short term.

Other critically important issues for digital transformation are around the actual uptake and use of the digital services. Particularly also considering the financial investments needed to achieve digital by default, there is no guarantee that the relatively low user uptake of digital government services in several countries can be shifted to a substantially higher uptake as a result of offering better quality digital services, as some governments have proposed in their strategies. For example, research findings from the UK show that, from 2009 to 2011, there was no change in the use of online government services, with a resilient 43 percent of Internet users reporting no use at all in the preceding twelve months (Dutton and Blank 2011: 28). Moreover, although information-seeking about government services was slightly higher, only 24 percent of Internet users reported the use of digital transactional services with local councils in Britain and only 21 percent used digital transactional services with the UK Central Government (Dutton and Blank 2011: 29).

For many individuals, the availability of transformed and better quality digital government services will not encourage them to use digital channels for public service provision for the first time, or use them more often. For instance, findings from a recent EU eGovernment survey show that, even though people can be daily Internet users, they can be unwilling to use digital government services for a variety of reasons, including preferring personal contact (62%), anticipating that the service requires face-to-face contact (34%), or seeing other channels as more convenient (19%) (European Commission 2013: 4).

Besides the fact that people may not be aware of the existence of digital government services, an important consideration for them might be that most people do not need to use government services, such as the renewal of a driver's licence, getting a building permit, or setting up a business, on a frequent basis. Another important consideration for people might be that, for privacy or security reasons, they prefer not to provide their personal information via digital channels, or conduct the transaction of important citizen identity documents, such as a driver's licence or a passport, (completely) online. Also, research findings from New Zealand point out that online standardized forms usually do not provide the option to customers to explain their unique circumstances to government. Consequently, digital service users held the view that government agencies are not always asking for the right information from them through these digital forms. They therefore preferred direct interaction with a public official by phone or face to face not only to make sure that government agencies understand their personal situation, but also to get instant confirmation of the requested service (Lips et al. 2010).

In order to make it more attractive for people to use digital services, the UK Central Government wants to encourage people to move from offline to digital channels through awareness raising, assisting with the use of digital services, and using a positive incentive scheme, including passing on lower costs to digital service users, allowing later deadlines for online process completion, and offering entries into prize draws for digital service users (Cabinet Office 2012a: 30). However, some groups of the population will not have any choice regarding the uptake of digital by default services, such as people highly dependent on government services. Examples are benefit claimants, families with low income, individuals dependent on health services, and senior citizens. With many lower-paid groups in society not having Internet access (Dutton and Blank 2011), these more vulnerable, government-dependent groups of the population will require assistance in some form or another with digital services, which may add to the costs involved with establishing digital government by default.

For example, in many countries, senior citizens become much more dependent on government services as soon as they retire. For many of them, they did not have much to do with government during their working lives but are now at a stage where they need to interact with government for getting superannuation or access to health services, for instance. Research in New Zealand has found that, besides not liking or quite understanding how to deal with government bureaucracy at this stage of their lives, this population group is not at all comfortable with using digital channels to do so (Lips et al. 2010). Moreover, Scandinavian countries are experiencing problems with senior citizens who can't use digital solutions for service provision any longer because of changing health conditions (e.g. dementia).

Another interesting development in Scandinavian countries around digital government by default is that, although youth may be very familiar with using digital channels, they often turn out to be illiterate in dealing with government. Consequently, governments in Scandinavian countries found that this customer group needed an "assisted government" support program for their first digital interactions with government agencies. In general, even though the shift towards consolidated and user-centric websites will make it easier for individuals to navigate around government, people often do not understand how government operates, and particularly also how personal information they provide in digital government transactions is processed, stored, accessed, or used (Lips et al. 2010). This lack of transparency around the management of digitized citizen identity information in government can lead to high levels of discomfort or even distrust amongst citizens, feelings which seem to be reinforced whenever data or security breaches in government are reported in the media.

# The Role of Digital Technology in Administrative Reform: Transformation or Reinforcement of Government?

Similar to earlier administrative reform waves, governments have rediscovered digital technology as the panacea for their problems. In so doing, digital government failures of the past, such as the common expectation of "build and they will come," seem to have been erased from governments' memories: again, the firm belief is that the supply of better quality and customer-centric digital services will make people shift from traditional to online channels. This time, however, there does not seem to be an escape for citizens and other government service users from adopting digital services forced upon them. At the same time, it is not at all clear either whether, as a result of implementing a digital by default reform program, governments will be able to achieve their main strategic objectives, such as substantial efficiency and cost savings. For example, in the UK, the National Audit Office reported research indicating that, while progress was made in making it easier for people to find government information and services online, no robust data was found on the costs or benefits of spending (National Audit Office 2013: 6).

In general, technology will not determine the outcome of digital by default reform initiatives: important issues around digital by default, such as the lack of leadership, user-unfriendly design, managing digital transformation, the complexity of public services, and the limited uptake of digital services, will not and cannot be solved by the technology per se. Instead, the outcome, including the possibility to transform the power relationships between government and individuals, will be determined by the ecology of games around the digital by default strategy in each country. Consequently, digital by default in the end might lead to digital transformation, or equally reinforce government as we know it today, with different outcomes possible in different countries. What has become clear, though, is the critical importance of a robust understanding of the public management issues and implications of digital by default and, with that, the critical role to play for senior government leaders responsible for this latest administrative reform initiative to enable digital transformation.

### ■ REFERENCES

Cabinet Office (2012a). *Government Digital Strategy*. London: Cabinet Office.

Cabinet Office (2012b). *Digital Landscape Research*. London: Cabinet Office.

Castells, M. (1996). *The Rise of the Network Society*. Oxford: Blackwell Publishing.

Chadwick, A. (2006). *Internet Politics: States, Citizens, and New Communication Technologies*. Oxford: Oxford University Press.

Coleman, S. and Blumler, J. (2001). *Realizing Democracy Online: Towards a Civic Commons in Cyberspace*. London: Institute for Public Policy Research.

Danish Agency for Digitization (December 2011). "eGovernment Strategy 2011–2015." *Digitaliseringsstyrelsen*. <http://www.digst.dk/Servicemenu/English/Policy-and-Strategy/eGOV-strategy> (accessed July 25, 2013).

Department of Broadband, Communications and the Digital Economy (2013). *Advancing Australia as a Digital Economy: An Update to the National Digital Economy Strategy*. Canberra: Australian Government.

Department of Internal Affairs (2013). *Government ICT Strategy and Action Plan to 2017.* Wellington: New Zealand Government.

Dunleavy, P., Margetts, H., Bastow, S., and Tinkler, J. (2006). *Digital Era Governance: IT Corporations, the State, and E-Government.* Oxford: Oxford University Press.

Dutton, W. H. (ed.) (1999). *Society on the Line: Information Politics in the Digital Age.* Oxford: Oxford University Press.

Dutton, W. H. and Blank, G. (2011). "Next Generation Users: The Internet in Britain." *Oxford Internet Survey 2011 Report.* Oxford: Oxford Internet Institute.

European Commission (2013). "Public Services Online: 'Digital by Default or by Detour?' Assessing User Centric eGovernment Performance in Europe—eGovernment Benchmark 2012. Final Insight Report." Directorate-General of Communications Networks, Content and Technology. Luxembourg: Publications Office of the European Union.

Foley, P. and Alfonso, X. (2009). "eGovernment and the Transformation Agenda," *Public Administration,* 87(2): 371–396.

Fountain, J. E. (2010). "Bureaucratic Reform and e-Government in the United States: An Institutional Perspective." In A. Chadwick and P. N. Howard (eds.) (2010). *The Routledge Handbook of Internet Politics.* Abingdon: Routledge, 99–113.

Heeks, R. (2006). *Implementing and Managing eGovernment: An International Text.* London: Sage.

Institute for Government (2010). *System Error: Fixing the Flaws in Government IT.* London: Institute for Government.

Kraemer, K. L., Dutton, W. H., and Northrop, A. (1981). *The Management of Information Systems.* New York: Columbia University Press.

Kraemer, K. L. and King, J. L. (2006). "Information Technology and Administrative Reform: Will E-Government be Different?" *International Journal of Electronic Government Research,* 2(1): 1–20.

Linders, D., Copeland-Wilson, S., and Bertot, J. C. (2012). "Open Government as a Vehicle for Government Transformation." In V. Weerakkody and C. G. Reddick (eds.), *Public Sector Transformation through e-Government: Experiences from Europe and North America."* New York: Routledge, 9–24.

Lips, A. M. B. (2011). "'E-Government is Dead—Long Live Networked Governance': Fixing System Errors in the New Zealand Public Management System." In B. Ryan and D. Gill (eds) *Future State: Directions for Public Management in New Zealand.* Wellington: Victoria University Press, 248–261.

Lips, A. M. B., Eppel, E. A., Cunningham, A., and Hopkins-Burns, V. (2010). *Public Attitudes to the Sharing of Personal Information in the Course of Online Public Service Provision,* Final Research Report, August 2010. Wellington: Victoria University of Wellington, <http://e-government. vuw.ac.nz/summary_IRD.aspx> (accessed July 25, 2013).

Lips, A. M. B. and Schuppan, T. (2009). "Transforming E-Government Knowledge through Public Management Research," *Public Management Review,* 11(6): 739–749.

Lyon, D. (1994) *The Electronic Eye: The Rise of Surveillance Society.* Minneapolis, MN: University of Minnesota Press.

National Audit Office (2013). *Digital Britain 2: Putting Users at the Heart of Government's Digital Services.* London: The Stationery Office.

Norwegian Ministries (2012). *Digitizing Public Sector Services: Norwegian eGovernment Program.* Oslo: Norwegian Ministries.

O'Neill, R. R. (2009). "The transformative Impact of E-Government on Public Governance in New Zealand," *Public Management Review*, 11(6): 751–770.

OECD (2009). *Rethinking e-Government Services: User-Centred Approaches*. Paris: Organisation for Economic Cooperation and Development.

Palfrey, J. and Gasser, U., (2008). *Born Digital: Understanding the First Generation of Digital Natives*. New York: Basic Books.

Price, A. (2013). "Does Assisted Digital Need a Rethink Already?" (April 4). <http://www.publictechnology.net/features/does-assisted-digital-need-rethink-already/37692> (accessed July 25, 2013).

The White House (2012). *Digital Government: Building a 21st Century Platform to Better Service the American People*. Executive Office of the President of the United States, Washington, DC: The White House.

Weerakkody, V. and Reddick, C. G. (eds.) (2012). *Public Sector Transformation through e-Government: Experiences from Europe and North America*. New York: Routledge.

# 12 The Wisdom of Which Crowd? On the Pathology of a Digital Democracy Initiative for a Listening Government

*Stephen Coleman and Jay G. Blumler\**

What is democracy without public discussion of the policies that will affect the everyday lives of citizens? What if there is plenty of such discussion, but it fails to connect to the institutional processes whereby public policies are articulated, deliberated, scrutinized, and implemented? Or, to put these questions in the terms of normative democratic theory: how can citizens be truly represented if the policies enacted in their name bear no conspicuous relationship to their expressed or considered values and preferences? Innovations in digital democracy seek to address such questions by presenting the potential to engage citizens more directly in democratic processes.

Since the emergence of the World Wide Web as a public network in the mid-1990s, communities, third-sector organizations, and governments at every level have initiated schemes designed to use digital information and communication technologies as enablers of democratic participation. These have included the provision of online services (ranging from tax collection to voting); making available hitherto restricted databases relating to local planning, budgets, or health risks; and the establishment of online spaces in which citizens can contact elected representatives, share local knowledge, volunteer their time for civic causes, and comment on policies and legislation. While many of these initiatives have done little more than replicate previously available citizen services in an online form, others have sought to change the terms of democratic engagement by making it easier for citizens to connect with decision makers and take collective action.

---

* This is a revised and updated version of Coleman and Blumler (2011).

Proponents of digital democracy—ranging from cyber-utopians who have imagined that "the Internet changes everything" to political realists who regard new information and communication technologies as promising tools for opening up a more informed, multivocal, accessible, and even deliberative polity—have argued that new forms of digitally enabled communication have a potential to broaden and deepen democratic engagement. Digital democrats tend to reject the views of earlier democratic theorists, who accorded only an occasional and minimal role for citizens in decision making, mainly confined to voting for those best qualified to arrive at policy judgments on their behalf. Innovations around digital democracy have opened up expectations of political representation as being less of a one-way service legitimized by a one-off mandate and more as a partnership. As the OECD (2001: 71) put it in a report entitled *Citizens as Partners*, governments are being pressured to place:

greater emphasis on citizen involvement.... It requires governments to provide ample opportunity for information, consultation and participation by citizens in developing policy options prior to decision-making and to give reasons for their policy choices once a decision has been taken.

Innovations around digital democracy include efforts to better link citizens with politicians and government, not just in service delivery but in decision making. The extensive diffusion of digital communication has spawned a number of ideas and ventures for making these connections a reality. They have included e-petitions (Wright 2012); online policy communities (Coleman 2012); online consultative panels (Sharp and Anderson 2010); city wikis (Mambrey and Doerr 2011); and an assortment of mechanisms to achieve two-way consultation and discussion between political authorities and citizens. It is with this last approach that this chapter is concerned. A recent review (Coleman and Shane 2012) describes an interesting range of such efforts and depicts positive outcomes when they are carefully prepared and are animated by a genuinely democratic spirit. Little is likely to be accomplished, however, if such exercises are mounted as fashionable gimmicks or for mainly pragmatic or partisan purposes.

## A British Case Study

To explore the tension between the democratic potential of digital technologies for enhancing civic participation (Coleman and Blumler 2009) and the temptation for governments to exploit such technologies with a view to appearing in touch, ultra-modern, and open to fresh input, the authors undertook a case study of the approaches to political consultation that were followed by the Conservative and Liberal Democratic parties (separately and in

Coalition government) before, during, and after the British general election of 2010. This method of investigation entailed a detailed analysis of all policy documents, statements, and actions by the Coalition partners (the Conservative and Liberal Democrat parties) relating to digitally enabled democratic engagement in the periods leading up to and after the election.

The extent to which such commitments to collaborative governance can amount to more than empty rhetoric, however, has exercised political commentators and practitioners. An earlier Labour government led by Prime Minister Tony Blair made use of people's panels, citizens' juries, "big conversations," e-petitions and ubiquitous polling, often derided as "government by focus group." Condemned on the one hand for its supposedly ephemeral regard to public whim, and on the other for being a mere gimmick, ignoring the input from citizens whose views conflicted with its own, it seemed as if listening power could never prevail. Despite such skepticism, articulated especially by journalists for whom every consultative initiative seemed proof of Machiavellian intent, Britain's main opposition parties—Conservative and Liberal Democrat—went into the 2010 general election proclaiming what appeared to be a radical new approach to more substantial co-governance.

In June 2009 Prime Minister David Cameron made a speech at a prestigious London university in which he sought to position the Conservatives as the radical party of the Internet:

The Internet is an amazing pollinator, spreading ideas and information all over the globe in minutes. It turns lonely fights into mass campaigns; transforms moans into movements; excites the attention of hundreds, thousands, millions of people and stirs them to action. And constantly accelerating technology makes information infinitely more powerful.[1]

And he went on to promise that "By harnessing the wisdom of the crowd, we can find out what information individuals think will be important in holding the state to account."

For the Conservatives, the Labour government's flirtation with e-politics (such as online policy discussions and e-petitions) had been a merely symbolic gesture towards "the wisdom of the crowd." Their declared intention was to go much further. Jeremy Hunt, who was to become a key government minister, wrote in an article in *The Telegraph* that

the Internet is not simply about the decentralising of information. It is about the decentralising of power. We ignore this at our peril, because it has already started to happen. The Government abandoned road pricing because 1.8 million people signed a petition against it on the No 10 website.[2]

---

[1] "Giving Power back to the People." Speech at Imperial College, London, June 25, 2009. <http://news.bbc.co.uk/1/hi/uk_politics/8119047.stm>.

[2] "If Politicians Want to be Trusted Again, They Must Learn to Listen," *The Telegraph*, 21 December. <http://www.telegraph.co.uk/news/newstopics/mps-expenses/6860666/If-politicians-want-to-be-trusted-again-they-must-learn-to-listen.html>.

A week later Hunt announced "a competition, with a £1million prize for the best new technology platform that helps people come together to solve the problems that matter to them." This would "be used by a future Conservative government to throw open the policy-making process to the public, and harness the wisdom of the crowd so that the public can collaborate to improve government policy." Hunt promised that "a Conservative government would publish all government Green Papers on this platform, so that everyone can have their say on government policies, and feed in their ideas to make them better." The underlying principle behind this idea was drawn from Surowiecki's 2004 bestseller, *The Wisdom of Crowds* (subtitled *Why the Many Are Smarter Than the Few and How Collective Wisdom Shapes Business, Economies, Societies and Nations*) which argued that crowds of people are more likely to arrive at intelligent conclusions than individual experts, and that reliance upon such aggregate knowledge is more likely to result in wisdom than appeals to evidence from research. A Conservative Party press release (December 30, 2009) declared that

Conservatives believe that the collective wisdom of the British people is much greater than that of a bunch of politicians or so-called experts. And new technology now allows us to harness that wisdom like never before. So at this time of year, when families and friends are getting together, we're announcing a new idea to help the British people get together to help solve the problems that matter to them.

And it concluded by asking, "When formulating and implementing policy, why should we not listen to the hundreds of thousands of experts out there?"

Although this should be interpreted as more than a rhetorical question, it raises deep and important issues of political philosophy and practice. Critics of the appeal to popular reason would argue that, far from being inherently wise, public opinion is often under-informed, fragmented, and self-serving; that the task of distinguishing between common sense and prejudice is formidable; that the job of an elected government is to carry out its electoral mandate rather than be permanently dependent upon the buzz of the crowd; and that aggregating disparate expressions of pop-wisdom could result in muddled policy. A party aiming to govern well should have answers to these criticisms that go beyond democratic-sounding pieties.

For our part, we believe that there are credible answers: that using communication technologies to gather and analyze public input with a view to stimulating public deliberation—which entails sharing, comparing, combining, and evaluating various claims and expertise—could help to nurture more informed, tolerant, and civic-minded public policy, enabling governments to interpret their mandates with greater sensitivity to contingent circumstances, and contribute to a richer contract between representatives and represented. If, however, a proposal of the sort outlined by the Conservatives were to be based only upon the gathering of hundreds of thousands of atomized opinions, without any attempt to engage different interests, values, and claims to wisdom with one another, it would be highly vulnerable to the criticisms we have outlined.

In its 2010 election manifesto, the Conservative Party announced its intention to have an online Public Reading Stage for legislation, that would provide an opportunity for the public to comment, stating that

In the post-bureaucratic age, new technologies make it easier than ever before to involve the public in the legislative process and harness the wisdom of crowds to improve legislation and spot potential problems before a Bill is implemented.

While this promised constitutional reform did not explicitly refer to a deliberative mode of public scrutiny of legislation, it would be hard to imagine the complexity of a parliamentary Bill being evaluated in any other way.

The 2010 election gave no single party a majority of seats in the House of Commons and resulted in the formation of a Conservative–Liberal Democrat Coalition government. The Liberal Democrats had long advocated policies for more devolved, community-based decision making, including the use of online tools to solicit public input. Whatever other matters of principle might have divided the new Coalition partners, a commitment to a new style of policy making appeared not to be one of them. Indeed, within weeks of his appointment as Deputy Prime Minister, Nick Clegg, leader of the Liberal Democrats, made a speech in which he claimed to be introducing no less than "the biggest shake up of our democracy since 1832:"

This government is going to be unlike any other. This government is going to transform our politics so the state has far less control over you, and you have far more control over the state. This government is going to break up concentrations of power and hand power back to people, because that is quite simply how we can build a society that is fair.[3]

Alongside promises to complete the reform of the House of Lords, limit the power of political lobbyists, empower parliament, and introduce a referendum on a new voting system, Clegg stated that "we'll do something no government ever has: we will ask you which laws you think should go." That is not quite the same as asking citizens which laws and policies should be introduced, but the radical tone of the Deputy Prime Minister's speech, combined with earlier Conservative promises to rely upon "public wisdom" as a source of policy, suggested a shift in the direction of participatory democracy of a kind that would indeed be politically transformative. So, what has happened since then?

Both its fiercest critics and most ardent supporters would agree that the Coalition government has introduced radical new policies, some of which will

---

[3] "New Politics." Speech at City and Islington College, London, 19 May 19, 2010. < http://news.bbc.co.uk/1/hi/8691753.stm >.

reshape key social institutions for years to come. The extent to which such radicalism has been a panic response to the financial crisis, a visionary and ideologically motivated attempt to break with the past, or a consequence of the Coalition chemistry is for others to judge. Our purpose in this chapter is to describe how these policies were introduced to the public and to assess the extent to which they have been formulated, scrutinized, and implemented in line with the principles of accountability and collaboration espoused by the Coalition partners.

While the Coalition government, after assuming power, introduced a wide range of radical policy initiatives, we focus here upon two that are likely to have some of the most far-reaching effects: the structural reforms to the funding of health care and higher education. Britain has a long tradition of providing state-funded access to health care and higher education. While some policies introducing market principles to aspects of the National Health Service and higher education were introduced in the past two decades, both institutions continued to be conceived as providing public goods, most effectively financed by the public purse and not amenable to the reign of the free market. Radical policies aimed at marketizing the delivery of health care and higher education were set out by the Coalition government. To what extent were options for change the subject of "ample opportunity for information, consultation and participation by citizens"? How far was "the wisdom of the crowd" harnessed so that the public could "collaborate to improve government policy"? In what ways were the introduction of these policies examples of citizens having "far more control over the state" than they had enjoyed hitherto?

## University Funding

On 12 October 2010 the Browne Review of Higher Education and Student Finance in England was published. Twenty-two days later (November 3) the government published its response, supporting Browne's key recommendations. Thirty-seven days later (December 10) the House of Commons voted to implement the government proposals. In the course of the fifty-seven days between the announcement of the Browne proposals and the parliamentary vote on them no government-sponsored public consultation took place. This was not only a case of the government failing to live up to its earlier rhetoric about instigating "the biggest shake up of our democracy since 1832;" but a failure to engage in public consultation of any description whatsoever.

Might the Coalition partners have concluded that there was no need to consult the public about this policy because they had only recently been elected with a mandate to do what Browne was recommending? Clearly, this was not the case. First, because one of the Coalition partners, the Liberal Democrats, had won votes at the 2010 general election on the basis of a very clear pledge to oppose any increase in tuition fees—indeed, to oppose tuition fees in principle. Second, the bigger of the Coalition partners, the Conservatives, had made no reference in their manifesto to increasing tuition fees or withdrawing the state's block grant to universities. Indeed, in the three televised prime ministerial debates that were screened during the 2010 campaign, no party leader made the slightest mention of a policy for higher education along the lines proposed by the Browne Review. Third, as Wring and Deacon (2010) have shown in an excellent analysis of national newspaper coverage of policies relating to university tuition during the election campaign period, "only 11 items across all newspapers…had tuition fees as their main focus, 22…referred to the issue in a subsidiary context and 38…mentioned it in one sentence or less." Wring and Deacon conclude that

the largest proportion of these articles addressed the Liberal Democrats' manifesto commitment to the revocation of tuition fees, which they have since reneged upon. The next most prominent category related to Labour's previous record on tuitions and their proposals. Conservative plans received less coverage than those of the minority parties. If there was a cross-party conspiracy to keep tuition fees off the political agenda, it is difficult to escape the conclusion that in media terms at least it was extraordinarily effective.

Given that the policy voted for in parliament in December 2010 had played no part in the governing parties' campaigns five months earlier (except insofar as the Liberal Democrats vowed to oppose any such policy), it cannot possibly be argued that the absence of any public consultation was justified because the government was simply carrying out its mandate. Might it be argued instead that, while there was no appeal to the public to support this policy by voting for it, the policy itself resulted from the government's divination of "the wisdom of the crowd"? In short, was the new policy for university funding and substantially increased tuition fees an idea that had arisen as a consequence of "people com[ing] together to solve the problems that matter to them," as Jeremy Hunt had put it?

Between July 9 and September 10, 2010 the new Coalition government ran what it called a Spending Challenge, intended to inform decisions made in its Spending Review. This comprised a website (<www.hm-treasury.gov.uk/spend_index.htm>) to which members of the public were invited to submit "ideas on how government could spend money more effectively, how it could save money by stopping some activities, and where it could reduce waste by taking practical steps to improve efficiency." Of the 48,000 suggestions submitted to the website, 4,000 failed the moderation policy. The remainder were published on the Spending Challenge website for the public to rank according to their preferences. According to the government, over 250,000 votes were cast by members of the public for various proposals submitted to the site. In its account of the exercise, the government asks the question, "What difference did the Spending Challenge make to the Spending Review?" and answers it as follows:

The Spending Review announces 25 ideas submitted to the Spending Challenge that will now be taken forward as policy by the Government. These ideas range from improving procurement processes, potentially saving £400 million a year, to stopping sending out letters along with back to work or training credits, saving £1.2 million a year. They show that small ideas can make a big difference, and that the Government has been keen to explore all possible efficiencies in the process of the Spending Review.

Alongside this, a number of suggestions have contributed to the Government's overall direction and priorities for reform. For example, a number of people suggested means testing some benefits, including child benefit, or minimizing tax avoidance—the Government has announced action in both these areas at the Spending Review.

Hardly any of the ideas submitted to the Spending Challenge referred to university funding or the level of tuition fees. In all, there were two related recommendations submitted:

- Increase Student Loans to cover the full cost of university education, taking the burden off the taxpayer
- Target government funding for courses, and grants, on the most valuable university courses

Neither of these recommendations were consistent with the radical policy that the Coalition government adopted within weeks of the Spending Challenge having closed. So, quite aside from criticisms of the method by which the government conducted this consultative exercise (to which we turn in detail further on), democratic legitimacy for the higher education policy cannot be claimed on the basis of crowd wisdom having been solicited and allowed to prevail.

In fact, the response to the government's new policy took the rather old-fashioned form of mass street demonstrations. Students and university staff vented their considerable frustration, not only in response to what seemed to them to be an unfair and culturally destructive policy, but because they felt that this unprecedentedly radical restructuring of higher education had been sprung upon them without sufficient consultation or public deliberation. It was precisely the openness, dialogue, and scope for collaborative governance that the Coalition partners had prided themselves upon that appeared to be missing.

## The National Health Service

When a second major national institution was radically reformed amidst widespread complaints that those affected were not appropriately consulted, the government's claim to be engaged in "the biggest shake-up of our democracy since 1832" began to take on an unintended meaning. In January 2011 the Coalition government introduced the Health and Social Care Bill, proposing to abolish primary care trusts and strategic health authorities, passing the job of commissioning health care (amounting to £80 billion annually) to consortia of GPs, and turning the National Health Service from a universal provider to a market purchaser of services. This proposal had been set out in neither the Conservative nor Liberal Democrat manifestos.

It is not our purpose here to evaluate the wisdom of this reform. We are interested in how this proposal accords with the government's claim to be engaged in a new kind of collaborative policy making. Criticism of the government focused precisely upon this failing. On January 17 the heads of six leading health institutions in the United Kingdom, including the doctors' grouping, the British Medical Association, and the Royal College of Nursing, co-signed a letter to *The Times* expressing "extreme concern" about the speed with which the proposed changes were being imposed. Dr Clare Gerada, chair of the Royal College of General Practitioners, complained: "Our members are worried about the pace at which these reforms are being implemented, the danger of fragmentation of services, and the emphasis on competition. They fear these reforms could cause irreparable and irreversible damage to the NHS." Dr Peter Carter, the Chief Executive of the Royal College of Nursing, warned that "the scale and speed of reforms place the NHS at risk of break up, with a potentially disastrous impact on patient care." The government's decision not to consult the public about the Health and Social Care Bill, on the grounds that it had already consulted on specific elements of a previous White Paper, has led the health workers union, Unison, to apply for a judicial review to stop it on the grounds that "the government has made promises that create a 'legitimate expectation' that the reorganisation proposals will be subject to consultation."

Quite aside from the value of hearing from those most likely to be affected by this radical new policy, the "legitimate expectation" of public consultation would seem to follow from the clear messages sent out by both of the Coalition partners to the effect that they were committed to a new way of governing which would be rooted in listening to what the public has to say.

A significant discrepancy exists between the way that the Coalition government said that it would relate to representative democracy and how it has. Of course, they had never promised—and would not have been taken seriously if they had—that it was their intention to follow every public recommendation that could be gathered via the Web or offline. But they had stated that their ethos would be one of deep listening: of not only conjuring up token opportunities for citizens to "have their say," but of engaging with and learning from public experience. The Coalition leaders might argue that such noble intentions were applicable to a time of stability, but that the scale of the economic meltdown had been such that a less consultative approach was called for. This was an unacceptable response for two reasons: first, because all of their pledges to listen, learn, and shake up democracy were made after the financial crisis began, when they must have been aware that far-reaching measures would be on the agenda; and second, because it is precisely at a time of high risk and low consensus that consultation is most relevant as a way of avoiding disastrous knee-jerks and of building consent for difficult decisions. It is hard not to conclude that the divergence between democratic claims and political practices reflect a profound failure by the Coalition government to understand the long-term danger of demoralizing an already skeptical electorate, thereby weakening the legitimacy of democracy per se.

## A Different Kind of Listening

How might the Coalition government have listened to the voices, experiences, and expertise of the public in a more productive fashion? Before making speeches about it, setting up websites, and offering prizes, they needed to think carefully about what becoming a listening government entails—culturally, technologically, and politically. Failure to think imaginatively about the practicalities of conversational democracy are not unique to this government: "New Labour" (as the Blair government termed itself) tended to employ simplistic, technocratic principles when it came to projects such as "The Big Conversation;" even the BBC, which understands national communication better than anyone else in the United Kingdom, has generally failed to think seriously about what interactivity really means for public communication and how to treat its audiences as consequential civic actors. Exchanging views, listening to others, and seeking common ground depend upon the enunciation, contestation, and enactment of principles of political communication that differ fundamentally from the command-style, vertical-transmission model that has characterized representative government for the past hundred years. Effective listening to the public entails first, making sure that there is a meaningful exchange of views rather than an almost endless succession of atomized positions; second, engaging in debate with the most prevalent as well as the most forceful views that emerge from public deliberation; and third, ensuring that citizens understand when and how their ideas will be considered by government and what sort of expectations they should entertain in relation to feedback and policy influence. We elaborate on each of these principles below.

There is a critical difference between the collection of fixed positions—or signatories to fixed positions, as in e-petitions—and a meaningful exchange of views. The former is aggregative; the latter deliberative. Aggregating knowledge can be useful in certain situations. For example, some statisticians argue that asking a thousand people to guess how many sweets are in a jar is more likely to come up with the correct number than by asking scientific experts. In such cases, "crowdsourcing" might make sense. But in the case of most political policy decisions there is no "correct" answer to be guessed, and individuals have material stakes in the outcomes, so crowd sourcing can be less relevant.

Politics arises because there are legitimate differences of values and preferences between people. Aggregating them tells us at best which values or preferences are in a majority. Deliberation starts from the basis that values and preferences are not rigid, but open to change as a result of reasonable discussion. The best deliberative exercises are ones in which all arguments receive a fair hearing; no voices are excluded, marginalized or mocked; all participants are open to learning something new from others; and there is an expectation that by the end of an argument people's positions might be different from the beginning. For example, a deliberative encounter between university students and Treasury economists might begin with the former demanding free university education funded by taxation and the latter insisting that universities need to pay their way by delivering services to consumers who can afford them, but one might hope that by the end of the exchange both sides would have a clearer understanding of the others' rationale and, possibly, a greater willingness to find some areas of common ground. The British government's Spending Challenge met none of those characteristics: it invited individuals to state their position and then disappear; it invited members of the public to vote for whichever cutting proposals they liked best; it involved no persuasion, no counter-arguments, and no search for common ground. The Spending Challenge was, indeed, a wholly non-deliberative exercise, despite the fact that the government hired a company called Delib to run it. Thus far, the Spending Challenge and another, similarly non-deliberative site called "Your Freedom," are the only online spaces the government has set up with a view to hearing from citizens. Based upon a non-discursive conception of citizenship, these projects are best regarded as online "suggestion boxes" of the kind that companies have long tucked away in the corner of offices so that staff can post occasional whinges, bright ideas, and anonymous rants. They fall far short of the promise of developing tools that will help people to "come together to solve the problems that matter to them."

The move from crowdsourcing to deliberation is essential for the kind of collective problem-solving that the government claims to want to promote. A second key principle is that government itself—sometimes in the form of Ministers, at other times in the form of civil servants speaking on behalf of government policy—must enter into the debate, as opposed to merely being the subject of debate or a remote respondent to public deliberation. Listening from afar is a form of political voyeurism; it is unlikely to convince participants in the discussion that they are being taken seriously, and it is too easily open to manipulation. This is not to say that government is obliged to engage with every message submitted by tens of thousands of people. The deliberative duty of government is to explain the first-order principles that have led it to arrive at second-order policies; to defend those first-order principles against others; and to accept that there might be other policies, based on their own or other first principles, that deserve to be considered. In short, governments should only enter into forms of dialogical-listening consultation if they are at least to some extent open to learning something new and arriving at policy positions other than those with which they started out. Appeals to the "wisdom of the crowd" can too easily become rituals in which governments seek to hear the echoes of their own dogmas. The deliberative approach to democracy is not simply a different method of evaluating arguments: it is based upon the challenging principle of being authentically open to new perspectives.

This leads to a third principle that would characterize a listening government. Rather than basing its claims upon a rhetoric of future promise, it would want to be judged on the empirical basis of whether or not it had actually interacted with, listened to, and learned from the citizens it represents. There is no way of knowing how many of the people who submitted 48,000 ideas and 250,000 votes in the Spending Challenge exercise felt that they had been taken seriously by government. Did they feel that they had had a fair chance to set out their arguments and persuade others; that the government had really heard what they were trying to say; that their input to the discussion had been reciprocated by honest feedback; and that, in at least some cases, they were responsible for influencing policy? We can quantify responses to none of these questions, but we can be sure, on the basis of long-standing research into the relationship between political participation and efficacy, that engaging in an activity that appears to have no consequence is usually followed by subsequent disengagement. Pseudo-involvement in decision making results in diminished future involvement, inefficacy, and a collapse of trust in decisions made. This is our greatest concern about the Coalition government: that it not only raised false hopes about changing the terms of democracy, but also that in shattering such hopes it will undermine the very public confidence that it and future governments depend upon for their legitimacy.

## Facing Up to Systemic Problems

There are three conclusions that could be drawn from what we have said so far. The first is that the Coalition parties were at best unrealistic and at worst disingenuous in setting out their plans to "shake up" British democracy. As we have already suggested, their dependence upon communication technologies as guarantors of government citizen connections, and their failure to embrace a deliberative approach to public voice, could be interpreted as either a cynical appeal to gimmickry or a naive failure to think through ideals to which they are genuinely committed. Either way, one conclusion might be that this lack of clarity around democratic radicalism could result in a squandered opportunity to use digital democracy to help revitalize politics.

A second conclusion might reflect upon the prescription that we have set out for "a different kind of listening" and argue that, even with the best will in the world accompanied by the most carefully conceived planning, these principles are more than any government could hope to introduce in one fell swoop. Mass public deliberation, politicians willing and ready to engage in such dialogue, significant consequences leading to enhanced efficacy—these objectives are surely best reached through the introduction of small-scale projects related to particular issues or communities. Not endless experiments, which we have referred to elsewhere as "pilotitis" (Coleman and Blumler 2009) but real-world democratic projects designed to show how government–citizen relations could be recast. Might it have made more sense for the Coalition to say that one or two government departments would be developing policies along these new lines?

A third conclusion to be drawn from this discrepancy between democratic rhetoric and apparent failure to listen might refer to something bigger than the Coalition government itself: the system of political communication that has come to prevail in Britain and many other liberal-democratic states whereby policy has become subordinated to presentation. One might argue that however well devised the government's commitment to dialogical consultation might have been, they were trapped within a media system in which the prominence of the latest headline, an inherent antagonism towards complex thought, the relentless speed of news circulation, the incessant competition for attention, and the crude partisanship of so much coverage renders any attempt to take time and think things through almost impossible. Could it be the case that neither deep listening nor rich deliberation are compatible with a political communication system that can only register winners and losers, policy triumphs and humiliations, black and white?

We conclude by suggesting that there is truth in all of these three observations. We do not dismiss the potential of digital democracy innovations, but question the approach taken in this case. The UK government has been less than consistent in its democratic commitments. Promoting a political culture characterized by a different kind of listening might most realistically happen on a small scale at first, learning along the way about what works best and how to scale up to national conversations and beyond. And the political communication system, which for so long has run against the grain of democratic inclusion, needs to be reconfigured, with journalists taking on a role as facilitators of public debate. While continuing their traditional function of making available pluralistic information and holding the powerful to account, a new role for journalists would be to create opportunities for citizens to act upon information and challenge power-holders. At the same time, the role of politicians within a reconfigured political communication system would be less about delivering a service to voter-consumers in the hope that they can persuade them that it is exactly what they wanted, and more about engaging with the principles of political co-production, whereby a deliberative public is invited to help make difficult decisions and work through their consequences. Taken together, these constitute a serious, feasible, but demanding political agenda. If, in a decade hence, the prevailing discourse is still focused upon the potential for dialogical governance and democratic uses of the Internet, there is sure to be great frustration at the failure to act decisively upon what has become a widespread desire for change. Rather than dwell upon the inconsistency of the present government, our aim in writing this chapter has been to shorten that period of frustration.

## ■ REFERENCES

Coleman, S. (2012). "The Internet as a Space for Policy Deliberation," in F. Fischer and H. Gottweiss (eds.), *The Argumentative Turn Revisited: Public Policy as Communicative Practice*. Durham, NC: Duke University Press, 149–179.

Coleman, S. and Blumler. J. G. (2009). *The Internet and Democratic Citizenship: Theory, Practice and Policy*. New York: Cambridge University Press, 2009.

Coleman, S. and Blumler. J. G. (2011). "The Wisdom of Which Crowd? On the Pathology of a Listening Government," *Political Quarterly*, 82(3): 355–364.

Coleman, S. and Shane, P. (2012). *Connecting Democracy: Online Consultation and the Flow of Political Communication*. Cambridge, MA: MIT Press.

Mambrey, P. and Dörr, R. (2011). "Local Government and Social Networking Technologies in Germany: The Example of Twitter." *Conference for E-Democracy and Open Government*, Danube University, Krems.

OECD (2001). *Citizens as Partners: Information, Consultation and Public Participation in Policy-Making*. Paris: OECD Publications.

Sharp, A. and Anderson, K. (2010). "Online Citizen Panels as an Advance in Research and Consultation—A Review of Pilot Results." *Commonwealth Journal of Local Governance* 6: 33–54.

Surowiecki, J. (2004). *The Wisdom of Crowds: Why the Many are Smarter than the Few and How Collective Wisdom Shapes Business, Economies, Societies, and Nations*. New York: Doubleday.

Wright, S. (2012). "Assessing (e-) Democratic Innovations: 'Democratic Goods' and Downing Street E-Petitions." *Journal of Information Technology and Politics* 9(4): 453–470.

Wring, D. and Deacon, D. (2010). "Patterns of Press Partisanship in the 2010 General Election." *British Politics* 5(4): 436–454.

# 13 Online Social Networks and Bottom-up Politics

*Sandra González-Bailón*

It is a common assumption that digital technologies have helped turn political engagement into a more decentralized process. Examples often cited include the 2011 political protests (from the Egyptian revolution to the Occupy Campaign); the actions of the hacktivist group Anonymous (which coordinates distributed attacks targeted at web servers to suspend online services of companies and governments); or the free culture movement (born to promote the creation and distribution of free online content). Examples more remote in the history of digital technologies include the anti-globalization movement (emerged in the late eighties) and the emancipatory struggles of minorities like the indigenous Zapatistas in Mexico—in both cases, the protests attained global visibility through the use of email distribution lists and alternative media sites like Indymedia. All these examples have in common is that the actors involved used digital technologies to coordinate their actions, and targeted online networks with their messages to reach larger audiences and involve more participants. Internet technologies allowed protesters to organize in a decentralized way, that is, without a central authority processing local information or overseeing strategies from above. This form of organization creates more flexible forms of collective action and it has radically changed the way in which grassroots politics operate. The aim of this chapter is to explain why, by examining the network mechanisms that are involved in this new form of organization.

This shift towards more decentralized forms of participation does not mean that online networks are horizontal structures where all connections matter in the same way. In fact, online networks are so instrumental for bottom-up politics (that is, for modes of participation that do not rely on hierarchical organizations, or institutionalized channels like political parties) because they are far from being horizontal: they form heterogeneous structures where some nodes are much better connected than others. It is this unequal connectivity that allows online social networks to be more efficient in the spread of information; it is also the reason why everybody in the network is at a short distance—or a few links away—from each other.

The assumption often made when accounting for the examples of collective action above is that the Internet has allowed larger groups of people to self-organize without formal structures (Shirky 2008). When formed online, social networks that are not necessarily political in nature can be quickly activated for political purposes (Earl and Kimport 2011). Although this chapter focuses on grassroots politics, the organizational power of online networks is also relevant for institutional forms of participation. In electoral races, for instance, online social networks can shape voting outcomes by allowing people to encourage others to vote for a candidate. The Howard Dean campaign in the United States back in 2004—part of his ultimately unsuccessful Democratic presidential nomination—was one of the first campaigns orchestrated using online technologies. Most significantly, the Obama campaign that followed in 2008 borrowed and built on many of the strategies implemented during the Dean campaign (Kreiss 2012). What made these campaigns so special was their ability to tap into social networks to elicit many small donations—which, on the aggregate, helped raise a significant amount of funds. In other words, these campaigns offer good examples of the power that interpersonal networks have to mobilize people and, in particular, of how digital technologies can be used to harness that power.

Online social networks have also transformed the operation and membership of advocacy and interest groups. The swift rise to prominence of platforms like MoveOn (a non-profit public policy advocacy group) and DailyKos (a progressive political blog) offer additional examples of how online social networks, and the audiences they bring, can empower organizations (Karpf 2012). This chapter, however, focuses on political engagement that takes place outside democratic institutions like parties and advocacy groups; the focus is on grassroots and non-institutional forms of participation. Social movements and political protests fall in this category. Although social networks have always been instrumental for the organization of collective action (Diani and McAdam 2003), online communication has allowed those networks to grow larger and faster, and to bring together people without the need for allegiance to a particular organization or authority. The question this chapter aims to answer is: How do online social networks (formed by people communicating with people) help those forms of political engagement emerge from the bottom-up and be sustained?

This chapter argues that online networks help people self-organize because they activate a number of mechanisms that rely on the connectivity of the network. What makes networks so important is that they make individual actions and decisions interdependent, diffusing information about previous behavior that will affect subsequent decisions and actions. This interdependence extends over the paths that networks create. Although the examples listed so far would seem to suggest that there is something inherently novel in digital technologies and in how online networks reconfigure communication flows

(Castells 2009), the fact is that online social networks operate through similar mechanisms to their offline counter-parts—if only with faster and wider effects. Social networks are capable of scaling up the consequences of interdependence, but this does not mean that the mechanisms governing their functioning are substantively different. In fact, the conceptual tools to understand why social networks (online or offline) give structure and muscle to bottom-up politics can already be found in early mass media and political communication research (Katz and Lazarsfeld 1955).

The chapter starts with a review of previous research on networks and political participation, and a summary of the features that make networks an important part of the political process. The review focuses on three dimensions: social influence and the effects of self-selection; information diffusion and the spread of behavior; and the feedback and cumulative effects that link individual actions to collective patterns. The structure of networks—whether they are forged online or offline—shapes the way in which dynamics like social influence or diffusion unfold. The following section explains why, presenting a series of old research questions that are now being revisited through the lens of online data. Section two follows up on this theoretical discussion using data drawn from online social networks. The aim is to debunk three claims: that online networks are horizontal structures; that online networks encourage polarization; and that online networks are always more efficient at facilitating large-scale diffusion of information. Section three brings the argument to a more concrete level by discussing how online networks, and the information they help flow, can be analyzed empirically in the communication environment created by social media. Special attention will be paid to how different choices when assembling and analyzing the data constrain the theoretical questions that can be considered. Overall, this chapter offers an outline of key theories and findings that should serve as a useful starting point for anyone wanting to do research on bottom-up politics in the digital era.

## Networks and Political Participation

Individuals are not isolated decision makers. They are part of primary groups and networks that create a frame of reference where opinions and behavior originate. Networks offer a map of those connections, and the communication patterns that arise from social interactions. They can be measured at the individual or the collective level, and although they have been the focus of analysis in social research for decades, online interactions (and the data trails they leave behind) are allowing us to understand their operation and dynamics in a more nuanced way—after all, social networks rely on human communication, and what Internet technologies allow us to do best is to communicate.

Communication creates the opportunity to influence others and be influenced by them: the information that flows amongst peers can change decisions and have a more relevant impact on actions than exposure to common sources of information like media. The study often cited as pioneering research on interpersonal influence aimed to understand how mass media affects voting behavior; but what the study concluded is that, in fact, personal contacts are more effective when it comes to helping voters make up their minds (Lazarsfeld et al. 1948). In discussing their unanticipated findings, the authors introduced the idea of the "two-step flow of information," which suggests that the media shapes opinions indirectly through the mediating role of opinion leaders: these are the people that are more exposed to news sources and pass on a digested version of the information through their personal networks (Katz and Lazarsfeld 1955). A significant amount of research has since tried to uncover what has been called the "social logic of politics" (Zuckerman 2005). Underlying these efforts is the realization that actors are not atoms that decide in isolation, but more like molecules (Katz 1957: 78), that is, part of larger structures that need to be analyzed to understand individual actions.

There are several features in these structures that are important for decoding bottom-up politics. On a local level, the focus of analysis is often placed on the size of personal networks, and the frequency of interactions. These dimensions have usually been analyzed using surveys that ask respondents to nominate discussion partners and use follow-up questions on the intensity of those interactions or the characteristics of discussants (Klofstad et al. 2009). Longitudinal analyses of these data have suggested declining trends in the size of discussion networks, which has been interpreted as a sign of weakening democracies (McPherson et al. 2006); this pattern, however has been contested for not taking into account the rising prominence of online social networks (Wang and Wellman 2010). Online interactions and the way in which they mediate communication have forced a shift in this theoretical discussion: they make the analysis of networks less dependent on surveys and questionnaires and more reliant on observational data.

In addition to size, another important dimension of social networks is their composition. The existence of diversity of opinions and disagreement in personal discussion networks has long been a focus for research (Huckfeldt et al. 2004), although the effects of disagreement on engagement and participation are still contentious issues. Online technologies are offering the means to test many of the assumptions made around self-selection and disagreement in networks. Experiments in Facebook, for instance, suggest that people are not that good at assessing the extent of disagreement that exists in their personal networks (Goel et al. 2010). This limits the extent to which people can self-select in groups of similar others because the assessment of how similar they are to friends or acquaintances is, often, inaccurate. Networks, in other words, always contain an amount of disagreement. The question—revisited in the next section—is whether online technologies are encouraging that disagreement or restricting it because of more polarized interactions.

The way in which personal networks connect to each other on the collective level is crucial to understanding the diffusion of behavior. Empirical research on this level of aggregation is not as rich as on personal discussion networks, given the difficulties of reconstructing networks for entire populations (a difficulty that some digital data alleviate, as the following sections will show). However, simulation studies that are used to overcome the lack of empirical data show that the structure of networks has a significant impact on chain reactions in, for instance, the decision to vote (Fowler 2005). The average degree (i.e. the number of contacts or discussants actors have in their local networks); the amount of local transitivity or clustering (i.e. the tendency of one's contacts to be connected to each other); and the existence of bridges (i.e. shortcuts connecting local networks that would be far apart otherwise) are all relevant structural properties when it comes to facilitating diffusion in a population.

That these features are important is not surprising: they are the properties that make networks small, a phenomenon that has been shown to have an impact on a wide range of collective dynamics (Watts 2004). These ideas are relevant because they link research on political networks back to the original study on the two-step flow of information. In particular, analyzing the structure of networks allows revisiting the question of where opinion leaders fall in the crossroads of connections. As explained above, the two-step flow model presumes that opinion leaders influence other people; networks allow tracing back the chains of influence and analyzing the relative position of some leaders compared to other leaders and to their followers.

Network dynamics are relevant not only because they affect individual decisions and practices but also because they shape collective outcomes: these can take the form of more votes on the aggregate or more people joining a political demonstration. Networks are instrumental not only in recruiting voters but also participants to political protests (Diani and McAdam 2003). Interpersonal connections activate chain reactions that might end up reaching a critical mass, on which collective action depends (Marwell and Oliver 1993). Every successful diffusion process has a point of no return, and networks—by making decisions interdependent—facilitate reaching that point beyond which diffusion becomes self-sustaining (Granovetter 1978). In the context of decentralized networks, initiating a chain reaction (to, say, recruit protesters) relies on the decision of specific individuals; but making that chain reach a large number of people is not in the hands of any of them: chains are shaped by the network position of those who decide to follow, and the position of those who follow the followers, and so on.

According to the network approach, there are three elements involved in a diffusion process. The first is sequential decision making: actors can see what other actors did before them, as when potential protesters check how many others are already demonstrating on the streets. The second element refers to the activation of thresholds, which happens when actors register that a sufficiently large number of people have already joined the collective effort: the leaders of a movement are driven by an intrinsic motivation to join first (so their thresholds are low), whereas the followers will only join once they see many others already active (so their thresholds are high). The third element are chain reactions: they are driven by sequential decisions and by how networks channel influence, which is similar to a domino effect; cumulative effects in the form of positive feedback loops make the rest of the process unfold (Schelling 1978: chapter 3). It is because of these three elements that networks provide the structure and the muscle of bottom-up politics: they are channels for the diffusion of information and behavior, but they also trigger mechanisms (i.e. threshold activation, chain reactions, cumulative effects) that amplify the impact of every individual action.

## Research on Online Social Networks

The previous section identified the mechanisms that make networks important mediators of grassroots politics. There are still, however many open questions about how they operate in the real world: networks are constantly changing and, with them, the position of opinion leaders and the position of their followers. Digital data are helping us understand the empirical intricacies of those mechanisms because they offer a higher resolution lens to observe social interactions (Lazer et al. 2009; Watts 2007). Recent studies illustrate the benefits of working with better data to analyze the three dimensions considered in the previous section: *social influence, information diffusion*, and *tipping points* as activated by interactions in networks.

Discussions on how online networks mediate social influence have often centered on the dangers of polarization—especially given the ability to self-select and personalize exposure to information that digital technologies afford by design (Sunstein 2007). This argument suggests that online networks can only amplify preconceptions and radicalize positions, undermining as a result a fundamental component of democracies: to have opinions and values challenged by those who think differently. The now classic example of ideological polarization in the blogosphere (Adamic and Glance 2005) has often been cited as evidence supporting this type of argument (which, up to that point, mostly relied on technological determinism). Other empirical studies soon followed to show that online social networks are biased towards the same old professional elites (Hindman 2009), and to confirm polarization using different subsets of the blogosphere (Baum and Groeling 2008; Hargittai et al. 2008). This line of research arrived to water down early optimistic claims of how digital technologies would transform political freedoms and empower individuals; it suggested that the concentration and polarization dynamics that shape offline politics are also leaving an imprint on online interactions.

More recent research on political talk in social networking sites, however, casts doubts on the polarization hypothesis: it shows that the extent of polarization depends on how communication networks are reconstructed, and that some users successfully provoke interactions across ideological divides (Conover et al. 2011). This is illuminating because it highlights the importance of operationalization: research on polarization in the blogosphere, for instance, does not often sample moderate or independent blogs, and these might have offered the middle ground where discussions from both sides of the divide converged. Research comparing segregation levels in online and offline news consumption, on the other hand, also finds no evidence that the Internet is becoming more polarized over time (Gentzkow and Shapiro 2011); instead, the evidence suggests that Internet news consumers with homogenous news diets are the exception: ideological segregation on the Web is low in absolute terms and significantly lower than offline segregation. In brief, it is by no means clear that online discussions and information exposure is more polarized today than it was before the Internet created venues for most public interactions.

The same technological determinism that prevailed in incipient discussions of polarization in online social networks applies also to claims about diffusion. Much in the same way as a technology that allows filtering does not necessarily increase the levels of polarization, networks that allow a fast diffusion of information do not necessarily lead to more cascades. Most case studies analyzing the virality of content or the rapid effervescence of collective action (Castells 2009: chapter 5) are based on success stories that, when put in context, emerge as the lucky outliers. Research with large-scale data, which reduce the effects of sample bias by including both failed and successful instances of diffusion, has shown that global information cascades occur only as a small proportion of all initiated cascades (Goel et al. 2012). These findings, replicated using different datasets and platforms, beg the following question: if online social networks are, by virtue of their structural properties, very efficient in transmitting information, but only occasionally give rise to information diffusion on a global scale, what explains those successful chain reactions? What happens in the rare circumstances when cascades grow large?

Network structure alone does not offer a set of sufficient conditions to answer those questions: content also matters. Research suggests that the domain of the information being diffused (i.e. politics versus entertainment, Romero et al. 2011) or the emotions triggered by that information (Berger and Milkman 2012) are also relevant factors in explaining the extent to which information spreads. Cascades are context-dependent and they are not driven by technology, although technology makes them grow faster—when they happen to grow.

Returning to the two-step flow of information hypothesis, research in online social networks has revealed that it is difficult to identify a subset of individuals who can be labeled as opinion leaders in terms of their demographics; however, they tend to have larger networks (Bakshy et al. 2011; Sun et al. 2009). The identification of opinion leaders is not independent of how "influence" is made operational, an empirical constraint that the next section will revisit. In the case of Twitter, for instance, possibilities include using the number of followers, the number of retweets (RTs) or the number of mentions as proxies to influence (Cha et al. 2010). Each of these alternative ways of measuring the influence of a given user offers different approximations to the same set of people and to the different roles they play in specific information contexts.

These and other recent studies confirm the idea formulated in early research on social influence: that individuals might be leaders in one domain but not in others. This implies that, depending on interests and the diversity of those interests, people will often act as followers and occasionally as leaders (Katz 1957). Because of this, the set of Twitter users following an opinion leader are even more important in the process of information diffusion than the leaders: in the end, leaders can only exert their influence if they have a contingent of followers who, with their actions, will help cascades grow large. The way in which these dynamics unfold in online social networks is important for the political process because they determine (a) who gets exposed to what information; and (b) how diffusion might spillover and shape offline behavior. The following section explores in more detail the way in which social networks can be measured and reconstructed using online communication, and why these methods affect the way in which we can address theoretical questions related to bottom-up politics.

## Measuring Online Social Networks

Many of the theoretical questions discussed in the previous sections are very dependent on how network data are collected and analyzed. Digital technologies offer broader and richer observations of how people communicate and interact, but they also add peculiarities to the data. This section summarizes a few of the measurement issues intrinsic to online networks with the help of one concrete example: political communication around the Occupy campaign on Twitter. Online communication has facilitated the emergence of global activism (Bennett 2003), but the formation of transnational networks, or the extent to which they can really be called "global," are questions that can now be assessed analysing the communication patterns of activists. These patterns can shed light into the structural properties of their decentralized organization (to identify, for instance, prominent actors), and into the dynamics of protest communication (which changes over time as events take place). Digital data are more granular than traditional sources of information like questionnaires or yearbooks tracking information at the level of organizations; but they require a careful collection and manipulation strategy in line with the theoretical aims—in this case, answer the question of how a social movement organizes on an international scale.

The process of collecting data from digital sources is a topic of its own that lies beyond the scope of this chapter (a good starting point is Hansen et al. 2011). Assuming that a sample of Twitter messages has already been collected—in this case containing variations of the hashtag #Occupy*—the question is how to use the sample to reconstruct the network of communication amongst protesters. Hashtags are labels self-assigned by users to identify streams of information that are relevant to particular issues. In this case, the selected hashtags track information relevant to the political movement that started in New York in September of 2011 and grew shortly afterwards to attain global awareness.

There are different ways of reconstructing communication networks using a sample of Twitter messages. Extracting the unique identifier of the authors sending messages, and crawling their local networks, allows mapping the global structure of who follows whom. This network creates the basic layer of interaction in the Twitter platform. On top of this structure, users can create more direct (and fluid) communication channels by mentioning other users in their messages. This network can be reconstructed using the @handle convention, which targets people by means of their username: every time a user mentions another user in a message, a directed link is formed between the two. Users can also help broadcast some of the messages they are exposed to via RTs, which allow reposting a message previously published by some other user; again, when a user RTs a message, a directed connection is created with the user who posted it first.

The networks formed by these two conversational conventions (RTs and mentions) are embedded in the same underlying structure of users following or being followed, but these networks have a different structure and allow different types of information flow. The analysis of political discussions introduced above, for instance, finds evidence of polarization in the network formed by RTs, but not in the network formed by @mentions (Conover et al. 2011). This suggests that Twitter users employ these conventions for different purposes: they are more likely to broadcast information of like-minded users, but they engage in discussions (as approximated via mentions) with users on the other side of the divide. These differences in communication flow would have gone unnoticed had the researchers focused on just one of the three possible networks.

Likewise, depending on the research question at hand, one level of analysis might be more meaningful than the others. The network formed by @mentions, for instance, is more relevant than the network formed by followers if the quest is to identify the users who are key in the diffusion of specific information, like messages related to a political protest (González-Bailón et al. 2013; González-Bailón et al. 2011). The network of followers creates the opportunity for information exchange (i.e. it opens the basic infrastructure for information diffusion), but interactions through message exchange create the streams of information that are relevant for a given political mobilization.

In the context of the Occupy campaign, there is yet a fourth way of reconstructing networks, namely by using the meta-information contained in the hashtags. Many hashtags used in the campaign are associated to cities as in #OccupyWallStreet for New York or #OccupyLSX for London. When any two of these hashtags are used in the same Twitter message, an implicit connection is created across cities: at the very least, the joint use of hashtags indicates that the message is relevant for the groups mobilized in the referenced cities. Using this meta-information, a spatial network of protest activity can be reconstructed, as illustrated by the map in Figure 13.1.

The network in Figure 13.1 can be disaggregated by looking at the actual individuals who sent those messages and their connections in the following/ follower structure (or in the @mentions or the RTs networks). This would

**Figure 13.1** Spatial communication network of the Occupy Campaign
*Note:* links between cities are based on "Occupy*" hashtags with an explicit location reference in the tag (i.e., #OccupyWallStreet for New York or #OccupyLSX for London); a link between locations was created when the hashtags were co-used in the same tweet. Darker lines indicate more messages. The data are aggregated for the time period April 30 to May 30, 2012, and are based on a sample of ~ 255,000 messages containing the hashtag "#occupy*" (only a subset of these messages used jointly two or more location-based tags). The pairs of cities most often co-mentioned are New York—Washington, Ottawa—Toronto, and Los Angeles—San Francisco. Thanks to Ning Wang for his work in collecting the data and drawing the map as part of the Oxford Internet Institute's project *Leaders and Followers in Online Activism*.

allow identifying the users who act as brokers, that is, those who link local groups and information flows to the international campaign and communication network. Which of all these possibilities offers the most appropriate reconstruction of the communication patterns driving the Occupy campaign is an empirical question, and it depends on the actual theoretical questions motivating the study: Is spatial diffusion the dimension of interest? Is it the dynamics of recruitment into the campaign? Is it engagement in protest activity over time? This section does not aim to answer these questions; instead, it aims to show that there are several ways in which we can measure online social networks, and that each illuminates a different aspect of grassroots or bottom-up politics.

This flexibility is not specific to Twitter data. Platforms like Facebook also allow different network layers to be reconstructed for the same set of users: in addition to the basic friendship ties, relationships can be assessed using posting behavior on walls or the tags applied to the same pictures (Lewis et al. 2008). Access to these data is often restricted and there are many privacy issues to take into consideration, but the point is that online interactions offer many ways of approximating communication networks, or how they change in different information domains and social contexts. This empirical versatility can only enrich our theories of why networks matter for the emergence of the collective dynamics that are relevant for grassroots politics.

## Conclusions

This chapter has used the theoretical insights drawn from early mass media and political communication research to assess a few claims about online social networks and how they mediate bottom-up politics. As argued in the introduction, this form of political participation takes place outside institutional channels, and does not rely on the coordinating power of any hierarchical organization; it relies, instead, on the collective dynamics that emerge from self-organized networks of communication. These networks are particularly important for grassroots initiatives mediated by Internet technologies. To explain why networks matter, this chapter has examined explanatory mechanisms on three dimensions: social influence, information diffusion, and critical mass dynamics (when global cascades are generated). These three dimensions are relevant for bottom-up politics because self-organization without a central authority relies on the activation of mechanisms in each of these levels—the network mechanisms discussed above are not specific to online networks, but they are potentially more efficient and scalable online.

In order to demystify common assumptions about how online social networks operate, this chapter has revised recent empirical evidence suggesting that polarization and self-selection are not necessarily higher online; that discussion networks are likely to contain disagreement (even when there is self-selection); and that even though online networks have the structural properties to facilitate a fast diffusion of information, cascades mobilizing a large number of people are still exceptional: they have been shown to be the exception rather than the rule across a number of online platforms. In addition, this chapter has also claimed that the identification of leaders and followers in online networks very much depends on how those networks are constructed. Leaders and followers swap roles in different information domains, and those who act as followers (and their position in the network) might turn out to be more relevant to explain diffusion: once a chain is started, it is followers who make chain reactions continue and grow.

The answer to the original question with which this chapter started (how do online social networks help political participation emerge from the bottom up?) requires a good understanding of how networks mediate—either to facilitate or hamper—influence, diffusion, and feedback effects. By presenting key evidence from recent research, this chapter has outlined the effects of these network mechanisms, and why they are important to understanding decentralized forms of political participation. Online social networks help people self-organize by activating mechanisms that rely on the connectivity of the network, and on the interdependence of their decisions and actions. The structure of social networks—whether they are forged online or offline—shapes the way in which dynamics like social influence or diffusion unfold. What online technologies have changed is the rate and breadth of information exposure: the boundaries of personal networks are less restrictive both in space and time, and the chains of influence they trigger can scale up faster.

More empirical research is needed connecting online networks (and their mechanisms) with grassroots and bottom-up politics. The link between online activity and offline behavior has just started to be investigated (Bond et al. 2012). It is also possible to measure the diversity of opinions expressed in networks using text-mining techniques, which can help identify the characteristics of the information that is more likely to be diffused. There is still much room for improvement, as we have only started to grasp how the study of online communication can help break new theoretical ground in the field of political participation. Our understanding of collective action and grassroots politics, however, will improve with the new data and approaches that Internet-mediated communication makes possible.

### ■ REFERENCES

Adamic, L. and Glance, N. S. (2005). "The Political Blogosphere and the 2004 U.S. Election: Divided They Blog." Paper presented at the 2nd Annual Workshop on *The Weblogging Ecosystem: Aggregation, Analysis and Dynamics*, WWW 2005, Japan.

Bakshy, E., Hofman, J. M., Mason, W. A., and Watts, D. J. (2011). "Everyone's an Influencer: Quantifying Influence on Twitter." Paper presented at the Proceeding of the Fourth International Conference on Web Search and Data Mining (WSDM 2011).

Baum, M. A. and Groeling, T. (2008). "New Media and the Polarization of American Political Discourse," *Political Communication*, 25: 345–365.

Berger, J. and Milkman, K. L. (2012). "What Makes Online Content Viral?" *Journal of Marketing Research*, 49(2): 192–205.

Bennett, W. L. (2003). "Communicating Global Activism: Strengths and Vulnerabilities of Networked Politics," *Information, Communication & Society*, 6: 143–168.

Bond, R. M., Fariss, C. J., Jones, J. J., Kramer, A. D. I., Marlow, C. A., Settle, J. E., and Fowler, J. H. (2012). "A 61-Million-Person Experiment in Social Influence and Political Mobilization," *Nature* 489: 295–298.

Castells, M. (2009). *Communication Power*. Oxford: Oxford University Press.

Cha, M., Haddadi, H., Benevenuto, F., and Gummadi, K. P. (2010). "Measuring User Influence in Twitter: The Million Follower Fallacy." Paper presented at the Proceedings of the International AAAI Conference on Weblogs and Social Media (ICWSM 2010).

Conover, M. D., Ratkiewicz, J., Francisco, M., Goncalves, B., Flammini, A., and Menczer, F. (2011). "Political Polarization on Twitter." Paper presented at the International Conference on Weblogs and Social Media (ICWSM'11).

Diani, M. and McAdam, D. (2003). *Social Movements and Networks: Relational Approaches to Collective Action*. Oxford: Oxford University Press.

Earl, J. and Kimport, K. (2011). *Digitally Enabled Social Change: Activism in the Internet Age*. Cambridge, MA: MIT Press.

Fowler, J. H. (2005). "Turnout in a Small World," in A. S. Zuckerman (ed.), *The Social Logic of Politics: Personal Networks as Contexts for Political Behavior*. Philadelphia, PA: Temple University Press.

Gentzkow, M. and Shapiro, J. M. (2011). "Ideological Segregation Online and Offline," *Quarterly Journal of Economics*, 126: 1799–1839.

Goel, S., Mason, W. A., and Watts, D. J. (2010). "Real and Perceived Attitude Agreement in Social Networks," *Journal of Personality and Social Psychology*, 99(4): 611–621.

Goel, S., Watts, D. J., and Goldstein, D. G. (2012). "The Structure of Online Diffusion Networks." *Proceedings of the 13th ACM Conference on Electronic Commerce (EC'12)*, New York: ACM Press, 623–638.

González-Bailón, S., Borge-Holthoefer, J., and Moreno, Y. (2013). "Broadcasters and Hidden Influentials in Online Protest Diffusion," *American Behavioral Scientist*, 57: 943–965.

González-Bailón, S., Borge-Holthoefer, J., Rivero, A., and Moreno, Y. (2011). "The Dynamics of Protest Recruitment through an Online Network," *Scientific Reports*, 1(197). doi: 10.1038/srep00197.

Granovetter, M. (1978). "Threshold Models of Collective Behavior," *American Journal of Sociology*, 83(6): 1420–1443.

Hansen, D., Shneiderman, B., and Smith, M. (2011). *Analyzing Social Media Networks with NodeXL*. Burlington, MA: Morgan Kaufmann.

Hargittai, E., Gallo, J., and Kane, M. (2008). "Cross-Ideological Discussions among Conservative and Liberal Bloggers," *Public Choice*, 134: 67–86.

Hindman, M. S. (2009). *The Myth of Digital Democracy*. Princeton, NJ: Princeton University Press.

Huckfeldt, R., Johnson, P. E., and Sprague, J. (2004). *Political Disagreement: The Survival of Diverse Opinions within Communication Networks*. New York: Cambridge University Press.

Karpf, D. (2012). *The MoveOn Effect: The Unexpected Transformation of American Political Advocacy*. New York: 0.

Katz, E. (1957). "The Two-Step Flow of Communication: An Up-to-Date Report on an Hypothesis," *Public Opinion Quarterly*, 21(1): 61–78.

Katz, E. and Lazarsfeld, P. (1955). *Personal Influence: The Part Played by People in the Flow of Mass Communications*. New York: Free Press.

Klofstad, C. A., McClurg, S. D., and Rolfe, M. (2009). "Measurement of Political Discussion Networks: A Comparison of Two 'Name Generator' Procedures," *Public Opinion Quarterly*, 73(3): 462–483.

Kreiss, D. (2012). *Taking Our Country Back: The Crafting of Networked Politics from Howard Dean to Barack Obama*. New York: Oxford University Press.

Lazarsfeld, P., Berelson, B., and Gaudet, H. (1948). *The People's Choice: How the Voter Makes Up His Mind in a Presidential Campaign*. New York: Columbia University Press.

Lazer, D., Pentland, A., Adamic, L., Aral, S., Barabási, A.-L., Brewer, D., et al. (2009). "Computational Social Science," *Science*, 323: 721–723.

Lewis, K., Kaufman, J., Gonzalez, M., Wimmer, A., and Christakis, N. A. (2008). "Tastes, Ties, and Time: A New Social Network Dataset Using Facebook.com," *Social Networks*, 30: 330–342.

Marwell, G. and Oliver, P. (1993). *The Critical Mass in Collective Action*. Cambridge: Cambridge University Press.

McPherson, M., Smith-Lovin, L., and Brashears, M. E. (2006). "Social Isolation in America: Changes in Core Discussion Networks over Two Decades," *American Sociological Review*, 71: 353–375.

Romero, D. M., Meeder, B., and Kleinberg, J. (2011). "Differences in the Mechanics of Information Diffusion Across Topics: Idioms, Political Hashtags, and Complex Contagion on Twitter." Paper presented at the International World Wide Web Conference, Hyderabad, India.

Schelling, T. C. (1978). *Micromotives and Macrobehavior*. London: Norton.

Shirky, C. (2008). *Here Comes Everybody: The Power of Organizing Without Organizations*. New York: Allen Lane.

Sun, E., Rosenn, I., Marlow, C. A., and Lento, T. M. (2009). "Gesundheit! Modeling Contagion through Facebook News Feed." *Proceedings of the Third International Conference on Weblogs and Social Media, ICWSM'09*.

Sunstein, C. (2007). *Republic.com 2.0*. Princeton, NJ: Princeton University Press.

Wang, H. and Wellman, B. (2010). "Social Connectivity in America: Changes in Adult Friendship Network Size From 2002 to 2007," *American Behavioral Scientist*, 53(8): 1148–1169.

Watts, D. J. (2004). "The 'New' Science of Networks," *Annual Review of Sociology*, 30: 243–270.

Watts, D. J. (2007). "A Twenty-First Century Science," *Nature*, 445: 489.

Zuckerman, A. S. (ed.) (2005). *The Social Logic of Politics: Personal Networks as Contexts for Political Behavior*. Philadelphia, PA: Temple University Press.

# 14 Big Data and Collective Action

*Helen Margetts, Scott A. Hale, and Taha Yasseri*

## Introduction

Increasingly, since so much of political life takes place online, most mobilizations in pursuit of public goods include a digital element and some take place almost wholly online. Most contemporary collective action, therefore, leaves a digital trail. This trail may be harvested to generate big data: that is, large-scale, real-time transactional data of political behavior. This kind of data presents a new avenue for social science research, distinct from and complementary to the survey research methods that have dominated the field since the 1960s. As explored elsewhere in this volume, big data is receiving massive attention and interest across the corporate world and scientific research communities (Mayer-Schönberger and Cukier 2013). Yet the potential of this kind of data for understanding political behavior in general and the dynamics of collective action in particular, remains underexplored (Hale et al. 2013).

This chapter uses one example of Internet-based collective action—electronic petitioning—as a case study to illustrate the potential for big data analysis of political activity. First, we provide a short background on online collective action in general and e-petitions in particular, using previous political science research on political attention to hypothesize that online mobilizations will be characterized by long periods of stasis and short periods of rapid change. Second, we analyze a big data set of Internet-based mobilizations, generated from continual scraping of two electronic petition platforms operated by the UK government over seven years, to show patterns of growth and the distinctive characteristics of the mobilization curves of successful and unsuccessful petitions on both platforms. Third, we discuss the implications of the findings for the use of big data in research, policy, and design. In particular, the analysis reveals that most petitions fail, that petition growth occurs in rapid bursts followed by periods of stasis, and that the first days of a petition's life are critical to its long-term success.

# Background

As discussed in Chapter 13, "Online Networks and Bottom-Up Politics," the 21st century has seen a prominent role for the Internet in collective action, from the dramatic events in authoritarian states of the Arab Spring, to a series of protests, demonstrations, and social backlash against austerity-driven cutbacks and state retrenchment in liberal democracies facing the consequences of the financial crash of 2008. Researchers have started to use innovative methods involving data mining to explore the spread and distribution of mobilizations across online social networks (see, for example, Ackland and Gibson 2006; Gonzalez Bailon et al. 2011; Aral and Walker 2011).

Methodologies of this kind open up new possibilities for political science research. As collective action moves online, it leaves a digital imprint, which can be harvested to provide what is now commonly known as "big data," a transactional audit trail of political participation. Data like this represents a shift for social science research into political behavior, which has traditionally rested on survey data, at least for any kind of political participation other than voting in elections. Big data is distinct from survey data in that it is real-time transactional data based on what people actually did, rather than what they think they did, or think they might do. It typically represents some kind of entire population, without the need to take a representative sample. Some commentators have even argued that such data renders the traditional methods of social science (e.g. sample surveys and in-depth interviews) dated in terms of understanding the social world, and represents a "coming crisis" for empirical sociology (Savage and Burrows 2007).

Big data represents an opportunity for social science research but also presents significant challenges. Transactional data often lacks demographic detail, and we do not know where people came from to any one interaction nor to where they go after the interaction. Therefore, it is often difficult to match up online activities across different platforms and to identify the underlying factors influencing behavior, such as age, income, gender, or personality. Similarly, while big data often represents the whole population of an online platform (e.g. all users filing electronic petitions to the government), the data usually sheds no light on the individuals missing from the set or the importance of these individuals (e.g. citizens without Internet access filing paper petitions). One typical definition of big data—datasets that are too large to be manipulated in a normal desktop computing environment—gives a clue to the technical challenges inherent in storing and analyzing them, which can be huge. Big data also introduces all kinds of ethical challenges into social science research: it may be collected unobtrusively, but that means that it has also been collected without explicit consent, in contrast to survey data for which rigorous ethical guidelines have been developed over decades. If the researcher does manage to attach demographic detail, then issues of privacy and data protection arise. The potential payoffs of overcoming these challenges are great: such data has rarely been available to social science researchers before the current decade, and may lead to new insights and theoretical developments.

The big data presented here relate to signing petitions to bring about policy change, which has long been among the more popular political activities. Petitioning is the collective act that people are most likely to undertake outside voting (Parry et al. 1992). Although the relatively low costs of signing a petition means that this act always appears low down in the ladder or scale of participation articulated by early scholars (such as Arnstein 1969; Almond and Verba 1961; Parry et al. 1992), it clearly falls within the category of collective action geared at the securing of public goods. As well as the political aim of bringing about policy change, various social benefits have been ascribed to the act of petitioning, such as the reinforcement of civic mindedness (Whyte et al. 2005). Petitioning moved online with the development of e-petition platforms as used by both governments and NGOs such as Avaaz and 38 Degrees, part of a growing portfolio of Internet-based democratic innovations (Smith 2009) that have received accolades for their democratic contribution (Escher 2011; Chadwick 2012). E-petitions are created, disseminated, circulated, and presented online, and although policy makers may discuss responses in offline contexts, such responses are usually disseminated online. So they are interesting examples of mobilizations with strong online imprints, which include the entire transaction history for both successful and unsuccessful mobilizations. The number of signatures on a single petition over time creates a unique mobilization curve showing how the petition grew over time. The data we present here makes it possible to look at differences in these patterns of growth in the 30,000 mobilization curves. We can then start to identify the distinctive characteristics of those mobilizations that succeed and those that fail with our digital hindsight. This is typical big data, of a kind which has not been used to study petitioning before: Jungherr and Jurgens (2010) used a smaller dataset to illustrate the viability of a big data (or computational social science) approach, but other studies of electronic petition platforms have used surveys (Lindner and Riehm 2011) or more qualitative approaches (Wright 2012).

So what would we hypothesize about petition growth curves? A possible hypothesis may be derived from previous research on agenda-setting in political systems. The most well-known model of how policy attention proceeds in a liberal democracy is that of "punctuated equilibrium," developed by the US authors Baumgartner and Jones and their "Policy Agendas" programme of research (see<www.policyagendas.org>; Baumgartner and Jones 1993; Baumgartner et al. 2006, 2009). The theory argues that policy attention to any issue will remain in long periods of stasis where little change occurs. Where issues do hit the policy agenda, it will be because some event has "punctuated" the equilibrium: all eyes (including the media, public opinion, interest groups, and politicians concerned) turn to the issue, money is spent, institutions are created, and policy change occurs (John and Margetts 2003; Baumgartner and Jones 1993; Jones and Baumgartner 2005). The theory of punctuated equilibria is multi-faceted and has been illustrated by a range of empirical data across policy areas and within different dimensions of attention, such as public opinion, budgetary change, and congressional attention (Baumgartner and Jones 2005), and in various countries, including the UK (John and Margetts 2003). Baumgartner and Jones do not discuss Internet-related activity to any great degree; however, we might hypothesize that the pattern of mobilizations around a petition would proceed in a similar way, thereby contributing to the same sort of issue attention cycle that has been observed many times over in agenda-setting research. Such a model would predict that the distribution of daily changes in attention would be leptokurtic. Leptokurtic distributions have a small number of large changes and a large number of very small changes, rather than the bell-shaped curve of a normal distribution. Given the scale-free characteristics and heavy-tailed distributions that characterize so much of Internet-based networks (Barabasi 2005) and fall into the leptokurtic class of probability distributions (Baumgartner et al. 2009), this hypothesis seems highly reasonable.

## Generating and Analyzing Big Data on Petitions

The big data presented here were generated from two e-petition platforms of the UK government. The first site was created by the social enterprise MySociety on the No. 10 Downing Street website in 2006 and ran until 2011, when it was closed by the incoming Coalition government. Over the course of its lifetime the site received more than 8 million signatures from over 5 million unique email addresses, a substantive subset of the UK population,[1] and some of these petitions had high policy impact, notably one against the Labour administration's proposed road pricing policy, which officials admitted to one of the authors of this chapter played a role in getting the policy scrapped. A new site with a different format was launched in 2011 by the Cabinet Office on the central government portal (see www.gov.uk).

To generate the data we accessed the earlier site (petitions.number10.gov. uk) daily from February 2009 until March 2011, when the site closed, with an automated script. Each day, the number of overall signatures to date on each

---

[1] <http://www.mysociety.org/projects/no10-petitions-website> (accessed July 13, 2013).

active petition was recorded. To overcome the ethical challenges associated with big data noted above, we recorded only the numbers of signatures and did not record the names of any signatories. In addition, the name of the petition, the text of the petition, the launch date of the petition, and the category of the petition were recorded. Overall, 8,326 unique petitions were tracked from the earlier site, representing all active, publicly available petitions at any point during the study. When the new site was launched in August 2011, we set the automatic script to scrape it every hour, recording the same details as the previous site. So our second dataset contains hourly data points for all the petitions submitted to the new site from August 5, 2011 to February 22, 2013 (a total of 19,789 petitions at the time of this analysis). Hourly instead of daily scraping offers the possibility of a more fine-grained analysis of the earliest hours of a petition.

The two sites ran under different policies for how the government would respond to petitions, offering different benchmarks for a petition gaining some measure of success. For the No. 10 Downing Street site, prospective petitioners were told that if their petition achieved 500 signatures, they would receive an official response. There were no other official measures of success, although one petition (the petition against road pricing noted above) did succeed in raising over one million signatures, which previous research has identified as a possible tipping point for mobilizations (Margetts et al. 2011). For the Cabinet Office site, the bar for an official response is unclear from the site, although the majority of petitions that have over 10,000 signatures do receive a response with the prefix "As this e-petition has received more than 10,000 signatures, the relevant Government department have provided the following response." More importantly, in the early days of the coalition administration, David Cameron promised that petitions obtaining more than 100,000 signatures would generate a parliamentary debate on the issue raised by the petition. All these information cues will have acted as possible drivers on individuals considering whether to sign a petition, and for this reason, we analyze the two datasets separately.

## Most Petitions Fail

The results from both datasets show just how few petitions actually attain success by any measure. First, we explored the data harvested from the first e-petitions site on the No. 10 Downing Street website, which produced a set of 8,326 unique petitions. The most immediate finding of interest was that 94 percent failed to obtain even the modest 500 signatures required to elicit an official response, the only measurable success indicator for the earlier site.

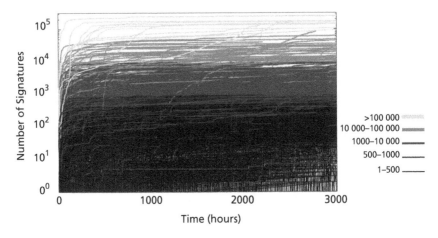

**Figure 14.1** Petition growth on Cabinet Office e-petitions site, 2011–13

*Note:* Graph shows N = 19,789 petitions, all created between August 5, 2011 and February 22, 2013. Note also that the y-axis uses a logarithmic scale and the lines are colored according to the final number of signatures each petition received.

The 500 signature mark seemed at first consideration a very low threshold that should have easily been passed.

Our second dataset tells the same story, suggesting that this finding may be generalized to other mobilizations rather than representing some characteristics of the No. 10 Downing Street platform. Figure 14.1 shows all petitions in this second dataset shaded by the level of success they achieved (10,000 for an official response, 100,000 for a parliamentary debate). The darkest blocks in the figure represent many thousands of petitions, while the single lines at the top denote the few that attained the stronger measures of success. Once again, it is immediately clear that the vast majority of petitions did not achieve any measure of success. Only 5 percent of petitions obtained the 500 signatures, which we calculated to compare with the previous dataset, and only 4 percent received 1,000. Only 0.7 percent attained the 10,000 signatures, which seems to be the bar for receiving some sort of official response, and only 0.1 percent attained the 100,000 required for a parliamentary debate.

Such a high failure rate illustrates both the completeness of the big data approach and the low costs for initiating a petition. First, the big data approach captures all petitions without requiring any minimum level of notoriety. It seems very likely that some of these petitions would not have made it into a more traditional dataset. Second, in online environments like e-petition platforms, the low costs of initiating a collective action mean that there are likely to be large numbers of unsuccessful mobilizations. And the finding that most mobilizations of this kind fail to take off in any sense chimes well with recent research into the spread or diffusion of initiatives across online networks. Goel et al. (2012), for example, analyze the diffusion patterns arising from online domains, ranging from networked games to microblogging services, and find that in all their seven cases, the vast majority of cascades are small, and are described by a handful of simple tree structures that terminate within one degree of an initial adopting seed. Even for the few large cascades that they observed, the bulk of adoptions take place within one degree of a few dominant individuals. An analysis of the network activity behind the petitions studied here seems likely to reveal a similar pattern.

## Petition Growth Patterns

Next, we tested our hypothesis that the distribution of daily change in signatures would be leptokurtic: that is, that most days the number of signatures on a petition will change very little, while on a very small number of days the number of signatures will change greatly. Such a finding would provide evidence that petitions grow in a lurching style characteristic of punctuated equilibria and accord with past work on policy change and agenda setting. To identify patterns in how petitions grow, the percentage change in new signatures was calculated each day for the No. 10 site. Most petitions had a long period of inactivity prior to their deadline date; so, to consider just how petitions grow, the data was truncated after the last signature on a petition, removing any final period of zero signature-per-day growth prior to the petition's deadline.

Leptokurtic distributions have a more acute peak close to the mean and larger tails. There is no statistical test to specifically classify a distribution as leptokurtic, but several tests in combination help demonstrate a distribution is leptokurtic (see John and Margetts 2003 for a discussion). The most rigorous test is the Shapiro-Wilk test (1965), which checks whether the points could possibly be drawn randomly from a normal distribution; leptokurtic distributions should reject the Shapiro-Wilk null hypothesis of normality. Visualizing the histogram and plotting a log-log graph, which should be nearly a straight line if changes are leptokurtic, provides further evidence of a leptokurtic distribution. Figure 14.2 shows a histogram of the percentage change in new signatures, adjusted so that the mean growth of each petition lies at zero. While most daily change is small, petition growth is punctuated by a few large changes. The distribution of growth is leptokurtic and strongly rejects the Shapiro-Wilk null hypothesis of normality with a W statistic of 0.17 translating to a p-value less than 0.000001. The distribution has a kurtosis score of 1,445 and a skewedness of 30.53, and also rejects the Kolmogorov-Smirnov test for a normal distribution ($p < 0.0001$). When we applied the same tests to the population of petitions that were successful in achieving 500 signatures (that is, excluding the unsuccessful ones), we found a similar leptokurtic distribution.

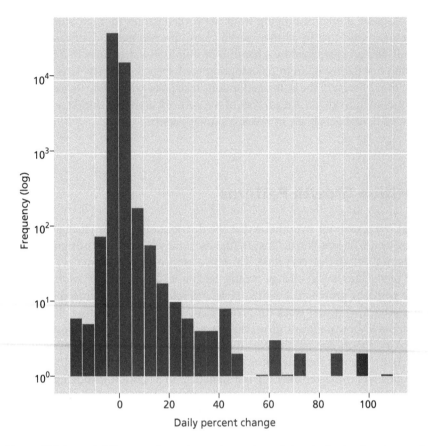

**Figure 14.2** Log of daily percentage change in number of signatories (centered around each petition's mean)

*Note:* Any final period in which petitions that gain no more signatures after a certain point before closing date has been removed from the daily percent change data (so the tallest bars do not include these "zero change" days).

## THE IMPORTANCE OF THE FIRST DAY

So, having identified punctuations, what can we say about where they are? The largest daily changes happened at the start in the life cycle of the petition. In the No. 10 dataset from the earlier site, nearly all petitions that succeeded in obtaining 500 signatures did so quickly. Successful petitions took a mean time of 8.4 days to reach 500 signatures, but a median time of only two days. In fact, 230 of the 533 successful petitions succeeded in obtaining 500 signatures on the day they were launched. Only a few petitions take a much longer time to reach the 500 signature mark: thirty-one petitions (6% of successful petitions) succeed after taking more than thirty days, and only five of these petitions reached the 500 signature mark after being active more than four months.

Looking at the distribution of the day on which the punctuation occurred, we see that all daily changes of more than 80 percent occurred in the first five days, and greater than 40 percent in the first eight days. Even for all changes over 40 percent, the median day is 1, and the mean is 2.2 and the third quartile is 1. Petitions are most active when they are first launched, and most petitions (presumably in the lack of outside stimulus) become digital dust after a couple of months despite typical deadlines of one year on the site.

This analysis shows that the early days of a petition are crucial, in particular the first day. Running a logit regression revealed that the number of signatures a petition received on its first day was among the most important factors in explaining the petition's success, and a linear regression showed that it was also an important factor in explaining the total number of signatures the petition receives during its lifetime. The number of other petitions started on the same day and, to a lesser extent, the category in which the petition was filed also had significant effects in explaining the total number of signatures. The day of the week a petition was launched was not significant (nor was there a significant difference between a weekday or a weekend start). Petitions tended to grow shortly after launch and then stop growing. This active period of growth for petitions has a mean length of fifty-seven days and a median length of twenty-seven days.

For our second dataset generated from the later, Cabinet Office petitions platform, we obtained similar results. Again, the first day was crucial to achieving any kind of success. Any petition receiving 100,000 signatures after three months had obtained an average of 3,000 within the first ten hours.

## How Does Collective Attention Decay?

We attempt to capture the characteristic of early rapid growth and decay that the data reveals, with a model of collective attention decay, drawing on Wu and Huberman (2007). In their model they calculate a novelty parameter relating to the rapidly diminishing novelty of news items on a news-sharing platform. Similarly, we sum up the rapidly diminishing growth rates of petitions by calculating an outreach factor which changes over time and dampens the fast initial growth that we observe (shown in Figure 14.3). This outreach factor summarizes the average ability of a petition to grow, and the relative growth of the logarithm of the number of signatures within an hour, averaged over the whole sample and shown as a function of adjusted time. Applied to the data from the Cabinet Office site, this shows that collective attention decays very fast indeed. After twenty-four hours, a petition's fate is virtually set (see Yasseri et al. 2014 for a full description of the model we used). If a petition hasn't captured public attention within its first day, it is highly unlikely to ever succeed.

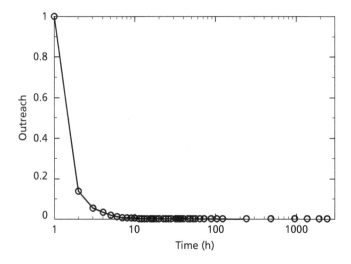

**Figure 14.3** Rate of change of collective attention paid to petitions created on the Cabinet Office site

## What Makes a Successful Petition?

Some issues (by far the minority) attract attention and very quickly gain a critical mass of petitioners and go on to attain some measure of success, before they can be are hit by the rapid decay of the outreach factor shown above. If such activity needs to take place on the day a petition is initiated, then one way is through the initiator of the petition disseminating the petition across their own contacts on online social networks (who may go on to disseminate it across their own), creating the foundations for viral spread. Petitioners who are successful in doing this are likely to be individuals who have larger than average online social networks or whose networks include other individual or organizational players with large-scale networks.

There may be other influences at work, connected to how potential signatories seeing a petition view the petition's likelihood of success. Over the past forty years, scholars have followed the sociologist Mark Granovetter in developing threshold models of mobilization, arguing that potential participants vary according to their threshold for participation (Granovetter 1978, 1983; Schelling 1978, 2006), and the distribution of thresholds will determine the success or otherwise of collective action. That is, some people will participate when very few other people have participated, some people will only participate when there are large numbers of other participants, and most people are somewhere in between. Under such a model, whether a petition can get enough signatures on the first day to avoid the average decay of the outreach factor will also depend on the existence of "starters," whose thresholds for participation are low (as well as those whose closeness to the petitioner has in this instance reduced their threshold for participation). These starters will act as a signal for people with higher thresholds and weaker ties to the petitioner to "follow" in signing the petition, thereby acting as a further signal for people with even higher thresholds to join. At some point, if the petition is successful, then the number of followers will reach critical mass, and attention to the mobilization will become widespread, breaking out of the petitioner's social network and gaining more general social media exposure and, ultimately, attention from traditional media outlets as well. In empirical studies using experimental methodologies, we have started to identify the existence of such starters with low thresholds, and to examine their distinctive personality characteristics, for example finding that those with extrovert personalities are more likely to be starters than those with high levels of introversion (Margetts et al. 2013). Similarly, we have identified possible levels at which evidence of critical mass will start to encourage people with higher thresholds to join (Margetts et al. 2011), finding it to be around one million other participants, for people considering whether to sign petitions on global issues. If these kind of models hold true for the context examined here, that is, that the majority of people are more likely to sign up for those petitions with the highest numbers of other signatories, then we might expect to find the sort of instability in online petitions as Salganik et al. (2006) observed for cultural markets, where people are more likely to prefer songs that they are told large numbers of other people like.

## Conclusions

The big data analyzed here has shown that most mobilizations around petitions fail to achieve any measure of success, even the modest measure of attaining 500 responses. It is likely that this finding could be generalized to other online mobilizations geared at collective goods, such as e-mail campaigns. It seems to fit the findings of recent work on diffusion patterns in online networks (Goel et al. 2012), suggesting that most online initiatives fail to attain any kind of viral spread. Internet-based platforms drastically reduce the start-up costs of mobilization, facilitating the existence of many initiatives that would not have got off the ground in an offline setting. So we would expect a high failure rate and this expectation is borne out by the findings presented here.

When growth does happen, it proceeds in rapid bursts followed by periods of stasis, leading to a leptokurtic distribution of daily change. Such a finding suggests that online mobilizations of the kind covered here (that is, aimed at attaining policy change) could play a role in the more general process of punctuated equilibria in policy change, as does public opinion more generally (for example, Jones and Baumgartner (2005) found a high correlation between public concern on an issue and Congressional attention). In the theory of punctuated equilibrium, the media plays a key role in terms of "lurching" from one issue to another and having a complex feedback relationship with public opinion to generate the instability that Baumgartner and Jones (1993, 2005) have modeled so extensively in previous research. The application of threshold models to the mobilizations around petitions, as discussed above, would suggest a similar source of instability from social media in collective action. But the sort of mobilizations we are looking at here are bubbling up relatively independently of the media, gaining media attention only when they obtain significantly high levels of support—the petition on road-pricing that successfully played a role in obtaining policy change, for example, received a great deal of media attention once it reached one million signatories. So, online petitions could be injecting an independent source of instability into the policy cycle. If mobilizations follow a pattern of very low levels of attention punctuated by occasional spurts which grow rapidly into full-scale mobilizations that merge with other elements of the political system to push policy change onto the agenda and the institutional landscape, then we can expect to see increasing turbulence in contemporary politics. Research that develops our understanding of the mechanics of this turbulence, for example by looking at the relationship between online collective action and policy change, will be important for scholars and policy makers alike as collective action continues to move into online settings.

We have established the importance of the first day in determining the success of petitions, which succeed quickly or not at all. This finding holds true across both versions of the UK government's e-petitions platform from which we have generated data, even though they had different features, including different measures of success. Initiators of petitions should pay attention to this result, maximizing their efforts on the first day. We cannot say from this data whether this finding could be generalized across other types of mobilization using other online platforms. In fact, we might hypothesize that it would vary across different types of social media platform, through variations in the outreach factor. And even within the general pattern we have observed, there may be differences in users' behavior depending on where they arrive at the site. For users starting at the homepage of the earlier No.10 Downing Street site, it was possible to view petitions overall or on a specific topic, and to sort petitions by the number of signatures or the date added. It was therefore easiest to look at petitions with the largest or smallest number of signatures and the oldest or newest petitions. On the newer Cabinet Office site, petitions can be sorted by signature or closing date, or viewed by government department, but not by topic. These variations may have shaped the likelihood of individual users actually finding a petition, and their incentives for signing it once they did so. In addition, we can expect different behavior from users of either site who arrive at the homepage (who may respond to these information cues by looking only at the newest petitions or the petitions with the most signatures contributing to the effects observed), or users following links shared via e-mail and social media, which would point to a specific petition that the contact was supporting (who may circumvent these information cues).

This chapter has, we hope, demonstrated the potential for big data approaches in political science research. The data we report here was automatically and non-obtrusively generated to provide a dataset of real-time transactional data of a kind that has rarely been available to political science researchers before. One of the aims of the research program of which this analysis forms a part is to develop the methods we have used to both harvest and analyze the data, addressing the technical, ethical, and logistical challenges of using big data in social science research. Such a task will require skills and expertise and conceptual approaches that span academic disciplines from both social science and the physical and life sciences. Of the authors of this chapter, one is a physicist, one a computer scientist, and one a political scientist. As big data is used more extensively in this kind of research, the ability to work across disciplines in this way will become increasingly important.

Future empirical work in this vein should also explore co-ordination with media coverage and mentions of the petitions on social networking sites (such as Facebook, YouTube, Google Search, and Twitter); we are now systematically gathering data on any mention of the petitions for which we have captured data across all these platforms. Much of the research work using big data generated from social media uses a single platform approach (particularly Twitter, from which data is relatively easy to retrieve), whereas any online activity tends to involve several. Looking carefully at the timing with which an issue gains attention in different parts of the political system, including the activist activities investigated here, may get us closer to establishing some sort of sequencing of attention and understanding the network activity behind the mobilizations. By identifying the influences of different types of social media platforms, such research can be of interest to those who initiate mobilizations, as well as those who study them. Designers of websites that involve civic engagement, such as e-petition sites, have various decisions to make, such as what kind of social information to provide (for example, about trending petitions or issues); whether participants are anonymous (as on the Cabinet Office site), or whether their names are made visible (as on the earlier No. 10 Downing St site and the German e-petitions platform), which has been shown to influence participation behavior (Margetts et al. 2013); and whether input from other social media platforms is incorporated into the petition site. Research of this kind, using big data across multiple platforms, can inform such design decisions in ways that maximize citizens' input to policy debates.

## ■ REFERENCES

Ackland, R. and Gibson, R. (2006). "Hyperlinks and Horizontal Political Communication on the WWW: The Untold Story of Parties Online." Mimeo., The Australian National University.

Almond, G. A. and Verba, S. (1961). *The Civic Culture*. Boston, MA: Little Brown.

Aral, S., and Walker, D. (2011). "Creating Social Contagion Through Viral Product Design: A Randomized Trial of Peer Influence in Networks," *Management Science*, 59(9): 1623–1639.

Arnstein, S. (1969). "A Ladder of Citizen Participation," *Journal of the American Institute of Planners*, 35(4): 216–224.

Barabasi, A-L (2005). *Linked*. New York: Penguin.

Baumgartner, F. and Jones, B. (1993). *Agendas and Instability in American Politics*. Chicago, IL: University of Chicago Press.

Baumgartner, F. R., Green-Pedersen, C., and Jones, B. (eds.) (2006). *Comparative Studies of Policy Agendas*. Special issue of the *Journal of European Public Policy*, 13(7).

Baumgartner, F. R. et al. (2009) "Punctuated Equilibrium in Comparative Perspective," *American Journal of Political Science*, 53(3): 603–620.

Chadwick, A. (2012). "Web 2.0: New Challenges for the Study of e-Democracy in an Era of Informational Exuberance," in S. Coleman and P. M. Shane (eds.), *Connecting Democracy: Online Consultation and the Flow of Political Communication*, Cambridge, MA: MIT Press, 45–75.

Escher, T. 2011. *Writetothem.com: Analysis of Users and Usage for UK Citizens Online Democracy*. London: My Society.

Goel, S. Watts, D., and Goldstein, D. (2012). "The Structure of Online Diffusion Networks," *Proceedings of the 13th ACM Conference on Electronic Commerce*: 623–638.

Gonzalez Bailon, S. Borge-Holthoefer, J. Rivero, A., and Moreno, Y. (2011). "The Dynamics of Protest Recruitment through an Online Network," *Scientific Reports*, 1(197).

Granovetter, M. (1978). "Threshold Models of Collective Behavior," *American Journal of Sociology*, 83(6): 1420–1443.

Granovetter, M. (1983). "Threshold Models of Diffusion and Collective Behavior," *Journal of Mathematical Sociology*, 9(3): 165–179.

Hale, S. A., Margetts, H., and Yasseri, T. (2013). Petition growth and success rates on the UK No. 10 Downing Street Website. In *Proceedings of Web Science: WebSci'13*. Paris.

John, P. and Margetts, H. (2003). "Policy Punctuations in the UK: Fluctuations and Equilibria in Central Government Expenditure since 1951." *Public Administration*, 81(3): 411–432. doi:10.1111/1467-9299.00354.

Jones, B. and Baumgartner, F. (2005) *The Politics of Attention: How Government Prioritizes Problems*. Chicago. IL: University of Chicago Press.

Jungherr, A. and Jurgens, A. (2010) "The Political Click: Political Participation through E-Petitions in Germany," *Policy and Internet*, 2(4): 131–165.

Lindner, R. and Riehm, U. (2011) "Broadening Participation Through E-Petitions? An Empirical Study of Petitions to the Germany Parliament," *Policy and Internet*, 3(1): 63–85.

Margetts, H. John, P., Escher, T., and Reissfelder, S. (2011). "Social Information and Political Participation on the Internet: An Experiment," *European Political Science Review*, 3(3): 321–344.

Margetts, H. John, P. Hale, S. A., and Reissfelder, S. (2013). "Leadership Without Leaders? Starters and Followers in Online Collective Action," *Political Studies*. doi: 10.1111/1467-9248.12075.

Mayer-Schönberger, V. and Cukier, K. (2013) *Big Data: A Revolution That Will Transform How We Live, Work and Think*. Boston, MA: Houghton Mifflin Harcourt.

Parry, G., Moyser, G., and Day, N. (1992). *Political Participation and Democracy in Britain*. Cambridge: Cambridge University Press.

Salganik, M., Dodds, P., and Watts, D. (2006). "Experimental Study of Inequality and Unpredictability in an Artificial Cultural Market," *Science*, 311(5762): 854–856.

Savage, M. and Burrows, R. (2007). "The Coming Crisis of Empirical Sociology," *Sociology*, 41(5): 885–899.

Schelling, T. C. (2006). *Micromotives and Macrobehavior*, 2nd edn. New York: W W Norton.

Smith, G. (2009). *Democratic Innovations: Designing Institutions for Citizen Participation*. Cambridge: Cambridge University Press

Whyte, A., Renton, A., and Macintosh, A. (2005). "e-Petitioning in Kingston and Bristol: Evaluation of e-Petitioning in the Local e-Democracy National Project," International Teledemocracy Centre, Napier University.

Wright, S. (2012) "Assessing (e-) Democratic Innovations: 'Democratic Goods' and Downing Street E-Petitions," *Journal of Information Technology and Politics*, 9: 453–470.

Wu, F. and Huberman, B. (2007) "Novelty and Collective Attention," *Proceedings of the National Academy of Sciences of the USA*, 104(45): 17599–17601.0

Yasseri, T., Hale, S. A., and Margetts, H. (2014) "Modeling the Rise in Internet-based Petitions." arXiv:1308.0239.

# 15 Empowering Citizens of the Internet Age: The Role of a Fifth Estate

*Elizabeth Dubois and William H. Dutton*

## Introduction

The ecology of actors and institutions defining Internet governance—the laws and policies governing the provision and use of the Internet—has been described as a mosaic (Dutton and Peltu 2007). It encompasses a wide variety of actors, and issues ranging from content regulation to standards for networking, such as the Web. In this mosaic, individual users of the Internet have seldom played a powerful role relative to that played by the representatives of governments, business and industry, and civil society, who are regularly engaged in setting up new institutional arrangements to govern the Internet, such as the Internet Governance Forum (IGF).

Public involvement in Internet governance has been limited for various reasons. One is a general early avoidance of Internet regulation at the national level by most liberal democratic nations (Eko 2008), who sought to encourage the diffusion of innovations around the Internet as a key technology-led economic development strategy. Second, most debate was focused on "technical" issues, such as on standards and naming and numbering issues that are esoteric for most of the public and relegated to a complex set of international institutions, such as the Internet Corporation for Assigned Names and Numbers (ICANN) and the IGF (e.g. Mueller 2002). These technical decisions can have real societal implications (DeNardis, chapter 22 this volume), but only a small community of individuals from business and civil society have followed these debates, given their complexity and perceived irrelevance to the concerns of users. Many other debates about global governance have been concerned with procedural and structural issues rather than the everyday experience of the individual or hard policy choices.

This is changing. Conversations within the Internet governance arena have been shifting as the technology becomes central to everyday life and work, and, simultaneously, individuals have begun to use the Internet as a tool to embed themselves in these new debates. One impetus is the emergence of national policies and legislation that could affect the everyday experience of the individual Internet user, such as by imposing stricter controls on the downloading of content. These policy changes have generated responses from members of the general public and particularly those individuals whom we call "networked individuals," who are enabled by the Internet to source their own information and networks and challenge policy makers.

Among an emerging set of examples of greater public participation in Internet governance is the public's response to legislation introduced in Canada, similar to legislative initiatives taken in the US, the UK, and other nations. This legislation, Bill C30, was tabled in the Canadian House of Commons in February 2012. C30 provides a case in point where networked individuals appeared to assert relatively greater communicative power in holding their government to account in response to legislation shaping Internet governance. It presents a useful case for understanding the potential for networked individuals to play a stronger role in Internet governance generally. Certainly in the case of C30, networked individuals appeared to demonstrate a powerful role in holding the government of the day more accountable in the area of Internet policy. We have described this role as the emergence of a "Fifth Estate," enabled by the Internet (Dutton 2007, 2009, 2010).

## The Fifth Estate

The concept of the Fifth Estate envisions the Internet as a platform through which networked individuals can perform a role in holding institutions such as the media and government more accountable. Networked individuals source information, independent of any single institution, using capabilities provided by search and social media. Users also create their own content in many forms, from posting photos on blogs to commenting on websites, providing even greater independence from other institutions and offering a mechanism whereby public opinion is directly expressed. This content can bypass or be amplified by the traditional mass media of the Fourth Estate, but in doing so it can fulfill many of the same functions of holding up the activities of government, business, and other institutions to the light of a networked public. As such, the Fifth Estate is not simply a new media, such as an adjunct to the news media, but a distributed array of networked individuals who use the Internet as a platform to source and distribute information to be used to challenge the media and play a potentially important political role, without the institutional foundations of the Fourth Estate. Composed of the distributed activities of one or many individuals acting on their own or collaboratively, but in a more decentralized network that crosses the boundaries of existing institutions, it is not equivalent to a social movement. Revolving sets of networked individuals can hold the leadership of social movements accountable like other institutional authorities in ways enabled by the Internet (Dutton 2009; Newman et al. 2012).

Did the engagement of networked individuals affect Bill C30? Do these patterns of engagement conform to what is described as a Fifth Estate? This chapter provides a case study of the politics of C30 in Canada that supports the emergence of a Fifth Estate and its relevance to Internet governance. The case cannot prove the idea of a Fifth Estate, but illustrates how networked individuals can exercise accountability in an important policy area, and therefore establishes the value of further research on this phenomenon.

## Conflicting Views on Internet Governance and Politics

The complex mosaic of actors shaping Internet governance is centered around the role of different institutional actors, such as the California-based ICANN and the International Telecommunication Union (ITU) based in Geneva. However, since 2010, individual citizens have appeared to be engaging in more issues related to Internet governance and regulation.

Indeed, networked individuals not necessarily linked to formal institutions, such as non-governmental organizations within civil society, contribute to a growing number of debates around particular issues of Internet governance. For example, the Internet "blackout" in response to the Stop Online Piracy Act (SOPA) was introduced in the US to enable law enforcement to better police the Internet. Wikipedia and other major sites on the Internet and Web protested against this anti-piracy law by blacking out all or parts of their websites (Kelion 2012). This is one illustration of individuals, and not only major Internet providers like Wikipedia, using their communicative power to influence Internet governance policy and its implementation.

Another example, which came just weeks after the SOPA blackout, is the Canadian Bill C30, a proposed piece of legislation entitled "An Act to enact the Investigating and Preventing Criminal Electronic Communications Act." Before C30 was tabled, some advanced copies noted the short title (most commonly used publicly) as "the Lawful Access Act." However, within an hour of tabling, a discrepancy in titles was observed by an opposition member and it was confirmed that the new short title, "Protecting Children from Internet Predators Act," was to be used instead. Though the government did not provide a clear explanation as to why the title was changed, opposition speculated the change was a communications strategy, rather than a decision made due to the substance of the policy (Schmidt and Fekete 2012). For example, in the officially retitled Bill C30, the terms "child" and "predator" appear only in the short title, and nowhere in the text of the Bill.

In response to C30, networked individuals used the Internet to engage in this Internet governance issue. They shifted the balance of power among institutions, arguably performing a "Fifth Estate" role in holding the government to account. The Internet allowed networked individuals to source and bring forward new information, and make connections among existing players, reframing the issue at hand, ultimately leading the government to abandon C30. Did networked individuals play a more powerful role, as a Fifth Estate, or was individual involvement in these debates ineffectual, as suggested by such competing perspectives as "slacktivism"?[1]

## The Approach: A Case Study of C30

We used a case study approach to critically examine whether networked individuals were able to influence governance debates. C30 is a relevant case since national policy appeared to develop in response to pressures from international Internet governance discussions and represents a unique instance of citizen engagement in Internet governance issues in Canada. Like any other single case study, results cannot be generalized to other cases. The value of the study lies in the ability to trace in detail the process by which a specific activity develops, such as the role of the Fifth Estate in shaping legislation related to Internet governance (Patton 2002; Agre 2002). This allows researchers to build an understanding of patterns of relationships and processes that might be validated by further research.

The case was first explored using news coverage and documents to track the course of events. We probed further as to the specific role of networked individuals through analysis of available content, such as Twitter posts, and two rounds of interviews with key participants and observers.[2] We needed to know how the activities of networked individuals fit into larger patterns of activities shaping the introduction and eventual demise of this legislation. A multi-phased approach increased confidence in the validity of observations and helped to draw causal inferences from the course of events (Ivankova et al. 2006; Lincoln and Guba 1985).

---

[1] The term "slacktivism" comes from a combination of "slacker" and "activism" and is sometimes referred to as "clictivism" with largely critical connotations (Morosov 2011).

[2] For a more detailed description of the case study methods, see Dubois and Dutton (2013).

**Table 15.1**  A Brief Chronology of Key Events Around Bill C30.

| | |
|---|---|
| Starting in late 1990s | Successive Liberal and Conservative minority governments put forward "lawful access" legislation without success |
| April 2011 | Conservative Party makes campaign promise to bring back lawful access legislation |
| May 2011 to February 2012 | OpenMedia hosts StopSpying Online Petition and coordinates other educational campaigns |
| February 13, 2012 | Introducing Bill C30, Min. Toews proclaims, "You can stand with us or with the child pornographers." |
| February 14, 2012 | Bill C30 is tabled in the House of Commons; initial advanced copies indicate short title "the Lawful Access Act," which is replaced with the short title, "An Act to Protect Children from Online Predators" |
| February 2012 | Online and offline response to C30; opposition from politicians, journalists, general public: (14th) Vikileaks, (16th) #TellVicEverything, and (18th) Anonymous threats |
| February 17, 2012 | House rises for regularly scheduled break; major amendments to C30 scheduled for consideration |
| May 15, 2012 | "Death" of Bill C30 announced by journalist |

# The Case: The Story of Bill C30

Bill C30: an Act to Protect Children from Online Predators, was tabled in the Canadian House of Commons by Public Safety Minister Vic Toews on February 14, 2012 (Table 15.1). The day before C30 was tabled, the Minister defended it against opposition parties' concerns. Arguing the bill enabled the government to protect citizens from harmful uses of the Internet, Toews infamously claimed, "You can stand with us or with the child pornographers." The statement gave rise to a range of public reactions. Opposition members of Parliament, members of the traditional media, experts from the private and public sector, including a Canadian non-profit grassroots organization focused on open and affordable Internet, called OpenMedia, and members of the general public, spoke out in opposition to the Minister's comments and to C30 itself. Importantly, OpenMedia had laid the groundwork for wider opposition to C30 both online, and offline, starting awareness and educational campaigns over eight months before C30 was even tabled. In addition to OpenMedia, online Twitter in particular was the site of many responses.

# The Political Run-Up to the Bill

Supporters of C30 claimed the Bill would update legislation to comply with international standards, providing law enforcement with tools needed to combat crime. Opponents claimed these new tools were, in fact, a mandate for surveillance without a legal warrant, a violation of privacy, and that they imposed unnecessary costs on telecommunication and Internet service providers.

The term "lawful access" is more commonly used to describe the kind of law C30 aimed to implement. In a legislative report on C30 the Library of Parliament define lawful access as "an investigative technique used by law enforcement agencies and national security agencies that involves intercepting private communications and seizing information where authorized by law" (Shaw and Valiquet 2012).

Legal experts argued that while policies that keep up with the Internet in order to protect citizens are needed, C30 failed to balance the citizen's right to privacy with law enforcement's ability to protect the public (Fraser 2012; Geist 2012). Moreover, no evidence that law enforcement agencies were at present denied access to information required to protect citizens existed (Geist 2012).

C30 was intended to provide law enforcement the investigative powers to combat computer and Internet-related crime. The first part of the Bill proposed a new law governing telecommunications service providers, requiring them to collect and store data and personal information of Internet users (subscriber name, address, phone number, email address, IP address, and local service provider identifier), and to provide this information to police or other law enforcement agencies when requested, even without a warrant. A second part called for amendments to the Criminal Code and other acts concerned with Internet communication and the modernization of some offenses, adapted to the Internet age, ranging from re-defining hate propaganda to dealing with the possession of a computer virus. The most controversial section involved the lack of a requirement for judicial oversight in order for data about users to be requested, stored, and accessed by law enforcement.

## Early Efforts to Prepare the Public

Prior to the introduction of this legislation, a non-partisan coalition of Canadians concerned with Internet regulation started an online "StopSpying Petition." OpenMedia, the organizing body, put forward a number of other actions aimed at increasing awareness and knowledge of what they branded the coming "surveillance bill." Over half a year before C30 was tabled, OpenMedia was using online tools to build a base of resistance against what they anticipated to be the lawful access policy, and its warrant-less access to subscriber information, which they described as "spying."

Despite opposition, the government tabled C30, re-framing it as a way to protect children and to provide police with the tools needed to keep Canadians safe. Two, apparently unforeseen, circumstances arose.

First, Minister Toews's comment that not to support C30 was to stand with the child pornographers, generated a swift response from politicians, journalists, bloggers, and members of the wider public. The statement attracted attention from many who felt they had legitimate concerns over surveillance. This response was prominent offline, such as debate within parliament, but it was the online reaction that generated the most media reaction. Second, the government's voting base was not happy with C30, seeing it as an affront to personal liberties and privacy rather than a way to crack down on crime (Ibbitson 2012a; 2012b).

Toews expected members of the opposition and left-leaning members of the press and general public to oppose the Bill. But he is unlikely to have expected the government's Conservative Party of Canada (CPC) supporters and right-of-center editorialists to question and voice their concerns with C30 through traditional media and online. Privacy commissioners, researchers, and others with technical and legal expertise also spoke out concerning the risks C30 presented, the potential problems, and the cost of its implementation.

## Online Response

The online response to C30 was immediate and significant in scale. First, a resurgence in the popularity of the StopSpying Petition hosted on the OpenMedia website emerged. Three other online initiatives became popular: Vikileaks, TellVicEverything, and Anonymous.

### VIKILEAKS

The Twitter account Vikileaks declared: "Vic wants to know about you. Let's get to know about Vic." Using public records from Toews's divorce proceedings, the anonymous tweeter made 140 character posts regularly for three days. On February 17, 2012 an *Ottawa Citizen* reporter uncovered that the IP address originated from the House of Commons by sending Vikileaks a unique url which was monitored. Soon afterwards a staff member of the Liberal Party of Canada (LPC) was identified as the creator of Vikileaks. A House of Commons Committee was called to review Vikileaks, and the Twitter account was shut down.

Vikileaks exemplified a networked individual using the Internet to access information the traditional media were not reporting, and disseminate that information with a political message. The micro-blogging style of Twitter and common use of "re-tweets" to re-post content others have created meant other individuals could easily share information coming from the Vikileaks account. Quickly Vikileaks' tweets became routinely posted, and the Vikileaks account itself gained over 8,000 followers in less than three days before shutting down. While the speed with which this information was shared is impressive, the action was criticized as "over the line" by the traditional media, as well as in parliament, on Twitter, and other websites. In the words of Foreign Affairs Minister John Baird it was "a nasty, dirty Internet trick" (Canada 2012). A Liberal politician, in an interview with the researcher, condemned Vikileaks as a "vicious attack."

## TELLVICEVERYTHING

On February 16, 2012, a second Twitter initiative became popular. A Canadian citizen concerned with C30, used the Twitter account "EnoughHarper" to create the hashtag #TellVicEverything. The logic was if Vic Toews wants access to our personal information, we will give it to him—all of it, including the mundane details of our lives. The hashtag, which served to link all related tweets, quickly became popular, trending globally on Twitter for a brief period and remaining as a top trending topic in Canada for two days. Tweets varied in topic. Some referenced the mundane details of life: "Dear @ToewsVic, I made these baked salmon-veggie bite thingies for lunch but they were just ok. Healthy tho. #tellVicEverything," while others were politically satirical, such as "Ooops! I think I accidentally deleted an email. Can I get your copy, @ToewsVic? #TellVicEverything." The goal, as the creator put it during an interview, was to "laugh Vic out." Journalists, politicians, campaigners, and bloggers joined in, tagging articles about C30 and the response, re-tweeting their favorite posts, and at times making posts of their own. It became viral for a short time, as a fun and inclusive way of presenting opposition.

## ANONYMOUS

The third online initiative came from hacker group "Anonymous" which, on February 18, 2012, posted a video to YouTube threatening Toews and the government if they did not drop C30 (see http://www.youtube.com/watch?v=OyOQFYeBIho). In contrast to the humorous #TellVicEverthing, the Anonymous message had a sinister and threatening tone. The computer-generated voice announced: "Mr. Toews you are now literally a joke in the eyes of the Internet, the Canadian public, and the world," and went on to warn "you will find yourself not only mocked but jobless and despised…Anonymous will not allow a politician who allows his citizens no secrets to have secrets of his own." Cleverly written with a clear message highlighting the role of Internet-enabled individuals, the video maintained the look and feel of an underground group. "You have underestimated the power of the Internet in the hands of the people," the voice said, a static headless photo as the only image in the entire video. "... Beneath this mask is more than flesh, beneath this mask there is an idea, Mr. Toews, and ideas are bulletproof," the voice concluded.

Upon uploading to YouTube the link was shared on Twitter and during the first two days nearly one quarter of all newspaper articles mentioning C30 in Canada also mentioned the Anonymous video (23.1% of articles on February 18, 25% of articles on February 19, 2012). Commentary relating to the threats was also common during television news broadcasts, in blogs, and elsewhere online. Anonymous continued to produce brief videos slowly leaking information about Toews, in the words of Anonymous "shining a light on [his] skeletons."

## The Aftermath of the Online Campaigns

By 15 February 2012 the Prime Minister announced major amendments to C30 would be considered. But later in the week, C30 was taken off the priority list and when members of Parliament returned to Ottawa a week later after a regularly scheduled break, few spoke of the Bill. On 15 May 2012, John Ibbitson published a piece titled "How the Toews-sponsored Internet surveillance bill quietly died" (2012a). Though the CPC responded claiming C30 was not dead, the House rose for the summer without further mention of C30.

## Reflecting on Key Patterns and Themes

OpenMedia helped establish and confirm opposition to legislation that would become known as the "surveillance bill." When C30 was tabled, a network of aware and educated individuals opposed to online surveillance was in place, apparently awaiting a spark. The fact that C30 was framed as a bill that combated child pornography may have been enough, but once Toews proclaimed "you stand with us or you stand with the child pornographers," he seemed to throw gas on the flames started by a series of online efforts.

A network of individuals opposed the legislation, united, not by institutionalized partisanship, but by opposition to increased surveillance of Internet use. These individuals were Internet users concerned that the proposed changes would affect their lives and the vitality of the Internet as a resource. They used the Internet strategically to oppose this legislation by harnessing their communicative power, enhanced by the Internet. Demonstrating the capacity to reject government framing of the bill, issues of child protection and crime became issues of surveillance and privacy. Though OpenMedia's organized and coordinated effort prior to the tabling of C30 is important, it is not clear it would have been as effective had not a large number of networked individuals picked up the call and both rallied behind the campaign and initiated other efforts to oppose C30. Many of the networked individuals had little to no contact with OpenMedia. None of the three core online initiatives were devised or formally supported by OpenMedia. This illustrates the degree to which the Fifth Estate is not a social or political movement, but the combined effort of networked individuals who source their own information and networks, enhancing their own communicative power.

The role of the Fifth Estate is most evident in the short-term actions of Vikileaks, TellVicEverything, and Anonymous. The strategy of Vikileaks was to find something people would talk about and repeat. The strategy of TellVicEverything was to find something people would talk about and repeat and be a part of. Finally, the strategy of Anonymous presumably was to find something with global recognition that people would talk about and repeat. While these three examples are only the most visible responses, as many other efforts existed, they show how a distributed group of networked individuals could provide new information, bringing in new participants with differing opinions to hold the government to account using multiple strategies and Internet application.

## The Significance of the Internet in Framing and Agenda-Setting[3]

A prevalent finding of media studies has been the importance of agenda-setting and the framing of issues by the media (McCombs 2004; McLeod and Detenber 1999). The core argument is that the media are effective at setting a list of priority issues, shaping what the public thinks about, though not determining what they think. C30 illustrates the significance of framing and agenda-setting, and the role networked individuals played in this political process, reconfiguring who took which side in the political conflict. As E. E. Schattschneider (1960) argued long ago, the outcome of the game of politics is shaped by the extent to

---

[3] This section builds on our other case studies (Huan et al. 2012).

which the spectators become involved and on what side they choose to join in. With this dynamic, the involvement of spectators can be changed by drawing the attention of more people to the conflict (agenda-setting), or redefining the issue (re-framing), which can lead some spectators to join a particular side or for some contestants to switch sides (Schattschneider 1960; Huan et al. 2013), such as when the minister lost members of his own party.

In the case of C30, the success of networked individuals was tied to their ability to challenge the official framing of the issues at stake. Moreover, it is clear that the CPC government itself sought to strategically reframe the issue from one of "lawful access"—where it had failed to gain a following—to one of child protection, seeking to enlist more support for their initiative. OpenMedia made use of an online petition, a mini-documentary, reports and analytics, and advertisement campaigns in order to establish and build a base of opponents to lawful access legislation and frame C30 as one concerned with surveillance and spying.

Rather than gathering support from citizens who valued a tough stance on crime, as the CPC may have hoped, networked individuals began to oppose the initiative on the grounds it was an invasion of privacy. This new spin on the issue, not "surveillance" nor "spying," but certainly in opposition to C30, engaged a larger audience which developed as networked individuals began to come into the game. In particular, CPC supporters became involved, but on the opposing side.

## The Distributed Bases of Networked Individuals

It is not clear if the role of networked individuals would have been sufficient if it were not for other bases of support within the media, government and opposition, and the general public. Networked individuals were able to source their own material, document and legitimate opposition from other quarters, and challenge the government. It is important to realize that networked individuals are not a single social movement, but a distributed set of individuals who choose to find information, enter debates, and support particular issues. For example, among the twenty-five most re-tweeted TellVicEverything posts over a seven-day sampling period, nine were made originally by politicians or journalists with seven others coming from accounts linked to either a legal expert or campaigner. Among the twenty-five most re-tweeted links, twelve were links to traditional media content. Further, among these, traditional media content linked to them was from a variety of sources, not necessarily with the highest expected visibility. This suggests that networked individuals used Twitter and the TellVicEverything hashtag to make information more visible and accessible across boundaries of time and space. Just as a wide range of individuals from all walks of life and across geographical boundaries might contribute to a Wikipedia article, so does a distributed group of networked individuals focus on an issue like C30.

In addition to bringing new information to light, networked individuals showed C30 was an important issue to many Canadians and thus worthy of traditional media attention. Further, as one campaigner interviewed claimed:

Twitter is useful because it takes the story and turns it into a joke but it keeps the story in the press for maybe another 8 hours, and I know it maybe sounds a little ridiculous but that's a big deal in the 24-hour news cycle. You can keep something going with a new angle. The media need something that's living, and if a story stops breathing the story's gone.

Other campaigners, bloggers, and politicians tended to agree, as one journalist clarified during an interview: "…did Twitter help keep the story alive? Sure, but the story was already pretty lively to begin with." In other words, the role of networked individuals is effective through their interaction with other political players, including complementarities with the government, media, and political parties. Of course, networked individuals come from these institutions as well as from the general public, business, industry, and civil society. The Fifth Estate is formed of individual efforts distributed across institutions for which the Internet has spanned boundaries.

The interaction among individuals involved in different initiatives is relevant. Vikileaks, TellVicEverything, and the Anonymous video, though separate acts initiated by different individuals/groups, affected one another. For example, among the 42,478 tweets collected for this case during a seven-day sampling period (February 17–23, 2012), the Vikileaks Twitter account was the third most replied to, OpenMedia's account was eighth, and an Anonymous account was fourteenth. In addition to referencing other acts through Twitter, comparison among campaigns was made in the traditional media, in blogs, and was also a theme in interviews conducted. Though the specific role of interaction among the separate initiatives was not targeted in the early stages of the case study, the importance of the relationships among networked individuals and these diverse, distributed initiatives became visible through the study.

# Clicktivism and the Modularization of Political Work

Why do networked individuals get involved in politics? Similar questions have been asked of participation in crowd sourcing generally, such as contributing to editing an article for Wikipedia or coding open-source software. One element in all these distributed collaborations is the degree to which tasks can be modularized, reducing costs of participation. The Internet and applications like the Web and micro-blogging, such as Twitter, allow campaigns to modularize tasks so they are relatively easy for people to complete, and are therefore capable of drawing a collective response. It takes only seconds to post a Twitter message with a particular hashtag.

Clicktivism is a theory that measures activist outcomes in number of hits involving tasks that can be enumerated (Bennet et al. 1999). Certainly, for all three initiatives most visible in the case of C30, the numbers of hits were impressive enough to be reported widely in the traditional media, but in particular TellVicEverything gained the most traction, in part due to its humor as well as its significance to the issue of privacy. Those who look negatively upon the clicktivist are comparing particular online activities to political movements or street protests, and diminishing their significance as "slacktivism" (Morozov 2011). Viewed from a Fifth Estate perspective, one reason online tweets and comments are beneficial is that they enable individuals to see that others have similar thoughts. Social comparison is a powerful psychological motivation and can fuel more online and offline activity.

## SUSTAINABILITY

Another potential limitation of online activity is that it is difficult to sustain over time. Online actions can be formed quickly, but also diminish rapidly without the institutional basis for sustaining their role (Dutton and Lin 2001). It is clear the C30 campaign demonstrated the base of support for public concern over privacy and surveillance, and that this base had the potential to be reactivated. Indeed, when the CPC contradicted journalist John Ibbitson's claim that C30 was dead in May 2012, the TellVicEverything hashtag witnessed a resurgence in popularity. All bloggers and campaigners interviewed agreed lawful access legislation would likely come back in some form and that #TellVicEverything and other online initiatives would likely serve as an enduring link connecting networked individuals who cared about Internet governance and privacy in Canada. Looked at differently, the lack of an institutional foundation means it is more difficult to stop the Fifth Estate of networked individuals distributed across society.

# Conclusions

The Fifth Estate relies on individuals' ability to use the Internet as a platform to collect and make use of information and connections and to turn that information and those connections into communicative power. They do this by harnessing affordances of the Internet—the speed, the ability to connect with people from many places, the ability to form a social bond without ever meeting face to face. By using the Internet to overcome barriers like time and geography, networked individuals bring new information, actors, and points of view to a given policy discussion/decision, that is, political conflict, which changes the balance of power.

In this case, citizens were uncharacteristically motivated to become engaged in a matter of Internet governance. Networked individuals became engaged in the debate over C30, recognizing surveillance and privacy as important issues affecting their lives as Internet users. Ultimately, this engagement affected the outcome of C30 which fell off the government agenda, but which could return, given the prominence of similar initiatives in other nations, such as the UK.[4] Related research has shown that the Fifth Estate has proven effective in shaping policy in other countries and across a range of issues, even outside the West, such as in China (Huan et al. 2012).

Networked individuals, in this case, used a number of Internet-enabled initiatives in order to both re-frame the debate around C30 and bring new players into the discussion. While the government also attempted to re-frame lawful access as an issue of crime and child protection, the opposition's framing of the issue as one of surveillance and privacy triumphed online and in traditional media. As notions of the Fifth Estate suggest, networked individuals were able to use the Internet in order to harness relatively greater communicative power.

While citizens have always been able to exert some level of communicative power, liberal democratic governance structures require citizens to relinquish a certain level of power to representative institutions like a parliament. Internet use today is not replacing those institutions with forms of direct democratic control, but it is allowing citizens to question the decisions of these institutions, provide input, and demand accountability. In other words, power is being checked and re-balanced, and with it the networked individual is becoming a player in public policy in new ways. In this chapter, we have described how Internet governance is being contested by those networked individuals who are intimately aware of the role of the Internet in their everyday lives and well informed about policy and government, and have described how they are able to do this because they are a distributed group of individuals empowered and coalesced through the Internet.

---

[4] The Data Communications Bill in the UK has been called a "snooper's charter" as it shares many features of C30, as does the US Stop Online Piracy Act (SOPA).

## ■ REFERENCES

Agre, P. (2002). "Real-time Politics: The Internet and the Political Process," *The Information Society*, 18(5): 311–331.

Canada (2012). House of Commons Debates, (Hon. Mr. Baird, CPC), 17 February: <http:// www.parl.gc.ca/housechamberbusiness/ChamberPublicationIndexSearch.aspx?arpist=s&ar pit=baird&arpidf=2012%2f02%2f17&arpidt=2012%2f02%2f18&arpid=True&arpij=False&a rpice=False&arpicl=&arpicpd=5396106&ps=Parl41Ses1&arpisb=Publication&arpirpp=10& arpibs=False&Language=E&Mode=1&Parl=41&Ses=1#Para2698318> (accessed September 10, 2012).

Bennett, D., Fielding, P., and Rockefeller, J. (1999), *The Net Effect: How Cyber-Advocacy is Changing the Political Landscape*. Merrifield, Va: e-advocates Press.

Dubois, E. and Dutton, W. H. (2013). "The Fifth Estate in Internet Governance: Collective Accountability of a Canadian Policy Initiative," *Revue française d'Etudes Américaines*, 134: 81–97.

Dutton, W. H. (2007). "Through the Network (of Networks)—the Fifth Estate," Inaugural lecture, Examination Schools, University of Oxford, 15 October, <http://webcast.oii.ox.ac.uk/?view= Webcast&ID=20071015_208> (accessed January 18, 2013).

Dutton, W. H. (2009). "The Fifth Estate Emerging through the Network of Networks," *Prometheus*, 27(1): 1–15.

Dutton, W. H. (2010). "The Fifth Estate: Democratic Social Accountability through the Emerging Network of Networks," in P. G. Nixon, V. N. Koutrakou, and R. Rawal (eds.), *Understanding E-Government in Europe: Issues and Challenges*. London: Routledge, 3–18.

Dutton, W. H. and Lin, W-Y. (2001). "Using the Web in the Democratic Process: The Web-orchestrated 'Stop the Overlay' Cyber-Campaign," *European Review: Journal of the Academia Europaea*, 9 (2): 185–199.

Dutton, W. H. and Peltu, M. (2007). "The Emerging Internet Governance Mosaic: Connecting the Pieces," *Information Polity*, 12: 63–81.

Eko, L. (2008). 'Internet Law and Regulation,' in W. Donsbach (ed.), *The International Encyclopedia of Communication*, Malden, MA: Blackwell.

Fraser, D. (2012). "The Hidden Gag Order in Bill C-30 (aka the lawful access bill)," Canadian Privacy Law Blog, <http://blog.privacylawyer.ca/2012/02/hidden-gag-order-in-bill-c-30-aka. html> (accessed September 10, 2012).

Geist, M. (2012). "Law Enforcement Renews Demand for Internet Surveillance Legislation," <http://www.michaelgeist.ca/tags/lawful+access/99999/4/0> (accessed September 10, 2012).

Huan, S., Dutton, W. H., and Shen, W. (2013). "The Semi-Sovereign Netizen: The Fifth Estate in China", pp. 43–58 in Nixon, P. G., Rawal, R., and Mercea, D. (eds.), Politics and the Internet in Comparative Context: Views from the Cloud, London: Routledge.

Ibbitson, J. (2012a). "How the Toews-Sponsored Internet Surveillance Bill Quietly Died," *Globe and Mail*, 15 May, <http://www.theglobeandmail.com/news/politics/how-the-toews-sponso red-internet-surveillance-bill-quietly-died/article4179310/> (accessed on 10 September 2012).

—— (2012b). "The Only Criticism Stephen Harper Listens to," *Globe and Mail*, May 16, <http:// www.theglobeandmail.com/news/politics/video-john-ibbitson-on-the-only-criticism-step hen-harper-listens-to/article4184556/?from=4179310> [video] (accessed September 10, 2012).

Ivankova, N. V., Creswell, J. W., and Stick, S. L. (2006). "Using Mixed-Methods Sequential Explanatory Design: From Theory to Practice," *Field Methods*, 18(1): 3–20.

Kelion, L. (2012), "Sopa: Sites Go Dark as Part of Anti-Piracy Law Protests," BBC News, January 18. <http://www.bbc.co.uk/news/technology-16612628> (accessed September 7, 2012).

Lincoln, Y. and Guba, E. (1985). *Naturalistic Inquiry*, Thousand Oaks, CA: Sage Publications.

McCombs, M. (2004). *Setting the Agenda: The Mass Media and Public Opinion*, Oxford: Polity.

McLeod, D. M. and Detenber, B. H. (1999). "Framing Effects of Television News Coverage of Social Protest," *Journal of Communication*, 49(3): 3–23.

Morozov, E. (2011). *Net Delusion*. London: Penguin Books.

Mueller, M. L. (2002). *Ruling the Root*. Cambridge, MA: MIT Press.

Newman, N., Dutton, W. H., and Blank, G. (2012). "Social Media in the Changing Ecology of News: The Fourth and Fifth Estates in Britain," *International Journal of Internet Science*, 7(1): 6–22.

Patton, M. (2002). *Qualitative Research and Evaluation Methods*. Thousand Oaks, CA: Sage Publications.

Schattschneider, E. E. (1960). *The Semi-Soveign People: A Realist's View of Democracy in America*. New York: Holt, Rinehart and Winston.

Schmidt, S. and Fekete, J. (2012). "Vic Toews will 'entertain amendments' to online surveillance bill," *National Post*, February 15. <http://news.nationalpost.com/2012/02/15/protecting-children-from-internet-predators-act-vic-toews/> (accessed on September 10, 2012).

Shaw, E. and Valiquet, D. (2012). "Bill C-30: An Act to enact the Investigating and Preventing Criminal Electronic Communications Act and to amend the Criminal Code and other Acts," Legislative Summary, Library of Parliament.

# Part IV

# Networked Businesses, Industries, and Economics

# 16 Scarcity of Attention for a Medium of Abundance: An Economic Perspective

*Greg Taylor*

## Scarcity in the Age of Digital Distribution

A conservative estimate puts the total number of web pages at around 7.5 billion so that, viewing one page every second, it would take at least 230 years to see the entire extant Web. YouTube receives over 72 hours of new video content every minute; one would need to watch 4,320 concurrent video streams merely to keep pace with this rate of upload. Wikipedia articles (of which there are 4 million in the English language), tweets (400 million posted daily), and emails (294 billion sent each day) similarly proliferate on a scale that far outstrips our capacity to consume them. In short, the new abundance of information is met with a scarcity of the attention needed to consume it.[1] Such is the shortage of attention that some advertisers pay in excess of $100 for access to a single consumer's "eyeballs." Indeed, whether a piece of content gets developed at all often depends upon whether it attracts sufficient attention to sustain a viable business model. The allocation of scarce attention, then, has real and deep economic and social ramifications. To understand these far-reaching implications, a framework for the analysis of scarcity and of resource allocation is needed, and such tools have been the stock-in-trade of economists for more than two centuries.

To begin to see the central role of attention in the online economy, it is useful to invoke one of the most fundamental and basic insights of economics: that prices in a competitive market are determined by the interaction of supply and demand. If the quantity of some commodity supplied in a market exceeds that demanded by consumers then firms face an incentive to reduce their prices so as not to be left with unsold inventory. It is natural to expect that consumers will respond to these lower prices by demanding more of the

---

[1] See Simon (1971) for an early discussion.

good or service in question. This process should be expected to continue until the price has fallen to the level at which supply and demand are equalized (see Figure 16.1(a), where this price is labeled $p^*$) so that the market is in some sense self-correcting; the market is then said to be in equilibrium. Similarly, if the price is below its equilibrium level so that there is an excess demand in the market then sellers could increase their price and still sell their entire supply as buyers compete for the right to purchase. One should therefore expect the price to drift upward, again restoring equilibrium.

One can think of the dynamics depicted in Figure 16.1(a) as being a simple representation of the market for advertising in the pre-digital era.[2] The prevailing market price for advertising opportunities in such a market is determined by the interaction of publishers' willingness to supply such opportunities and advertisers' collective demand for them. If, for example, a new newspaper enters a local news market then the supply of advertisement opportunities in that market will increase causing excess supply: one should then expect the price of an ad to fall in order to restore equilibrium in the market. In terms of our diagram, such an increase in the supply of advertising space can be depicted as a rightward rotation in the supply curve so that the quantity of ad space supplied increases at every price (Figure 16.1(b)). The arrows in the figure indicate that—in accordance with the intuition above—a reduction in the scarcity of advertising opportunities results in an increase in the quantity of advertisements sold but a fall in ad prices.

One effect of digital technology has been to dramatically reduce the cost of distributing content, with the consequence that the number of publishers has exploded to include individual bloggers and small outlets as well as large, established media organizations. Moreover, since every blog and niche website is capable of functioning as an advertising platform, the dramatic growth in content production has been coupled with the potential for an equally unprecedented reduction in the scarcity of advertising inventory. We can easily incorporate such a change into our model of the industry. Take another look at Figure 16.1(b), but now think about what would happen if we made the supply increase larger (so that the supply curve rotates even further to the right). The larger the increase in supply, the less scarce is advertising space, and the further must the price fall in order to restore equilibrium.

The simple market dynamics summarized in Figure 16.1(b) are illustrative of a broader brand of pessimism with regard to the future of the advertising-funded media, and prompt an interesting question: How can the continued availability of high-quality content, whose provision is costly,[3] be

---

[2] For a broad and thorough overview of the literature on the economics of advertising, see Bagwell (2007).

[3] It is important to draw a distinction between fixed costs (one-off, up-front costs of production), and marginal costs (the incremental costs associated with serving one more consumer). The digital

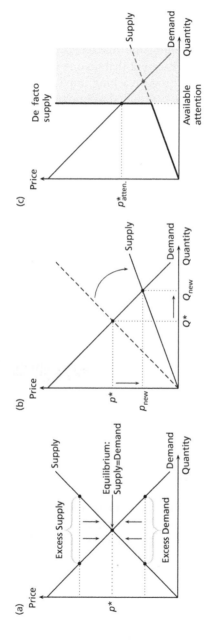

**Figure 16.1** (a) Convergence to equilibrium price, $p^*$, and quantity in a competitive market; (b) the effect on equilibrium price and quantity of a reduction in scarcity of a commodity; (c) equilibrium price when subject to a scarcity of attention

reconciled with a radical fall in the price of the advertisements whose sale funds that provision? An important part of the answer to this puzzle lies in acknowledging that the advertising business is not about selling ad space per se. Rather, publishers create value for advertisers by providing them with access to consumers' attention, and it is the supply of this attention that is ultimately relevant in determining the market value of an advertisement opportunity—indeed, an advertisement that no one will ever see has very little value! This distinction has broad-reaching implications for the future of the ad industry: whilst it is true that digital technology enables near limitless expansion of ad space, attention is fundamentally scarce. In Figure 16.1(c), taking the supply of consumer attention as given, we obtain the de facto supply curve depicted by the bold, kinked line. Beyond the level labeled as "Attention available," this curve becomes vertical: publishers cannot increase their supply (of attention) beyond this level because doing so would carry us into the shaded region within which the available attention of consumers is exhausted and consumers are subject to information overload—unable or unwilling to process any additional advertising messages. Significantly, note that the equilibrium price for *scarce* attention ($P^*_{atten}$ in Figure 16.1(c)) is higher than the price ($P^*_{new}$) of *non-scarce* ad space.

Attention, then, plays a central role in the digital content ecosystem: it is the scarcity and consequent value of attention that underpins the viability of the online advertising industry which, in turn, finances commercially provided content and services en masse. Given this centrality, the remainder of this chapter is concerned with the economics of marshaling and managing attention, and the consequent implications for online media and advertising markets.

## Attracting Attention

### THE TWO-SIDED BALANCING ACT

The scarcity of attention ensures that great rewards await organizations that can deliver eyeballs into the advertising market. Attention, though, is a peculiar commodity that must be attracted before it can be sold. This moves such organizations into the realm of so-called two-sided platforms, whose study was pioneered by Caillaud and Jullien (2001, 2003), and Rochet and Tirole (2003).[4] A two-sided platform is a service that intermediates between

---

distribution of content can be carried out at almost zero marginal cost, but publishers continue to invest significantly in the fixed costs of content production such as journalism and infrastructure expenditure.

[4] For an overview with applications to media markets, see Anderson and Gabszewicz (2006).

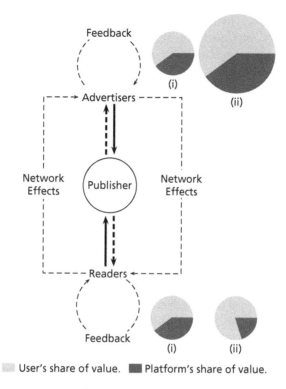

User's share of value. ■ Platform's share of value.

**Figure 16.2** A two-sided media market

two distinct groups that value interactions with each other. In the case of advertising-funded media markets these two groups are consumers and advertisers, whilst the platform is a publisher that enables the transmission of advertisement messages. A schematic illustration of a two-sided media market is presented in Figure 16.2. The interesting thing that distinguishes two-sided markets from their one-sided counterparts is the presence of cross-side network effects: advertisers care about the number of readers (or, more precisely, the amount of attention) that they can reach via a given publisher, so the publisher becomes more attractive to advertisers as its readership increases. Likewise, readers should be expected to care about the extent to which the media they consume is bundled with advertisements.[5] These network effects also give rise to feedback: increasing a publisher's readership may attract more advertisements which, in turn, affects its value to other readers.

---

[5] One might typically expect readers to prefer publishers with fewer advertisements, but Kaiser (2007), for example, finds that consumers positively value advertisements in some contexts.

A central question in the economics of two-sided markets is how a platform should price its intermediation services given these links between the two sides. The use of the publisher's platform generates value for consumers and advertisers, represented by the pie charts labeled "(i)" in Figure 16.2. A positive price charged by the publisher for access to content or advertising services can be thought of as appropriating some of this value, and the dark wedges in the pie chart reflect the piece of the "value pie" thus retained by the publisher. Now, suppose that the publisher changes its pricing policy—reducing the price charged to its readers. Such a change is represented in the pie charts labeled "(ii)" in Figure 16.2. On the reader side of the market, the share of the value enjoyed by readers (the size of the light-grey segment) has increased owing to the lower price. This makes the publisher more attractive to readers so that its readership should be expected to increase. Meanwhile, on the advertiser side of the market, the increase in the readership (and the commensurate increase in the amount of attention available) causes the total value of the platform (the size of the "value pie") to increase. Thus, whilst the publisher extracts less value from the consumer side of the market after its price cut, it is compensated with a piece of a bigger pie on the advertiser side—even if its advertisement price per unit of attention is left unchanged. In essence, the publisher is subsidizing readers in order to grow its supply of attention so that the profitability of its advertising business can be maximized.[6] A careful balancing of these two effects will typically ensure that the publisher is better off overall than under the no-subsidization regime. This is why, for example, newspapers are typically sold to readers at a price insufficient to cover the cost of the editorial process,[7] and why search engines—arguably amongst the most powerful knowledge tools ever wielded by mankind—are available to users at no pecuniary cost.

There are various factors that influence the optimal pattern of subsidization. One important dimension is the sensitivity of demand to the size of the user base on the opposing side of the market. Indeed, one might be inclined to ask why it is that readers rather than advertisers are subsidized. The simple answer is that advertisers typically value an additional reader more highly than readers value an extra advertisement, so that attracting readers to the platform is a more powerful means of building value. More generally, the more

---

[6] We say that readers are being subsidized because the price that they pay for access to content is lower than would be the case in the absence of indirect network effects. Subsidization thus does not preclude the possibility of a price greater than zero.

[7] More recently, free daily newspapers such as *Metro* have grown their market share precisely because they so heavily subsidize readers (providing the newspaper for free) in order to expand their advertising audience. Such newspapers are therefore a pro-typical example of two-sided pricing. This kind of strategy is not unique to the media: Adobe provides free PDF reader software to build a large user base and maximize the value of its professional PDF authoring solution, whilst nightclubs have historically run "ladies' night" events to grow their female patronage, in the hope of subsequently attracting more fee-paying males. Other examples abound—see, for example, Table 1 in Rochet and Tirole (2003).

sensitive is advertiser demand to the size of the readership, the more can the platform gain by attracting additional readers so that a larger subsidy should be expected. Similarly, if readers are particularly price sensitive, then a small price cut will attract many additional readers so that larger subsidies are more effective when the target users are price sensitive.

Another key issue is the presence and intensity of competition. An interesting feature of two-sided markets is that a publisher that captures many readers will be in an extremely strong competitive position in the advertising market vis-à -vis one with a low readership. Thus, the presence of competition can foster extremely aggressive subsidization behavior as platforms compete for scarce attention that will give them an advantage in their ad business. The clearest manifestation of this is in the online world, where vast swathes of commercial media and online services are made available at no pecuniary cost precisely because attention is so scarce and the number of publishers so large.

## INFORMATION CONGESTION

The two-sided pricing model is pervasive in media markets, but some organizations seek to sidestep such market arrangements and instead force their way into consumers' attention: e-mail spam and ad clutter are manifestations of such behavior. This is problematic when consumers are prone to information overload because such unsolicited messages are not mediated by a well-functioning market mechanism that appropriately allocates consumers' attention. Instead, consumers themselves must decide how to allocate their scarce attention across the multitude of messages that they receive—a process that cannot be expected to function efficiently because evaluating the value of competing messages is a task that itself consumes attention. As a consequence, there is likely to be a crowding-out effect as some useful messages go unseen whilst consumers' attention is exhausted by useless ones (Anderson and de Palma 2009; van Zandt 2004). Put another way: when access to a consumer's attention is not appropriately priced, firms send too many ads and overloaded consumers struggle to identify the best messages to look at in a sea of spam.

It is important to emphasize that this congestion inefficiency arises in the absence of a market for attention. If such a market were in place then sending additional ad messages would amount to an increase in demand for access to attention (e.g. a rightward shift in the demand curve in Figure 16.1(c)), which causes the equilibrium price to rise. As the price of attention increases in this fashion, the advertisers whose messages are most likely to be of no interest to consumers find that it is no longer profitable to transmit messages at all.

Thus, only the most valuable messages are sent when attention is properly priced and the congestion/crowding-out problem is mitigated. In the absence of appropriate attention pricing, a tax on unsolicited messages has the potential to increase welfare by deterring the sending of undesirable messages in an analogous fashion to a higher price. Indeed, if messages can be well-targeted then even the senders of spam messages can find themselves better off when subject to such a tax (van Zandt 2004). The intuition for this result is that, by mitigating the information congestion problem, the tax ensures that message senders are better able to contact those consumers whose attention they value the most.

# The Allocation of Attention

## THE TARGETING OF ADVERTISEMENTS

We have thus far concerned ourselves with the raw scarcity of attention and the desire to gather it en masse in a fairly blunt fashion. Technology, though, is also providing more nuanced ways of allocating attention so as to maximize the value that can be extracted from it. One such advance is the growing importance of targeted advertising. Targeting is by no means new: advertisers have long undertaken to target their advertisements by, for example, placing car ads in motoring magazines and holiday advertisements within a newspaper's travel section. This kind of "contextual" targeting can now be automated. Google AdSense, for example, is an ad platform that algorithmically determines the topic of a web page and automatically displays relevant ads alongside it. The proliferation of niche media platforms such as highly specialized websites, and the consequent division of audiences into smaller, more homogeneous segments, appear to have facilitated a growth in the accuracy and importance of this kind of ad targeting (Esteban and Hernández 2012). Moreover, new markets have appeared that involve a kind of quasi-contextual targeting. These include search advertising where the consumer specifies a highly idiosyncratic context by entering a search phrase and the search engine returns advertisements targeted at that context.

Technological developments have also given rise to new ways of targeting advertisements. An important growth area in this regard has been behavioral targeting, which uses data on consumers' past behavior to determine which advertisements are likely to be relevant. For example, a consumer with a browser cookie indicating that they have visited a car review website at least five times in the last six weeks might be labeled as an "auto-intender" and targeted with car advertisements. Another emerging technology is so-called social advertising, whereby advertisements are targeted according to ties within a social network. A growing body of evidence suggests that targeting measures such as these are an effective way of extracting additional value out of a finite supply of attention (see, for example, Goldfarb and Tucker 2010b; Tucker 2012) and investment and adoption in this area has been robust.

More generally, industry advocates have argued that targeting is crucial for the sustainability of the online media ecosystem—financing the provision of new, high-quality content that would otherwise not be viable.[8] There are, however, important caveats to attach to this sentiment. Consumers are, at the very least, suspicious of targeting technologies—and of their implications for personal privacy in particular (Goldfarb and Tucker 2010a; Turrow et al. 2009). Moreover, even putting privacy concerns aside, there is reason to think that targeted advertising is not unambiguously good for consumers. In Taylor (2012), for example, I show that targeting technology can drive up the prices of advertised products. More precise targeting also makes each advertisement more effective on average which, holding all else equal, makes the transmission of advertising messages more attractive for advertisers. This has the potential to induce higher levels of advertising, worsening the kinds of information overload discussed in the previous section. Johnson (2009) provides a model of this issue in which firms decide on the volume of advertisements to transmit and consumers who receive too many undesirable ads can elect to block them. Blocking is socially inefficient to the extent that the time and resources used to transmit and then block an ad are wasted—better to have not sent the ad in the first place. This result notwithstanding, ad avoidance has important social benefits: Blocking advertisements decreases the value of transmitting them in the first place so that firms send fewer advertisements overall—partially alleviating the information overload problem. Thus, once one takes firms' use of optimal advertising strategies as given, some degree of ad avoidance is socially desirable.

There are also broader issues relating to the effects of targeting on the structure of the media industry. Since it is primarily online media which benefit from targeting technology, improved targeting can cause a decline in the viability of offline media.[9] This may be problematic if, for example, some consumers do not have access to online media, or if consumers value diversity in the channels through which they access media products. On a related note, regional newspapers have historically coexisted with their larger national counterparts—enjoying the advantage of a more (geographically) homogeneous audience attracted by content tailored to local interests. This has allowed such media organizations to sustain themselves by catering to an advertising

---

[8] See, also, Taylor (2012) on this point.
[9] See, for example, Bergemann and Bonatti (2011) for a model.

market consisting primarily of local firms that are ill suited to broader exposure. Behavioral targeting technologies stand to undermine this advantage by enabling large publishers to precisely target advertisements based on the location of the viewer in a fashion previously only possible for niche outlets[10]—ensuring that the finite attention of local consumers is properly matched with the appropriate advertisers in spite of the publisher's broad reach (Athey and Gans 2010). Note that the scarcity of attention has an important role here because, absent such scarcity, a publisher lacking targeting technology could induce more advertiser–consumer matches simply by increasing the volume of ads shown to each consumer.[11] Targeting is effectively softening the effect of scarcity for large-scale publishers by allowing them to use the available attention more effectively, but has much less of an impact on niche publishers that were already able to contextually target ads. Any development that increases the profitability of large media outlets relative to small ones, argue Athey and Gans, should be expected to favor the existence and success of the former relative to the latter, so that targeting may lead to a decline in local news and other relatively niche content. This issue is likely to be particularly acute in circumstances where dealing with many niche publishers entails burdensome transaction costs for advertisers that are reduced considerably when transacting with a single large publisher or ad platform.

Traditionally, the readership of a publication constituted its supply of attention which, when coupled with demand for access to that attention, would give rise to an equilibrium price. Targeting, though, allows the publisher to divide its audience into many segments and "supply" each segment to advertisers individually. Moreover, the advertisers that demand access to the attention of consumers with an interest in, say, fashion may be distinct from those that wish to contact auto-intenders. Thus, each segment of consumers that the publisher is capable of targeting is potentially the focus of its own sub-market, with the supply, demand, and price of attention varying across these markets. With relatively coarse targeting this is not likely to be problematic but, as Levin and Milgrom (2010) note, excessive sub-division of markets can cause serious problems for their performance. One such problem is that precise targeting enables advertisers to "cherry-pick" advertising opportunities, so publishers may find themselves with unsold inventory that is not particularly attractive to any potential buyer—undermining their overall profitability and therefore their incentive to invest in content innovation. A more subtle issue is that

---

[10] For example, the IP address of a computer can be used to identify the city in which it is located with a relatively high degree of accuracy.

[11] Physical factors such as the number of pages in a magazine also constrain the number of advertisements per consumer and thus have a similar effect to attention scarcity for the purposes of Athey and Gans's model.

dividing attention into many markets makes each market thinner in the sense that demand stems from fewer potential buyers (advertisers). This becomes problematic, from the publishers' perspective, when markets become so thin that there is insufficient competition between buyers to drive prices up to their competitive level.

## ALLOCATING ADVERTISING OPPORTUNITIES BY AUCTION

In addition to thinning the market, targeting introduces practical challenges for a publisher or ad platform. If targeting permits the segmentation of a publisher's attention into millions of advertising sub-markets, then simply pricing and allocating ads in each of these markets becomes a daunting task. Consider search keyword advertising as an example. A Google search for "books" returns a list of so-called organic search results and, along the right edge of the page, a list of advertisements. Advertisements closer to the top of this list attract more attention and should intuitively be more expensive. The advertisements for such a search thus require up to ten prices—one for each ad slot. A search for "Oxford hotel" returns a completely different list of advertisements and—since hotel ads are likely to have a different value to book ads—these require an entirely new set of prices. A search for "digital camera" produces yet another set of ads, and so on. Determining the appropriate price for each slot associated with each search query when handling billions of queries each day thus becomes an important challenge.

Fortunately, people have for centuries been effectively solving the problem of pricing and allocating items of uncertain value by means of an auction—a set of rules for determining the price and assignment of goods according to bids proposed by a set of bidders. Indeed, Google and others have successfully solved their advertisement allocation problem with the judicious application of the extant economic theory of auctions.[12] A Google ad auction proceeds roughly as follows: for each search keyword, would-be advertisers enter a bid into Google's system, which then allocates the top slot to the highest bidder, the second best slot to the second highest bidder and, more generally, the nth best slot to the nth highest bidder. The twist is that the price paid by each successful bidder is not its own bid, but rather the bid of the advertiser in the slot below it.[13] An example profile of bids and the corresponding allocation is shown in Table 16.1.

[12] Google promotional materials explicitly acknowledge "Google's unique auction model uses Nobel Prize-winning economic theory…" (<www.google.com/adsense/afs.pdf>, accessed August 3, 2012). The theory in question is that of William Vickrey, and dates to the early 1960s.

[13] The firm in the last slot does not have an advertiser below it, and instead pays the highest losing bid.

**Table 16.1** An example profile of bids and the corresponding outcome of a generalized second price auction with three ad slots to allocate

| Bidder | Bid | Slot Allocated | Ad Price Paid |
|--------|-----|----------------|---------------|
| Firm A | £10 | Best | £7 |
| Firm B | £7 | 2nd best | £6 |
| Firm C | £6 | 3rd best | £3 |
| Firm D | £3 | none | n/a |
| Firm E | £2 | none | n/a |
| ⋮ | ⋮ | ⋮ | ⋮ |

This kind of auction is known as a generalized second price (GSP) auction, and was first studied by Edelman et al. (2007) and Varian (2007) who have shown it to have a number of interesting properties. Chief amongst these is that GSP auctions produce equilibrium allocations that are efficient—that is to say, they allocate the best advertisements to those firms that value them the most. Recall that an important motivation for introducing such auctions is the difficulty in allocating large volumes of advertisements and it is reassuring to know that the auctions perform well in this regard. The second important motivation for the introduction of ad auctions was the problem of price determination; here, too, GSP auctions have interesting properties. In particular, the natural outcome of competitive bidding in a GSP auction is a special set of prices (known as Vickrey-Clarke-Groves prices) that correspond to the prices that would ordinarily arise in a competitive market.[14] Taken together, the efficiency and competitive prices induced by a GSP auction imply that such auctions are an effective way to decentralize the problem of implementing the kind of well-functioning market outcomes depicted in Figure 16.1. An ancillary benefit of GSP auctions is that they provide a way to consolidate the markets for each ad slot associated with a given keyword into a single auction—somewhat mitigating the problem of market thinness highlighted by Levin and Milgrom (2010).

As well as putting the "right" ads in front of consumers, GSP auctions have a more fine-grained role to play in allocating attention. The basic idea is that, when consumers start their search at the top of the list of advertisements, ad slots close to the top will be most valuable. Advertisers will then compete fiercely to win these slots with the result—as we have seen—that the best slots are allocated to those advertisers who value them the most. But what does it mean for one firm to value the top slot more than another? In this context, an advertiser is likely to value an ad highly if it is especially likely to convert the advertising opportunity into a sale. Thus, the top slots are most likely to be allocated to firms that have a

---

[14] The insight that VCG prices are competitive is due to Leonard (1983).

high probability of offering precisely what the consumer happens to be search-ing for—vindicating the consumers' strategy of considering the top advertisers first. This line of reasoning, originally due to Athey and Ellison (2011) and Chen and He (2011), implies that besides selecting the best set of advertisements, GSP auctions order the ads in a way that channels attention towards where it is best used. Another way of thinking of this is that a firm's presence in the top slot is a signal of relevance; essentially, the firm is saying to the consumer, "I am willing to pay so much to get here in the best slot because I am very confident that you are going to want to buy what I am selling."

## ADVERSE INCENTIVES FOR THE ALLOCATION OF ATTENTION

Of course, consumers decide which ads look useful based on the explicit con-tent of the advertisement as well as the ad's position. Given jurisdictional and other difficulties in enforcing honesty in advertising regulations online, what is to prevent advertisers from promising the world in order to attract additional attention? The answer is that search ads (and, more generally, around two-thirds of all online ads) are priced per-click, with advertisers only paying when a con-sumer clicks on their ad. This discourages inflationary, unsubstantiated claims that attract many (costly) clicks but ultimately produce few additional sales.[15]

It is not just advertisers that face incentives to manipulate the distribution and use of attention in ways that may be construed as dubious by observers. One obvious issue is that advertisements compete for attention with the content served alongside them. Publishers may therefore wish to use obtrusive adver-tisement technologies such as pop-up ads, which are effective at attracting atten-tion (Goldfarb and Tucker 2010b) but are generally disdained by users. In other instances, publishers face an incentive to distort content if doing so increases the value of their advertising resource. Ellman and Germano (2009), for exam-ple, present a model in which publishers under-report news that is damaging for advertisers,[16] whilst Berman and Katona (2010) show that one-upmanship in an attempt to top search rankings (a process known as search engine opti-mization) can lead publishers to divert resources away from substantive con-tent provision whilst simultaneously undermining the usefulness of search engines. Indeed, the incentives of search engines themselves have also been subject to scrutiny. Search engines may wish to degrade their organic search results in order to induce more consumers to click on advertisements (Taylor 2013; White 2012). A related issue is that search engines may wish to bias their organic search results to favor links to their own services over those of rival

---

[15] Baye et al. (2004) make this argument informally, whilst a formal model may be found in Taylor (2011).

[16] The reporting of tobacco-related illness is one prominent example of such practice.

publishers (de Corniére and Taylor 2013; Edelman 2011). The relative lack of transparency surrounding the functioning of search algorithms and publishers' content strategies makes a full assessment of these issues difficult, and ensures that they remain the subject of an ongoing policy debate.

## Conclusion

The advent of digital distribution has brought an era of both abundance and scarcity. The potential for infinite duplication of content throws into sharp relief the extent to which the availability of attention is the defining constraint in online media and advertising markets. More than ever before, organizations are responding with new schemes to attract and distribute attention. Such innovations cement the profitability of online advertising providers, and thus serve to underwrite the viability of many online content and service platforms. However, the rapid pace of change has come with the introduction of new kinds of market arrangements that are without historical precedent. Whilst some appear to function well, others give rise to incentives that run contrary to what consumers and policy makers might consider ideal. There is thus a need for careful scrutiny and continued research in this rapidly evolving environment: there remains much to be done and time is scarce!

### ■ REFERENCES

Anderson, S. P. and A. de Palma (2009). "Information Congestion," *RAND Journal of Economics*, 40(4): 688–709.

Anderson, S. P. and Gabszewicz, J. J. (2006). "The Media and Advertising: A Tale of Two-Sided Markets," in V. A. Ginsburgh and D. Throsby (eds), *Handbook of the Economics of Art and Culture*, volume 1. Amsterdam: Elsevier, 567–614.

Athey, S. and Ellison, G. (2011). "Position Auctions with Consumer Search," *Quarterly Journal of Economics*, 126(4): 1213–1270.

Athey, S. and Gans, J. S. (2010). "The Impact of Targeting Technology on Advertising Markets and Media Competition," *American Economic Review*, 100(2): 608–613.

Bagwell, K. (2007). "The Economic Analysis of Advertising," in M. Armstrong and R. Porter (eds), *Handbook of Industrial Organization*, volume 3. Amsterdam: Elsevier, 1701–1844.

Baye, M. R., Morgan, J., and Scholten, P. (2004). "Price Dispersion in the Small and in the Large: Evidence from an Internet Price Comparison Site," *Journal of Industrial Economics*, 52(4): 463–496.

Bergemann, D. and Bonatti, A. (2011). "Targeting in Advertising Markets: Implications for Offline vs. Online Media," *RAND Journal of Economics*, 42(3): 417–443.

Berman, R. and Katona, Z. (2010). "The Role of Search Engine Optimization in Search Rankings." Working Paper.

Caillaud, B. and Jullien, B. (2001). "Competing Cybermediaries," *European Economic Review*, 45(4–6): 797–808.

Caillaud, B. and Jullien, B. (2003). "Chicken & Egg: Competition among Intermediation Service Providers," *RAND Journal of Economics*, 34(2): 309–328.

Chen, Y. and He, C. (2011). "Paid Placement: Advertising and Search on the Internet," *Economic Journal*, 121(556): F309–F328.

de Cornière, A., and Taylor, G. (2013). "Integration and Search Engine Bias," Working Paper.

Edelman, B. (2011). "Bias In Search Results? Diagnosis and Response," *Indian Journal of Law and Technology*, 7: 16–32.

Edelman, B., Ostrovsky, M., and Schwarz, M. (2007). "Internet Advertising and the Generalized Second-Price Auction: Selling Billions of Dollars Worth of Keywords," *American Economic Review*, 97(1): 242–259.

Ellman, M. and Germano. F. (2009). "What do the Papers Sell? A Model of Advertising and Media Bias," *Economic Journal*, 119(537): 680–704.

Esteban, L. and Hernández, J. M. (2012). "Specialized Advertising Media and Product Market Competition," *Journal of Economics*, 106(1): 45–74.

Goldfarb, A. and Tucker, C. E. (2010a). "Online Display Advertising: Targeting and Obtrusiveness." Working Paper.

Goldfarb, A. and Tucker, C. E. (2010b). "Privacy Regulation and Online Advertising." Working Paper.

Johnson, J. P. (2009). "Targeted Advertising and Advertising Avoidance." Working Paper.

Kaiser, U. (2007). "Do Media Consumers Really Dislike Advertising? An Empirical Assessment of a Popular Assumption in Economic Theory." Working Paper.

Leonard, H. B. (1983). "Elicitation of Honest Preferences for the Assignment of Individuals to Positions," *Journal of Political Economy*, 91(3): 461–479.

Levin, J. and Milgrom, P. (2010). "Online Advertising: Heterogeneity and Conflation in Market Design," *American Economic Review*, 100(2): 603–607.

Rochet, J.-C. and Tirole, J. (2003). "Platform Competition in Two-Sided Markets," *Journal of the European Economic Association*, 1(4): 990–1029.

Simon, H. A. (1971). "Designing Organizations for an Information-Rich World," in M. Greenberger (ed.) *Computers, Communication, and the Public Interest*. Baltimore, MD: Johns Hopkins Press, 37–72.

Taylor, G. (2011). "The Informativeness of On-Line Advertising," *International Journal of Industrial Organization*, 29(6): 668–677.

Taylor, G. (2012). "Attention Retention: Targeted Advertising and the Provision of Media Content." Working Paper.

Taylor, G. (2013). "Search Quality and Revenue Cannibalisation by Competing Search Engines," *Journal of Economics & Management Strategy*, 22(3): 445–467.

Tucker, C. E. (2012). "Social Advertising," Working Paper.

Turow, J., King, J. Hoofnatle, C. J., Bleakley, A., and Hennessy, M. (2009). "Americans Reject Tailored Advertising and Three Activities that Enable It." Working Paper.

van Zandt, T. (2004). "Information Overload in a Network of Targeted Communication," *RAND Journal of Economics*, 35(3): 542–560.

Varian, H. R. (2007). "Position Auctions," *International Journal of Industrial Organization*, 25(6): 1163–1178.

White, A. (2012). "Search Engines: Left Side Quality versus Right Side Profits," Working Paper.

# 17 The Internet in the Law: Transforming Problem-Solving and Education

*Richard Susskind*

The interaction of the Internet and the law gives rise to two distinct fields of research and practice.[1] The first is the law relating to the Internet, a discipline that addresses substantive legal issues such as privacy, censorship, copyright, defamation, and computer misuse. In this area of the law, academic and practicing lawyers assess and advise upon the legal implications of existing and emerging Internet technologies. The second field, which is the subject of this chapter, concerns the manner in which Internet techniques and technologies can be used in support of the practice of law and the administration of justice. The purpose of this chapter is to consider three of the numerous ways in which the Internet can be harnessed by lawyers and in the courts: Internet-based dispute resolution; online tools to enhance access to justice; and legal e-learning. Although many of the examples are based on UK developments, what is discussed is of direct application across the globe.

## Internet-Based Dispute Resolution

Judges in the courts are commonly regarded as sitting at the heart of the process of dispute resolution. At the same time, they are often portrayed, by the media and in fiction, as old fashioned and otherworldly. The reverse is so. Most judges in Western jurisdictions have become committed users of IT, keen to

---

[1] The arguments and findings presented in this chapter are drawn from two books: *Tomorrow's Lawyers* (Susskind 2013) and *The End of Lawyers?* (Susskind 2008), in which the issues discussed are set out at much greater length.

embrace systems that offer practical benefits in their everyday work, such as e-mail, word processing, and online research. Looking beyond these rudimentary applications, how profoundly could the Internet and IT affect the work of the courts? There are numerous possibilities here, from e-filing of documents into the courts, through case management technology, to electronic display of evidence in the courtroom. A glance at the website of the Center for Legal & Court Technology (<www.legaltechcenter.net>), based at William & Mary Law School, in the United States, gives a sense of the many options here.

One clear and yet simple application of technology would tackle the outmoded administration of much of the work of courts. Around the world, this remains labour intensive, cumbersome, and paper based. A visit to most courts in Western jurisdictions reveals a working environment that is less efficient and automated than most ordinary offices in the country, whether in the public or private sector. In many countries, judges complain of antiquated systems, outdated working practices, excessive running costs, inefficiencies, errors, and delays. In turn, court users suffer, and the reputation of the justice system is adversely affected. And yet, the inertia is considerable. In his *Access to Justice* reports, for example, Lord Woolf made a series of recommendations in the mid-1990s for the computerization of much of the operation of the civil justice system in England and Wales (Woolf 1995; 1996). Very few have been implemented. The lack of progress can be attributed to two main factors: insufficient investment by the Government and the Treasury, who have not considered civil justice to be a priority, and the Ministry of Justice's poor track record of successfully procuring and delivering large-scale technology projects. These shortcomings are mirrored in many other countries.

Proponents of judicial and court technology insist that the lack of progress so far should not deter us from looking ahead and anticipating change that is likely for tomorrow's lawyers if not for today's. Their broad claim is clear—if courts and tribunals were easily affordable, widely accessible, and delivered a swift service, an argument could be made for ignoring the new and emerging technologies. But the 21st century court system is creaking. Too often, it is inefficient, slow, and too costly. For instance, around one million civil justice problems in England and Wales are said to go unresolved every year (Genn et al. 2007), and projected cuts in public legal funding will greatly add to this level of legal exclusion. Access to justice is in grave danger of being available only to the rich.

In principle, if the advantages of the Internet and IT that have been secured in overhauling the paperwork in other sectors were enjoyed by the courts, the antiquated filing systems for court administration could be replaced by an automated, streamlined, and largely paper-free set of systems that would be less costly, less prone to error, more efficient, and more accessible. In turn, an efficient and well-equipped court system, populated by satisfied lawyers, would be a system in which the public would have greater confidence. The prize is a glittering one—inexpensive, swift, proportionate, inclusive resolution of disputes.

Looking at the long-term future of courts and dispute resolution, one fundamental question sets the agenda—is court a service or a place? To resolve disputes, do parties and their advisers need to congregate together in one physical space, in order to present arguments to a judge? Why not have virtual courts or online dispute resolution?

The terminology is not firmly settled but, generally, when reference is made to "virtual courts," this is to a fairly conventional courtroom set-up into which some video link is introduced. Take-up has been greatest in criminal cases, where there are child or intimidated witnesses; and, increasingly, for bail and remand hearings, conducted through links between prisons and courts. In some civil cases, witnesses from outside the UK have given evidence remotely, as have otherwise inaccessible expert witnesses. The idea is that the witnesses or the accused appear on large screens, suitably located in hearing rooms, and this saves time and money or protects the vulnerable. In 2010, the Ministry of Justice in the UK published a report on this subject (Ministry of Justice 2010). On the face of it, the findings suggested that the costs of the enabling technologies would outweigh the benefits secured. But the costs of the systems are plummeting, especially if procured in bulk. Significantly, the report did establish that a video link between a police station and a court can be used successfully to conduct a first hearing in the majority of criminal cases—in the pilot, it reduced the average time from charge to first hearing, it cut down the failure-to-appear rates, and saved the costs of transporting prisoners from prisons to courts.

The growing use across society of video-calling and video conferencing—from Skype to telepresence—suggests there is much scope for virtual courts, if not for trials then for earlier hearings, when judges could sit in their chambers and participants could attend remotely. For tomorrow's lawyers, appearance in physical courtrooms may become a rarity. Instead, virtual appearances may become the norm, and new presentational and advocacy skills will be required. It is not being suggested that virtual courtrooms will be pervasive in the short or medium term. Virtual hearings are relatively rarely held, for example, in England, other than, occasionally, to enable vulnerable witnesses to give evidence, and for some remand hearings. But, as one measure to help reduce the disproportionate costs of many conventional hearings, it is a safe prediction that they will be in common usage in the long term.

In the virtual courtroom set-up, one or more judges sit in some kind of hearing room, dispensing justice in the traditional manner. The break from tradition here is that some participants appear virtually across a video link rather than in person. But there is a step beyond the virtual hearing and this is known as online dispute resolution (ODR). With ODR, no traditional courtroom is involved. Instead, the process of resolving a dispute, especially the formulation of the solution, is entirely or largely conducted through the Internet (Wahab et al. 2012). A leading example of ODR is Cybersettle, an American web-based system that was launched in 1998 (<www.cybersettle. com>). Cybersettle is claimed to have handled over 200,000 claims of combined value in excess of $1.6 billion. Most of the cases have been personal injury or insurance claims. It uses a process known as "double-blind bidding" —a claimant and defendant each submit the highest and lowest settlement figures that would be acceptable to them. These amounts are not disclosed but if the two ranges overlap, a settlement can be achieved, the final figure usually being a split down the middle.

Another sort of ODR is mediation across the Web. An online mediation can be undertaken when a face-to-face mediation is logistically difficult, perhaps because of the locations of the parties or when, relative to the size of dispute, it is too costly to assemble. Mediation is one form of ADR (alternative dispute resolution), a way of sorting out differences beyond the courts. Instead, the mediator, as a third party, assists parties to negotiate settlements, usually on a private and confidential basis. Using a mix of Web-based tools and human mediators, through e-mail exchanges and online discussion areas, conflicts can be resolved electronically by e-mediation. Parties to a dispute can, in this way, settle their disagreements across the Internet without convening in a meeting room.

A blend of ODR techniques is used to sort out disagreements on eBay. About 60 million disputes arise each year amongst eBay users. It is unimaginable that these would all get resolved in conventional courts. Instead, ODR is used— swiftly, efficiently, and generally to good effect (Rule and Nagarajan 2010). The Ministry of Justice in England and Wales has also embraced ODR. Its Money Claim Online system (<https://www.moneyclaim.gov.uk>) was launched in 2002 and enables users, with no legal experience, to recover money owed to them without needing to handle complex forms or set foot in a County Court. The service covers claims, such as unpaid debts, up to a value of £100,000. It allows a claimant to request a claim online, keep track of the status of the claim and, where appropriate, request entry of judgment and enforcement. It is said to handle more than 60,000 claims annually.

Very few law firms have yet taken ODR seriously. In fact, even though the European Commission has adopted a regulation on ODR, most lawyers have not heard of online dispute resolution. In the long run, however, in a world in which the Internet is embraced so widely in people's working and social lives, it is not radical to expect it to become the dominant way to resolve all but the most complex and high–value disputes.

Virtual courts and ODR may, however, be seen as threatening everyday conceptions of fair trials. For example, victims of crimes and their families, alongside aggrieved and wronged parties in civil disputes, may feel shortchanged by a lack of physical meeting. An IT-enabled resolution may not provide the closure that some regard as a central part of the judicial process. On the other hand, if virtual trials or ODR deliver a much speedier resolution, more quickly even than "a reasonable time," this may well offset the disappointment of not being vindicated in person. Further, and crucially, it may be that virtual courts and ODR might be confined to preliminary hearings and most final trials would be conducted in the traditional manner.

There may be a different concern—that a hearing or trial should be in a publicly accessible forum, so that any wrongdoer's acts are publicly declared and denounced. This could clearly be achieved across the Internet in the case of virtual courts, but it is less obvious how ODR could be publicly viewed. Interestingly, this concern could equally be a call for televising or broadcasting hearings, which would render them radically more public. Tens of thousands of people each day are said to view the proceedings of the UK Supreme Court live on the Sky News website.

As to the actual fairness of decisions, there is no obvious reason why judges or online mediators should be any less impartial, independent, or just, when physically remote from some or all litigants, witnesses, and lawyers. It will of course be crucial, in the pursuit of fairness, that there is no actual difference between the soundness of decisions and findings delivered online as compared with those that flow from conventional hearings.

Other important questions abound. What about the reliability and credibility of evidence taken remotely? Will judges, juries, and lawyers be at a disadvantage if they cannot look across the courtroom directly into the eyes of witnesses? Or will close-up, three-dimensional video on large, high-resolution monitors permit improved scrutiny? Should lawyers, in virtual trials, be with their clients at the camera-end of proceedings or in the hearing rooms near the judges? If the experience of giving evidence remotely is, as is likely, less intimidating than being in a physical courtroom, will this be conducive to evidence that is more or less convincing, or decisions that are more or less authoritative and well founded?

More generally, flowing from the thinking of Judith Resnik and Dennis Curtis in their magisterial book, *Representing Justice* (Resnik and Curtis 2011)—what will be the impact of public perceptions of justice, if one of its main icons, the courtroom, is displaced? Could well-designed ODR indeed become symbolic of a new, more inclusive era for dispute resolution? While virtual trials and ODR may seem alien or outlandish for policy makers and opinion formers of today, few of these individuals hail from the Internet generation. Future generations, for whom working and socializing online will be second nature, may feel very differently. Indeed, for tomorrow's clients, virtual hearings and ODR together may improve access to justice and offer routes to dispute resolution where none would otherwise be available.

It is too early to answer in a conclusive way many of the questions just posed. No doubt, more empirical research and analysis are needed. But, on the face of it, there are no overriding concerns of law or principle that should call a halt to the ongoing and advanced computerization of courts.

# Online Tools to Enhance Access to Justice

Franz Kafka sets the scene hauntingly in *The Trial* (Kafka 1983). He tells of a gatekeeper who inexplicably refuses to grant a man access to the law. This unfortunate man from the country had not expected any problems. After all, he thinks, "the law should be accessible to everyone at all times." So it might be thought. Yet, as noted, research in England and Wales concluded that around one million civil justice problems go unresolved each year (Genn et al. 2007). This legal exclusion is a grave social problem and is loosely referred to in legal circles as the "access to justice" problem.

Thinking more widely, no one today can pretend to have mastery over anything other than small parts of any modern legal system. And yet all citizens, under the law, are taken to have knowledge of all legal provisions that affect them. Given that most citizens do not know most of the law and cannot afford to obtain conventional legal advice, there is a very clear social problem here. The problem perhaps comes most sharply into focus when people contemplate taking an action through the courts system. From a lay perspective, as well as appearing to be unaffordable, the courts also seem to be excessively time consuming, unjustifiably combative, and inexplicably steeped in opaque procedure and language. It was with such problems in mind that, in 1995 and 1996, Lord Woolf, then a Law Lord and later the Lord Chief Justice of England and Wales, published *Access to Justice,* his two seminal reports on the future of the civil justice system (Woolf 1995; 1996). These reports have been the focus of discussion around the world since their appearance.

Lord Woolf's terms of reference confined his attention to the resolution of disputes. And for many judges and policy makers since, the idea of improving access to justice has come to mean improving the way disputes are resolved. A wider view can be taken and is proposed here. To be entirely or even substantially focused on dispute resolution in the pursuit of justice is potentially to miss much that we should expect of our legal systems. It is contended that better access to justice should embrace improvements, not just to dispute resolution, but also to what can be called dispute containment, dispute avoidance, and legal health promotion.

Dispute containment concentrates on preventing disagreements that have arisen from escalating excessively; and it is lawyers as well as the parties themselves who need to be contained. Dispute avoidance is a theme that in-house lawyers often raise: they speak of legal risk management, or to put it metaphorically, putting a fence at the top of a cliff rather than an ambulance at the bottom. It is unusual to find a regular human being, whether a Chief Executive or a consumer, who would prefer a large dispute neatly resolved by lawyers to not having one in the first place. Legal health promotion extends beyond the preventative lawyering of dispute avoidance to ensuring that people are aware of, and able to take advantage of, the many benefits, improvements, and advantages that the law can confer, even if no problem has arisen.

With these four dimensions of access to justice in mind, obstacles arise when the plight of the non-lawyer is reflected upon. The first obstacle for the non-lawyer is recognition, the process by which someone with no legal insight realizes that they would benefit from legal help. Sometimes it is obvious—when a claim arrives through the letterbox or a decision has been made to move house. But often non-lawyers may not know that they are in a situation in which there is a legal problem to be resolved, contained, or avoided, or that there is some benefit to be secured. Paradoxically, it seems a person needs to be a lawyer to know if and when he or she would benefit from legal help. The second challenge, even if a non-lawyer has recognized that he or she would benefit from legal help, is to select the best source of legal guidance, whether that be finding a suitable lawyer or some other kind of adviser or even online help. The third dimension is the delivery of legal service itself. And here there are a wide range of options. In relation to this third challenge, it is far from clear that conventional lawyers in traditional law firms are always the best placed or most affordable sources of guidance for clients. It seems all but inevitable that cuts in public legal funding brought about by grim economic conditions will lead to legal and court services that are less affordable and less accessible. A major and urgent social challenge is to find new ways of providing legal help, not least to citizens and to small businesses.

One clear alternative to the provision of legal help by lawyers is for skilled and often voluntary non-lawyers to advise people on their problems, rights, and responsibilities. Another option is to provide citizens and businesses with online legal resources so they can take care of some of their legal affairs on their own; or, when guidance is needed, they can work more efficiently with their legal advisers. If there can be online services that provide medical guidance, why not have something similar for law? Such online legal facilities come in three forms: first, as free web-based services, provided by a variety of commercial and not-for-profit organizations; second, as subscription-based tools from conventional law firms; and, third, as chargeable offerings from other businesses, such as legal publishers.

In practice, though, how might the Internet actually help secure access to justice in all the various aspects just noted? In the first instance, addressing the first obstacle, IT can and will continue to be of use in assisting non-lawyers to *recognize* that they might benefit from some kind of legal input. One approach would be for people to register their social and working interests and for legal alerts to be delivered automatically to them when there are new laws or changes in old law that apply to them. Another tack would be online triage—when a citizen has a grievance of some sort, a simple online diagnostic system could ask a series of questions, require some boxes to be ticked, and could then identify if the user has a legal issue, and if so, of what sort and who is best placed to sort it out.

A further possibility would be the embedding of legal rules into systems and procedures. Consider the game of Solitaire. In the past, this was played only with physical cards and not electronically. It was possible, when using these playing cards, to place, for example, a red 4 beneath a red 5, although this would clearly have been in breach of the rules. But it would have been physically possible. In contrast, when Solitaire is played on a computer, such a move is not possible. Any attempt to place a red 4 below a red 5 will be met with a refusal by the system to do as clicked. The difference is that, with the electronic version, the rules are embedded in the system. Failure to comply is not an option. In years to come, in many dimensions of our lives, it is likely that legal rules will similarly be embedded in broader systems and processes. This would mean that non-lawyers will no longer have to worry about, or have the responsibility of, recognizing when legal input is required.

A final use of IT to help non-lawyers recognize when they need legal help could be through what can be called "communities of legal experience." When a PC user is confronted with some incomprehensible error message from Windows, he or she may cut and paste the message into Google, and find that someone, out there in the online world, has already provided an explanation and solution to the problem. So too in law, in open source and wiki spirit, large communities of legal experience will likely build up so that people will learn of legal issues that affect them, not formally through notification by their lawyers, but informally through their social networks. There are concerns here, however. For example, the extent to which the legal insights of lay people are reliable or applicable in any given situation can be questioned. And there may be liability issues here too—if guidance gleaned from a legal wiki gave rise to some loss, who will be held responsible?

IT will also play a role in helping clients *select* their lawyers and other sources of guidance. There will be online reputation systems, like those services that offer collective feedback on hotels, which will provide insight from other clients on their experiences with particular law firms and lawyers. There will also be price comparison systems, which will allow non-lawyers to assess the respective prices of competing legal providers. And there will be auctions for legal services—not generally for complex bespoke work but for routine and repetitive work.

As for the role of IT in the delivery of legal *service*, increasingly people will turn for basic guidance, on procedural and substantive issues, not to lawyers, but to online legal services. Online information already plays a central role in the daily lives of so many people that there is no reason, especially for those who cannot afford otherwise, why legal help should not be similarly accessed. Equally, users will also turn to the Internet for the production of standard documents, such as basic wills and landlord and tenant agreements and to communities of legal experience to determine how fellow lay people have sorted out their difficulties in the past.

Yet another prospect will be to build social networks of lawyers or legal advisers who are willing, in their own time, rather than on a face-to-face basis, to provide guidance, in a variety of ways, across the Internet (either directly to citizens or indirectly to advice workers).

Although these systems are being discussed here as though they belong to the future, there are already innumerable examples of operational online legal services. In the words of William Gibson, the science fiction writer, "The future has already arrived. It's just not evenly distributed yet." It is early days to be sure, but within a few years these systems, it is predicted here, will be commonplace in helping non-lawyers to recognize when they need legal help and to select the best sources of advice, as well as in actually offering them practical guidance. And this is not just the pipe dream of some Internet enthusiasts. Significantly, recent research found there is considerable enthusiasm amongst consumers for the online delivery of reliable legal support and advice (Legal Services Board 2012).

Some of these uses of online legal services would be disruptive of traditional law firms. But, at the same time, many of these techniques would make the law available to people who would otherwise have no affordable sources of legal help. This is the realization of the "latent legal market" —those countless occasions in the lives of many people when they need legal help and would benefit from legal help but, until now, have been unable to secure this assistance (whether to resolve, contain, or avoid problems, or indeed to afford them some benefit). Online legal services therefore will liberate the latent legal market.

## Legal e-Learning

Looking beyond the services provided daily by judges and lawyers, the Internet is also set to play an increasing role in education and training across the legal profession. In his erudite book, *Transforming Legal Education*, Paul Maharg demonstrates beyond any sensible discussion that legal education is indeed ripe for digital overhaul (Maharg 2007), while Brian Tamanaha, in his compelling text, *Failing Law Schools*, gives good reason to believe that change in legal education, at least in the United States, is long overdue (Tamanaha 2012).

Consider the conventional law lecture. The students assemble and in the British way (in contrast with the Socratic method favored by many prominent US law schools), the audience is "spoken at" for just under an hour. Many lawyers, when reminiscing about their legal undergraduate years, will say that the time they spent listening to some of their less inspiring lecturers was not time wisely spent. These lecturers were not trained as orators. Some mumbled and rambled; others simply read from their notes; while only a very few were wonderfully articulate and inspirational.

Proponents of first-generation e-learning see no reason why the conventional law lecture and the Socratic method of teaching should not be replaced by online lectures, presented by wonderful and inspirational speakers from other universities who make webcasts of their lectures available. It would be a shame, of course, if undergraduates were never to experience the enjoyment of assembling amongst friends in a crowded lecture hall and hearing an outstanding live performance. But the old ways should not be preserved in the delusion that this is the norm. The best lecturers should be identified, nurtured, and encouraged to speak regularly, and students should be urged to attend and listen. And these lecturers should also be invited to create webcasts for the benefit of others. There could be a TED equivalent of world-class law lectures (<www.ted.com>).

What, though, is the role for the not-so-great lecturers? Are they rendered redundant by the professorial rock stars, with their over-subscribed live performances and massively downloaded webcasts? Not at all. The rest should move steadily from being the law lecturer who acts as "the sage on the stage" to more of a teacher or coach, playing more of a counseling and tutoring role. Much in the way that the Universities of Oxford and Cambridge have conducted small tutorials since the 19th century, the emerging role for the law teacher should be that of the "guide on the side," building on the lectures that students have (generally) attended virtually. As the dominant, face-to-face approach to teaching, educating, lecturing, instructing, and training in the law is called into question by e-lectures, it is submitted that the job specification of the law teacher should change, shifting from a didactic responsibility to a more facilitative role. And this shift will also have direct effect on the ongoing education of qualified lawyers. Some commercial providers in the UK and US offer stand-alone web-casts, accredited under various continuing education schemes. Busy lawyers do not need to attend training courses and conferences to keep up to date. They can do this from their desktops.

Many more ambitious e-learning techniques have become well established. In 2009, a five-year review of e-learning at the College of Law in England was undertaken (Susskind 2009). This established that electronic tutorials and online supervision had substantially changed the learning experience of law students on the College's Legal Practice Course. More than 400 "i-Tutorials" had been developed. These were a type of webcast: online, head-and-shoulders video recordings of legal experts, with slides on the side. Students found these mini-lectures convenient. They could be stopped, started, and replayed, and they were portable too, in that they could be viewed on laptops and handhelds. While many law firms and law schools have dabbled in webcasting, the College led the way in industrializing and professionalizing the production process.

More controversially, the College had also gone a step further and developed a "supervised" mode of e-learning. On this mode there was one-to-one supervision by tutors, but it was virtual rather than face-to-face, so that the students rarely attended the College. In spirit, this created what could be regarded as an "electronic Oxbridge" —the strengths of the traditional tutorial system are embraced (the pressure, stimulation, and personal attention of a personal expert tutor) but achieved in an affordable and practical way. Lectures, again, were replaced by i-Tutorials, and tutors kept in touch with students by e-mail. Other tools, such as instant messaging, Skype, and webinars were to be introduced to improve the experience. The feedback from students was largely enthusiastic. The online facilities were said to be flexible, re-usable, green, and ideal for part-timers or those who live far from the College. And, on the supervised mode particularly, students welcomed the one-to-one attention from tutors.

However, here as in so many areas of legal technology, lawyers and observers should not fall into the trap of thinking that what we have today is all that will be on offer tomorrow. Maharg's work takes us beyond the world of electronic lectures and web-casts into the universe of simulation-based training and transactional learning. Based on his practical experience of using these methods, he compellingly argues that online simulations will enable students actually to engage in legal transactions, to experience the running of a legal practice, to be assessed reliably, to engage in collaborative learning and, in turn, to change quite fundamentally what and how they learn (Maharg 2007). He used these techniques extensively in the Scottish Diploma in Legal Practice and most dramatically he designed a fictional town, Ardcalloch, in which students play the part of solicitors in virtual law firms and are provided, amongst many other facilities, with characters, institutions, professional networks with whom they can communicate, virtual offices in which they can work, simulations of actual legal transactions, and a remarkable collection of resources that lend authenticity to the environment including newspaper clippings, photographs, wills, bank books, advertisements, and much more. A full history of Ardcalloch has been written, adding still further to the sense of reality that the designers have been at pains to create. Very crudely, this simulated learning environment is akin to *Second Life* for law students (although it is not 3-D).

Once again, the potential for e-learning in this broader sense extends well beyond law schools. Using techniques and technologies not unlike Maharg's, it is likely that trainee lawyers will serve as much of their apprenticeship by immersing themselves in simulated learning environments, as they will by sitting alongside more senior lawyers. In this way, not only will they be exposed to a richer and more stimulating range of training experiences, but also they will avoid the drudgery and repetition of traditional trainees' work.

Legal e-learning, therefore, need not simply be an IT-based or Internet-based instantiation of traditional legal education technique. Instead, the new technology allows lawyers to learn, and even work, in fundamentally new ways.


# Conclusion

This chapter highlights the transformative potential of the Internet and related applications: they are challenging judges to reappraise the manner in which disputes are resolved; they are urging lawyers and policy makers to revisit the ways in which access to justice is sustained in society; and they are encouraging educators to rethink the manner in which lawyers are trained.

Two broader themes in the current legal literature are echoed here. The first is that traditional methods of delivering legal service are, in various respects, failing to meet the needs of clients and are likely to change fundamentally in the coming years (Kowalski 2012; Morgan 2010; Harper 2013). The second is that information technology can and should play a central role in helping lawyers streamline and re-invent their working practices (Black 2012; Kimbro 2012).

In general, this chapter favours the changes that the Internet will bring to the law—more affordable and swifter resolution of disputes, easier access to justice, and improved training of lawyers. However, the anticipated developments also carry concerns. In particular, policy makers and legal technologists must be sensitive to the possible exclusion of the "hard to reach": those whose financial or social circumstances currently mean that the law is too forbidding, costly, or in other ways, inaccessible, are likely also to be amongst the digitally deprived. One way of meeting this concern is to encourage the new technologies to dovetail with the legal services offered through the voluntary sector.

On the other hand, there is potential here greatly to extend the reach of the law and legal support. In developing countries, where many citizens are unlikely to be aware of their legal entitlements or how to enforce them, there is the promise of legal support through mobile devices, and of educating the young on the rule of law and their legal rights, through web-based tools.

These possibilities and risks are of considerable significance. The law is, or ought to be, the prime method of social control. Existing and emerging Internet applications, if wisely deployed, could greatly deepen the impact and reach of the law, not just by restricting or obligating, but by empowering and enabling the people in whose name it is created.

## ■ REFERENCES

Black, N. (2012). *Cloud Computing for Lawyers*. Chicago, IL: American Bar Association.

Genn, H. et al. (2007). "Developing Capable Legal Citizens: The Role of Public Legal Education." <http://www.pleas.org.uk> (accessed July 13, 2013).

Harper, S. (2013). *The Lawyer Bubble*. New York: Basic Books.

Kafka, F. (1983). *The Trial*. Harmondsworth: Penguin.

Kimbro, S. (2012). *Limited Scope Legal Services: Unbundling and the Self-Help Client*. Chicago, IL: American Bar Association.

Kowalski, M. (2012). *Avoiding Extinction: Reimagining Legal Services for the 21st Century*. Chicago, IL: American Bar Association.

Legal Services Board (2012). *Understanding Consumer Needs from Legal Information Sources*. London: LSB.

Maharg, P. (2007). *Transforming Legal Education*. Aldershot: Ashgate.

Ministry of Justice (2010). *Virtual Court Pilot: Outcome Evaluation*. London: Ministry of Justice. <http://www.justice.gov.uk> (accessed July 13, 2013).

Morgan, T. (2010). *The Vanishing American Lawyer*. New York: Oxford University Press.

Resnik, J. and Curtis D. (2011). *Representing Justice*. New Haven, CT: Yale University Press.

Rule, C. and Nagarajan, C. (2010). "Leveraging the Wisdom of Crowds: The eBay Community Court and the Future of Online Dispute Resolution." Paper prepared for Dispute Resolution Conference 2010, organized by the Continuing Education Society of British Columbia.

Susskind, R. (2008). *The End of Lawyers?* Oxford: Oxford University Press.

Susskind, R. (2009). "The College of Law E-learning: 5-year Review." <http://college-of-law.co.uk> (accessed July 13, 2013).

Susskind, R. (2013). *Tomorrow's Lawyers*. Oxford: Oxford University Press.

Tamanaha, B. (2012). *Failing Law Schools*. Chicago, IL: University of Chicago Press.

Wahab, M., Katsh, E., and Rainey, D. (eds.) (2012). *Online Dispute Resolution: Theory and Practice*. The Hague: Eleven International.

Woolf, H. (1995). *Access to Justice—Interim Report*. <http://www.justice.gov.uk> (accessed July 13, 2013).

Woolf, H. (1996). *Access to Justice—Final Report*. <http://www.justice.gov.uk> (accessed July 13, 2013).

# 18 The Digital Divide and Employment: The Case of the Sudanese Labor Market

*Laura Mann*

## Introduction: Addressing Youth Unemployment and Access to Information

In 2005, a group of Harvard students developed the mobile phone application *Souktel* as a solution to the high youth unemployment problem in Palestine. The application allows jobseekers to upload qualifications and experience onto a central system via SMS (short message service) messages. It then allows employers to filter and contact relevant candidates. The service has been rolled out across Palestine, Somalia, Morocco, Jordan, Tunisia, and Egypt. In 2012, African-based entrepreneurs developed similar services, launching *mKazi* and *Duma* in Kenya, *Job Express* in Nigeria, and *mPawa* in Ghana. These entrepreneurs frame the problem of youth unemployment in a similar way. Jacob Korenblum, the founder of *Souktel*, explains:

[Y]outh unemployment hovers at around 40 per cent for 18 to 25 year-olds—almost double the jobless rates of adults. At *Souktel*, we believe this problem stems largely from one source: a lack of resources to help youth find work. Schools are cash-strapped, with none of Palestine's four largest universities offering a full-service career centre. Outside the classroom, only 34 per cent of Palestinian youth have regular web access. Young women face an even tougher time getting online, as most Internet cafes are dominated by males. Newspapers only advertise senior positions; social networks are limited to a small circle of family and friends. The result of this information shortage? Unemployment which could otherwise be avoided...However, in countries across the developing world, most youth do have basic cell phone access, even in rural areas.

(Korenblum 2010)

The problem is thus conceived primarily as one of information access. Unemployment could otherwise be avoided if people had better access to information about jobs. Nancy Wang, cofounder of *mKazi*, similarly describes how "[t]here is 70% mobile penetration in Kenya, but we are talking about 5 computers for every thousand people. A mobile tool like *mKazi* which sends personalised job alerts through basic mobile phones via USSD (Unstructured Supplementary Service Data) and SMS will bridge this gap" (Mulupi 2012). In Nigeria, Jeremy George, ForgetMeNot Africa's CEO (the producers of *Job Express*) likewise describes how: "[t]he OECD's research shows that a major concern for many young Africans is that jobs are only given to people with connections or relatives...*Job Express* helps to level the playing field by giving job applicants a direct method of application" (quoted in Matinde 2012). While it is acknowledged that job information largely flows through those with connections, these entrepreneurs claim that their systems can circumnavigate nepotism and democratize access.

This chapter examines these ideas in relation to Sudan's graduate labor market. It suggests that this simple framing oversimplifies the real problems. Difficulties in finding employment opportunities are not only due to lack of access to information, but also concerns over the validity of information. How can employers validate the reliability of information online—a problem that presents itself in many contexts around the world? In the next section, I examine wider theories about job information and technology before proceeding to a description of a case study of the Sudanese labor market, which provides an empirical perspective on these issues.

## The Strength of Weak Ties and the Rise of Network Society

The well-known expression "It's not *what* you know, but *who* you know" nicely sums up the job-seeking experience for most professionals. In 1973, Mark Granovetter published *the Strength of Weak Ties*, demonstrating how jobseekers are three times more likely to hear about jobs from social contacts than from formal means. He further demonstrated how the majority use "weak ties," contacts that job-seekers do not know well. He explains:

A natural *a priori* idea might be...that those with whom one has strong ties would be more motivated to help with job information. There is, however, a structural tendency for those to whom one is only *weakly* tied, to have better access to job information one does not already have. Acquaintances, as compared to close friends, are more prone to move in different circles than one's self. Those to whom one is closest are likely to have the greatest overlap in contact with those one already knows, so that the information to which they are privy is likely to be much the same as that which one already has.

(Granovetter 1995: 53)

Granovetter defined the strength of tie by frequency of contact before the information exchange. Of those in his sample who found their job through contacts:

16.7 per cent reported that they were seeing their contact 'often,' 55.6 per cent 'occasionally,' while 27.8 per cent saw him 'rarely' (N=54).

(Granovetter 1995: 53)

Since Granovetter, a generalized theory has been promulgated, stressing that weak ties are common in richer, formalized, and democratic communities, while strong ties are the hallmark of poorer, younger, chronically unemployed, closed, or politically corrupt communities (Bian 1977; Falcon 1995; Kasinitz and Rosenberg 1996; Ioannides and Loury 2004). Ronald Burt has similarly hypothesized that "structural holes," the breaks between networks, prevent information from traveling freely. Those able to bridge structural holes act as "brokers" linking networks with new sources of information (Burt 1992). Communities that fail to bridge into different networks are said to be pulled down by "neighborhood effects," ensuring solidarity but increasing isolation from others (Elliott 1999). Conversely, communities able to move across structural holes are said to be more flexible, innovative, and efficient in their allocation of resources and people.

Such theories have gained particular importance with the diffusion of ICTs. Economists such as Michael Spence have argued that the Internet has the potential to transform information flows within economies, relaxing geographic and social boundaries and allowing individuals to maintain contact with weaker, more distant ties (Spence 2002; Howard et al. 2001; Ellison et al. 2007). Citing Metcalfe's law, Spence describes how: "the value and hence, the speed of connecting accelerates as the [number of members in the network] increase[s]," thereby producing a "network effect" (Spence 2002: 437). This effect gives weak ties their velocity in ICT-mediated environments.

Manuel Castells has likewise argued that networks have become the dominant organizing principle in society (Castells 2010a). It is not merely the rise of new technologies that has produced this change, but rather their convergence with a certain historical evolution stemming from economic globalization and new social movements (Castells 2010a). These wider historical changes have produced more institutionalized forms of trust and looser networks of socialization (Polanyi 1944; Sennett 1977). When institutions mediate trust between strangers, ICTs can have their strongest impact.

So the discussion therefore proceeds: will ICTs have similar implications worldwide, despite major differences in the socio-economic make-up and technological infrastructures of countries? If people are given the capacity to share information easily, will they do so? Proponents of interventions such as *Souktel, mKazi, Job Express,* and *MPawa* appear to suggest so. While Internet penetration is still weak, they argue, mobile phone networks can effect similar change. In his third volume of *Network Society,* however, Manuel Castells appears to suggest otherwise.

The rise of Network Society, Castells writes, has simultaneously produced a Fourth World marginalized by a technological apartheid. In particular, he singles out Sub-Saharan Africa. Castells provides a fairly sophisticated justification for this assertion, drawing on the work of prominent Africanists such as Frimpong-Ansah, Davidson, Fatton, Leys, Bayart, and Lewis to assert that Africa's marginalization primarily derives from a weak institutional environment, co-created by colonial systems of government and the liberalization of Africa's export-oriented economies. These developments led to "the erosion of political institutions as stable systems" and their replacement with "close-knit circles of personal and ethnic loyalties" (Castells 2010b: 98). In such circumstances, Network Society accentuates existing economic and social cleavages.

Claudia Goldin and Lawrence Katz have likewise suggested that rising US inequality partly stems from the technological modernization of the economy without a corresponding modernization of the education system. In the first half of the 20th century, education kept up with technological change, but as the century moved into the 1980s, technological innovation outpaced education, and the United States became more unequal (Goldin and Katz 2008). Central to the development of the Network Society is therefore the creation and maintenance of stable, high-quality education systems that level out opportunity.

Such discussions imply that confronting unemployment in the developing world should be accomplished through a concerted restoration of primary, secondary, and tertiary education, and through the renovation of public institutions that allow weaker ties to form between communities. Of course, for ICT for Development (ICT4D) entrepreneurs on the ground today, they cannot wait for such changes. They must design and manage their systems to account for these deficiencies. The entrepreneurs at the beginning of this chapter mentioned both the institutional weaknesses of universities and the monopolization of opportunities by elites; yet their systems do not seem to address these issues head-on. Without tackling these problems, how do ICTs change access to information and opportunity among graduate job seekers?

# Methodology

This chapter draws on a focused case study of the role of networking in the Sudanese labor market, conducted by the author over the course of eighteen months between 2008 and 2010. The fieldwork included 159 interviews conducted with managers, jobseekers, civil servants, and professionals about the changing nature of the job search over time. In addition, a 300-person survey was conducted in 14 organizations and with 100 users of public buses. These surveys were based on those used by Mark Granovetter, asking how current employees had found out about their jobs. A number of focus groups were also conducted in hospitals, engineering firms, a recruitment company, and a scholarship NGO. In all cases, pseudonyms have been used for research participants.

In the manifold diversity of Africa and the Middle East, one should not generalize too much. Sudan shares a number of similarities with other countries, but it is also unique in many respects. The country has seen a massive expansion in higher education, similar to other countries in North Africa and Sub-Saharan Africa (Heyneman 1997; Teferra and Altbachl 2004; Schofer and Meyer 2005; Romani 2009). It has seen its economy liberalized and its state companies privatized. These changes have taken place within a heavily politicized environment. While most African and Arab countries have undergone similar economic transformations, there is of course, much social and political diversity behind each case (Tangri and Mwenda 2001; Reno 1997; Meagher 2007). This chapter does not therefore intend to suggest Sudanese trends are purely indicative of the rest of the continent and its neighbors. Rather, through an exploration of the Sudanese case, common threads can be teased out. How does information access relate, not just to infrastructure and technology, but also to wider social and institutional structures? Can technological provision really overcome social and political monopolization of power and opportunity? Or does the monopolization of information by elites reflect deeper structural barriers to trust and coordination among strangers and weaker ties? If so, how can mobile and web applications integrate trust-building processes that bring outsiders into information networks? These questions will be explored in more detail in the conclusion.

# The Privatization of Job Information

The Sudanese graduate labor market is characterized by strong and strengthening ties. However, these ties should not be understood as reflecting traditional kinship or tribal relations, but rather as contemporary phenomena, at least in the formal economy where a restricted but meritocratic labor market previously existed. In order to demonstrate this point, some brief historical background is necessary.

Sudan was first colonized by the Ottoman Empire in the 1820s, but slowly came under British influence as the century progressed. In 1881, a Sudanese religious leader emerged, proclaiming himself the *Mahdi*, or the "guided one." From 1885 to 1898, his followers attempted to assert control over the country in a shaky, turbulent rule. During this time, the French moved from West Africa towards the Nile. Fearing French influence in East Africa, a joint Anglo-Egyptian force re-conquered Sudan in 1899 and established a condominium government dominated by British administrators (Collins 2008).

With the memory of the Mahdist uprisings fresh in their mind, the colonial state was wary of political consciousness. It therefore restricted education and civil service employment to the bare minimum (Sanyal and Yacoub 1975). It made strong political alliances with the religious sects of the Khatmiyya and the Mirghani, preferring these groups to their urban educated counterparts, whom the British feared would call for greater political autonomy. The Umma Party, linked to the religious sect of the Ansar, and the Democratic Union Party (DUP), linked to the Khatmiyya sect, monopolized power after independence. From 1956 to 1989, Sudan experienced three periods of democracy (dominated by the Umma and the DUP) interrupted by two dictatorships: the Abboud regime and the Numayri regime. Neither dictatorship ultimately succeeded in threatening the two parties' entrenched control over the state.

The British established Gordon Memorial College (which later became the University of Khartoum) and prestigious regional high schools like Hantoub, Wadi Sedna, Rumbek, and El Fasher in smaller cities and towns. These high schools acted as "grammar schools" for the University of Khartoum, allowing clever boys from across the country to come to Khartoum and enter the professional labor market. In the lead up to independence, Cairo University opened a Khartoum Branch in 1955 and ten years later, an Islamic University opened. Shortly thereafter, a private women's college opened and two public universities in the 1970s: Juba University in 1977 and Gezira University in 1978. Gezira University focused on agriculture and medicine (the largest government agricultural scheme was in close proximity) and Juba University on the demands of Southern development after the signing of the Addis Ababa peace agreement between North and South in 1972. Before the Islamist coup in 1989, the country had increased its public and private universities from one to six: a modest increase.

The limited number of universities made it easy for graduates to get jobs after university. All students received internships during their studies and many were offered work in state institutions at graduation. Others would find work in private companies or overseas, where their qualifications were well regarded. Although government institutions like the *lujna ikhtiyar* (or selection committee) played a strong role in recruitment, Khartoum was also beginning to form a socio-economic network around education and civil service employment. While the elite classes monopolized access, others could climb the hierarchy provided they did well in regional schools. A baseline level of trust was established and graduates were rare and valuable. In 1989, this network of power would come under aggressive attack.

The National Islamic Front (NIF, which later became the National Congress Party, NCP) came to power in a military coup. The Islamists had little appeal outside Khartoum and were unable to compete with the sectarian parties of the Umma and the DUP on the national electoral stage. They immediately set about dismantling the old system of privilege and patronage. They initiated a *tamkeen* (or empowerment), re-shuffling personnel in the military, civil service, and parastatal companies. They privatized the economy, favoring party members while penalizing unaffiliated managers. They launched an "Education Revolution," purging university campuses of political opposition and "Islamizing" and "Arabizing" the curriculum (Breidlid 2005; Bishai 2008; El-Tom 2007). Public universities mushroomed from three to twenty-four in a seven-year period and financial responsibility shifted onto universities and parents. Private universities soon followed. University intake rose from 6,080 in 1989 to 13,210 the following year and to 132,047 by 2008 (Assal 2010: 5). Educational quality plummeted and qualifications lost much value. Within ten years of taking power, the new Islamist government had produced a very different kind of labor market. They had weakened the sectarian parties' control over the state, but in so doing, they had destroyed broader social networks and institutionalized trust. The next section looks at what these changes did to the job-search.

## Getting a Job ... in Khartoum

These political and educational changes have profoundly altered patterns of communication in the economy, such as in the advertising of jobs. Figure 18.1 shows variations in the source of information that individuals use to find out about jobs, broken down by age. We find that older generations are more likely to hear about their jobs from central work offices or through newspaper advertisements. Younger generations are increasingly reliant on information from personal contacts. A similar trend can be observed when using sources of information about jobs by period of recruitment. Those hired before the Islamist takeover and the Education Revolution were much more likely to use direct application and "open advertisements."

Figure 18.2 shows strength of tie by age. Here, strength of tie refers to frequency of contact period to the start of the job. If someone had seen the contact frequently prior to the job, she would be a "strong tie." Figure 18.2 demonstrates how ties in the labor market appear to be growing stronger over time. A similar trend was again observed when using period of recruitment. One thing that must be noted is the prevalence of "weak ties" within Sudanese families. In many cases, respondents who had not communicated with their

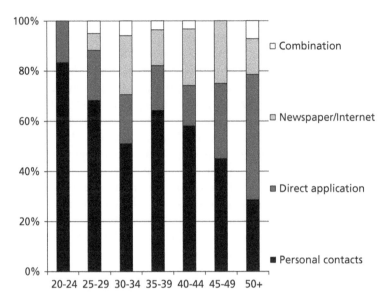

**Figure 18.1** Source of information about job by age
*Source:* Author

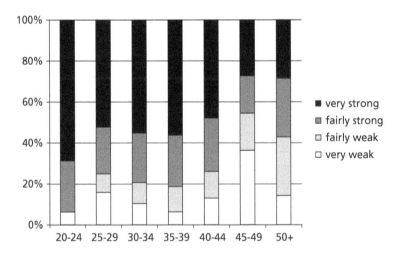

**Figure 18.2** Strength of tie by age
*Source:* Author

contact before the job also indicated that the contact was a family member. In one case, the respondent wrote: "The contact was my cousin and I met him on the day that he told me about the job and on the same day, I got the job." In this way, frequency of contact may not be a good indicator about the strength of tie when we consider Granovetter's characterization of strong ties as driven by motivation and weak ties as being driven by the structure of the information network. In Sudan, a weak tie (measured by frequency) could also be driven by strong family motivation. Nevertheless, the survey suggests that "strength of tie" weakens with age and appears to be strengthening over time. Older respondents hired in earlier periods were able to use weaker ties, but younger respondents appeared to depend more heavily on strong ties for information about jobs.

There are three possible explanations for the growing "strength of tie." First, older jobseekers might be more established and less reliant on ties for information. Second, the "weaker" ties of earlier periods might reflect a bias: information obtained from weaker ties might lead to more permanent employment. Third, the expansion of education and the corresponding increase in competition might have increased the value of information about jobs and made individuals less likely to share. This third explanation was suggested by graduates and employees who spoke of the "great value" of job opportunities and how people were unwilling to share information widely. One IT specialist described the competitiveness of a position in the Kuwaiti ICT company, Zain:

I had an interview at Zain during Ramadan. We were 500 (they said we are a short list!) competing for only one position. I met many of my colleagues from work, university, even from other banks that are far better than my bank. I realised what Zain means to Sudanese Engineers. As their ad slogan says: "Wonderful world". I was sad to meet one of my university seniors who taught me ABC in computer networks. I was sad because I felt he should be in a higher position, that he shouldn't be looking for a position that requires only two years of experience. Anyways, life isn't always fair.

Such opportunities in select companies are so valuable that all levels of applicants compete. The survey revealed a propensity for people with steady jobs to share information, while those with less secure or undesirable jobs to "horde." Responding to the question "Have you recently told anyone you know about a job?" one respondent who was desperate to change his job, replied: "No, I will apply myself and then I will tell my closest friends only." In another, responding to whether or not he agreed with the statement: "*Wasta* (personal intermediation) helps you find out about a job but it does not help you get a job," the respondent replied: "*Wasta* helps you find out about the job before it has been advertised and squeezes the time of advertisement so qualified people cannot apply for the job."

Has graduate unemployment merely strengthened the motivation of strong ties to share information, or has it also changed the structure and distribution of information between weak and strong ties? Several factors suggest strong ties have also become "structurally" privileged. In other words, Granovetter's key theory must be questioned in the Sudanese context. For example, responding to the statement, "*Wasta* helps reveal information about jobs but it does not help you actually get the job," many younger respondents strongly disagreed, citing the distinction between a contact who tells you about a job and a *wasta* who can influence the process as well. While university colleagues of a similar age might have information about jobs, older generations had more direct control over recruitment decisions. The small world of Khartoum with its restricted batch of graduates has been replaced by a large Khartoum with thousands of unemployed graduates with questionable qualifications. Graduates need the help of the older generation to get their foot in the door.

The threat of "hundreds and thousands" of CVs has made managers unwilling to publicize opportunity widely. In the words of one HR manager,

you get applications, but irrelevant. Elsewhere, you find people apply with the criteria that are mentioned in the advertisement, but here, everybody, when they see an advert, because people are very desperate, so you get like thousands of CVs (resumes) but the relevant ones are very few.

Many other HR managers described how they would no longer advertise positions. One manager revealed that in some cases "[p]eople are hired in companies through birthday parties, dinners, lunches…[and] family gatherings…I would say 80% of cases in Sudan hire this way nowadays." As the number of graduates expands and pressure increases, managers and HR personnel are encouraged to favor close relatives and friends above strangers or weaker ties. Many can no longer attend weddings and Friday prayers for fear that old school friends will besiege them with requests. Wealthier individuals have moved into new city districts, far from the close-knit neighborhoods of their youth. One older engineer complained that these new districts breed a different social etiquette. He described how people would come together during Ramadan in older areas: tables are brought out into the streets and neighbors share their evening meals as a community. In the new neighborhoods, he declared, social relationships are "only on your phone," and "the streets are empty" during Ramadan. While the value of social networks grows more precious, they also grow "tighter" as influential people try to shield themselves from wider social demands.

It is not just the graduates who benefit from this closed structure of communication. Managers continually explained that they wanted someone they could trust. They did not want "a random graduate off the street." Sanctions have intensified this sentiment. Due to the regime's former relationship with Osama bin Laden and the ongoing conflict in Darfur, international banks and credit card companies cannot conduct business in Sudan, so the bulk of business is done through cash transactions. Sanctions also limit access to software and business tools that would allow more institutionalized trust to form in organizations.

The legacy of the *tamkeen* (empowerment) period has also influenced the personalization of recruitment. "Ibrahim," a former civil servant in the

Ministry of Finance, estimated that 45% of state employees lost their jobs during *tamkeen*. Because *tamkeen* was accompanied by a political privatization process, private companies also developed a defensive, inward attitude. For these reasons, managers explained that it was very difficult to trust graduates whom they did not know.

The economy has become more private and less accessible to young people. Any semblance of institutionalized trust has vanished from the domestic education system. Nevertheless, the growing economy needs qualified individuals, capable of navigating international business and Sudanese consumer preferences alike. These individuals are increasingly hard to identify. Instead of asking state bodies and universities for such candidates, managers are increasingly using their own social networks, and private recruitment companies, and headhunting outside of the country. Strong ties are not only bound by motivation. The significance of strong ties is also embedded in the structure of information resources. Institutions no longer mediate trust, and allow weaker ties to play a structural role in the circulation of information.

## ICTs and Job Information

The survey also reveals counter trends. There has been an increase in private recruitment companies and Internet advertisements in recent years. Recruitment companies typically favor those with foreign qualifications, higher levels of English, and existing work experience. However, some fresh graduates without experience may also benefit if they can demonstrate competence to recruitment agents.

The most effective company, *Gizek,* trains and assesses graduates over time. In this way, *Gizek* does not merely relay information; rather it creates it, providing trusted advice about which individuals hold promise. This "quality control" is valuable to employers and does allow some fresh graduates to gain access to employment who otherwise might not. Quality costs, however, since companies like *Gizek* reside in the private sector, where both jobseekers pay and subscribers pay to see information and opportunity.

Similarly, the Internet functions as a kind of qualitative filter for managers. Responding to the question, "What kinds of communication do you regularly use?" 57 percent of respondents with experience abroad listed e-mail as a daily form of communication, while the corresponding figure with no experience abroad was 13 percent. Those who have lived abroad presumably want to keep in touch with friends overseas. Sudanese people living abroad might also be more exposed to ICT and might be better able to afford to use it. What is interesting however, is how these outside experiences impact their lives once they return.

As managers shift their advertisements online, they can effectively target particular groups without exposing themselves to wider pools of desperate young people. When asked about the possibility of introducing a mobile phone-based system like *Souktel* to Sudan, managers gave mixed replies. Many felt that such a system was not appropriate, arguing that the problem was not the transmission of information about vacancies—they would often receive too many applications—but the quality of the information they received back—they were not sure whether those who ostensibly had qualifications were really qualified. Some conceded that in many cases, they receive hundreds of applications from people who are not even remotely qualified for a position. In other instances, there were many candidates who were theoretically qualified but turned out to be unsuitable in an interview. Others lied about their qualifications.

Managers went so far as to suggest that widening access might worsen the situation for them. They did not want *more* applicants: they wanted *better* applicants, and perhaps more succinctly, they wanted to *know* which applicants were really better, rather than which applicants simply had lots of qualifications. One HR manager explained that a mobile matching system had been introduced by the company *Sudani* but had failed as the company found it difficult to recruit participating employers. A more successful kind of service has been *Sudanjobs*, a recruitment website set up by a young Sudanese entrepreneur. It is similar to *Souktel* but has one major difference: it does not use SMS, a highly accessible platform, but Internet, a more restricted platform.

While Internet usage is growing rapidly (Zain and Ericsson 2009), many graduates must still go to Internet cafes in order to surf the Web. Some research participants reported that they had email addresses but could not remember their passwords. Others used it so infrequently that they lost access and therefore had to start new accounts. Others yet had never had an email address before. *Souktel* is right in stressing the more democratic nature of SMS over email, but this ease of access also makes it less attractive to employers. ICT does not just widen access to information; it also allows individuals to limit access to information by playing on the "digital divide" and specifically by using more elaborate and sophisticated interfaces.

Designers can use technology to make things more accessible, but they can also use it to filter access. The head of *Sudanjobs* explained that the "Internet is more sophisticated. It reaches the right kind of people." This sentiment was also reflected in the comments of HR managers who said they preferred advertising on the net. One said, "I want someone who can use a computer. If they cannot apply for a job online, then they won't be able to work here." He explained how the Web acted as "his sieve." The information exchange within the recruitment relationship is therefore not just a mere information exchange. The method of transmission plays a role in constructing the way in which that information is to be evaluated. The more sophisticated the transmission and the more insulated from social pressures, the trustworthier it appears.

This chapter puts forth the thesis that the Internet is being used to circulate information about jobs precisely because it is an effective filter and that most graduates do not use it (see also Fountain 2005). When the masses begin to log on, HR managers may simply find other ways to filter applicants, perhaps by retreating into the social barriers that exist within the Internet itself, using intranets, using social media sites with privacy features, or simply by using personal emails within their own address books.

## Conclusions: Pausing for Reflections

ICTs have the potential to transform the way that individuals in developing economies network and share information. Nevertheless, such interventions need to make sense to users, speaking to their needs and desires. In the case of job information in economies with high youth unemployment, those needs and desires are varied: job-seekers want better access to information but managers want better information about job-seekers. Put succinctly, ICT4D entrepreneurs have partly misidentified the problem to be solved. It is not merely a lack of access to information, but also a lack of validation about information. The digital divide can thus be seen as a barrier for graduates without Internet access, but a resource for managers wishing to limit access to information to certain groups. Internet and mobile diffusion affects groups differently and technological provision alone cannot overcome the monopolization of power and opportunity held by elites. Open access involves convincing elites that wider access benefits them as well.

The Sudanese case study imparts short- and long-term lessons. In the short term, ICT4D entrepreneurs can learn from the success of recruitment companies like *Gizek*. These companies have come to occupy a niche because they move beyond information access and transmission. They give managers what they need. Through their training and observations, they create new trustworthy streams of information about applicants: personal characteristics, levels of English, presentation skills, and the reliability and accuracy of qualifications. There is a strong need for *trustworthy* information about jobseekers.

Different kinds of employers may have different kinds of information needs. A mobile-based application might be helpful to employers seeking low-skilled laborers, but Internet apps might be more suitable for employers recruiting highly skilled laborers. As one moves up the skills scale, more information and trust are needed to evaluate competence. Networks bring employers and job seekers part of the way, but the next steps of engendering a greater level of trust and confidence in the authenticity of information require further work, and most often, informal and interactive channels of communication. Developers and entrepreneurs building applications for the labor market need to work closely with managers in order to understand their information needs, and their anxieties over the authenticity and quality of applicants. As is the case with many kinds of ICT innovations, the hard work might not be in the technical invention, but rather in creating a complete infrastructure that integrates social intelligence by encouraging users to evolve both sides of the information exchange over time. Such trust-building can overcome the limitations of online networking, by building in complementary channels for communication. This idea can be applied to other kinds of online networking, such as dating and e-commerce sites. Here, applications often initiate the first contact between people who then go on to communicate by email, phone, or in person in order to strengthen levels of confidence and trust. In other words, scholars and practitioners need to look at the bigger picture of communication. They should not confine themselves to thinking about information access, but also to the reception and evaluation of information. How trustworthy is information? Do existing sources of information adequately signal value and difference? How can new kinds of information that widen access within and between networks be identified or created? How can online applications create opportunities for online and offline trust-building exercises to allow contacts to develop relationships and interpersonal knowledge over time?

In the long term, this case study has shown that graduate unemployment in Sudan has as much to do with politics and education as it does with the ICT infrastructure. Without restoring and caring for institutions of learning, it is unlikely that ICTs will produce the same kinds of networking as they have in parts of the world characterized by a "Network Society." Without upgrading universities, the digital divide is likely to continue to be used by managers seeking better-educated, more elite groups of applicants. The uneven diffusion of ICTs appears to deepen inequality further. Likewise, the extensive network of mobile phone users is unlikely to produce "network effects" unless common institutions that can build trust between communities of weak ties and strangers are restored.

### ■ REFERENCES

Assal, M. (2010). "Highly-Skilled Sudanese Migrants: Gain or Drain?" *CARIM Analytic and Synthetic Notes* (13) Highly-Skilled Migration Series. Florence: European University Institute, Robert Schuman Centre. <http://cadmus.eui.eu/dspace/handle/1814/13450> (accessed April 27, 2013).

Bayart, J. F. (1993). *The State in Africa: The Politics of the Belly*. London: Longman.

Bian, Y. (1997). "Bringing Strong Ties Back in: Indirect Ties, Network Bridges, and Job Searches in China," *American Sociological Review*, 62(3): 366–385.

Bishai, L. (2008). "Sudanese Universities as Sites of Social Transformation," United States Institute of Peace. Special Report 203, February.

Breidlid, Anders (2005). "Education in the Sudan: The Privileging of an Islamic Discourse," *Compare: A Journal of Comparative and International Education*, 35(3): 247–263.

Burt, R. (1992). *Structural Holes*. Cambridge, MA: Harvard University Press.

Castells, M. (2010a). *The Rise of the Network Society*, Volume I: *The Information Age* Oxford: Blackwell Publishers.

Castells, M. (2010b). *The Rise of the Network Society*, Volume III: *End of Millennium*. Oxford: Blackwell Publishers.

Collins, R. O. (2008). *A History Of Modern Sudan*. Cambridge: Cambridge University Press.

Davidson, B. (1992). *The Black Man's Burden: The Curse of the Nation-State*. New York: Times Books.

Elliott, J. (1999). "Social Isolation and Labour Market Isolation: Network and Neighborhood Effects on Less-Educated Urban Workers," *Sociological Quarterly*, 40(2): 199–216.

Ellison, N. B., Steinfield, C., and Lampe, C. (2007). "The Benefits of Facebook 'Friends:' Social Capital and College Students' Use of Online Social Network Sites," *Journal of Computer-Mediated Communication*, 12(4): 1143–1168.

El-Tom, M. E. A. A. (2007). *Higher Education in Sudan: Towards a New Vision for a New Era*. Khartoum: Sudan Centre for Education Research Occasional Monograph Series.

Falcon, L. (1995). "Social Networks and Employment for Latinos, Blacks, and Whites," *New England Journal of Public Policy* 11(1): 17–28.

Fatton, R. (1992). *Predatory Rule: State and Civil Society in Africa*. Boulder, CO: Lynne Reiner.

Fountain, C. (2005). "Finding a Job in the Internet Age," *Social Forces*, 83(3): 1235–1262.

Frimpong-Ansah, J. (1991). *The Vampire State in Africa: The Political Economy of Decline in Ghana*, London: James Currey.

Goldin, C. and L. Katz (2008). *The Race Between Technology and Education*. Cambridge, MA: Harvard University Press.

Granovetter, M. (1973). "The Strength of Weak Ties," *American Journal of Sociology*, 78(5): 1360–1380.

Granovetter, M. (1995). *Getting A Job: A Study of Contacts and Careers*. Chicago, IL: University Of Chicago Press.

Heyneman, S. P. (1997). "The Quality of Education in the Middle East and North Africa (MENA)," *International Journal of Educational Development* 17(4): 449–466.

Howard, P., Raine, L., and Jones, S. (2001). "Days and Nights on the Internet: The Impact of a Diffusing Technology," *American Behavioral Scientist*, 45(3): 383–404.

Ioannides, I. M. and Loury, L. D. (2004). "Job Information Networks, Neighborhood Effects and Inequality," *Journal of Economic Literature*, 42(4): 1056–1093.

Kasinitz, P. and Rosenberg, J. (1996). "Missing the Connection: Social Isolation and Employment on the Brooklyn Waterfront," *Social Problems* 43: 180–196.

Korenblum, J. (2010). "Fighting Youth Unemployment with Mobile Phones," CNBC News, December 2.

Lewis, P. (1996). "From Prebendalism to Predation: The Political Economy of Decline in Nigeria," *Journal of Modern African Studies*, 34(1): 79–103.

Leys, Colin (1994). "Confronting the African tragedy," *New Left Review*, 204: 33–47.

Matinde, V. (2012). "ForgetMeNot Africa Launches a Job Application Service," Human IPO News, July 24.

Meagher, K. (2007). "Manufacturing Disorder: Liberalization, Informal Enterprise and Economic Ungovernance in African Small Firm Clusters," *Development And Change* 38(3): 473–503.

Mulupi, D. (2012). "Kenya Job Alerts App Goes Viral," ITWeb Africa, June 26.

Polanyi, K. (1944). *The Great Transformation*. New York: Farrar & Rinehart.

Reno, W. (1997). "African Weak States and Commercial Alliances," *African Affairs*, 96: 165–185.

Romani, V. (2009). "The Politics of Higher Education in the Middle East: Problems and Prospects," Middle East Brief 36. Waltham, MA: Brandeis University.

Sanyal, B. and Yacoub, E. S. A. (1975). *Higher Education and Employment in The Sudan*. Paris: International Institute for Educational Planning.

Schofer, E. and Meyer, J. W. (2005). "The Worldwide Expansion of Higher Education in the Twentieth Century," *American Sociological Review*, 70 (6): 898–920.

Sennett, R. (1977). *The Fall of Public Man*. New York: Alfred A. Knopf.

Spence, M. (2002). "Signaling in Retrospect and the Informational Structure of Markets," *American Economic Review*, 92(3): 434–459.

Tangri, R. and Mwenda, A. (2001). "Corruption And Cronyism in Uganda's Privatization in the 1990s," *African Affairs*, 100: 117–133.

Teferra, D. and Altbachl, P. G. (2004). "African Higher Education: Challenges for the 21st Century," *Higher Education*, 47(1): 21–50.

Zain and Ericsson, 2009 "Economic Impact of Mobile Communications in Sudan," Briefing paper. <http://www.ericsson.com/res/thecompany/docs/sudan_economic_report.pdf> (accessed April 27, 2013).

# 19 A Critical Perspective on the Potential of the Internet at the Margins of the Global Economy

*Mark Graham*

Information and Communication Technology have inspired hopes, fears, and expectations of social, political, and economic change. Specifically, it is the technologically mediated reconfigurations, and speeding-up, of movements of information that have led many to talk about the transformative and even revolutionary effects that ICTs can have.

This chapter focuses on the overlaps between the Internet and economic networks in traditionally marginal parts of the world. A pervasive idea exists that the Internet can liberate economic information from many of its traditional geographic constraints, and so ultimately benefit the world's poor by removing frictions, barriers, and intermediaries that stand between producers of goods and commodities in the Global South and consumers of those things in the Global North.

Such ideas are examined through a case study of Internet use in the Thai silk industry. Thai silk is a high-cost product typified by long commodity chains connecting producers and consumers, in which the actual producers of silk receive very little of the value of the fabric that they produce. The case study demonstrates that while the Internet is allowing sellers of silk to expand their markets and reach out to new customers, few of these benefits are being accrued by the actual producers of silk. The benefits provided by Internet-enabled mediations and reconfigurations of commodity chains are therefore not being captured by those most in need.

The chapter concludes by arguing that many of our, often unrealistic, expectations of the power of ICTs in the contexts of marginal economies are based on particular spatial ontologies, or ways of imagining, the Internet. The Internet is undoubtedly an important transformative tool for many at the margins of the world's economy, yet there are ultimately many entrenched social, economic, and political relationships and obstacles to change that cannot be easily dispelled by removing barriers to the flows of information.

## Hopes for ICTs in the World's Economic Margins

Hopes for the transformative power of ICTs have been especially pronounced in the poorest parts of the world for a few interconnected reasons. First, the South has traditionally faced the biggest barriers to the transmission and communication of information non-proximately. ICTs can alter the relationships between people and information in key ways: they can change the speed at which information is transmitted over space (thus altering geographic frictions), they can change the cost of transmitting information (altering economic frictions), and they can change the accessibility of information and communication networks by altering barriers to entry.

In the poorest parts of the world, the time–space paths of most people have traditionally been highly constrained by distance. Simultaneously, they have also been lacking in the technological mediations that have the potential to alter either geographic or economic frictions. Because of this, the potential of the Internet to reconfigure time–space paths of people and information in global cores will be different than at global peripheries. For instance, access to a mobile phone and Wikipedia will mean something entirely different to a person in New York who already has access to a fixed landline phone and lives close to a public library than to a person in Bujumbura who had access to neither type of information or communication affordance. It has followed that many governments and development agencies have seen broadening access to ICTs in the Global South as a way to 'leapfrog' stages of economic development. This has led some prominent voices such as Jeffrey Sachs to claim that "mobile phones are the single most transformative technology for development" (quoted in Etzo and Collender 2010: 661).

Second, and relatedly, is the idea that ICTs in the Global South will be able to radically reconfigure flows of capital and commodities. For many policy makers, the reduction of geographic frictions that techno-mediated changes in connectivity are thought to bring about, can allow for both better functioning markets and better access to markets: the idea being that both changes will ultimately result in economic development and tangible benefits for people currently excluded from selling their goods and services.

The UK's Department for International Development (DFID), for instance, claims that "weak, inefficient or non-transparent markets and societal institutions, including governments, hinder economic growth, deter private sector innovation and investment, and weaken the ability of society to respond to the needs of the poor." In markets characterized by opaque economic information and significant barriers to non-proximate information flow, sellers often only know local prices and can thus be locked into selling to middlemen and intermediaries who have local footprints (see also Grover and Ramanlal 1999). This could mean village weavers selling their goods cheaply to a local intermediary rather than to a buyer in the nearest city due to lack of knowledge about the urban market value of their cloth, or fisherpeople similarly selling their catch for a low price in one port, not knowing that the price for their fish is significantly higher just a few miles away (Coyle 2005 in Carmody 2012).

Further exacerbating the poor position of producers is the issue of clientelization (Eggleston et al. 2002). In an environment of high information search costs, producers of goods (such as farmers) are not just pushed into dealing with intermediaries, but are also often locked into long-term relationships with those dealers. This can be problematic because sellers are thus unable to "independently assess the integrity of the dealer, or the reasonableness of the prices he offers, by comparing purchase prices across many markets and many dealers" (Eggleston et al. 2002: 67).

Many of these examples of what economists refer to as weak, inefficient, or non-transparent markets are enacted because of a paucity of information. Because of their geographic positionalities (i.e. their non-proximate position to relevant information sources), many sellers are unaware of demand, and many buyers are unaware of supply, allowing the lion's share of value to be captured by intermediaries rather than producers and farmers (who are often the poorest in society). But in markets with efficient and transparent flows of information, it becomes difficult for intermediaries to capture excessive amounts of value in the chains of commodities that exist between producers and consumers (UNCTAD 2003: 163).

Poon and Jevons (1997: 34) state that "because the Internet creates a 'borderless' virtual business platform on which suppliers, customers, competitors and network partners can freely interact without going through the pre-defined channels on the value chain, members of the same business network or of different networks can bypass the traditional interaction patterns and form virtual value chains." As such, "the Internet has diminished many of the information asymmetries (and hence power asymmetries) between sellers and buyers" (Gereffi 2001: 1628). Firms in "developing nations" can use transparency brought about by the Internet to find new customers in order to "escape local de facto monopolies" (UNCTAD 2005). In a borderless world, it is argued that historical competitive advantages such as firm size become irrelevant because the Internet can "level the competitive playing field by allowing small companies to extend their geographical reach and secure new customers in ways formerly restricted to much larger firms" (OECD 1999: 153), such as by allowing villagers to better understand the market price for their crops in nearby towns (Anderson 2005).

There are important counter-arguments to some of these positions. Some of the most sustained criticism is leveled by those who see the spreading of ICTs as a way of enabling and giving shape to processes of neo-colonialism and exploitation (Gurumurthy and Singh 2009; Roy 2012). Early dependency theorists observed that the integration of "Third World" economies into first world markets created a state of dependence. Dos Santos (1970: 231) describes such dependence as "a situation in which the economy of certain countries is conditioned by the development and expansion of another economy to which the former is subjected." Drawing on the work of dependency theorists and post-colonial theorists, commentators such as Sardar (1996) see the Internet "as a new phase in a long history of the West's attempt to colonize not only the territory and the body but also the mind of the Third World 'other'" (Schech 2002: 18).

From this perspective, by taking places out of their isolation and placing them in a global village, such places are thrust into the hegemony of Western knowledge and capitalism (Pieterse 2001). Producers then grow dependent on unstable market conditions and distant consumer preferences (Dahles and Zwart 2003). Profitable elements of local cultures (such as silk making) are packaged and integrated into the network, while others are potentially ignored, both by distant consumers and local people. This dynamic can also have harmful effects on the crafts being produced: "the decline of craftsmanship, their simplification, the denigration of aesthetic and material culture and the loss of their symbolic and functional value, [...and] the subjection of indigenous groups to the external exigencies of the commercialization process" (Dahles and Zwart 2003: 146).

Nonetheless, this chapter mostly concerns itself with the hopes rather than the fears of ICTs in the world's economic margins. The arguments above (both the hopes and the fears), interestingly move beyond viewing the Internet as a tool for disintermediating commodity chains, and also see it as a technology with the power to accomplish an unfettered geographic expansion of markets. Purcell and Toland (2004: 241) claim: "ICT[s] offer the opportunity to reduce the barriers of distance, and give...countries better access to the global economy." According to the International Telecommunication Union, the Internet "provides developing countries with a unique opportunity to compete in market places that were beyond their reach" (Ntoko 2007: 1).

The ideas that the Internet will allow for geographic expansion and disintermediation are deeply intertwined, and rest on a particular spatial ontology. For both geographic expansion and disintermediation to occur, the Internet needs to bring consumers and producers into the same online marketplace. To do this, the Internet needs to take on an ontic (i.e. a physical or material) role. The assumption here is that the Internet can bring into being both an ethereal alternate dimension that is infinitely accessible (from any connected portal on the planet), and fixed in a distinct (cyber-) location (the virtual marketplace in which all producers and consumers transact with one another). Using the Internet to transport producers and consumers into co-presence in a virtual marketplace thus means that both physical barriers and the intermediaries who throughout history have served as a bridge over physical distance are rendered largely irrelevant (to the transactions that are supposed to happen between producers and consumers).

With the assistance of ICTs, many governments and development organizations therefore see the potential for significant change and an ability to bring development to the poor by bypassing entrenched economic power relations. For such reasons, there are substantial hopes vested in the potential for information and communication technologies in the Global South. ICTs are able to reconfigure time–space paths of people and information, and fundamentally alter economic flows and the functioning of markets: in doing so, potentially providing benefits to the most marginal and disconnected in society.

## Digital Divides in the Thai Silk Industry

It is useful to ground some of these important expectations in a concrete example of the intersections between ICTs and marginal economies. As such, this section reviews some of the results of my research into the role of the Internet in the Thai silk industry (Graham 2010; 2011a; 2011b; 2013).

The Thai silk industry has existed for thousands of years and remains an important part of the Thai economy and Thai social practices. Statistics vary considerably on the matter, but it is estimated that there are over 150,000 and as many as 500,000 households, mostly in north-eastern Thailand, that are dependent on the production of silk for supplemental income (UNCTAD/WTO 2002).

Many unique weaving patterns have been handed down from mothers to daughters for generations. For instance, when interviewing a weaver in Khon Kaen province, I was told, "I have been weaving some of these designs since I was born." The weavers sitting next to her laughed at the statement, but then agreed that they too have been producing certain distinct styles since they were taught to weave. Almost any weaver in the north-east can point to unique designs and patterns that they have seen and woven all of their lives and that are distinct to their village, town, or province (Conway 1992).

The Thai silk industry is distinct in Southeast Asia in its predominant use of handlooms (see Figure 19.1). Reeling and weaving are most often performed by hand by rural women and elderly household members. But Thai silk producers are currently in a worrying economic position. The old global Multi-Fibre Arrangement (MFA), which expired in 2005, set export limits to wealthy

**Figure 19.1** Digital divides in the Thai silk industry
*Source:* Author

countries on textiles. With its expiration, Thailand's National Economic and Social Development Board and the World Bank (2005) warned that Thai silk is highly uncompetitive in comparison to Chinese and other imported fabrics. They estimate that large reductions in labour costs or increases in productivity are needed.

Although Thai silk tends to be expensive, labour costs in the silk industry are paradoxically already extremely low (silk weavers are some of the lowest-paid workers in the country). In the north-east, stories abound about mothers being unable to persuade their daughters to take up weaving because of the relative allure of factory work in Bangkok and Central Thailand. It is the many intermediaries and merchants that instead tend to capture much of the value of any particular piece of cloth. On the other hand, while increases in productivity might initially seem desirable, the necessary adoption of hybrid or foreign higher-yield silk would eliminate domestic varieties that are the basis for traditional Thai hand-woven silk products.

Policy makers are then faced with a dilemma: saving an industry that is economically important for thousands of people without undermining the unique cultural practices and traditions associated with silk that are important for many Thais. It is this moment of crisis and worry that has given rise to many people in government, in civil society, and in the private sector seeing the Internet as a partial solution to these issues.

The Internet could, in theory, reinvigorate the Thai silk industry in two ways (reminiscent of the two hopes for the transformative power of the Internet described at the beginning of this chapter). First, it could allow sellers to use new types of visibility afforded by the Internet to move beyond traditional time–space paths and networks of Thai silk to reach out to new and distant consumers. Second, it could increase economic transparency in the market for Thai silk, ultimately allowing producers to sell to consumers without the need for long chains of intermediaries.

Much effort has been spent trying to use the Internet to save the Thai silk industry. The former Prime Minister of Thailand, Thaksin Shinawatra, recognizing that Thailand could not compete with China on mass-produced products, often argued that Thailand needed to blend its unique heritage with ICTs in order to thrive in a global economy. He stated, for instance, that

We are looking inward to our original strengths, our unique local know-how, and matching them with new marketing and communications technology. The aim is to create a new class of entrepreneurs who could marry local skills with international technology and hence move up the value chain. (Phongpaichit and Baker 2002: 3)

These ideas were put into practice in Thailand's ten-year ICT policy framework in which the government declares "e-commerce as the national trade strategy" and the necessity to "proactively engage in international trade" (UNCTAD 2003: 84). A pillar of the policy framework was the setting up of a large government economic stimulus program to market and sell Thai handicrafts in trade fairs and through the Internet.

My research, therefore, was designed to study this coming-together of the Internet and a dying craft industry. I spoke to 126 silk producers and merchants and analyzed the websites of 139 Thai silk sellers to explore key research questions. These questions were designed to understand the intersections of the Internet and the Thai silk industry, and identify some of the real potentials and barriers of the Internet for people in the world's economic margins.

The study asked: (1) how people in the silk industry imagine and envision the effects of the Internet, and how they use new types of visibility afforded by the Internet to represent their businesses and their work online; (2) whether sellers are actually using the Internet to sell to new and distant customers; (3) whether the Internet is being employed to disintermediate commodity chains and allow more direct links between producers and consumers; and (4) whether the Internet and integration into new commodity chains is altering the types of silk produced by weavers and ultimately reshaping the ways in which cultural practices are reproduced.

The work found that many sellers choose to portray the Internet as a tool that has brought about significant benefits to actors in the Thai silk industry. Many of these portrayals centred on the notion of 'directness' or distintermediation that could be enabled by the Internet. Some sellers focused on the benefits of this directness to consumers:

Most [pieces of silk] are acquired directly from the artists or workshops that produce them. This allows us to offer lower pricing and provides greater control over the quality and designs of the products. [<www.asianartmall.com>]

The crafts that you see on our site are supplied direct from source which helps us to keep our prices very competitive, against other Thai and non Thai suppliers. [<www.chiangmaicraft.com>]

Others chose instead to highlight the benefits to the producers of silk:

World of Thai Silk online fabric shop connects you directly to Thailand's rural village weavers as well as the wholesale fabric of the largest weaving mills. No matter how distant you are from these villages, now you have access to them online. [<www.bangkok-thailand.com>]

We also aim to provide a platform for the skilful Thai craft people. Many of those live in remote villages and do not have access to the world market. [www.thailandfashion.net]

It is hoped that an expanded market for their silk craft can be developed. We are encouraging the female weavers to produce more of their "folk art" silk for a market previously beyond their reach. [<www.thaivillagesilk.com>]

In both cases, there is an idea that the Internet can bring into being direct connections and a form of proximity between producers and consumers that didn't exist before. These claims about altered commodity chain topologies and imagined proximities are then used as a base for powerful arguments that then result in an accrual of economic and cultural benefits for producers and/or consumers (i.e. lower prices and the sustainability of the industry).

However, most of these statements about directness, new positionalities, and disintermediation actually come from intermediaries, rather than producers of silk who are disintermediating commodity chains. North-eastern producers have, for the most part, been unable to establish online presence, and it is merchants located primarily in Bangkok or outside of Thailand who have instead positioned themselves as virtual bridges in the buying and selling of silk. It is conceivable that proximity to markets (in terms of positions on the commodity chain) plays a factor in encouraging Bangkok merchants to create websites, as they adapt to the needs or desires of their customers.

Not only are intermediaries more likely to use the Internet to sell silk than producers, but both producers and merchants who use the Internet often see no noticeable change in the topological length of their commodity chains. Firms that use the Internet are actually more likely than those that do not to sell silk to intermediaries and are more likely to buy silk from intermediaries. In the Thai silk industry, instances in which the Internet is being used to shorten commodity chains are exceptions and aren't representative of common experiences with the Internet.

This isn't to say that the Internet has no geographical effects: Internet users are actually more likely to sell both non-locally and non-proximately. Specifically, amongst producers and merchants who do not have websites, there is a distance-decay pattern that can be seen: Thai customers are by far the most important, followed by customers elsewhere in Asia. No such statement can be made about producers or merchants that use websites, as their important customers are far more geographically dispersed. In some ways, then, the Internet seems to be altering the manner in which distance is experienced by firms in the Thai silk industry. Absolute distance is made less relevant and less of a barrier for firms with an online presence.

## Pak Thong Chai

Why then is the Internet being used so well in expanding markets geographically, and yet at the same time is so ineffective at breaking down existing commodity chain structures? One reason is likely a lack of economic transparency throughout the commodity chain. Intermediaries limit knowledge about weavers to customers, and limit knowledge about customers to weavers.

An example of this can be seen in the town of Pak Thong Chai in north-eastern Thailand. Pak Thong Chai is one of the hubs of the production of plain silk in

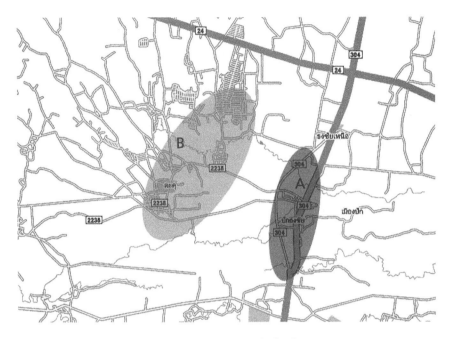

**Figure 19.2** Pak Thong Chai, Nakhon Ratchasima, Thailand
Google Maps (base map) and author

the region (see Figure 19.2). Location A on the map is the center of town and contains a cluster of fifteen to twenty shops like the one in Figure 19.3. Most of these shops are designed for a comfortable shopping experience: they are sometimes air-conditioned, have polished wood interiors, and bilingual staff who offer visitors water and coffee.

Location B is where much of the actual weaving of silk occurs. It is an altogether different place. For outsiders, many of the weaving groups in this area are extremely challenging to find. They are situated in small side-streets devoid of signs. The purchasing experience is also an entirely different one: there is no polished furniture, no air conditioning, and no pretty displays of products (Figure 19.4). The weavers here rarely interact with end-customers; something evident from my conversation with the group leader in location B. He told me:

> I don't know much about the shop that buys from me; they show up here at my house when they need more. I just know that they want the silk in long pieces. The price always varies, but sometimes if I really need money I have to sell it for 100bt a yard and lose money on the sale.

This conversation is symptomatic of many other stories recounted to me in the area. In very few cases, in the north-east of Thailand, do the actual weavers of

**Figure 19.3** Silk shop
*Source:* Author

silk ever communicate directly with the consumer, and because of this there is very little transparency within, and a lack of knowledge about, distant nodes on the commodity chains of Thai silk[1].

For instance, I asked all silk sellers that I spoke with to tell me about what their customers do with their silk. A large number of people told me that not only did they not know, but they also didn't care as long as they kept buying from them. The head of another weaving group in Pak Thong Chai that sells large amounts of silk to local merchants told me that:

> There is such a long chain of people, and I really just don't know where it goes. I don't know if the retailers that buy from us export our silk.

Others did have a vague idea of what happens to their silk, but were still lacking any specific details. The head of another weaving group recounted:

---

[1] As an example, there is a pervasive myth among Thai consumers outside of the north-east that most Thai silk comes from Chiang Mai and the northern region of Thailand (hundreds of miles away from the north-east). On numerous occasions when telling Thais about my project, they insisted that I should be spending more time in Chiang Mai. What actually happens is that many merchants from Chiang Mai travel to cities in the north-east, buy silk, and rebrand it in their shops.

**Figure 19.4** Spinning platform
*Source:* Author

I know that some of the people who buy from me export my silk, but I have no idea to where.

The example of Pak Thong Chai succinctly illustrates that the problem faced by people in the silk industry is not remoteness or distance from markets. Both places in Figure 19.3 are equally far removed from important and distant markets. In other words, the issue faced by many is not distance from markets, but rather a lack of transparency and an absence of functional information about markets.

More broadly, in the Thai silk industry, the Internet is undoubtedly allowing a few people and firms (most of whom are merchants in Bangkok) to sell in new markets, and is enabling some reconfigurations of economic positions. It is helping some people to reach out to customers all over the world (e.g. the merchants with websites described earlier in this chapter). But, while the Internet can theoretically allow people like the weavers in Pak Thong Chai to bypass existing nodes in commodity chains, it is difficult to see how that would work in practice. The actual producers of silk have little experience of marketing to distant consumers. Furthermore, this unfamiliarity with selling to other nodes on the commodity chain seems to have made many people skeptical about ever using the Internet for business purposes.

Some had never used the Internet, but nonetheless had an understanding of its potentials. One seller noted, "The reason I don't have a website now is because of copying. I will probably do it in the future, but I will decide which silk to show online." Others also had no direct experience with the Internet, but instead were pessimistic about its benefits. The head of a weaving group told me, "I prefer selling face to face so that people can touch. If I had a website, people might not buy anything. We had some people come around and tell us that they were putting our silk on a website. I don't know the name of it though.... They never call though so it doesn't matter." Finally, others were still hostile to the idea of using the Internet. One weaver shook her head in disgust when I asked what she thought about the Internet and told me: "Other people have told me that colors are different on the Internet. It is not sure for selling and people might not pay money. What would I do then?"

In sum, there are three important points to take away from the case of the Thai silk industry. First, many sellers with websites choose to highlight the idea that the Internet brings about transparency and directness in the commodity chains of Thai silk. Ironically, it is primarily intermediaries (as opposed to producers) that use the Internet to sell silk. Sellers with websites are more likely to sell their silk internationally, but also more likely to sell to other intermediaries. The second key point is therefore that the Internet does not appear to be facilitating a process of disintermediation in this industry. Finally, relationships in the silk industry tend to be opaque, not because of an inability to communicate information and economic signals non-proximately, but because of a range of other micro-level barriers. Producers who are functionally illiterate, mono-lingual, and inexperienced in basic mathematics necessarily rely on intermediaries to do the work of brokering transactions.

We need to then ask why there are such powerful assertions about the disruptive and disintermediating potentials of the Internet and yet the benefits have been mostly captured by people and firms that the Internet was supposed to make irrelevant. Why do we expect the Internet to bring about transparency in the commodity chains of silk when economic transparency is clearly reliant on so much more than the technologically mediated ability to transmit information? I assert that many of the hopes that we have for benefits that can be accrued to the underprivileged and disempowered through disintermediations, directness, transparency, and the bringing into being of virtual marketplaces all rest on a very particular ontology of space.

# Reimagining the Internet

Development discourse is replete with suggestions that the Internet can *connect you directly, make the work smaller,* and *expand markets.* More broadly, much of the power embedded in discourses about the 'digital divide' lies in the fact that they are able to postulate movement across space.

In some cases, much of the spatiality embedded into rhetoric about the 'digital divide' refers to the geography of the divide itself. That is, a divide can be thought to exist between the North and South, East and West, urban and rural, etc. But to many people who talk about 'digital divides,' the Internet takes on an ontic role. The Internet (or a 'cyberspace'), is conceived of as an ethereal alternate dimension which is simultaneously infinite and everywhere (because everyone with an Internet connection can enter) and fixed in a distinct location, albeit a non-physical one (because despite being infinitely accessible all participants are thought to arrive into the same marketspace, civic forum, and social space). The Internet then turns into Marshall McLuhan's idea of a global village.

Employing this 'global village' conceptualization of the Internet, this ontology that sees the Internet as bringing into being a space that is simultaneously infinite and fixed, then the 'digital divide' becomes not a statistical divide between people or places, but rather an existential divide between those that can access a shared cyberspace, and those who remain rooted to the material world and constrained by traditional barriers of time and space.

It is then easy to see how expectations and claims about the Internet rarely seem to have matched up to its effects in the Thai silk industry. Ideas of transparency, directness, and proximity all appear to be grounded in the type of ontology described above. By rendering material time–space paths and barriers less relevant, and by providing a new virtual space in which goods and information can be exchanged, the Internet was thought to offer an effective solution to the silk industries' woes that are based on persistent barriers of long commodity chains and distances between producers and consumers. However, use of the Internet in the Thai silk industry has not had the expected effects.

First, the Internet appears to be partially fulfilling its geographical potentials. Absolute distance is made less relevant and less of a barrier for firms that have an online presence, with Internet users more likely than others to sell internationally. But at the same time, despite facilitating trade with new markets, the Internet doesn't appear to be facilitating the transparency and directness that so many hoped that it would.

It is important to note that the Internet is actually not being used by most producers of silk. Many of the people interviewed either saw too many difficulties or no economic value in attempting to use the Internet to sell silk. Instead, it is more often employed by merchants in Bangkok and abroad. Furthermore, merchants found most success selling to other companies rather than to end-customers. This means that many people are effectively using the Internet to add commodity chain positions rather than disintermediating those chains: a point which runs counter to much that is written about the potentials of the Internet.

In the places it is being used by producers, it is rarely an effective tool. The producers of silk who had used the Internet were quite unfamiliar with the requirements or tastes of any distant markets. This is because intermediaries often occupy a crucial (and useful) organizational position on the commodity chains of silk. Put another way, the Internet changes the relative spatial positionalities of intermediaries, yet does little to alter their economic, cultural, and educational positionalities.

This chapter has argued that because of very specific ontologies that we tend to use when thinking about the Internet and its social and economic effects, we can often have unrealistic expectations about the transformative potentials of the Internet in the world's economic margins. Reducing a digital divide does not automatically bring a virtual, transparent, and direct marketplace into being that can transcend the distance between producers and consumers. The ability to engage in non-proximate trade in most cases requires an Internet connection, but is also clearly contingent on a range of other economic, cultural, political, and technological positionalities, barriers, and costs. Not everyone has the education, experience, linguistic knowledge, willingness, or desire to innovate, and interpersonal networks necessary to reconfigure commodity chains; and Internet-access alone is rarely sufficient to fundamentally reconfigure entrenched, and often unfair, economic networks and relationships in the world's economic margins.

## ▦ REFERENCES

Anderson, N. (2005). "Building Digital Capacities in Remote Communities within Developing Countries: Practical Applications and Ethical Issues. Information Technology," *Education and Society* 6(3): 1–15.

Carmody, P. (2012). "A Knowledge Economy or an Information Society in Africa? Thintegration and the Mobile Phone Revolution," *Information Technology and Development* (4 October): 1–16.

Conway, S. (1992). *Thai Textiles*. Bangkok: River Books Press.

Coyle, D. (2005). "Overview. Africa: The Impact of Mobile Phones," *Vodafone Policy Paper Series.*

Dahles, H. and Zwart, E. (2003). "Tourism and Silk Trade in Post-Civil War Cambodia," *Pacific Tourism Review*, 6: 143–157.

Dos Santos, T. (1970). "The Structure of Dependence," *American Economic Review*, 60: 231–236.

Eggleston, K., Jensen, R., and Zeckhauser, R. (2002). "Information and Communication Technologies, Markets, and Economic Development," in G. Kirkman et al. (eds.), *The Global Information Technology Report 2001-2002: Readiness for the Networked World*. New York: Oxford University Press, 62–75.

Etzo, S. and Collender, G. (2010). "The Mobile Phone 'Revolution' in Africa: Rhetoric or Reality?" *African Affairs*, 109(437): 659–668.

Gereffi, G. (2001). "Shifting Governance Structures in Global Commodity Chains, With Special Reference to the Internet," *American Behavioral Scientist*, 44(10): 1616–1637.

Graham, M. (2010). "Justifying Virtual Presence in the Thai Silk Industry: Links Between Data and Discourse," *Information Technologies and International Development*, 6(4): 57–70.

Graham, M. (2011a). "Disintermediation, Altered Chains and Altered Geographies: The Internet in the Thai Silk Industry," *Electronic Journal of Information Systems in Developing Countries*, 45(5): 1–25.

Graham, M. (2011b). "'Perish or Globalize:' Network Integration and the Reproduction and Replacement of Weaving Traditions in the Thai Silk Industry," *ACME: Journal of Critical Geographies*, 10(3): 458–482.

Graham, M. (2013). "Thai Silk Dot Com: Authenticity, Altruism, Modernity and Markets in the Thai Silk Industry," *Globalizations* 10(2): 211–230.

Grover, V. and Ramanlal, P. (1999). "Six Myths of Information and Markets: Information Technology Networks, Electronic Commerce, and the Battle for Consumer Surplus," *MIS Quarterly*, 23(4): 465–495.

Gurumurthy, A. and Singh, P. J. (2009). "ICTD – Is it a New Species of Development?" *IT For Change Perspective Paper*. <http://idl-bnc.idrc.ca/dspace/bitstream/10625/41794/1/129457.pdf> (accessed June 25, 2012).

Ntoko, A. (2007). "e-Business: A Technology Strategy for Developing Countries." International Telecommunication Union. <http://www.itu.int/ITU-D/e-strategies/2007/publicationsarticles/wmrcjune00/ntoko.html> (accessed June 25, 2012).

OECD (1999). *The Economic and Social Impact of Electronic Commerce*. Paris: OECD Publications.

Phongpaichit, P. and Baker, C. (2002). "The Only Good Populist is a Rich Populist: Thaksin Shinawatra and Thailand's Democracy." Working Paper Series 32. <http://www.cityu.edu.hk/searc/WP36_02_PasukBaker.pdf> (accessed June 25, 2012).

Pieterse, J. N. (2001). *Development Theory: Deconstructions/Reconstructions*. London: Sage.

Poon, S. and Jevons, C. (1997). "Internet-Enabled International Marketing: A Small Business Network Perspective," *Journal of Marketing Management*, 13: 29–41.

Purcell, F. and Toland, J. (2004). "Electronic Commerce for the South Pacific: A Review of E-Readiness," *Electronic Commerce Research*, 4: 241–262.

Roy, A. (2012). "Ethical Subjects: Market Rule in an Age of Poverty," *Popular Culture*, 24(1): 105–108.

Sardar, Z. (1996). "alt.civilizations.faq: Cyberspace as the Darker Side of the West,". in Z. Sardar and J. R. Ravetz (eds), *Cyberfutures: Culture and Politics on the Information Superhighway*. New York: New York University Press, 777–794.

Schech, S. (2002). "Wired for Change: The Links Between ICTs and Development Discourses," *Journal of International Development*, 14: 13–23.

Thailand's National Economic and Social Development Board and the World Bank. (2005). *Thailand Northeast Economic Development Report*. Bangkok: Thailand's National Economic and Social Development Board and the World Bank.

UNCTAD (The United Nations Conference on Trade and Development) (2003). *E-Commerce and Development Report*. Geneva: United Nations.

UNCTAD (2005). *Information Economy Report*. New York: United Nations.

UNCTAD/WTO (2002). *Silk Review 2001: A Survey of International Trends in Production and Trade*. Geneva: International Trade Centre.

# Part V

# Technological and Regulatory Histories and Futures

# 20 Next-Generation Content for Next-Generation Networks

*Eli M. Noam*

## The Nature of Internet Television

Marshall McLuhan memorably stated that "the medium is the message" (McLuhan 1964: 9), that is, that the nature of the distribution system defines its content. If so, the next generation of the Internet, ultrabroadband at gigabit rates over fiber optic networks, will have an impact on the styles of content. In this chapter I will analyze the types and styles of content most likely to emerge with this new technology of distribution.[1] I will engage in a data-driven analysis of price trends of media consumption, distribution cost, and several other factors. This analysis will determine the historic rate by which media have become more bit-intensive and enriched in terms of sensory signals. Projecting this rate ahead permits us to predict the type of media content of the future.

The question of content is critical for any economic analysis of the viability of an ultra-broadband infrastructure. It is common to rush into talk of technology or rollout strategy without first considering the utility to users. If one builds an oil pipeline one must first be sure that there is an oil supply at one end and demand for it at the other. The economic case for investment in super-broadband must rest on its meeting a demand/price combination that is not satisfied today.

What would super-broadband connectivity be used for? There is no evidence of a major need for significantly more powerful types of email, website browsing, or professional at-home applications beyond basic-quality video. Ultrabroadband provides transmission rates of over 1 Gigabits per second, 50–500 times as fast as typical broadband rates of DSL or cable modem service. To what purpose, then, would many millions of residential users conceivably

---

[1] An earlier version of this article appeared as Noam, E. (2008). "If Fiber is the Medium, What is the Message? Next-Generation Content for Next Generation Networks," *Communication & Strategies*, special volume: 19–34.

want the vastly more powerful connectivity of ultrabroadband? For residential households, the answer to this question has to be video entertainment, broadly defined.

But what kind of video would this be? If one asks even knowledgeable people what types of enhancements to video services a super-powerful Internet pipe would produce, the answers normally include:

- More specialized and "long tail" programs
- More individualized content
- Anytime, anywhere video entertainment
- More user-generated content
- More independent and foreign content
- More interactivity and games

Yet these answers are largely incorrect. Of course, ultrabroadband will be associated with these elements. However, they do not require upgrade to ultrabroadband transmission rates: regular broadband is sufficient. If the economic base of ultra-broadband rests on these applications it will fail as a new medium. Ultra-broadband-capable infrastructure must be supported by different content applications.

And indeed, different generations of television technology have affected content. In the US case, for example, when the first generation of TV was broadcast over a limited amount of spectrum, the number of channels was small and the resolution of its picture was relatively low and nationally standardized. Content was in consequence oriented to the broad center of the taste distribution, often described as the "lowest common denominator." It was characterized by content that was broad-based, middle of the road, middle-brow, national with some localism added, and an advertising-based economic model. Because audiences were huge due to the limited number of channels, the budget for programming was substantial.

The subsequent second TV generation saw the development of cable, satellite, and home video for television. These allowed for the creation of an alternative TV transmission infrastructure. Today, advanced cable TV operates at about 1 Gigahertz. This is about twenty times as much as the typical seven over-the-air terrestrial channels (IDATE 2011). The extra transmission capacity was used first in a horizontal fashion—resulting in more channels employing the traditional technology of analog, 6MHz, one-way TV. Narrowcasting and long-tail content emerged, and new channels included such highly specialized offerings as the Anime Network, the Martial Arts Network, the Baby Network, and the Boating Channel. As audiences fragmented, content budgets dropped even for the bigger channels. Low-cost quiz shows, reality programs, and "talking head" content proliferated. Theatrical films, both recent (for extra pay) and old became a staple. In the 2000s, TV moved to a fully digital transmission (Seel 2012). This, by itself, did not change very much, but it brought TV much closer to the computer sector, and this ended the next generation of the online TV video medium.

The emerging next TV generation is mostly based on new transmission platforms. Internet TV (representing diverse content) and mobile TV (with ubiquitous availability) are the main components of this generation. The development of these new forms of TV was due in part to the increased transmission capacity on the last-mile access that came with broadband Internet (using the transmission media of DSL over copper phone lines, coaxial cable, fiber lines, and broadband wireless such as LTE). But the main distinguishing aspect of transmission was not so much in its overall increase but in its individualization, that is, the ability of each user to receive communications independently of other users. This is known as "asynchronous" transmission, the opposite of the synchronous broadcast technology. Furthermore, the new type of communication permitted a return channel, that is, it is 2-way, and interpersonal, in other words, social Broadband allows individuals not only to receive but also to create their own content transmission, individually as well as interactively (Smart 2010). Lastly, the cost of transmission of information becomes substantially distance-insensitive, thereby enabling a wider reach of content distribution than in the past.

Thus, the strengthening of transmission rates impacts content distribution and leads to it having much more of the following:

1. More standard TV at different times. Services such as Hulu create free avenues for users to view regular broadcast content online and on-demand.
2. Even more specialized programs for niche audiences than before. Examples might include TV from other countries; specialized feeds (e.g. "The Women's Field Hockey Channel" from the Olympics); and other types of long tail content.
3. Global aggregation of nationally thin audiences.
4. User-generated content such as that found on YouTube, Daily Motion, etc., even with a lower quality of resolution.
5. Increased downloading of movies. Studios are increasingly considering downloads as part of their traditional release sequence, and some films may even be offered at the top of the sequence. Hindering these efforts, however, are fears of piracy as well as current low download speeds and low picture qualities.

For all the diversity of such individualization, one must understand that it does not require any increase in transmission capacity at the edge of the network in its costly access network segment.

Why is that? Transmission is only one technology dimension underlying new-style TV. A second one is the enhanced storage. This is often overlooked. With powerful and cheap storage, users can access a wide array of video content stored on many locations. The increased storage capacity and individualization mean that the nature of TV transmission changes. Instead of pumping to individuals hundreds of channels simultaneously, of which only one or two are actually watched at any given time, online TV needs to send out only one or two channels at any given time to the user. This means that the transmission requirement of the end user at the last-mile access segment is actually not particularly high in comparison to the requirements of having hundreds of channels simultaneously transmitted. A household which uses simultaneously VoIP voice service, plus maybe two high definition TV channels, plus some gaming, requires no more than 35 Mbps (Giunta 2006). This is about the rate available already to millions of households. User-generated content and peer-to-peer applications are similarly not reliant on large last-mile access transmission beyond those of regular broadband. Instead, these require storage and a strong core network. Storage is required on both the user end and by intermediaries such as YouTube and DailyMotion. Similarly, online video games do not require ultrabroadband. Even seemingly complex interactive multiplayer games do not use all that much transmission capacity. On average, *Counter Strike* operates at about 40 Kbps. The limiting factor is the processing capacity on the central node, which restricts players' data stream.

Thus, the bandwidth of ultrabroadband—1 Gbps and more—seems excessive for such requirements. What then would one use it for, if at all? Greater bandwidth creates two capabilities: the first is the *widening* of content options. This was discussed and described above. And the second is the *deepening* of content, which is based on the increasing *richness* of content in terms of the bit rate of information supplied per time unit to human sensory receptors.

The most obvious dimension of increased richness in video media is simply the increase in picture quality. The distinguishing factor between standard and higher definition displays has to do with the number of pixels, which allows a greater level of detail to be displayed. A standard display will possess 525 (or 625, depending on the country). A high-definition display (HDTV) provides twice that number. More advanced are so-called 4K and 8K TV with still more vertical and horizontal lines of pixels, a wider aspect ratio (1:2), more bits per pixel, more frames per second, and much better audio (Sugawara 2008). These new generations of picture quality represent an impressive move forward in the clarity of the moving image. Is such an advance truly necessary? Traditionally, satisfaction levels in video quality have been shortsighted; each generation persuaded itself, and was persuaded by marketers, that it was using a technology that was life-like in video and audio quality. Each generation eventually moved to higher levels of quality and soon wondered how it could have endured the past poor resolution.

The second dimension and driver in media richness is a product of larger screens. As digital displays become flatter than the boxy CRTs, they can become larger, while homes and apartments remain roughly the same size. As a result, people will sit at a wider angle to their screen and its pixels. This requires sharper pictures, that is, a higher resolution such as 4K and 8K resolution, with a much larger number of pixels.

Three-dimensional displays, as well, will improve on the richness of the media experience. Technically many of its elements are already offered, and technologies that do not require the wearing of special glasses are on their way. Other sensory modalities beyond sight and audition might also find their way to an enriched TV content, such as elements of feel. Vibration is already being set into home-theater seats.

## The Economics of Bits

All of the above trends of individualization and increasing richness of experience are interesting to note but have a pronounced technological ring. One is reminded of past scenarios envisioning a helicopter in every garage, electric power too cheap to meter, and other utopian scenarios. If the question is where residential fiber will take video media, the answer is not just technological, but also economic. People will use more bits if their price drops. They will consume these bits by spending more time in the consumption of bits relative to other activities; and they consume more bits per time unit, that is, consume a "richer" medium in sensory terms.

It is necessary to look at the underlying economics. To this end we now turn to bit cost trends. Willingness to pay for media is composed of two elements: the content cost, and the distribution cost.

$$\text{Cost of Media Consumption } P(C) = \text{Cost of Distribution } P(D) + \text{Cost of Media Information } P(I) \tag{1}$$

$$\text{Cost of Media Information } P(I) = \text{Quantity of bits } Q(B) \times \text{price per bit } P(B) \tag{2}$$

$$\text{Quantity of bits } Q(B) = \text{Consumption time } T(C) \times \text{Bits per time unit (BpT)} \tag{3}$$

Substituting, we get

$$P(C) = P(D) + T(C) \times BpT \times P(B) \tag{4}$$

We can express this as

$$BpT = (P(C) - P(D)) / (T(C) \times P(B)) \tag{5}$$

Equation (5) expresses the bits per time unit of the medium, which is our measure for media richness, as a function of the price of media consumption per unit of time, the price of distribution per time unit, consumption time, and the price per bit. We now look at these components empirically. To do so we measure the prices and costs for various media, ordered by the time of their introduction, plus a few more years for maturity to be achieved. And this is what we find:

First, the price P(C) which people are willing to pay for entertainment has remained fairly constant over time, adjusted for inflation. It is approximately 0.1 cents per second, or about $3.60 per hour. The rate of decline per year has been merely 0.5 percent. When the cost for individualized consumption is higher than such an amount, people engage in sharing consumption, such as going to film theaters or watching broadcast television as part of a mass audience. When cost drops over time, people shift to individualized consumption for that medium, such as home video or pay TV. They share consumption for the still more expensive, often new, media, until they, too, become affordable (see Figure 20.1).

Thus, the left hand of equation (5) above shows almost no upward or downward trend for a century for consumers' payment for media per time unit, adjusted for inflation, even though several components of media cost have declined considerably. The price per second is about 0.073 cents. The growth rate is almost flat, at 0.08 of one percent.[2]

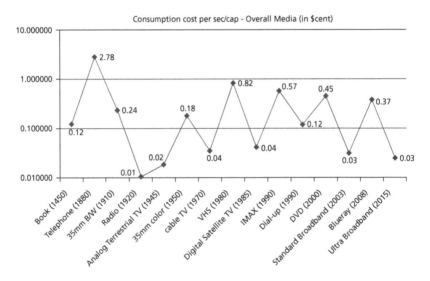

**Figure 20.1** Media consumption cost per second, per capita[3]

---

[2] Here and subsequently, the estimated OLS regressions are lnY = a +blnt + u, where t is time.
[3] We identified the historical prices for different mediums per media unit (e.g. price for one book, record, DVD, etc.), or per monthly subscription rates, plus cost of time if the medium incorporates advertising. Historical prices are adjusted for inflation to 2008 dollar equivalents. We divide by the time spent with each medium or media product. We arrange the media by their time of appearance as a consumption item.

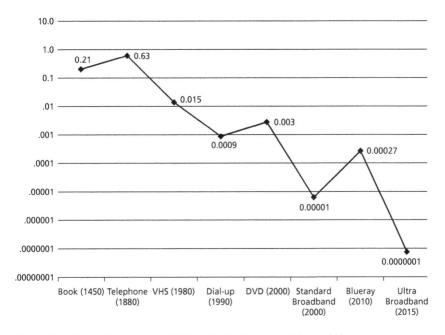

**Figure 20.2** Distribution cost per Mbit/capita (individualized channels)[4]

Of the right-hand elements of equation (5), the price of distribution P(D), as measured in the price of transmission of bits per second, has declined enormously over time, at a rate of almost 10 per cent (9.68%) per year since 1880 (see Figure 20.2). With this cost component dropping rapidly, and with the willingness to pay per media time unit stable (P(C)), the component of payment for the information itself (P(I)) has been able to rise. This consumption could rise both in terms of time units (T(C)) and in the consumption of bits per time unit BpT. The former has not risen much, given the reality of work, transportation, sleep, and other time-consuming necessities of life. According to studies such as those by the media investment bank Veronis Suhler Stevenson, media consumption is 9.67 hours per day, or about 3,530 hours per year (Stevenson 2007a). This includes multitasking with other media and other activities. It is hard to imagine how much extra time could be allocated to media consumption. Indeed, in one year, 2006, that number even declined slightly according to the US Census (Stevenson 2007b). Over the past decades, media consumption time has risen only modestly—15 percent over the past three decades, for an annual compound growth rate of 0.47 percent—even though its composition has changed.

---

[4] The distribution cost per media product is divided by the Mbit per unit of each media.

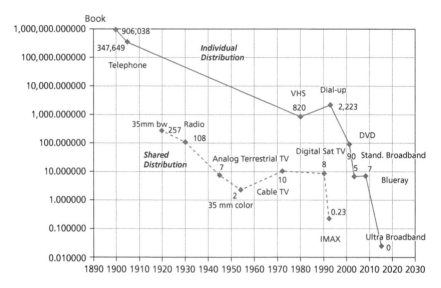

**Figure 20.3** Consumption cost per Gbit/cap[5]

Meanwhile, the price per bit has declined sharply, by an 8 percent compounded annual growth rate, as can be seen in Figure 20.3.

If we put these elements together, we observe that what has risen, then, is not the time units of media consumption but their quantity per time unit, in terms of bits. Media enrichment can be calculated by equation (5):

$$BpT = (P(C) - P(D)) / (T(C) \times P(B)) \tag{5}$$

We can express the changes logarithmically:

$$\ln BpT = \ln[P(C) - P(D)] - \ln T(C) - \ln P(B)$$
$$= -2.15 - .47 - (-8.0) = 5.38 \tag{6}$$

Thus, the consumption of bits per time unit of media use has risen, by this calculation, by a 5.38 percent compound annual growth rate. This relationship is roughly confirmed by the directly measured empirical trend, as shown in Figure 20.4 which exhibits a compound growth rate of 8 percent.

We can be more specific. Our data shows that the bit richness of print (books), once the dominant medium, was .00013 Mbit per second of consumption. Radio's bit rate was typically about 0.096 Mbps. Standard analog television required about 2.5 Mbps. HDTV is 19.6 Mbps. The next generations of TV

---

[5] The cost per second (see Figure 20.1) is divided by the Mbit/sec transmission rate.

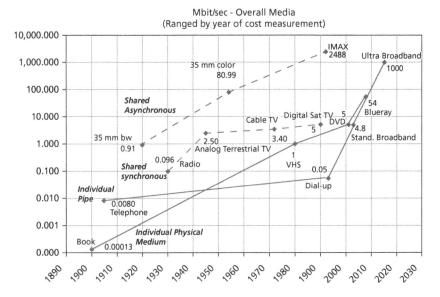

**Figure 20.4** Transmission rates of different media[6]

display, 2K and 4K, have compressed bitrate needs of about 180 Mbps and 640 Mbps respectively. In each of these generations, visual imagery becomes more pronounced. In the print medium, a relatively few content bits are carefully crafted by the author, and the reader supplies the imagination process which enriches the experience. As the bit rate for a medium grows, the visual imagery that is supplied by the medium rises. The growth rate of this enrichment, as measured above, is about 8 percent per year. In the process, the sensory content of a medium keeps rising. It becomes ever more realistic, approaching reality with its sounds and images.

## Implications for Content

What kind of television will such enrichment in terms of bits yield? There is no need to engage in futuristic imagining of the nature of content. Instead, we can follow the trends of media in the past. And here one can observe the following path. The basic dynamics of a new medium are that when it is first introduced it tends to be relatively expensive, and in that period of high cost

---

[6] Rates of data transmission for telephone, dial-up Internet, DSL, Broadband, etc. from http://en.wikipedia.org/wiki/Bitrate (accessed 7 April, 2013). For traditional media, bandwidth is calculated by the number of bit equivalents of the information per second.

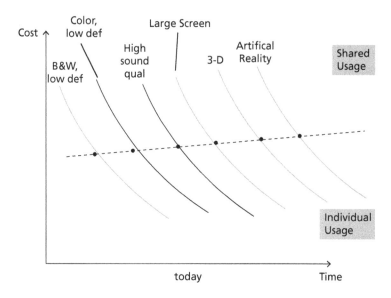

**Figure 20.5** Trends of media prices and usage patterns (schematic)

it is mainly consumed by elite users individually or in small groups. Soon the medium leads to the creation of a system of mass shared usage, which lowers the cost for each individual user, defrays the high fixed cost over multiple users, and enables the creation of high-cost productions of content. Examples include theater plays, public concerts, and operas, all of which moved from high-priced individualized consumption to low-cost shared consumption through shared distribution technologies of large halls, film theaters, broadcast TV, and cable and satellite distribution. At this stage, consumption is by necessity synchronous, that is, hundreds or even millions of users share the content simultaneously. But this is not the end of the story. In time, content and distribution costs decline still further and eventually move to a range that is affordable for ordinary individuals (see Figure 20.5). Once this occurs, the medium starts to become individualized and asynchronous again.

Therefore, by looking at the present use of shared media, and assuming a certain rate of price decline per bit, we can predict the future of individualized media usage and its timing. It allows us to predict the next individual content type and medium by looking at existing shared communications styles.

The nature of a medium affects its content. When visual images could not be easily stored and transmitted, before film, the major medium was print. The print medium generated extraordinarily subtle works—novels, poems, all aimed at creating images in the imagination—using the compressed, bit-parsimonious technology of the written word. The human mind had to supply much of the processing and imagination. Film changed this. It explicitly filled in the visual details. Early film was probably the most unsubtle form of mass media expression ever. The less expensive bits are, the more visual the medium becomes. The less expensive the visual aspects are, the more they dominate. A weaker capacity for visuals favors story line, character development, and dialog. With no sound, the early film medium relied primarily on action, painted in the broad strokes of slapstick comedy, simplistic plots, and uncomplicated characters. But still, the film medium could present visual tableaus that had not existed before and which quickly outperformed the visual capabilities of the acting stage. Thus, within the following ten years of the new medium, new genres appeared in film, and new forms of expression were pioneered. The genres of science fiction (*A Trip to the Moon*, 1902), Western adventure (*The Great Train Robbery*, 1903), and voyeur content (*The Gay Shoe Clerk*, 1905). Without sound, these were heavily visual and physical. The first feature-length film with sound and embedded dialog came in 1927 with *The Jazz Singer*, and this advance soon enabled more subtle films with dialogue, ideas, and wit.

Two decades later, with the emergence of television with its black-and-white, low-resolution visual content, theatrical film was prompted to upgrade its technology and content. Color and wide-screen Cinemascope became standard. Sound improved enormously. Higher-quality 70mm film was introduced, allowing filmmakers greater ability to include fast-moving action, fine detail, close-ups, and convincing special effects. In content terms, theatrical films included themes of sex and violence, and provided spectacles with huge supporting casts and special effects. These films dominated worldwide. In contrast, Europeans had much lower budgets for advanced visuals, and so they shot black-and-white films with a greater portion of dialogue and character development, and much less in the way of action or special effects. Intellectually interesting, but not visually flashy, such films were more like books on screen.

In the 1980s, computer animation began to emerge. In time, stars' faces were superimposed on others' bodies, and computer-generated characters were on the verge of substituting for human actors.

The combination of computer animation (especially in video games) and 3-D displays will create a new entertainment approaching total sensory captivation. This new entertainment would allow for user participation and some user control. Imagine dazzling computer-generated special effects. Add virtual reality and game elements. Imagine the avatars and participation in virtual worlds. A total immersion becomes possible, in which viewers become participants, inserting themselves with undivided attention into the action, in the center or on the sidelines, *Zelig*-like. This is where new content creators will go.

## Implications for the Content Business

Now that we have a better idea of what ultra-broadband content will look like, the question is, who would supply it? To produce such content is expensive, and it will be scarce in its early phases. It requires creativity, many programmers, visual artists, special effects experience, performance testing, and constantly improved versions. This type of content exhibits strong economies of scale on the production side and network externalities on the demand side. Providers positioned to take best advantage of these factors are characterized by large budgets; ability to diversify risk and distribute over multiple platforms; strong branding; access to large audiences; and an ability to coordinate specialized inputs. Premium content then will be supplied by large and complex providers. Long-tail content, on the other hand, can be readily produced by just about anyone with a broadband connection. This means that there will rarely be sustained profit in it. There will be room for experimental developers for such content, and should it prove successful these suppliers will likely be acquired by the larger players. Other content is likely to be developed through interactive communities of individual non-commercial developers, or through a multiplicity of small specialist commercial firms coordinated by large integrators.

Hollywood studios already spend heavily on premium content. For *Terminator 3* (2003), $20 million was spent on computer-generated special effects alone. In the same year, the *Attack of the Clones* listed 572 technicians (Epstein 2005). Premium ultrabroadband content is likely to be still more expensive. Is there really a demand to justify it? The answer would appear to be yes, given the ever-rising levels of stimulation that media consumers seem to require. In terms of global demand, if 100 million households use such content for two hours per week at $5, the annual revenue generated is $52 billion, with maybe half going to distribution and to content production respectively.

The globalization of media will also be affected. Contributing elements are 1) the price of international transmission is dropping rapidly, 2) Internet penetrations are increasing rapidly, and 3) ultrabroadband content has economies of scale. US firms are likely to play a major role in such content. They are early entrants, with large domestic audiences, leading software and hardware suppliers, access to risk capital, global talent, and established distribution channels.

## Conclusions

To summarize, we find that:

1. Individualizations of content style—of space and time, of consumption mode, or of source—do not require ultra-broadband on the user level.

Storage and transmission are substitutes for one another. In fact, as storage becomes less expensive, it requires less transmission than in the past. For regular quality TV, to enable more content diversity, the proper approach would be to store more programs and make access and download possible. Synchronous channels make sense only for large audiences or live-critical content—such as sports events.

2. The price people have been willing to pay for media entertainment per time unit has been fairly steady over a century, adjusted for inflation, at about 4.4 cents per minute.

3. The price of distribution of content has been dropping at a compound rate of 8 percent.

4. The bit quantity of media content has risen at a steady clip, at the rate of about 5.5 to 8 percent per year.

5. This enrichment of media content leads to genres and styles that are individualized, immersive, and often interactive.

6. For the first time, entertainment at home will be technically superior to that in a shared communal environment.

7. It is only a matter of time, given the trends of steady enrichment of media content in terms of signals, until media content will be richer in sensory terms than real life.

Thus, should technology continue to influence content as it has, we can look forward to ultra-broadband content that is highly individualized, customizable, and of unprecedented sensory richness. Ultra-broadband pipes will require appropriate ultra-content in order to be economically viable. Yet to realize these new content forms and genres will take time and creativity, trial and error. The implication for the infrastructure providers is that to fill their pipes with users, they must help to develop ultra-broadband content. If they do not support new content creation, or if they restrict access, they will find that they have created a theater with nobody ready to perform. This interaction of new generation infrastructure networks with new generation content leaves much room for entrepreneurship, innovation, and originality. And it provides the analysts of media with important new topics of study on the nature of culture, entertainment, and news in the next electronic environment.

### ▨ REFERENCES

Epstein, E. J. (2005). *The Big Picture: The New Logic of Money and Power in Hollywood.* New York: E. J. E. Publications.

Giunta, T. (2006). "The Next Generation Network: Ultra-Broadband IPTV." *Motorola.* <http://www.docstoc.com/docs/20046807/The-Next-Generation-Network-Ultra-Broadband-IPTV> (accessed April 20, 2013).

IDATE (2011). *Next Gen TV, TV Trends 2011—Live Service, Catch-Up TV, VOD & OTT, STBs, 3D, TV Widgets & Apps*. Montpellier: Author. <http://www.idate.org/private/idate/etudes/_730/M11217_Report.pdf>. (accessed April 8, 2013).

McLuhan, M. (1964). *Understanding Media: The Extensions of Man*. New York: McGraw-Hill.

Noam, E. (2008). "If Fiber is the Medium, What is the Message? Next-Generation Content for Next Generation Networks," *Communication & Strategies*, special volume: 19–34.

Seel, P. B. (2012). "Digital Television and Video," in A. E. Grant and J. H. Meadows (eds.), *Communication Technology Update and Fundamentals*, 13th edn. Boston, MA: Focal Press, 65–82.

Smart, J. (2010). "Tomorrow's Interactive Television," *The Futurist*, November–December: 41–46.

Stevenson, V. S. (2007a). *Communication Industry Forecast: 2007–2011*. New York: VSS.

Stevenson, V. S. (2007b). *New VSS Forecast Released*. <http://www.thefreelibrary.com/New+Veronis+Suhler+Stevenson+Forecast%3A+Shift+to+Alternative+Media...-a0167296406> (accessed April 20, 2013).

Sugawara, M. (2008). "Super Hi-Vision—Research on a future ultra-HDTV system." *EBU Technical Review*. < http://tech.ebu.ch/docs/techreview/trev_2008-Q2_nhk-ultra-hd.pdf> (accessed December 6, 2013).

# 21 Data Privacy in the Clouds

*Christopher Millard*

## Introduction

"Cloud computing" (also known as "the cloud") is essentially a means of providing computing resources as a utility service via the Internet. Cloud services range in scope from the provision of basic processing and storage capacity through to fully featured online services such as webmail and social networks. The cloud market is evolving very rapidly, with substantial investments being made in infrastructure, platforms, and applications, all delivered "as a service." The appetite for cloud resources is enormous, driven by such developments as the deployment on a vast scale of mobile apps and the rapid emergence of "Big Data." Estimates of the scale of the market for core cloud services vary but it has been predicted that by 2016 it will be worth over $43 billion in the United States and more than $206 billion worldwide (de Borja 2012). The wider economic and social impact of cloud-enabled services is likely to be far greater than those numbers indicate. Whether they are aware of it or not, members of the public are increasingly dependent on cloud infrastructure and services as a technological underpinning for their lives as private individuals, as consumers, and as citizens.

As cloud computing has moved into the mainstream, questions have increasingly been asked about protection of, and responsibility for, "personal data" (broadly meaning information about identifiable individuals) that is processed in cloud environments. After a brief introduction to both data privacy and cloud computing, this chapter will focus on four key issues in this field. First, what information in cloud-computing environments is, and what should be, protected as personal data? Second, who is, and who should be, responsible for such data? Third, what is the international impact of data privacy laws? In particular, which laws apply to personal data in clouds, how do restrictions on cross-border transfers of personal data affect cloud-computing activities, and what happens when access to cloud data is requested or demanded by third parties such as law enforcement authorities, regulators, and courts? Finally, we will look at the likely future development of data privacy, and consider some alternative approaches to providing effective protection for personal data in clouds.

The global legal and regulatory environment for data privacy in clouds is complex, with many relevant laws at both national and local level. There have been various attempts to harmonize data protection rules at the transnational level and such initiatives continue. In addition to legislation and regulatory frameworks that focus specifically on protection of personal data, cloud activities involving personal information may be subject to numerous legal rules such as duties of confidentiality, contractual obligations, and remedies for defamation. Indeed, regulation of the Internet has evolved rapidly over the past couple of decades on many different fronts. Cloud computing is just one element of online activities, and data privacy is a specific aspect of the legal and regulatory framework applying to the cloud. Certain activities that are facilitated by the cloud, such as social networking and the use of "big data," will be mentioned, but the main emphasis will be on cloud computing as such, and on the implications, for cloud providers and users, of legal and regulatory frameworks that apply specifically to the processing of personal data in clouds.

As regards terminology, the body of law that regulates personally identifiable information is typically referred to in Europe and Asia as "data protection." In the United States, and some other jurisdictions, it tends to be called "information privacy" or "data privacy." Although important distinctions can be drawn between these concepts, for simplicity the terms will often be used interchangeably in this chapter. The main geographical focus will be Europe, which has the longest tradition of attempting to co-ordinate national data protection laws. Europe also currently has the largest number of data protection laws of general application to public- and private-sector activities, though as we will see that is unlikely to remain the case for much longer.

## What is Data Privacy?

Privacy, as a distinct legal concept, can be traced back to an article published in the *Harvard Law Review* in the late nineteenth century (Warren and Brandeis 1890). In that paper the authors reviewed the long history of protection under English law for various individual liberties and private property. They extrapolated a general "right to privacy," at the heart of which was a "right to be let alone." Eight decades later, popular concerns about the use of computers in both public and private sectors led to the adoption of a swathe of data protection laws, starting in Germany in 1970 (Millard 2012). Since then, some ninety countries around the world have enacted legislation intended to protect individuals' rights to privacy by restricting the way in which information about them may be processed in the private sector. Europe still has the greatest number of jurisdictions with data protection laws and most of those laws are based on transnational harmonization measures, notably a Convention adopted by the Council of Europe (Council of Europe 1981) and a Directive on data protection adopted by the European Union (EU DPD 1995). The global balance is shifting, however. As the adoption of national privacy laws has accelerated in recent years, many countries in the Asia-Pacific region have enacted, or are considering proposals for, data protection legislation (Greenleaf 2012).

The United States remains an outlier. Although it has had a federal law regulating privacy in the public sector since 1974, private-sector processing of personal data is subject to a complex, but not comprehensive, patchwork of sector-specific laws and regulations both federally and in the states (Solove and Schwartz 2011). There are, however, growing calls for a more coherent, and less parochial, approach to privacy legislation. Recent proposals from the US Administration (The White House 2012) and the Federal Trade Commission (FTC Report 2012) have recognized the potential benefits for both consumers and businesses of "interoperability" in relation to privacy laws, a theme that resonates with the European Commission's approach to increased harmonization in *Safeguarding Privacy in a Connected World* (European Commission 2012).

At the heart of most existing data protection laws is a set of principles intended to ensure that personal data is:

- Processed only with consent or some other legal justification;
- Processed fairly and lawfully;
- Adequate, relevant, and not excessive for specific, identified, purposes;
- Accurate and, where necessary, kept up to date;
- Kept in an identifiable form only for so long as is necessary;
- Protected against unauthorized or unlawful processing and against accidental loss or destruction.

In addition, most data protection laws restrict the transfer of personal data to jurisdictions that are deemed to lack an adequate level of protection and also establish a regulator with enforcement powers. Almost all laws provide for a range of rights and remedies for individuals in relation to their personal data, including access to data and a right to insist that inaccurate information be corrected or erased.

Much could be said about the core data protection principles and the specific rights of individuals, all of which can be both complex and controversial when applied to online activities. In the limited space available here the focus will be on the key issues arising from cloud-computing arrangements and, in particular, the scope of the data privacy obligations placed on cloud providers and the corresponding protections and remedies available to customers of cloud services.

## What is Cloud Computing?

At its simplest, cloud computing is a way of delivering computing resources as a utility service via the Internet. As such, the cloud may prove to be as disruptive an innovation as was the emergence of cheap electricity on demand a century or so ago (Carr 2008). In slightly more technical terms, cloud computing is an arrangement whereby computing resources are provided on a flexible, location-independent basis that allows for rapid and seamless allocation of resources on demand. Typically, cloud resources are provided to specific users from a pool shared with other customers with charging, if any, proportional to the resources used. The delivery of cloud services often depends on complex, multi-layered arrangements between various providers. Many permutations are possible but cloud computing activities are often described as falling into one or more of these three service categories:

- Infrastructure as a Service ("IaaS")—computing resources such as basic processing and storage;
- Platform as a Service ("PaaS")—tools for developing and deploying applications;
- Software as a Service ("SaaS")—end-user applications.[1]

Cloud deployment models can also be viewed in various ways but a widely used classification is:

- Private cloud—where the relevant infrastructure is owned by, or operated for the benefit of, a single large customer or group of related entities;
- Community cloud—where infrastructure is owned by or operated for, and shared amongst, a specific group of users with common interests;
- Public cloud—where infrastructure is shared amongst different, varying users using the same hardware and/or software;
- Hybrid cloud—involving a mixture of the above, for example an organization with a private cloud may "cloud burst" processing activities to a public cloud for "load balancing" purposes during times of high demand (Mell and Grance 2011).

The cloud sector is expanding rapidly with cloud service providers ranging from major technology companies to small start-ups. While some providers specialize in a specific type of cloud service and/or market, others offer cloud products covering the spectrum of cloud activities. In addition, there is an

---

[1] Examples of IaaS are Rackspace's Cloud Servers and Amazon's EC2 (Elastic Compute Cloud); examples of PaaS are Microsoft's Windows Azure and Google's App Engine; examples of SaaS are Facebook and Salesforce's online customer relationship management service. For a more detailed discussion, see Millard 2013.

emerging group of integrators, who provide various types of cloud consultancy and systems integration services. The importance of such intermediaries looks set to grow (Hon et al. 2012a).

Most cloud service arrangements, especially for consumers and SMEs, are set up via non-negotiable, standard-form, "click-through" contracts. Such terms of service tend to favor cloud providers and often contain specific provisions, including in privacy policies, which are disadvantageous to customers and may be unenforceable, or even illegal. Terms and conditions may be complex and obscure and it is not uncommon for cloud providers to claim the right to change them unilaterally and without notice (Bradshaw et al. 2011). Transparency is generally regarded as a fundamental pre-requisite to effective privacy protection and it is also important that affected individuals have an appropriate degree of control over the way that information about them is used. Cloud providers, and the contractual terms on which they operate, vary significantly in the way they address (or fail to address) these and other privacy issues, such as data security.

A relatively small, but growing, number of cloud contracts is negotiated, typically where cloud customers insist on specific arrangements and cloud providers consider that the financial or strategic value of a deal merits special treatment. Although such deals typically involve corporate or government customers, privacy and security provisions are amongst the most commonly negotiated terms and can be deal breakers (Hon et al. 2012a).

## What Information in Clouds is Regulated as Personal Data?

Regulatory obligations imposed by data protection laws tend to apply on an "all or nothing" basis. In the member states of the European Economic Area (EEA),[2] and many other jurisdictions with data privacy laws, the key test is whether information constitutes "personal data." This is typically defined along these lines: "any information relating to an identified, or identifiable, natural person" (EU DPD 1995). If information is personal data then "data controllers" (see the next section called "Who is Responsible for Personal Data in Clouds?") are subject to a raft of compliance obligations, some of which may prove highly onerous, or even impossible, in specific situations. Even stricter rules apply to a subset of personal data defined in the EU DPD as "special category" data, also known as "sensitive data," or "sensitive personal data."

---

[2] The EU DPD has been implemented throughout the EEA, which comprises the 28 EU member states plus Iceland, Liechtenstein, and Norway.

Conversely, if information is not personal data, or if it ceases to be personal data (for example, as a result of anonymization), it may not be subject to any restrictions under data protection laws. This binary approach can be problematic, especially when applied to complex processing scenarios such as those that arise frequently in cloud-computing arrangements. To complicate matters further, regulators and courts that are supposed to use the same concepts may disagree fundamentally as to what is and is not "personal data" (Millard and Hon 2012).

It is the inclusion of "identifiable," and not just "identified," in the definition of personal data that tends to be most problematic, including in the context of cloud computing. If "identifiable" individuals are automatically included, even if their identities are disguised securely, and regardless of whether they are ever actually identified, then a vast category of information that is only *potentially* personal data will be regulated. This has been described as the "European Union's expansionist view" and can be contrasted with the "United States' reductionist view" whereby only information that has been specifically associated with a particular person constitutes "Personally Identifiable Information (PII)." An alternative approach might be to protect and regulate the processing of information about both identified and identifiable individuals, but with different legal requirements for each category (Schwartz and Solove 2011).

The answer to the question of whether personal data is being processed or not may vary depending on the type of cloud service and precise deployment model used. In some cases, for example a social networking service, it may be clear that the service provider is processing personal data, partly provided by users and partly generated through operation of the service. The question then is who should be responsible for the relevant processing activities (see the next section called "Who is Responsible for Personal Data in Clouds?"). In other cases it may be more difficult to establish whether information that is being processed in a cloud environment should be regarded as personal data. For example, should encrypted or anonymized data be regulated as personal data in the hands of a cloud service provider that does not have the decryption key or the means to re-identify the individuals concerned? Such scenarios are common. A customer may use strong encryption to make personal data indecipherable prior to uploading the encrypted data to a SaaS cloud backup or archive service. Similarly, a customer of an IaaS service may use the cloud service provider's computing resources to process personal data on virtual machines in a way that prevents the service provider from having access to any identifiable information. Why should the personal data controlled directly in this way by the customer be treated as still being personal data in the hands of the cloud service provider in either of these examples? To take the argument a step further, why should the responsibilities of a cloud provider depend on the steps that their customers take to anonymize or encrypt their data (Hon et al. 2011)?

This takes us beyond the definitional question about personal data to the key question of responsibility for personal data in clouds.

# Who is Responsible for Personal Data in Clouds?

Under data protection laws in EEA member states and various other jurisdictions, it is assumed that anyone who processes personal data will be either a "data controller" or a "data processor," or possibly both. A "controller" determines the "purposes and means" for processing personal data. Laws based on the EU DPD impose various obligations on controllers vis-à-vis the "data subjects" whose information they process, including compliance with the principles summarized in the section called "What is Data Privacy?" Controllers also have obligations to regulators that may include filing registrations, paying fees, and reporting data breaches in certain situations. A failure by a controller to comply with its obligations may expose the controller to regulatory intervention (including financial penalties), civil liability and, in some cases, prosecution for a criminal offense.

A "processor" processes personal data on behalf of a controller. This may seem a straightforward definition but drawing clear distinctions between controllers and processors is often difficult, especially where a service provider has a degree of autonomy in determining the "means" used to process a controller's data. This categorization issue can arise in conventional outsourcing deals, but it is likely to be both more common and more complex in cloud-computing arrangements.

In some cases, such as social networking and webmail, service providers may both provide a processing service for users and also have significant control over what they do with the information that is provided by users. As such they are likely to be viewed as data controllers, at least to the extent that they use the data for their own purposes such as data mining, profiling, and targeted marketing. Each user may also be a controller, although use of a social network or webmail service by an individual for private purposes may be exempt from regulation, as "processing...by a natural person in the course of a purely personal or household activity" (EU DPD 1995, Article 3(2); Article 29 WP 163, 2009; Article 29 WP 169, 2010). In other cases, a cloud provider may play a fairly traditional service provider role as a data processor, for example by providing backup and disaster recovery services for non-encrypted data. Still further down the cloud stack, a customer may simply be leasing general-purpose computing infrastructure and the cloud provider may have neither knowledge of, nor control over, any activities that involve the processing of personal data.

In such a case the cloud provider will not be regarded as a controller of such data, but it also makes little sense to treat the provider as even a processor.

By analogy, if I sell or lease to you a conventional computer system for you to use on your premises to process personal data in your business, you will be the controller of the personal data, and the mere supply of equipment will not make me a processor. In a cloud infrastructure arrangement, instead of supplying you with a physical computer for you to use at your premises, I may provide you with one or more virtual machines that are hosted on hardware at my server farm. I may, however, still have no more knowledge of, or control over, your data than if you were doing the processing yourself on equipment under your direct control at your premises. So what is the difference? Under EEA rules, even simple storage of personal data is a type of processing that is likely to be regulated. This means that if you store personal data on equipment located in my server farm, I will be a data processor as defined by the EU DPD, and possibly even a joint data controller because I determine aspects of the "means" of storage.[3]

Why does any of this matter? The reason is that the characterization of participants in cloud arrangements as controllers and/or processors has significant legal consequences. For example, as regards data security, Article 17 of the EU DPD states that controllers "must implement appropriate technical and organizational measures to protect personal data against accidental or unlawful destruction or accidental loss, alteration, unauthorized disclosure or access, in particular where the processing involves the transmission of data over a network, and against all other unlawful forms of processing." If a controller delegates any processing activity to a processor, then the controller must put a contract in place to regulate the processing and must ensure that the processor provides and complies with "sufficient guarantees in respect of the technical security measures and organizational measures governing the processing."

In a conventional outsourcing transaction, the respective roles and responsibilities of a customer and its service provider(s) will typically be the matter of extensive negotiations. A detailed contract, or set of contracts, will usually be prepared that, in the EEA at least, will include specific provisions to address the EU DPD's Article 17 requirements regarding control and security. Although similar negotiations do occur in relation to some cloud arrangements, the majority of cloud contracts are offered on a "take it or leave it" basis (Hon and Millard 2012b). Moreover, in an opinion on cloud computing, the Working Party of national regulators established under Article 29 of the EU DPD has asserted: "the processor can subcontract its activities only on the basis of the consent of the controller...with a clear duty for the processor to inform the controller of any intended changes concerning the addition or

---

[3] For a more detailed discussion of the issues with additional examples, see Hon et al. (2012b).

replacement of subcontractors with the controller retaining at all times the possibility to object to such changes or terminate the contract. There should be a clear obligation of the cloud provider to name all the subcontractors commissioned" (Article 29 WP 196, 2012). Compliance with this requirement may be difficult, or impracticable, in many cases where a specific cloud-computing arrangement depends on multiple providers each of which may play a different and changing role in delivering a complex package of services to a particular customer (see the section called "What is Cloud Computing?"). Moreover, it is not clear how a customer with modest technical and legal resources, such as a typical SME, will be in a position to evaluate, and deal appropriately with, all the information that an SaaS provider might need to provide regarding its sub-contracting arrangements with providers of IaaS, PaaS, and perhaps also other SaaS services.

Another fundamental problem with the established controller/processor model is that it may be inappropriate, or impossible, for a particular cloud customer to dictate terms regarding security and other key processing criteria to a large cloud provider with perhaps millions of customers. This point is acknowledged, but not resolved, by the UK Information Commissioner's Office which has observed: "a cloud customer may find it difficult to exercise any meaningful control over the way a large (and perhaps global) cloud provider operates. However, simply because an organization chooses to contract...on the basis of the cloud provider's standard terms and conditions, does not mean that the organization is no longer responsible..." (ICO 2012, para 31). Similarly, it may be impracticable and inappropriate for a particular customer to insist on conducting an audit to assess a public cloud provider's security arrangements, not least because an audit by one customer may compromise security for others.[4]

## WHAT IS THE INTERNATIONAL IMPACT OF DATA PROTECTION LAWS?

The EU DPD has a very long-arm reach in two key respects, both of which are controversial. First, national laws in the EEA regulate processing worldwide to the extent that it is "carried out in the context of the activities of an establishment of the controller on the territory of the Member State" (EU DPD 1995,

---

[4] This much is accepted by EEA data protection regulators who concede that an independent third-party audit commissioned by the cloud provider may suffice. Nevertheless, they insist that "businesses and administrations wishing to use cloud computing should conduct, as a first step, a comprehensive and thorough risk analysis." Reference is made to reliance on "independent verification or certification" but it is not clear whether this can be a complete substitute for a risk analysis (Article 29 WP 196, 2012).

Article 4(1)). This means, for example, that the processing of personal data in the United States by a US-based cloud service provider on behalf of a company established in France may be subject to French data protection law. This is particularly important for SaaS providers outside the EEA that have customers in the EEA. Second, EEA data protection laws apply where a controller established outside the EEA "makes use of equipment" situated in the EEA (EU DPD 1995, Article 4(3)). This test has been interpreted extremely broadly by EEA regulators and may be triggered by a non-EEA controller merely setting a cookie on a device in the EEA. It also means that a non-EEA cloud customer that uses a cloud service provider with equipment in the EEA may become subject to one or more European data protection laws. So, for example, a US-based customer that has data stored on a server farm in Ireland may be subject to Irish data protection law. Moreover, this may not be obvious as the US customer may have entered into a cloud service arrangement with a US cloud provider that happens to use a server farm in Ireland for load-balancing or backup purposes. The rules on "establishment" and "use of equipment" are complex and may have consequences that are counter-intuitive in specific cases (Hon et al. 2012).

In addition to their broad jurisdictional reach, EEA data protection laws also contain tough, and controversial, restrictions on the export of personal data to non-EEA countries that lack an "adequate" level of protection. Various justifications exist for transferring personal data to "inadequate" countries, including use of standard contract clauses that have been approved by the European Commission and reliance on participation by a data importer in the so-called US Safe Harbor. However, the data transfer rules are also complicated and compliance can be very cumbersome (Hon and Millard 2012a). Taken together, the long-arm jurisdiction rules, combined with the restrictions on exports of personal data from the EEA, may make Europe unattractive as a location for cloud businesses and infrastructure.

Cloud computing has highlighted fundamental problems with the location-based approach to regulating personal data, data controllers, and data processors, but the EU's preoccupation with the physical location and movement of data was already anachronistic. European data protection concepts had largely crystallized at a time when computers were few in number, large and expensive, and when input and output options were limited and typically involved the physical movement of media such as punched cards and magnetic tapes. All of this made it relatively straightforward for regulators to identify and monitor the automated processing of personal data. Keeping track of data processing became steadily more difficult as online transfer technologies evolved in the 1970s and 1980s and commercialization of the Internet from the mid-1990s made it increasingly easy and inexpensive for governments, businesses, and consumers to transfer information worldwide. Billions of network-enabled devices are now in use, with vast amounts of personal data being transferred globally every second. Export control regimes for personal data that deem most countries of the world to be "inadequate" and that impose cumbersome restrictions on international transfers are, for all practical purposes, obsolete (Millard, 1997).

## WHAT IS THE FUTURE OF DATA PRIVACY IN THE CLOUDS?

Data privacy laws are in a state of flux. Significant reviews of established frameworks are under way and the pace of adoption of new laws in countries that have not previously had data protection legislation is accelerating. Work has begun on updating the (non-binding, but influential) OECD Privacy Guidelines, while in Europe there are proposals both to overhaul the Council of Europe Convention and to make far-reaching changes to the EU data protection framework. Development of the Asia-Pacific Economic Cooperation (APEC) Privacy Framework, with its Information Privacy Principles (also non-binding), appears to have stalled, but data privacy laws are being introduced, or strengthened, in various jurisdictions in the Pacific Rim. Meanwhile, there is a growing trend to adopt data privacy laws in Latin America as well as in the Middle East and Africa (Greenleaf 2012).

These international efforts to expand and upgrade data privacy laws are a positive sign, both in terms of an increased focus on protection for individuals and a growing acceptance of the need to facilitate effective compliance by establishing greater "interoperability" between different legal regimes. However, notwithstanding these various initiatives, we remain a long way from a coherent international framework for protecting personal data. Moreover, although a more radical approach to reform remains possible, the current international debate is largely predicated on "more of the same" in terms of the existing expansive approach to regulating the processing of "personal data," largely regardless of context or risk, and the imposition on data controllers and data processors of complex and bureaucratic compliance obligations including impracticable and unenforceable restrictions on data exports.

Is there a better way to provide effective data privacy safeguards in the clouds? More specifically, how might we move beyond the current formalistic, complex and uncertain rules that determine what is regulated as "personal data," and who is responsible for processing such data? Is there also a more effective way to ensure that national privacy safeguards are not undermined as a result of offshore processing or control of data? To answer these questions we must revisit some of the core issues discussed earlier in this chapter.

In relation to the questions of what should be protected as personal data in clouds and who should be responsible (see the sections called "What Information in Clouds is Regulated as Personal Data?" and "Who is Responsible for Personal Data in Clouds?"), in both cases it would help to adopt a purposive, or functional, approach in place of the current procedural, or formalistic, approach. Under a purposive/functional paradigm, instead of trying to squeeze cloud data into the current "all or nothing" binary models of what is personal data and who has responsibility, the focus could be on who has effective control over personal data and who is best placed to ensure appropriate safeguards for individuals. Under such a purposive/functional approach, considerations of risk and accountability would assume much greater importance and the issues of categorizations and regulatory formalities would have much less importance.

Such a paradigm shift would also make sense in relation to cross-border aspects of data protection law. As noted in the section called "What is the International Impact of Data Protection Laws?," continuing attempts to regulate the physical location and movement of personal data may both miss the point in terms of protecting individuals and be distinctly "cloud-unfriendly" from the perspective of cloud service providers and their corporate and government customers. The geographic location of data is no longer the key factor in determining whether personal data will be protected from unauthorized access or use. For example, strongly encrypted data hosted on a server outside the EEA is likely to be much "safer" than unencrypted data stored within the EEA on laptops, tablets, and smartphones. Remote processing of data is an essential feature of many cloud-computing arrangements. Many major cloud providers that provide services in Europe make use of server farms and other infrastructure outside the EEA, and such processing may occur even where the provider also has infrastructure within the EEA. The specific cross-border arrangements may not be obvious, or even predictable, because transfers of data may occur automatically within distributed cloud architectures. So from both the perspective of providing effective protection for individuals and from the point of view of making compliance appropriate and feasible, "more of the same" in terms of applicable law and data export controls is not a good basis for protecting personal data in clouds on a global basis.

Of the various current international initiatives to reform data protection law, the European Commission's proposal to replace the current EU DPD with a Regulation (EU DPR Proposal 2012) is likely to have the greatest impact. It represents the most comprehensive attempt to modernize data protection, and the history of the EU DPD suggests that an EU DPR would influence the evolution of data protection laws globally and not merely in Europe. The EU DPR Proposal is far too long and complicated to be considered in detail here. However, a few features stand out from the perspective of protecting personal data in cloud environments, some likely to be positive, others negative.

On the plus side, the EU DPR Proposal includes several provisions that represent a positive attempt to shift the focus away from bureaucratic compliance and toward a more proactive, and indeed preventive, approach to protecting personal data based on risk. In particular, the EU DPR Proposal contains various provisions that are intended to promote data protection by design and by default, techniques that have been tried and tested and found to be beneficial in other jurisdictions, especially in Canada. In addition, although controversial, the proposal for more draconian sanctions, including fines of up to 2 percent of worldwide turnover, might lead to businesses taking data protection compliance much more seriously, from board level on down.

It is not all good news, however. Notwithstanding the frequent invocation by EU officials of "the cloud" as a catalyst and justification for new EU data protection laws, in its current form the EU DPR Proposal is not particularly "cloud friendly." In particular, the opportunity to establish a lighter-touch approach to regulating the processing of personal data that has been securely encrypted or anonymized would be wasted and the arrangements for regulating data controllers and data processors would become even more complex (indeed, probably completely unworkable) if applied to multi-party, multi-layered, cloud infrastructures, platforms, and services. Moreover, cumbersome and restrictive controls on international data transfers, together with ongoing uncertainty regarding applicable law rules, would be likely to make the EU unattractive, both as a location for data centres and as a base for cloud service providers. To date, these fundamental issues have been overshadowed in many public debates by a focus on the so-called "right to be forgotten." In fact, although it might be problematic for Internet intermediaries such as search engine operators, this right is neither particularly novel (at least in the EU) nor is it likely to make a great deal of difference to individuals, as it is very similar to existing EU rights to have data corrected or erased. To the extent that the right to be forgotten is defined in broader terms, expectations that are raised about rewriting history, or comprehensively deleting specific information, are likely to lead to disappointment in practice.

The social and economic significance of both personal data and cloud computing will continue to grow as more and more relationships and transactions are mediated via online services involving storage and processing of data in remote locations. These developments are likely to result in an ever greater focus by legislators, regulators, businesses, and the general public on data privacy in the clouds.

### ■ REFERENCES

Article 29 Data Protection Working Party (2009). "WP 163—Opinion 5/2009 on Online Social Networking." <http://ec.europa.eu/justice/policies/privacy/docs/wpdocs/2009/wp163_en.pdf> (accessed April 18, 2013).

Article 29 Data Protection Working Party (2010). "WP 169—Opinion 1/2010 on the Concepts of 'Controller' and 'Processor.'" <http://ec.europa.eu/justice/policies/privacy/docs/wpdocs/2010/wp169_en.pdf> (accessed April 18, 2013).

Article 29 Data Protection Working Party (2012). "WP 196—Opinion 05/2012 on Cloud Computing."<http://ec.europa.eu/justice/data-protection/article-29/documentation/opinion-recommendation/files/2012/wp196_en.pdf> (accessed April 18, 2013).

de Borja, F. (2012). "IDC Report: IT Cloud Services Market to Reach \$43.2 Billion by 2016," *Cloud Times*, 30 November. <http://cloudtimes.org/2012/11/30/idc-report-it-cloud-services-market-2016/> (accessed April 18, 2013).

Bradshaw, S., Millard, C., and Walden, I. (2011). "Contracts for Clouds: Comparison and Analysis of the Terms and Conditions of Cloud Computing Services," *International Journal of Law and Information Technology*, 19(3): 187–223.

Carr, N. (2008). *The Big Switch: Rewiring the World, from Edison to Google*. New York: W.W. Norton.

Council of Europe (1981). "Convention for the Protection of Individuals with regard to Automatic Processing of Personal Data," *European Treaty Series*, No. 108.

European Commission (2012). "Safeguarding Privacy in a Connected World: A European Data Protection Framework for the 21st Century." <http://eur-lex.europa.eu/LexUriServ/LexUriServ.do?uri=COM:2012:0009:FIN:EN:PDF> (accessed April 18, 2013).

EU DPD (1995). "Directive 95/46/EC of the European Parliament and of the Council of 24 October 1995 on the protection of individuals with regard to the processing of personal data and on the free movement of such data," *Official Journal of the European Communities* L 281, 23/11/1995: 31–50.

EU DPR Proposal (2012). "Proposal for a Regulation of the European Parliament and of the Council on the protection of individuals with regard to the processing of personal data and on the free movement of such data (General Data Protection Regulation)." *COM (2012) 11 final*. <http://ec.europa.eu/justice/data-protection/document/review2012/com_2012_11_en.pdf> (accessed April 18, 2013).

FTC Report (2012). "Protecting Consumer Privacy in an Era of Rapid Change." Federal Trade Commission. <http://ftc.gov/os/2012/03/120326privacyreport.pdf> (accessed 18 April 2013).

Greenleaf, G. (2012). "The Influence of European Data Privacy Standards outside Europe: Implications for Globalization of Convention 108," *International Data Privacy Law*, 2(2): 68–92.

Hon, W. K., Hörnle, J, and Millard, C. (2012). "Data Protection Jurisdiction and Cloud Computing—When are Cloud Users and Providers subject to EU Data Protection Law?" *International Review of Law, Computers and Technology*, 26(2–3): 129–164.

Hon, W. K. and Millard, C. (2012a). "Data Export in Cloud Computing: How Can Personal Data be Transferred Outside the EEA?—The Cloud of Unknowing, Part 4," *SCRIPTed*, 9(1): 25–63.

Hon, W. K. and Millard, C. (2012b). "Cloud Computing vs Traditional Outsourcing—Key Differences," *Computers and Law*, 23(4).

Hon, W. K., Millard, C., and Walden, I. (2011). "The Problem of 'Personal Data' in Cloud Computing: What Information is Regulated?—The Cloud of Unknowing," *International Data Privacy Law*, 1(4): 211–228.

Hon, W. K., Millard, C., and Walden, I. (2012a). "Negotiating Cloud Contracts: Looking at Clouds from Both Sides Now," *Stanford Technology Law Review*, 16(1): 79–128.

Hon, W. K., Millard, C., and Walden, I. (2012b). "Who is Responsible for 'Personal Data' in Cloud Computing?—The Cloud of Unknowing, Part 2," *International Data Privacy Law*, 2(1): 3–18.

Information Commissioner's Office (2012). "Guidance on the Use of Cloud Computing." <http://www.ico.org.uk/for_organisations/data_protection/topic_guides/online/cloud_computing> (accessed April 20, 2013).

Mell, P. and Grance. T. (2011). "The NIST Definition of Cloud Computing." *Recommendations of the National Institute of Standards and Technology, Special Publication 800–145*, Washington, DC: US Department of Commerce.

Millard, C. (1997). "Impact of the EU Data Protection Directive on Transborder Data Flows," *Information Security Technical Report*, 2(1): 47–49.

Millard, C. (2012). "Communications Privacy," in Walden, I. (ed.), *Telecommunications Law and Regulation*, 4th edn, Oxford: Oxford University Press, 605–652.

Millard, C. and Hon, W. K. (2012). "Defining 'Personal Data' in E-Social Science," *Information, Communication & Society*, 15(1): 66–84.

Millard, C. (2013). *Cloud Computing Law*. Oxford: Oxford University Press.

Schwartz, P. and Solove, D. (2011). "The PII Problem: Privacy and a New Concept of Personally Identifiable Information," *New York University Law Review*, 86: 1814–1894.

Solove, D. and Schwartz, P. (2011). *Information Privacy Law*, 4th edn. New York: Aspen Publishers.

Warren, S. and Brandeis, L. (1890). "The Right to Privacy," *Harvard Law Review*, 4: 193.

The White House (2012). "Consumer Data Privacy in a Networked World: A Framework for Protecting Privacy and Promoting Innovation in the Global Digital Economy" (includes proposed Consumer Privacy Bill of Rights). <http://www.whitehouse.gov/sites/default/files/privacy-final.pdf> (accessed April 20, 2013).

# 22 The Social Media Challenge to Internet Governance

*Laura DeNardis*

Emerging social media technical architectures and business models pose several challenges to individual civil liberties and to the Internet's historic openness and interoperability. A number of excellent scholarly enquiries have examined the salutary relationship between social media and political transformation and ways in which social media platforms expand freedom of expression and facilitate new forms of citizen journalism and alternative media (Howard et al. 2011). This chapter examines an antithetical question focusing not on social media content and usage but on the evolution of the technical and transactional infrastructures concealed beneath content and how these infrastructures potentially constrain the future of individual civil liberties and technical openness. There are many definitions of social media (boyd and Ellison 2007). This chapter defines social media as possessing three characteristics: the affordance of user-generated content, the ability for individuals to directly engage with other individuals and content, and the ability to select and/or articulate network connections with other individuals. With this capacious definition, social media encompasses social-networking platforms, content aggregation sites, and various forms of interactive media and journalism.

The technical architectures and business models enabling these broad forms of social media present four challenges to Internet freedom and governance. Most social media alternatives are freely available to users and financially supported by online advertising business models. This financial model is only sustainable if information intermediaries are able to collect and aggregate personal information about their users and then target the delivery of online ads based on *ad hominem* user profiles. This chapter begins by examining the implications of this relinquishment of individual privacy, whether visible to users or not, as the price for free Internet goods. Second, there is an increasing disconnect between perceptions of online anonymity and the technically embedded identity infrastructures that, at the very least, enable direct traceable anonymity.

Some social media platforms inherently require real-name identification, but even the ones that do not require real names have underlying identity infrastructures based on unique technical identifiers. This chapter addresses this erosion of the possibility of anonymous speech, governance trends toward real identification mandates, and the long-term implications of this shift for freedom of expression. Third, the increasing deployment of proprietary social media platforms is challenging the Internet's underlying principle of global interoperability and universality. Finally, the chapter concludes with an examination of the ways in which social media platforms provide centralized and privatized points of control for concentrating government censorship and surveillance. In all of these examples, the mediation of the technical and social values at stake—whether privacy, anonymity, expressive freedom, or interoperability—rests with the private sector, raising a broader insight into how Internet governance is evolving in practice.[1]

# Online Advertising as Faustian Privacy Bargain

Social media industry revenue models involve trading individual privacy for free information goods (Anderson 2009). Much scholarly and policy attention has addressed the evolution to free *information* and the implications of this shift for traditional and dominant media industries. Less attention has been devoted to the similarly transformative shift from models of *software* as purchased consumer goods to industry models of software as entirely free consumer goods. Social media software and services such as Orkut, Twitter, and Facebook are essentially free. The public similarly uses email products like Gmail and search engines like Bing, Google, and Yahoo! without having to pay for these services. Even online content hosting sites like Flickr and YouTube are free to users. This business model has created an entirely new industry even while posing enormous challenges to the revenue approaches of traditional media. The opportunity to use free software and free online services is so entrenched and ingrained that users sometimes do not even think about how they are freely given these information software products.

The provisioning of free software goods does not necessarily stem from pro bono altruism: it is simply based on a different business model. The operating expenses of a company like Google are enormous, totaling billions of dollars per quarter.[2] Revenues are similarly massive. Rather than the flow of currency

---

[1] A lengthier treatment of these concepts is provided in L. DeNardis (2014), *The Global War for Internet Governance*, New Haven, CT: Yale University Press.

[2] "Google Announces Second Quarter 2012 Financial Results," July 19, 2012. <http://investor.google.com/earnings/2012/Q2_google_earnings.html> (accessed August 6, 2012). Google's operating expenses for the quarter were $4 billion; other cost of revenue (e.g. data center operational expenses) totaled $2.41 billion.

occurring between users and social media providers, it flows between these providers and an ecosystem of third-party paid online advertising. Revenue generation has shifted from subscribers to third parties.

The underlying currency is not only the attention economy of hundreds of millions of eyes absorbing advertisements. The value added for advertisers is the data about individuals that is collected and aggregated during usage of information intermediation software like social media and search engines. Yochai Benkler explains the benefits of this removal of material barriers to information production for individual freedom and autonomy (Benkler 2006). But these barriers to information production have fallen because of the availability of free software platforms and the hidden and mechanized monetization networks that support them. The free software movement has famously advocated for free as in free speech rather than free as in free beer. The questions that need to be asked are whether what has actually unfolded is free as in free beer and what the implications are for freedom of expression.

Social media embedded advertising is not monolithic. Embedded in social media are several distinct forms of online advertising, each with a different set of implications for individual privacy. Contextual ads are targeted commercial messages that appear alongside the information a consumer is viewing or contributing via social media. The content of these advertisements is dependent upon the information appearing on the page. Behavioral advertising involves the tracking and retention of user activity (e.g. websites visited, links clicked, sales conversions made) over a period of time and subsequently serving ads that target the individual's likely consumer preferences as determined by this behavior. It is increasingly standard practice for an individual's behavior to be tracked over numerous unrelated websites by a private third party that has no direct relationship or contractual agreement with this individual. Location-based advertising has become one of the most common forms of online ad serving. Internet users are tethered to mobile devices fixed directly to location at any moment in time, whether via a Wi-Fi connection, a connection to a cellular base station, or via a GPS. Location-based ad platforms serve ads tailored to this location, such as listing a nearby retail store or restaurant. There are many other kinds of online ads, such as the old-fashioned online classified ad approaches like Craigslist, or stealth advertising and ad-vertainment approaches in which the paid message is a Trojan horse appearing like a product review or form of entertainment content.

The tracking of individual behavior and the retention and sharing of this data for financial gain is the underlying basis of online social media business models and a significant challenge to Internet governance. Data retention can produce harms such as identity theft and social and economic injury. When consumers understand how online advertising works, this can produce chilling effects on freedom of expression. On the other hand, abrogating all individual data retention and targeted advertising would erode the business models that have brought free online platforms to users and all the benefits to freedom of expression and innovation that accompany these platforms. The salient Internet governance challenge involves finding the balance between acceptable approaches to directing targeted ads to individuals and allowing the new business models that have helped make platforms freely available to anyone. The related question involves who should decide what constitutes this acceptable balance.

Governance of online advertising can occur in five ways: international agreements among governments; statutory frameworks within sovereign nation states; voluntary best practices among corporations involved in online advertising; private user agreements between individuals and the platforms they use; and individual and technologically mediated user choice about what and how data is collected, retained, and shared.

Many countries have statutory frameworks that address specific aspects of online privacy, such as laws against identity theft, protection of financial and health transactions, or prohibitions on collecting information from children, spam, or taking street-view pictures for map applications. For example, the European Union has a strong "Data Protection Directive" and recognizes the protection of personal data as a fundamental human right. As technologies and business models change, translating these types of protections into practice is increasingly complicated.

Many social media platforms provide privacy policies that inform users about how these corporations gather, retain, and share personal information. These policies reveal a great deal about how data is aggregated and shared. Information that, to the user, "seems" private is not actually private. Information is scanned or gathered during almost all transactions. Some of this data is content-based but some is also more specific to a user's location, physical hardware, or logistical circumstance. Specific examples of information collected about individuals include IP addresses, mobile phone number, time of call, unique hardware identifier, and physical location (based on Wi-Fi, global positioning system, or cellular signal information).

The routine collection of this type of personally identifiable information is quite a departure from the Internet's original design of locating intelligence at endpoints and using IP addresses as virtual identifiers rather than tying an information exchange to individual identity or usage context.

Individual data collection is at the heart of online advertising and new business models. It is yet unclear how this balance between new business models and individual privacy will unfold but its resolution will be a significant Internet governance decision, with implications both for individual rights and industry stability. At a minimum, disclosure of these policies and user choice about what information is shared seems extremely reasonable and would help eliminate the introduction of additional laws that would possibly homogenize the degree of privacy for everyone and invite additional regulatory interventions on an emerging industry.

## Trending Away from Anonymity

There is a disconnect between the perception of online anonymity and the actuality of a multilayered identity infrastructure beneath content. The historical traditions of the Internet and its underlying technical architecture have been to afford anonymous communication, or at a minimum, traceable anonymity in which law enforcement could secondarily obtain identity information from a service provider. Peter Steiner's famous 1993 cartoon in *The New Yorker* portrayed a web-surfing dog along with the caption "On the Internet, Nobody Knows You're a Dog." On social media, some know you're a dog, as well as your relationship status and favorite song.

At the level of content, there still is the appearance of anonymity. Someone can establish a Twitter account with a pseudonym or create a blog that reveals nothing about one's personal identity. But the identity infrastructures within the technologies that enable these content transactions erode anonymity. For example, if someone sets up a blog using a domain name they register, the WHOIS database (pronounced "who is") enables anyone to look up who has registered the domain name. The database includes not only the registrant's name but also physical address and email address. Technical identifiers are more deeply embedded: at the hardware level via mobile phone device identifiers and unique binary addresses on Ethernet cards; at the logical level via Internet Protocol addresses, globally unique phone number, unique software attributes on a computer, and cookies; and at the geographical level with location-based information easily traced via Wi-Fi antenna position, GPS, cellular base station triangulation, or the network segment of an IP address.

These technically situated identification mechanisms allow for traceable anonymity, meaning that a law enforcement agency can approach a network or application provider and request the real identification of the individual associated with a unique technical identifier, or combination of identifiers.

Some social media approaches have progressed beyond this traceable anonymity to require the use of real-name identifiers. Facebook requires its subscribers to use their real names and information and prohibits them from providing false information. There are many justifications for pushing back on anonymity, not just in social media but more broadly: discouraging anonymous cyberbullying; providing accountability; and promoting civility in comment sections on media sites (Citron and Norton 2011). But in the global networked environment, real-life identification requirements of social media platforms that ban anonymity also provide openings for repressive governments to crack down on dissent and free expression. Narratives linking social media usage with revolutionary uprisings can sometimes overlook the ways in which governments exploit social media to suppress expression. Governments can monitor platforms in advance of protests and identify pictures of individuals who have been photographed already participating in protests.

Real identification requirements on social media platforms at least present individuals with some choice about whether to participate, although being photographed and tagged online by others can occur even if someone has never used social media. But explicit requirements for real identification registration have evolved beyond technical identity infrastructures and social media usage policies. Much of this follows from the ways in which Internet access has evolved. There are increasing global requirements for the presentation of ID cards at cybercafés. For example, India has established rules requiring cybercafé owners to obtain the identity of its patrons with some form of official identification. Anything that requires a billing arrangement, such as a mobile phone subscription or home Internet access service, also necessitates the presentation of an individual identification card such as a driver's license.

An open question of Internet governance is whether national governments will increasingly mandate real identification requirements to accompany online usage and speech, not just in cybercafés but via any type of access. Indeed, statutory restrictions on anonymity are on the rise (Froomkin 2011). Whether real identification is mandated by service providers, social media platforms, or national governments, this move away from anonymous or pseudonymous speech will have implications for freedom of expression and for the character of political discourse and culture on the Internet. As in many other areas of Internet governance, these policy decisions, whether enacted by private industry or sovereign nation states, have to balance competing values—in this case freedom of expression and privacy versus law enforcement, national security, and civil discourse.

## Losing Internet Interoperability

The design of social media platforms is also pushing back against a historically important priority of Internet governance known as interoperability, a design approach enabling the seamless exchange of information among computing devices. A common protocological language enables computing devices to embed standard data formats, software interfaces, and network characteristics that enable interoperability among devices adhering to these standards, regardless of manufacturer or geographical location. The Internet works because of these standards, the blueprints that provide universal order to the stream of 0s and 1s that represent emails, movies, audio, and other types of information. Examples of these standards include the fundamental TCP/IP protocols on which the Internet is designed, as well as standards enabling information exchange between a web server and browser (e.g. HTTP), voice over the Internet (VoIP), and the encoding and compressing of audio (e.g. MP3) and video (e.g. MPEG).

While it is easy to take this interoperability for granted in the 21st century, only decades ago, computing devices made by one manufacturer could not exchange information with a different manufacturer's computers. These products were based on proprietary (undisclosed) specifications and the basic business model was precisely to not have products be compatible. In this way, a business purchasing a manufacturer's products would be locked into this single vendor for future purchases. Examples of the proprietary network protocols of this era include IBM's Systems Network Architecture, Digital Equipment Corporation's DECNET, Novell's Netware, and Apple's Appletalk. Even in the early days of online consumer services, such as email, there were completely non-interoperable proprietary systems such as American Online, CompuServe, and Prodigy. Someone using America Online could not "speak" to someone using Prodigy. It was a difficult industry transition from these incompatible systems to a new environment, based on standard and openly published Internet protocols like TCP/IP, which provided interoperability regardless of computing device, email program, or operating system.

Traditional Internet governance norms have privileged design principles such as universal searchability, information portability, and inherent interoperability among systems made by different companies. In a challenge to the innovation and interoperability these open approaches have enabled, social media platforms actually diminish interoperability and instead promulgate business models based on proprietary architectures. Different social media systems are not inherently interoperable or universally searchable. Uniform Resource Locator (URL) universality is not a design priority. There is lack of data portability in that social media users are not able to easily transport their own information from one platform onto a different social media platform. Social media companies could provide this interoperability but have instead adopted design approaches that create proprietary and somewhat autonomous systems.

For example, Skype is a communication system enabling users to interact with other Skype users via voice calls, instant messaging, and video. Purchased by Microsoft in 2011, the system has grown rapidly because it is both easy to use and free. Skype software is available for complementary download and the cost of Skype-to-Skype calling is free over an existing Internet connection. However, a Skype user wishing to call a non-Skype user over the Internet requires a service subscription. The inherent approach of this system is proprietary in that it technically constrains interoperability with other voice or video systems unless unlocked. Skype uses a proprietary signaling system not inherently compatible with other Voice over the Internet (VoIP) systems. This is a business model decision rather than a technical constraint.

Such proprietary, or partially proprietary, approaches are a considerable shift from the natively interoperable approach of traditional Internet applications such as email and web access. Any email client (e.g. a Gmail address) can generally exchange email with any other system (e.g. a Yahoo! address) without requiring technical translation or an additional fee. Any web browser can technically access any website. These systems are natively compatible. The interoperability and associated growth and innovation of the Internet would not have been possible if email had remained proprietary.

Web inventor Tim Berners-Lee has warned that social media approaches have also eroded the universal accessibility of information, instead creating fragmented information spaces (Berners-Lee 2010). The technical design of the Web created a globally consistent means for finding and reaching a website from any browser anywhere in the world. Uniform Resource Locators (URLs), also sometimes called Uniform Resource Indicators (UNIs), enabled this universality. Unfortunately, social media systems have eschewed this universal approach for more siloed architectures in which both search functionality and hypertexts among information are relegated within each social media system rather than interoperable between systems.

Social media systems are wildly popular and experiencing considerable market growth. Yet from the standpoint of Internet governance and Internet freedom, social media business models and architectural design choices are moving the Internet from a relatively universal, interoperable, and open standards-based network to a more balkanized environment in which information is partitioned, protocols are increasingly proprietary, and the only applications permitted are those authorized by gatekeepers.

# Implications of Social Media Choke Points for Freedom of Expression

Social media technical approaches also aggregate public content *in medias res* rather than decentralizing content at end points. This centralization inherently positions private companies as arbiters of freedom of expression and also creates concentrated technical points of control for Internet security attacks and government censorship and surveillance, usually delegated via private ordering. In other cases, governments ban a social media service outright, such as China's prohibitions on Twitter usage. Even when government-imposed censorship and surveillance is not present, this private mediation constrains what individuals can express because it requires permission and administration by an information intermediary.

Twitter terminated the personal account of a British journalist during the 2012 London Olympic Games. The reporter had been posting tweets criticizing aspects of NBC's Olympic coverage including some of its editing and the time delay making Americans wait to view certain events until the prime time recorded broadcast. The reporter also tweeted an NBC executive's email address to encourage viewers to complain about these delays. Twitter claimed that the suspension was due to this publication of the executive's email, which was deemed a violation of Twitter rules. This decision was met with a great public outcry, in part because of the perception that the company's decision was influenced by its promotional partnership with NBC during the Games. Twitter fairly quickly reinstated the account, admitting that it was a Twitter employee who prompted NBC to file a complaint, and stating that the company should not be monitoring and flagging content (Macgillivray 2012).

In addition to this direct private mediation of content, social media platforms also serve as levers for external parties wishing to censor specific voices. This censorship can happen without the cooperation of the social media platform, such as through Internet security attacks that disrupt the entire platform, or through censorship requests in which a government orders the information intermediary to take down specific content or suspend a specific account.

Most major social media platforms and information intermediaries have been the target of distributed denial of service (DDoS) attacks, orchestrated virtual sit-ins in which a targeted site is bombarded with so many requests that it becomes unavailable for legitimate use. A telephone analogy would be the effects of thousands of simultaneous calls to a 911 dispatcher, flooding the system so that legitimate calls could not connect. This type of attack does not involve unauthorized access or modification of the targeted site but effectively disables the system by overwhelming it with requests. One such attack in 2009 interrupted global access to Twitter, as well as Google's Blogger and YouTube platforms, Facebook, and LiveJournal. Such an extensive assault requires attacks launched simultaneously from tens of thousands of hijacked computers whose owners are often unaware of this activity.

Even though this episode disrupted social media service for many users, the purpose of the attack was actually to silence an Eastern European (Georgian) blogger named Cyxymu. Russian activists carried out the attack to censor Cyxymu's blog postings during a tense territorial dispute between Georgia and Russia. This incident was hardly the first DDoS attack motivated by political conflict, but illustrates the collateral damage to freedom of expression when an intermediary platform is disrupted to silence particular voices.

Private social media companies also grapple with direct government requests to remove content or block individuals from their sites. The inability of governments to directly block digital content has drawn their attention to information intermediaries and their underlying support infrastructures. This phenomenon is known as delegated censorship. Many of these delegated requests attempt to enforce national laws related to hate speech, defamation, privacy, blasphemy, pornography, or political speech restrictions. Delegated censorship requests sometimes also are attempts by repressive governments to silence citizen journalists, independent media, or political opponents.

In deciding which requests to execute, social media companies have to navigate numerous national legal contexts, each with its own unique set of laws, such as those that outlaw the online distribution of Nazi propaganda, laws against hate speech against various groups of minorities, laws against insulting a monarch, and laws against defamation. It is also difficult for social media companies to legitimate the veracity of each appeal.

Some companies have decided to publicly reveal the types of requests it receives to censor content. For example, Google's "Transparency Report" presents a snapshot of the types of state requests the company receives to remove content from its various platforms such as YouTube, Google+, its Orkut social media platform, and other online properties. Examining some specific cases of what the company has refused to remove, or not, provides insight into the challenges information intermediaries face, particularly because of the differing circumstances of national legal frameworks and cultural norms. With wording taken directly from the Google transparency reports, the following are just a few of the government-initiated content-removal requests with which the company did or did not comply.

Examples of Google Compliance with Government Content-Removal Requests

- Requests from Thailand Ministry of ICT to remove 149 videos allegedly insulting the monarchy (removed 70%) (2011)
- Request from United Kingdom's Association of Chief Police Officers to terminate five user YouTube accounts (2011)
- Brazilian electoral court order to remove four Orkut profiles due to political campaign-related content (2011)
- Request from United Kingdom's Office of Fair Trading to remove 93,360 fraudulent/scam advertisements (2010)
- United States court order for the removal of items from Google Groups in a defamation case (2010)

Examples of Google Non-Compliance with Government Content-Removal Requests

- Request from Canadian passport office to remove a YouTube video of a Canadian flushing his passport down the toilet (2011)
- Request from Pakistan's Ministry of Information technology to remove YouTube videos satirizing the Pakistan army and politicians (2011)
- United States local law enforcement request to remove a blog post alleged to personally defame a law enforcement official (2011)
- Request from Polish Agency for Enterprise Development to remove search result critical of the agency (2011)
- Request from local ministry in Kazakhstan to remove a YouTube channel supportive of its political opposition (2010)

Social media companies have become powerful intermediaries determining when information is or is not censored, just as they have direct power over allowing the publication of certain content, and just as they are tasked with the responsibility for battling denial of service attacks and other Internet security breaches with collateral damage to freedom of expression.

The evolution of the Internet's architecture into this dominant model of private intermediation calls attention to this privatization of Internet governance. A core objective of freedom of speech is to enable a communicative context necessary for the preservation and advancement of democracy (Post 2009). As these cases demonstrate, communicative contexts of freedom of expression are increasingly exercised through intermediary technologies and shaped by these same technologies, which are in turn controlled by the private companies that operate them.

The degree to which digital media create a robust public sphere for the formation of public opinion and the democratic legitimation of the state depends not only on state protections and interventions but on the architecture of underlying technical protocols, content intermediaries, and infrastructures. In all of the examples presented in this chapter—privacy, anonymity, interoperability, and expression, individual civil liberties are constructed and mediated by private ordering. Social media have engendered both the technical mediation of the public sphere and the privatization of civil liberties. This development in the governance of the online public sphere directly follows from both the evolution of social media technical architecture and business models.

As these private intermediaries increasingly establish policies about basic civil liberties online, the broad Internet governance community—governments, international institutions, private industry, consumer groups, and technical design communities—must grapple with the types of processes and transparency that are necessary to increase the legitimacy of privately mediated governance. How these governance questions unfold will determine the future of the Internet's openness and technical universality and the degree of individual freedom of expression in the online public sphere.

## ▓ REFERENCES

Anderson, C. (2009). *Free: The Future of a Radical Price*. New York: Hyperion.

Benkler, Y. (2006). *The Wealth of Networks: How Social Production Transforms Markets and Freedom*. New Haven, CT: Yale University Press.

Berners-Lee, T. (2010). "Long Live the Web: A Call for Continued Open Standards and Neutrality," *Scientific American*, 303(6): 80–85. doi:10.1038/scientificamerican1210-80.

boyd, d. and Ellison, N. (2007). "Social Media Sites: Definition, History, and Scholarship," *Journal of Computer-Mediated Communication*, 13(1): Article 11.

Citron, D. and Norton, H. (2011). "Intermediaries and Hate Speech: Fostering Digital Citizenship for the Information Age," *Boston University Law Review*, 91:1435.

Froomkin, M. (2011). "Lessons Learned Too Well." Paper presented at the Oxford Internet Institute's *A Decade in Internet Time: Symposium on the Dynamics of the Internet and Society.* September 22, 2011.

Howard, P. N., Duffy, A., Freelon, D., Hussain, M., Mari, W., and Mazaid, M. (2011). "Opening Closed Regimes: What Was the Role of Social Media during the Arab Spring?" *Project on Information Technology and Political Islam*, Research Memo 2011.1. Seattle, WA: University of Washington.

Macgillivray, A. (2012). "Our Approach to Trust & Safety and Private Information." Twitter official blog posting on July 31, 2012. <http://blog.twitter.com/2012/07/our-approach-to-trust-safety-and.html> (accessed August 7, 2012).

Post, R. (2009). "A Progressive Perspective on Freedom of Speech," in Jack M. Balkin and Reva Segal (eds.), *The Constitution in 2020.* New York: Oxford University Press, 179–186.

# 23 Beyond the Internet and Web

*Yorick Wilks*

## Introduction

What will the future Web or Internet be like? Will it be more of the same, though with many added applications, or will it be something very different? Pessimists warn that the Internet is ruining education, social interaction, and perhaps civilization itself;[1] meanwhile, philosophical visionaries (such as Clark 2008) claim the Web is the start of a totally new phenomenon in human history, the "group mind," a powerful notion that implies both the breaking down of barriers between individual minds, as well as barriers between a single mind and its electronic environment. What are the possible paths to the future of the Internet and what difference will they make for society?

The striking shifts everyone continually sees on the Internet and World Wide Web are mostly the appearance of novel applications, whether Web services in general, impressive government services for citizens, or novel forms of social software. One might say, not totally seriously, that one end point in the development of the latter would be a rumored site that answers the question "What shall I do now?" This site is said to advise you what to do given what you usually do at that time and what it knows of your tastes and habits. For some this is an exciting prospect; but it represents a dead end, the cul-de-sac down which some believe the Internet is leading us, until we are bereft of any real interests, willpower, taste, or discrimination.

The novelties we see can appear either as special applications from the Internet itself through devices like tablets and smartphones, or can be reached by browsing the World Wide Web on any device. This chapter is not so much concerned with new applications, as with the underlying browsable Web and its foundations: are those shifting with time, or are they rather a fixed substratum with all change coming from different apps implemented on top? The case made here is that there is indeed a serious foundational shift under way: one from the classic World Wide Web (WWW) to what we shall call the Semantic (alternatively, Data) Web (SW), and that this shift brings back into discussion many 20th-century philosophical disputes on what it is to have meaning.

Some mention should be made at the outset about the relationship of the terms in which we discuss the WWW and SW here to the common use of the terms "Web n.0" where n began as 2 (Web 2.0) and has been cited at ranges up to 6 and beyond. Tim Berners-Lee has dismissed all such terms as jargon and he may be right; they are certainly a distraction.[2] Web 1.0 is fairly well understood as the WWW of documents, images, and videos. Web 2.0 has become a term widely used to refer to the WWW as a portal or platform for a wide range of user-driven activities from provision of user-created content up to self-publishing and the use of social network sites (SNS), such as Facebook, Twitter, and others. Nothing in that description assumes any change in the underlying architecture of the WWW, although many Web 2.0 applications, such as Facebook, are private spaces, walled off from the Web (see DeNardis, chapter 22 this volume). Some commentators use Web 3.0 to refer to what we are here calling the SW, along the lines of the original article with that name by Berners-Lee and others (Berners-Lee et al. 2001). What then is this SW, and what might it give us that the WWW has not?

## The Semantic Web

Another way to ask what kind of object the SW is to be is to ask the question: "How are we to understand what the objects in the SW actually *mean*?" This was never an issue with the WWW because the objects on it—usually text words or images—only meant things to people who were reading its documents. The WWW no more knows what the words in its documents—or the people in its pictures—mean than a television set knows what it is showing. Yet, the SW is no longer simply an aspiration that started life in a magazine article (2001) but a serious research subject worldwide, with its own conferences and journal. It is an attempt to have a successor to the WWW that knows what the objects it contains mean, and so can reason about them and assist humans so as to provide much more useful services.

The SW does not yet exist in a fully demonstrable form, but it is a topic for research about which fundamental questions can be asked, as to its representations, their meanings, and their groundings in reality. "Grounding" is a crucial word and refers to ways in which digital entities inside a computer that exist as just binary code can relate in clear and unambiguous ways to real things out there

---

[2] <http://news.bbc.co.uk/1/hi/technology/4132752.stm> (accessed January 10, 2013).

in our world. This chapter will argue that the concept of the SW has two distinct origins, and this persists in two differing lines of SW research: one, closely allied to notions of documents, to the humanities, and to processing natural language by computer, and the other related back to Artificial Intelligence (AI) and logic. These differences of emphasis carry with them quite different views about what it is to interpret a representation of some piece of knowledge on the Web, and what that method of interpretation has to do with meaning in spoken and written natural language, which is the only kind of meaning that humans in general understand.

I will simply assume that natural language (by which I just mean the language that we speak and write) is, in some clear sense, humans' primary method of conveying meaning, and that other methods of conveying meaning (formalisms, science, mathematics, codes, etc.) are parasitic upon it, in that they could not exist if humans did not already have language. This is a view once associated firmly with the philosophy of Wittgenstein (1953).

The initial presentation of the SW was by Berners-Lee, Jim Hendler, and Ora Lassila in 2001 in the *Scientific American*. They argued that if a web-like structure of knowledge or data could reason about itself in the right way, it could provide far more intelligent services. Their example was how one could make an appointment with a doctor for an elderly relative by consulting at the same time the doctor's availability, the relative's schedule, the transport needed, and so on. One can do more of these things online than ten years ago, but they had in mind a comprehensive change in the Web so that it "understood its own contents" in some sense. This Semantic Web, they argued, would need very complex notions like "trust" if it was to provide this kind of service, because you would need to trust such a web if you were going to use it to affect the life of an elderly or vulnerable person.

## Annotation and the SW

In the original *Scientific American* paper it was argued that the computers behind the Semantic Web would have to have notions like trust, logic, and proof, and it is these, and their traditional interpretations, that have caused both critics and admirers of the SW to say that the SW is really Good Old-Fashioned Artificial Intelligence (GOFAI) by another name, because those concepts (except perhaps trust, a more recent addition) were always important to AI: AI was originally founded to explore notions like proof by computer, but quickly extended to machine vision, language processing, and robots. But much of the machinery of the proposed SW in that article had to do with much simpler notions like Namespaces and the language XML,[3]

---

[3] <http://en.wikipedia.org/wiki/XML> (accessed January 10, 2013).

which are the notations used to specify items and rules that actually run the machinery of the WWW itself and its websites. These notions are all the products of what we may broadly call natural language processing obtained from the annotation of texts by a range of technologies we may conveniently gather under the name Information Extraction (Cowie and Wilks 2000). Information Extraction was a technology that descended from old humanities' techniques of adding marks, or annotations, to texts to indicate something about the words in them.

Those who developed the SW idea in terms of making texts "machine-understandable" through annotations, used this maturing technique of Information Extraction for this purpose. Classic Information Extraction detects objects of the following sorts in large-scale text corpora, and does it by learning from the annotations of such objects that humans have first made by hand in real texts:

- Named entities (e.g. the Eiffel Tower)
- The semantic types of those entities (e.g. a country or a person or, in this case, a building)
- Actions and relations between entities (e.g. the Eiffel Tower being in France, France being larger than Belgium, and so on).

The presence and nature of these relations among entities is then indicated either by annotating the text itself (with a notation known as SGML, a traditional "mark-up language") or by recording it separately from the text in a notation called XML (XML) and generally known as meta-data—data about the content of a text. This latter notion is very close to the way in which information about the content of a text has been stored by the somewhat different technology of Information Retrieval (IR), which searches for documents, in places such as libraries or on the Web. This is what Google search originally did by searching only for a text's key words, words which can also be thought of as meta-data, words as data about a text and which define its content. Information Extraction searches inside documents for things and facts, and IR searches for documents in a collection just by searching terms that describe them and not the documents themselves.

Information Extraction has been a resounding success as a technology, extracting facts from a wide range of sources on the Web, especially newspapers in real time, and providing services to individuals and companies. For companies it provides, for example, the extraction of financial information in Japan on the single day when companies all file their annual reports and at a speed that would be impossible for human annotators and analysts. Information Extraction's further developments have included the widespread use and deployment of sentiment analysis—answering questions like "Is this text saying something positive or negative?" —and of automated question answering (QA), of the kind shown in the IBM winning program Watson that won a *Jeopardy* contest on television against human experts.[4]

It is useful to remember that available information for science, business, and everyday life, still exists overwhelmingly as text: 85 percent of business data still exists as unstructured data (i.e. text).[5] So, too, of course does the WWW itself, though the proportion of it that is text is probably falling as video increases. If we think about all that information contained in texts on the WWW, then we can ask how could a SW that knew the contents of those texts be created except by information being extracted from natural text and stored in some other form, such as a database of facts extracted from text or annotations on text items. These forms are, of course, those provided by large-scale Information Extraction.

## Semantic Web Style Applications

Information Extraction-based services are one place to look for SW-style applications. These services have been based on pioneering annotation engines like Sheffield's X-Media,[6] and existing SW applications include Apple's recipe annotator based on its Rich Snippets technology, where users can annotate recipes themselves and then retrieve results later, when needed in the kitchen or while doing the shopping.[7] The German application iPopulator[8] extracts information from Wikipedia pages that have been automatically annotated and provides automatically the kind of summary panel one finds at the top of many Wikipedia pages (see Figure 23.1).

So far we have considered only the annotation of texts, which is where the notion began in the humanities community and where, in some form, the procedure goes back centuries to biblical annotations in monasteries. However, the most striking advances on the annotation of Web content are perhaps the annotations of images, and it is there that the scope for new and more striking services is strongest.

A US-government-sponsored competition (TRECVID) has for years invited research groups to compete to annotate images:[9] there are some hundred or more things that can be found and annotated automatically in images

---

[4] <http://www-03.ibm.com/innovation/us/watson> (accessed January 10, 2013).

[5] <http://en.wikipedia.org/wiki/Business_intelligence> (accessed January 10, 2013).

[6] <http://www.x-media-project.org/> (accessed January 10, 2013).

[7] <http://support.google.com/webmasters/bin/answer.py?hl=en&answer=173379> (accessed January 10, 2013).

[8] <http://www.hpi.uni-potsdam.de/naumann/projekte/completed_projects/ipopulator.html> (accessed January 10, 2013).

[9] <http://trecvid.nist.gov/> (accessed January 10, 2013).

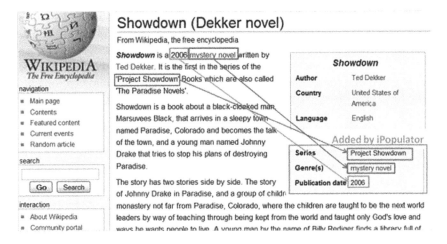

**Figure 23.1** Summary panel on a sample Wikipedia page

in TRECVID: a person sitting down or walking, someone baking a cake, a male person, two people kissing, someone scoring a goal at football, and so on. Usually this is done by sophisticated programs that examine the tent of video images and find one that they want from thousands of hours of video (or still images). Sometimes this is done by using text or voice associated with the video images (such as a football commentator or a news reader in time synchronization with the video). For example, to find a video of footballer Fernando scoring a goal—something many people might want to find on the Web—a program can scan the sound track of a commentator and find a place where it is said "Fernando scores" because searching voice automatically is usually easier than interpreting images in the same way. There are also fairly accurate techniques for face recognition. We can therefore foresee an annotated SW where all human faces are annotated with their names, either automatically or because they have been hand-tagged, such as on a social site like Facebook. It will then become increasingly easy for a journalist to search the whole Web for, say, an image containing both a famous politician and a notorious criminal. Through this discussion of understanding content on the Web, such as names associated with faces, we have returned to the clear possibility of the very thing we noted earlier that we don't have at home in 2013—essentially a Web TV that *does* understand what it is showing.

Understanding content on the Web also means being able, for example, to answer questions on the Web rather than just search for documents, which is what browsers do: the documents you retrieve may answer a question you have, but that is not the same as getting a real answer, for doing that requires understanding documents in a way searching for them does not. As already discussed, searching for documents is called Information Retrieval (IR), and you might think this difference is just about *size*. For, if we could find a document the size of a single sentence that was most relevant to a question we had then IR would be doing question answering (QA). But that is not so because, if we look for the sentence most relevant to a question (which is what IR does) it might well find the question itself on the Web—nothing could be more relevant than that. Yet that would not be exactly the answer to the question—to know something is an answer to a question we have first to understand it—which is what the name of the game is here. This kind of advance is not all being made under the heading "Semantic Web": for example, Yahoo! calls it understanding content, and has an app called "Searchmonkey." The name of the task does not matter.

In this section we have looked at some real and near-term possibilities for providing real content on the SW, content that the Web itself "understands." One possibility that opens up, and one some will dislike, is that a Web that understands its content may then go on to have its own point of view on that content.

## The SW and the Single Point-of-View

One concern some have about the SW is that it will require that everyone using it share a single point of view on all issues, often embodied in a hierarchy or map of concepts underlying a SW and called an ontology (Brewster et al. 2005). If true, this would be a serious drawback to its use from a social and user's point of view since the Internet has always championed diversity and the importance of individual needs and choices. At its simplest, an ontology is the structure that tells you a cup is an instrument for drinking, and at its most complicated it can be a standard logic-based representation of the whole of medical knowledge such as SNOMED.[10] Indeed, one could say to any skeptic about the existence of the SW that the place to see it coming into being is in one of the giant ontologies being built in almost every formal medical and scientific domain, without which modern research is unthinkable.

Many popular criticisms of the SW argue that agreed ontologies are difficult to obtain.[11] This is true in everyday life, but if extended would mean that science and medicine cannot be formalized at all, a view completely at odds with current developments in e-Science (see Wilks and den Besten 2010) practice, and indeed the whole history of science itself.

---

[10] <http://en.wikipedia.org/wiki/SNOMED> (accessed January 10, 2013).
[11] <http://halfanhour.blogspot.com/2007/03/why-semantic-web-will-fail.html> (accessed January 10, 2013).

However, it is very important to remember that, even in science, there can be, and are, rival medical ontologies across the globe and that not all of them express the same viewpoint on medicine and the treatment of disorders. Just as some people could employ news filters on the WWW to give them only news that agrees with their own point of view, it would be perfectly possible for individuals to have their own individual SW, expressing their own ontology and personal viewpoint on any issue.

A highly personal SW could be used to promote a point of view on the Internet, as well as to use filters or annotations to prevent one seeing any web pages incompatible with the Koran, for example, and that might be an "Internet-for-me" that I could choose to live with. However, there is no reason why the SW, or any annotated web of documents or images must, as some of its critics, such as Ted Nelson, have argued (e.g. Nelson 2004), *necessarily* impose a single point of view. He argued that the use of a general ontology behind the WWW necessarily implied seeing only a world compatible with that ontology, and that it might be just plain wrong. The technology of annotations, as discussed earlier in this chapter, is perfectly able to record two quite different, even incompatible, sets of annotation data (as meta-data) for the same texts, and no uniformity of point of view is either necessary or desirable.

It is worth remembering that the underlying page-rank technology of Google (Page et al. 1998) is itself very much a point-of-view phenomenon, not in the sense of controlling logical consistency with an ontology, but in promoting, under a measure of rank, what is most believed by a population, as measured by being most linked to. This is the basis of the criticism many make of WWW search in general, arguing that what is most believed is not necessarily what is true, and referring to the period when, for example, most people are said to have believed the Earth was flat, even though scientists believed it was round, and we may take it as true that it really was round at the time. It is by no means clear that page-ranking is a good perspective on knowledge in general, even though there are an increasing number of phenomena where human aggregates through "crowd sourcing" seem better able to predict events than experts, a subject that has been of much interest (Surowiecki 2004) to economists and other social scientists. This has a clear relation to ontologies and other information structures built not from expert authority but from amalgamations of mass input, sometimes described as the "wiki" movement or "folksonomies."[12] This movement might, in time, undermine the whole SW concept in a quite different way, since it lacks any concept of "authority" and "trust" which are central to the SW.

The point-of-view and Internet-for-me issues are of wider importance than speculating about, say, religious or pornographic censorship: they are

---

[12] <http://www.flickr.com/> (accessed January 10, 2013).

important because of the notion they raise of there being any *correct* view of the world, one that the SW and its associated ontologies could conceivably control by controlling the meanings of terms (the subject of this chapter) as well as the wider issue of consistency with a received view of truth. The nearest thing we have to a received view of truth in the 21st century, in the Western world at least (and the restriction is important), is that of science, not least because the Web was developed by scientists and serves their purposes most clearly, even though they do not now control the Internet as they did at its inception. One could see the SW as an attempt to ensure closer links between the future Web and scientific control. This emerges a little in what I shall call the view of scientists as the Guardians of Meaning in a later section below. It is a crucial notion because, although scientists controlling the meanings of web terms may not sound dangerous, this possibility would sound far more insidious if the controllers were governments or companies. In a democratic world we should surely prefer a web where no one controlled what its terms meant.

## The Semantic Web as Trusted Databases

Since Tim Berners-Lee invented the term, it is important to see what he meant by SW and how his own views have evolved since the original article that introduced the term. He no longer uses his original phrase "Semantic Web," but prefers "Linked Data Web," but I, like many others, will go on using the older term here. SW conveys Berners-Lee's original vision, which was not the WWW that we have, although that was what was produced first. His original vision, inspired by his own work at CERN with databases, was in fact much closer to what we are calling the Semantic, or Linked Data Web (see Wilks 2010). His earliest diagrams from Geneva show links to interpretations of symbols and as he put it later: "The great need for information about information, to help us categorize, sort, pay for, own information is driving the design of languages for the Web designed for processing by machines, rather than people. The web of human-readable documents is being merged with a web of machine-understandable data".[13] That is exactly the transition we are discussing in this chapter: from documents we read to material the Web itself can read and understand.

Berners-Lee's own writings emphasize databases as the core of the SW. Databases are structures the meanings of whose features are kept constant and trustworthy by a cadre of guardians of their integrity, a matter quite separate from both logical representations (dear to GOFAI) and from any

---

[13] <http://www.w3.org/People/Berners-Lee/ShortHistory.html> (accessed January 10, 2013).

language-based methodology such as I described earlier as Information Extraction. Berners-Lee's view deserves extended discussion and consideration that cannot be given here, but it will inevitably suffer from the difficulty of any view (like GOFAI) that seeks to preserve predicates, features, facets or whatever from the ways the senses of words, or any symbols, change and drift with time. We still "dial numbers" when we phone, even though that action no longer means what it did a few decades ago. We have no dials now; hence, not even number-associated concepts are safe from the ravages of time. Any foundation for the Web, therefore, that believes its terms can be protected from a change of meaning—as Berners-Lee sometimes seems to—cannot work. We shall return to this theme in the last sections of the chapter.

## Annotation and the Philosophers

Philosophers have not been very sympathetic to the notion of annotation, which we claimed underlies much of the attempt to have a SW that encodes its own meanings.

David Lewis (1972) raised the classic philosophical objection to any attempt to encode meaning in this way: his target at the time was the theory in linguistics which attempted to attach semantic codings or markers to the syntactic structures produced by Noam Chomsky's theories (by means of markers like ANIMATE attached to words for animate things like "dog"). Lewis called all such efforts "markerese" and said they could not possibly provide meanings for English words because the markers were themselves just more English words, so the whole process was circular. Yet these annotations are exactly what computer processes like Information Extraction attempt to provide on a large scale.

The quickest objection to Lewis's criticism is that dictionaries have for centuries provided the meanings of English words to millions of happy consumers by giving definitions couched in other English words. We do not need here to step into the philosophical controversy Lewis stirred up, but only note that Information Extraction and the annotation movement generally simply take his criticism head on and proceed to provide such mark-ups, either by a human or computer annotation, and see this simply as an engineering project, one whose value will be proved, or not, by the outcomes and values it provides.

Lewis (1972) believed that semantics, which is to say the giving of meanings, could not be provided by words but must be provided by formal symbolic representations of the real objects in the world, that lie outside the symbolic realm: that meaning must in some way "pop out" of the world of symbols to get at real meanings like tables and chairs. The problem is that it is very hard to see exactly what it would be like to do that. As the philosopher Wittgenstein emphasized many years ago, words do not attach as simply and unambiguously to things in the world as we sometimes think, a topic I discuss further below.

## Meaning and the SW

The central question about the meaning of terms in an electronic system like the SW that understands the meanings of the terms it contains is how it does that: how are its terms given meaning at all? The most original notion in Berners-Lee's design is the URI: a Uniform Resource Indicator, a notion very close to what we now call a URL, a Uniform Resource Locator, which is what appears in every browser's window to show the web page or object we have reached. However, they are not quite the same and a URI can be thought of as either a URL or as a URN (a Uniform Resource Name). Berners-Lee himself explained it as: "A *resource* is anything that might be identified by a URI" (Berners-Lee 2005). A simple way of thinking about it is that a URN is something's name, such as the ISBN name of a particular book title, whereas a URL is its address, which is where to find a book as a document. Both can be thought of as hyperlinks, where clicking on the first would normally take you to a (formal) description of a particular book, but clicking on the book's URL might well take you to its full text.

That is the classical story about names and meaning in the SW but, things are much more complicated. Remember that the aim of Berners-Lee's resources, like the real referents of his and of all his philosophical predecessors, is to reach something non-symbolic, a real datum or meaning outside the world of words and other symbols. But this cannot be done from inside a computer and without a hand to point with. This is a complex issue that can bring in the huge corpus of the philosophy of meaning, and accounts linking the Semantic Web to philosophy (Wilks 2008; Halpin 2011). The short answer is that within a world of symbolic computation there is no hope of linking terms to real hard meanings that lie outside the computer or the Web itself.

## Guardians of Meaning

Let us turn, as a final philosophical excursion, to another modern philosopher who made a major claim relevant to our underlying question. Putnam (Putnam 1975/1985) has set out a case about meaning which has the effect that ordinary speakers of languages often do not, *and cannot,* know what words mean and so cannot identify anything distinctively as their referents. This, if true, has consequences for what it is for a URI to point at its meaning, for if language users cannot identify what their words refer to, why should the SW be able to? Putnam goes further and argues that, in the class of cases that interest him, scientists or other experts *can* identify such referents, and so they become an elite, or the Guardians of Meaning, one might say, who safeguard the real referents of words.

The kind of case Putnam described is that of the metals Aluminum and Molybdenum, which, although they appear to be similar whitish metals, are in fact chemically different, so that scientists can distinguish them but laypeople cannot. So, says Putnam, an ordinary person does not really know the meaning of "Aluminium" because he or she cannot pick it out from Molybdenum. The opposition to this view, which is what one could call the Wittgensteinian attitude to meaning (Wilks 2008) is that speakers of a language do determine what its terms mean, or that meaning is in its use, as this general attitude is known. If that is correct then there is no possibility of "locking meanings away safely somewhere" watched over by guardians: not in a laboratory with tests nor in a dictionary with definitions. Berners-Lee's own URI-based views of meaning in the SW, which originated as a service for scientists, have clear analogies with Putnam's.

## URIs as a Public Language

Wittgenstein's views on the nature of language have been touched on in this chapter but not described in any detail. They were complex but their relevance here is that they assumed that a language is a public matter, and so, in a SW, URIs and their names are themselves part of a public language over which no authority has control. Only the users of that language are in control by how they use it. Like any public language, URIs may be ambiguous or redundant; nonetheless their users and creators cannot wholly control them. There is clearly a sensible pressure to let the term used in a URI (or URL) reflect what it actually points to, rather than be always wholly arbitrary (as a company name URL will be arbitrary because proper names normally are). Halpin (2011) puts this issue as a problem for the future of the SW as follows:

What is apparent from any analysis of the Semantic Web is that there appear to be too many URIs for some things, while no URIs for other things. As differing users export their data to the Web in a decentralized manner, new URIs are always minted, and so running the risk of fracturing the Semantic Web into isolated "semantic" islands instead of becoming a unified web, as the same URIs are not re-used.

But this is exactly how language itself functions, where we have many terms and phrases "for the same thing," and many ambiguous descriptions. Nor do we have any formal social way of sorting this out with each other: people either understand us, and go on talking to us, or they do not, which leaves some people feeling isolated unless they adapt to social norms of communication.

## Conclusion

This chapter has touched on a number of views of what the SW is, or will be, one of which we identified with Berners-Lee's own, which he usually puts in terms of databases of information to be used for social purposes and needs. I argued that we need to think about the SW's development (with its unconstrained creation of URLs by users) in terms analogous to the way a language develops in the hands of its users, without any formal constraints at all, whether imposed by scientists or other experts, or by companies or politicians. Languages develop in the mouths and hands of their users, and their terms cannot be artificially constrained by authorities of any kind. This applies also to the SW, and implies that technical and scientific experts will not be able to control the meanings of key web terms, much as they clearly want to. Making the future Web democratic is thus linked to a certain attitude to how language develops and both adapts and maintains its meanings, within the Web and in the real social world. It might sound paradoxical, but the argument of this chapter is that we will go beyond the Internet and Web as we know it and get to a more people-friendly web precisely by making it machine friendly, by realizing Berners-Lee's original vision of a web that machines themselves understand.

### ■ REFERENCES

Berners-Lee, T. (2005). Keynote lecture in BCS Workshop on the Science of the Web, London.

Berners-Lee, T., Hendler, J., and Lassila, O. (2001). *Scientific American*, May: 29–37.

Brewster, C., Iria, J., Ciravegna, F., and Wilks, Y. (2005). "The Ontology: Chimaera or Pegasus," *Proceedings of the Dagstuhl Seminar on Machine Learning for the Semantic Web*, February 13–18, 2005.

Clark, A. (2008). *Supersizing the Mind: Embodiment, Action, and Cognitive Extension*. Oxford: Oxford University Press.

Cowie, J. and Wilks, Y. (2000). "Information Extraction," in R. Dale, H. Moisl, and H. Somers (eds.), *Handbook of Natural Language Processing*. New York: Marcel Dekker, 241–269.

Halpin, H. (2011). "Sense and Reference on the Web," *Minds and Machines*, 21(2): 153–178.

Lewis, D. (1972). "General Semantics," in D. Davidson and G. Harman, (eds.), *The Semantics of Natural Language*. Amsterdam: Kluwer.

Nelson, T. (2004). "A Cosmology for a Different Computer Universe: Data Model, Mechanisms, Virtual Machine and Visualization Infrastructure," *Journal of Digital Information*, 5(1) <http://journals.tdl.org/jodi/index.php/jodi/article/view/131/129> (accessed December 6, 2013).

Page, R., Brin, S., Motwain, R., and Winograd, T. (1998). "The Pagerank Citation Algorithm: Bringing Order to the Web," in 7th WWW Conference.

Putnam, H. (1975/1985). "The Meaning of 'Meaning,'" in H. Putnam (ed.), *Philosophical Papers: Mind, Language and Reality*,,Vol. 2, Cambridge: Cambridge University Press, 239–297.

Surowiecki, J. (2004). *The Wisdom of Crowds*. New York: Random House.

Wilks, Y. (2008). "What Would a Wittgensteinian Computational Linguistics Be Like?," in *Proceedings of Convention for the AISB*, Aberdeen, Scotland.

Wilks, Y. (2010). "Happy Surprises: The Development of the World Wide Web and the Semantic Web,". in H. Margetts, Perri 6, and C. Hood (eds.), *Paradoxes of Modernization: Unintended Consequences of Public Policy Reform*. Oxford: Oxford University Press, 101–116.

Wilks, Y. and den Besten, M. (2010). "Key Digital Technologies to Deal with Data," in W. H. Dutton and P. Jeffreys (eds), *World Wide Research: Reshaping the Sciences and Humanities*. Cambridge, MA: MIT Press.

Wittgenstein, L. (1953). *Philosophical Investigations*. Oxford: Oxford University Press.

# INDEX

Bold entries refer to tables and figures.